W9-BBE-213

LOST STATESMAN

VICKY
SAINT-GEORGES
De vièvre
Dec. 1955.

Reproduced by courtesy of the artist and the editor of The New Statesman

DC 407
M4
W4
1958

ALEXANDER WERTH

LOST STATESMAN

THE STRANGE STORY OF
Pierre Mendès-France

'Your courage and vitality have
given me an impression of French
leadership which I had not sustained
since the days of Clemenceau.'
SIR WINSTON CHURCHILL
TO PIERRE MENDÈS-FRANCE

'Des malheurs de la France
voici le responsable numéro Un.'
'CARREFOUR'
ON PIERRE MENDÈS-FRANCE

SEP '58

SEP '58

ABELARD-SCHUMAN
NEW YORK AND LONDON

55432

FIRST PUBLISHED IN U.S.A. 1958

© Copyright 1958 by Alexander Werth

Printed in Great Britain by
Taylor Garnett Evans & Co. Ltd., Watford, Hertfordshire
for the publishers Abelard-Schuman Ltd.
404 Fourth Avenue, New York 16

CONTENTS

v

INTRODUCTION

WHEN Pierre Mendès-France resigned in May, 1956, over the Algerian issue, after four agonizing months as Minister of State without portfolio—and without any say—in that Republican Front Government which he himself had done so much to create, Guy Mollet, the Socialist premier, used this strange and suggestive phrase: 'Don't throw stones at him; he is a sincere and tortured man.' Was not Mollet, in saying so, betraying at least a slight feeling of guilt towards the man whom he himself had done so much to 'torture'?

This, then, is the story of a 'sincere and tortured man'; it is also the story of the man whom Claude Bourdet once described as 'our most serious and lonely statesman'.

Lonely—Mendès-France has been lonely nearly all his life. No other leading public figure in France has been in such a chronic state of eclipse as he. This, in a sense, is the story of his three—or one might even say, four—eclipses, of which the last one—of May, 1956—may perhaps continue for a very long time.

Mendès-France had often had stones thrown at him. Was it because he was too unadaptable? Was it because he despised his fellow-men, and especially his fellow-politicians too much? Was it because he saw problems much more clearly than most, but, in trying to solve them, never quite made enough allowances for human weaknesses, traditions and habits, and wanted to impose cut-and-dried solutions on a nation that has been notorious, especially since 1945, for its procrastination? Was it not also because he was not making enough allowances for the irrational element in human and national conduct? Was it finally, because Mendès-France, though admitted even by his enemies to be one of the best political minds in France, was himself not only vaguely, but sometimes acutely, conscious of being an 'outsider'—of never quite belonging to French political life and to that Radical Party to which, for over 25 years, he had stuck through thick and thin, even though, temperamentally, there are few *milieux* in France where Mendès-France could feel less at home than in that easy-going party, so rich in amiable muddlers, fumblers, compromisers, 19th century optimists and colonialist racketeers? A party which, in the words of Philip Williams, 'exists for the specific purpose of protecting its clientèle from painful sacrifices and clear-cut choices'.[1]

[1] Philip Williams, *Politics in Post-War France* (London, 1955), p. 105.

A party, in short, which, by and large, was the very antithesis of what Mendès-France stood for.

On balance, the story of Mendès-France is, so far, the story of a man who failed. Whose fault was it? Was it the fault of Mendès-France? Or was it the fault of France? Or the fault of what De Gaulle calls 'the system', the rules of which Mendès-France has obstinately refused to accept?

It has often been said by his admirers that if only Mendès-France had been head of a government for four years, he would have transformed France into a much more efficient, socially better-organised, industrially more powerful country than she is. It is said that he would with sufficient powers at his command, have stopped the war in Indo-China long before 1954, and turned North Africa into another 'California', inhabited by a happy and contented Franco-Moslem community. He would have broken France of her drinking-habits and taught her to pay her taxes honestly and fairly.

But he did none of these things. Was it not Mendès-France's fundamental error never fully to have appreciated the *undertones* of French political life, of French psychology?

To take a striking recent example. Mendès was, in his own way, quite right to be outraged by Edgar Faure's decision to dissolve the National Assembly in December, 1955; but, at the same time, he tended to overlook the simple psychological fact that, in the whole of France, nobody really cared a hang whether Faure dissolved the Assembly or not, and that the dissolution was, if anything, welcomed, rather than condemned. Or to take another, even more striking example of Mendès's failure to appreciate the undertones of French mentality: he thought it fair enough that *L'Express*—his chief election mouthpiece—should dwell on certain atrocities committed by the French in Algeria. He did not quite realize that there were powerful, though dormant, anti-Arab feelings in the country, and that a my-country-right-or-wrong attitude had made great headway in France throughout 1955. With Tunisia and Morocco half-gone, the old myth inculcated over the last hundred years into every French schoolchild that Algeria was 'part of France' suddenly acquired a new reality, a new vitality, among a surprisingly broad section of French public opinion. When, in March, 1956, Jacques Soustelle spoke of the need of a real nation-wide *sursaut* to 'save Algeria for France', he was using words that were not falling on deaf ears, and words which it would have been impossible, at any time, to apply to Indo-China.

It was a little like that all his life; his almost infallible logic came up against habits and prejudices, whether in 1936, or 1945, or 1955 or 1956. As he once remarked: 'It's good to put iodine on a wound, even if the patient squeals'. A revealing remark; and yet the French do not like their leaders to make them 'squeal'.

Only once did he fully succeed: but even this success was a negative one—it was when, in the nick of time, he negotiated the Indo-China armistice. And even this one outstanding success of his career was never forgiven him by his enemies who—long after the event—claimed that they could have obtained better terms (which was untrue) and that he was little short of being a traitor.

In Britain, in the United States, in almost all foreign countries, there is a Mendès-France Myth. It was strongest in 1954, after the Geneva settlement on Indo-China, but also for a long time afterwards—for example when Mendès-France became the St. George who was going to slay the Monster Booze. His manner, his tempo, his personality were different from those of any other French politician the outside world had seen since the War.

As Sir Winston Churchill wrote to him in the famous 'Empty Chair' letter of January 12, 1955:

> Your courage and vitality have given me an impression of French leadership which I had not sustained since the days of Clemenceau. Pray accept my earnest compliments.

It was no idle compliment; that was the impression Mendès-France had given the outside world. He had, for a short time, given France the same impression—but only for a short time, so long as his services were thought indispensable.

But there was something disturbing about the man. As Jacques Fauvet wrote in *Le Monde* on June 18, 1954, just before his investiture:

> Just because he doesn't accept certain rules of the game, the man seems to worry and indispose even those who constantly complain of parliamentary routine. He didn't, before making his investiture speech, consult any of the groups. . . . Mendès is suspected of either despising office so much that he doesn't care on how many toes he treads, or else of wanting office so desperately that he is willing, if necessary, to adopt the policy of his enemies.

And then these challenging and perhaps penetrating words:

> Everything concerning Mendès-France is not so much a matter of pure politics as a question of personal and psychological reactions. . . . He has the flattering, but slightly alarming reputation of being a man *hors série*, who might be accepted *intuitu personæ, intuitu rationis*, without the blessing of any party.

And yet, abroad Mendès-France is a Myth, a Legend—a Legend in which even the people least interested in French politics, the people who can be least bothered with them, have believed, and still believe, even to this day.

The Mendès Myth was, indeed, to remain alive abroad, even after the fall of the Mendès Government. Even at the end of 1955 the Washington correspondent of the *Monde* wrote that Mendès-France continued to be the best-known and most popular Frenchman in America, and that American tourists going to Paris all wanted to see three Paris 'sights': the Eiffel Tower, the Folies-Bergère and—Mendès-France!

When my book, *France 1940-1955* was in the press, my friend, the late Robert Hale, suggested it might be a good idea to get an opinion on it from a leading French personality. 'Who, would you say?' I asked. 'Obviously,' he said, 'Mendès-France. Only man in France worth a thruppenyworth of gin!'

This book is neither an attempt to justify the Mendès-France Myth, nor is it an attempt to 'debunk' it. Or rather, it is, inevitably, a little of both. What this book really aims at is to show Mendès-France against the background of French political life during the last 25 years, and to show just why this man of extraordinary knowledge, ability and experience has still proved, by and large, a failure and a misfit. And why also, when looked at rationally from outside, his Algerian policy was right from the start, and yet continued, irrationally, to be rejected by the bulk of French public opinion.

From the very early stages of his political career, as this narrative will show, Mendès-France, for all his dazzling initial successes, was pursued by an evil fate. Had he been born ten years earlier, one can well see him play a major part in the history of the Third Republic in the 1920's. As it was, he entered political life in a small way around 1928—during the very last years when there was still room for optimism. His intellectual calibre, his technical knowledge, his reformist drive were greater than those of any other Radical in the 1920's—with the possible exception of Caillaux. He had a better analytical brain and greater technical competence than Herriot or Daladier, let alone Chautemps or Sarraut. But he was not born in time to become a statesman in the 1920's—the only time that he remembered when there was room for a genuine faith in Progress. I have always been struck by the nostalgia with which I heard Mendès speak of his early days as a Radical *militant* between 1928 and 1932: 'In those days I was full of youthful optimism and idealism, and I was convinced that Democracy had come to stay, and that, with appropriate reforms, we could make it a fairer and more equitable democracy'.

Was it one of Mendès-France's weaknesses to have been too consistent throughout his career, and to have believed, from start to finish, in the capitalist order, though never in *laissez-faire* capitalism? He thus always tended to fall between two stools: he was neither a Socialist, nor a capitalist in the old sense. He believed in what so many British contemporaries believed in—a planned or rather, 'guided' economy on a capitalist basis; he belonged, as one commentator described him, to the 'intelligent part of the French bourgeoisie'—that part of the bourgeoisie for which there was extremely little room in France.

Even so, in the 1920's, he might well have made his mark as an economist with profound knowledge, new ideas, and bold, imaginative solutions. But in reality, he did not enter active politics until 1932, the year when he was first elected deputy at the age of 25. 1932: the date is worth noting. In France, 1932 was at the tail end of an era of democratic normality. And it is ironical to recall what a great impression Mendès-France made with that first great speech on France's economic and financial position which he delivered at the Radical Congress at Toulouse in November, 1932; it was the occasion on which his future arch-enemy, Martinaud-Déplat hailed young Mendès as 'a future great Finance Minister!' But 1932 marked the end of an epoch; in the new epoch about to open there was little room for Mendès-France. Already Mendès was putting forward ideas which, at the time, were new: he rejected as a shibboleth the sanctity of a perfectly-balanced budget, and in speaking of finance, he uttered the —at that time still unorthodox—truth that whatever financial measures were taken to meet the effects of the world slump, '*none should be taken which would weaken France economically*'.

There were new ideas in the air—the New Deal, and other forms of state intervention in the economic life of capitalist nations, and Keynesian economics, which Mendès-France was one of the first in France to study.

But it was Mendès-France's tragedy that no sooner had he come into public prominence as an outstanding economic mind—especially through his speech at the Toulouse Congress—than France entered on an era where common sense and sweet reasonableness were thrown to the winds.

What began in France, soon after Hitler had set up the Nazi regime, was an era of acute conflicts and inflamed passions, an era when it was difficult, if not impossible, for a man like Mendès-France to play any major part. He stayed in the background, dismayed and full of foreboding, and sought consolation in a happy domestic life, in constant technical self-improvement, and in that curious sideline—

local government—which, during the last twenty years, Mendès-France has always found personally so much more human and so much more satisfactory than his uneasy parliamentary and government career.

No doubt, Mendès welcomed the Popular Front, but perhaps more for emotional and political reasons than as an economist. He was as fully aware as anybody of its economic weaknesses; but felt, nevertheless, that, even economically and socially, it represented a step in the right direction, though many of its features—such as the 40-hour week—were thoroughly unsound.

At heart he also knew that, with Nazi Germany overshadowing the whole of Europe, no worse time could have been chosen for the Popular Front experiment in France. And when, in 1938, he was offered by Blum his first government post, he hastened, together with Blum, to place this second Popular Front experiment into the context of the great international tragedy threatening Europe and the world. The Blum-Mendès plan was, in fact, a strident call to greater military preparedness: but it was, above all, something in the nature of a political demonstration, because no one could have any illusions about this second Blum Government lasting more than a few weeks.

Other men, seeing more eye-to-eye with Chamberlain than Blum, and claiming that appeasement alone could prevent World War II, had, in fact, taken over long before, and the second Blum Cabinet—in which Mendès held his first government post—was an anomaly and an anachronism. Again Mendès-France was unlucky.

And then came the agony of Munich, and the semi-dictatorship of Daladier, and that ugly Daladier-Bonnet era when a man like Mendès-France was—as so often in later years—reduced to silence, and could do little more than express his anger and anguish by abstaining in the more outrageous votes glorifying the conduct of Daladier and Bonnet.

Mendès-France felt particularly vulnerable during those years, those 'horrible years of 1937, 38 and 39' as he later wrote. For all his discretion, he was treated by scurrilous papers as a 'warmonger', and morally, at any rate, the outbreak of war came to him as a relief.

Acutely conscious of the discrimination he had suffered during the last pre-war years, he was determined to show his complete and utter 'Frenchness' in the most simple and direct way—by fighting for France.

But again luck was against him. Few men had better reason than Mendès-France to be embittered by the fearful *méchanceté* of so many of his fellow-Frenchmen. An absurd charge of desertion was trumped up against him; and he spent many months in Vichy jails, maligned and insulted with impunity by the men of Vichy and their countless underlings. His war experiences did not teach him to love his fellow-Frenchmen, or the human race generally. After his dramatic escape from prison—an extraordinary example of single-mindedness and personal courage—Mendès found himself an outcast in Vichy France, with nearly everybody around him a real—or potential —enemy.

Like de Gaulle, Mendès loved France, and, like de Gaulle, he had little love and respect for his countrymen. '*C'est un misanthrope*', one of the people knowing him best once told me, '*mais un misanthrope malgré lui.*'

As Fauvet remarked, it is often hard to make out whether he is morbidly ambitious—so much so that he will pursue the policy of his enemies in order to remain in power; or whether he is wholly indifferent to power. It *is* often difficult to make out. In 1954-55 he was ready to compromise with his enemies—but was it in order to remain in office, or was it not rather because, on balance, he thought it in the interests of the country that he should stay on?

Despite his deep contempt for so many of his fellow-humans, the dominant impression one has of Mendès is still that he is not personally vain and ambitious, but that he has a profound sense of mission and a powerful reformist zeal. He is also deeply conscious—usually, but not always rightly so—of 'knowing best'.

When de Gaulle—one of the few men whom he deeply admired, even without wholly agreeing with him—took him on at Algiers as *Commissaire* of Finance, Mendès became conscious of a tremendous mission. It was he, and only he, he thought, who could put France on her feet financially after the Liberation. He had his sharp, cut-and-dried, 'Crippsian' solutions to France's economic and financial troubles. He was not enamoured with the CNR (*Conseil National de la Résistance*) programme—which he thought amateurish and out-of-date ('a mere imitation of the old Front Populaire programme—these people hadn't the technical knowledge and experience to produce anything better', he later wrote). The Mendès Plan was the best thought-out, technically soundest plan for France in 1944-45; but it failed. It failed because France was not fired by Mendès's missionary zeal; it was turned down because he had not made enough allowances for the *undertones* of French life—with its hatred of fiscal 'inquisition' and with those hundreds of milliards of banknotes hoarded by a peasant population reluctant to submit to controls, however salutary these might be in the long run. . . .

And so in 1945 Mendès dropped once again out of public life, respected but unmourned, except by a few.

There followed nine years of eclipse or semi-eclipse. For four years Mendès confined himself to a number of technical jobs on the Economic and Social Council of UN and the like. Then in 1950 he emerged as The Critic. A harsh, merciless critic of the successive governments of the Fourth Republic, with their easy-going ways, their industrial and economic backwardness, their scrounging on the United States, and their senseless and ruinous war in Indo-China.

1950-53—these were perhaps the happiest years in Mendès-France's life; he was a man to whom a large part of France was looking for criticism and advice; his was the great analytical brain that was showing France what was wrong with her financies, her economy, her colonial policy. For three or four years, the intellectual élite of France—a great power in the land—were hanging on Mendès's lips. Every speech he made was now an event of national importance, and his investiture speech in 1953—when he failed by only a handful of votes to become head of the government—was like a revelation, like a breath of fresh air in the *immobiliste* France of Queuille, Pleven and Bidault.

But when at last, in 1954, Mendès-France became head of the French Government, it was already too late to save Indo-China. He made peace there on the best possible terms, and despite a catastrophic military situation. The natural reflex of France was to be grateful to him.

Public opinion was impressed by his vigorous manner in rejecting the delaying tactics of the last ten years, and in expressing his constant determination to 'get things done'.

By a bold stroke, he 'began' to settle the vast problem of North Africa and seemed to have achieved a remarkable success in the smallest of the three countries, Tunisia. He then decided to cut the Gordian knot of EDC; swept on by the success of his Indo-China and Tunisia settlements, he felt that public goodwill—that goodwill for which he had waited for years—would help him over many other hurdles.

His psychology was at fault, though. By yielding on German rearmament, he weakened himself on the Left, yet without strengthening himself on the Right: the Right were determined to strike him down at the first opportunity.

So a counter-legend was started to the effect that his two great successes had, in reality, been two great failures. The time was not ripe yet for accusing Mendès-France openly of treason—but that was

to come eighteen months later, when the *affaire des fuites* was used as
an occasion for a great smear campaign against him; and when, at the
MRP Congress in May 1956, Pierre-Henri Teitgen treated him as a
half-traitor who, in the words of Clemenceau, deserved not twelve but
only six bullets through his skin.

The English legend of 'Mr. France' was being demolished stone
by stone, over this period of 18 months. Nothing could be proved, but
there was 'guilt by association'; there were endless innuendoes that
not all was clean or clear; had not Roger Stéphane called on him at
Louviers on such-and-such a date?—the very Stéphane who *had* published military secrets on Indo-China in *France-Observateur*?

It was enough: something wasn't quite above-board where
Mendès-France was concerned. Whereas Vichy tried him as a deserter,
the MRP in 1956 were—without any definite charge whatsoever—
making many people believe that there was something wrong about
him; that he was, in some mysterious way, to blame for the loss of
Indo-China; that he was 'quite definitely' to blame for the loss of
Tunisia; that but for Tunisia, there wouldn't have been the Aurès
rebellion in November 1954, and, consequently, no war in Algeria.

The Counter-Legend had penetrated into people's minds so deeply
that Guy Mollet lacked the courage—or thought it inexpedient—to
make a fuss over the semi-charges and innuendoes at the *fuites* trial
and at the MRP Congress.

I remember how at Le Bugue, in the Dordogne in the summer of
1954, people were pathetically grateful to Mendès-France (*'un type
formidable'*): it was he who had stopped the rot in Indo-China, it was
he who had saved so many young people from being sent to Indo-
China to be killed.

In the summer of 1956 when one mentioned Mendès-France, the
same people would screw up their faces and say: *'Non, c'est pas ça. . .'*
He had failed; Indo-China was forgotten; but what had he achieved
in North Africa, after all? Maybe a temporary reduction of tension in
Tunisia in the summer of 1954—but then what? Things in North
Africa had since then gone from bad to worse, hadn't they?

The truth is that even in Tunisia, Mendès had been unlucky. After
all the terrible damage done in North Africa in the three previous
years by the MRP, after all the distrust that had been sown among
the Arabs, it was too late in 1954 to do what could have been done
so easily, and with such gratitude from the Tunisians themselves, in
1951 or 1952. Mendès's Tunisian venture would have been no gamble
in 1951; it could only be a gamble in 1954. He was so conscious of it
that he did not dare, while in office, to tackle Morocco as well as
Tunisia.

For years, the grand opportunity of turning North Africa into 'another California' had been missed; now it was desperately late in the day to do anything constructive. To stop the rot at that late stage was infinitely difficult. To let Mendès deal with North Africa in 1954 was almost like assigning to him the rôle of liquidator.

And yet—and here he showed courage, though not perhaps enough discretion and tact—he tried desperately, even after his fall, to believe in a generous and peaceful solution of the North African problem. He believed that reforms could still save North Africa for France, but bold and far-reaching reforms; for there was a terrible lot that France had to live down.

What he did not realise was that the time for sweet reasonableness was over once again. In Algeria he was faced with a situation which was different from that of Tunisia, while in France he miscalculated the vigour of the widespread desire in the country to 'assert itself'. The outcry of the Algerian French against the appointment of Catroux, 'the Mendès-France nominee' was even more strident than had been the outcry of the French in Morocco against Grandval, another 'Mendès-France nominee'. And this outcry echoed throughout France itself. There is little doubt that if not Mollet, but Mendès had gone to Algiers on that 6th of February, he would have been hit by something harder than mere rotten tomatoes. . . .

The wave of French nationalism over Algeria was rapidly mounting during those early months of 1956; and this was to continue for a very long time.

The era known as National-Molletism had set in. This was not, of course, the same as National-Socialism in Germany or as Fascism in Italy. But it had some features in common with both. Just as Hitlerism was a revolt against the 'humiliation' of Germany by the Treaty of Versailles, and Fascism a revolt against the thought that Italy had been cheated of the fruits of victory by the peace-makers of 1919, so National-Molletism was largely a reaction against the widespread French feeling of national humiliation. The humiliations had started in 1940, and even before; and after the Liberation, France had been given a back seat among the 'Great' Powers. And then there had been other humiliations: Syria, Indo-China, Tunisia, Morocco, not to mention the rearmament of Germany which had been forced on France against her will.

'No more retreats: Algeria is the last trench of French greatness' —that was the dominant French reaction in 1956. And this 'defence of Algeria' assumed some strangely chauvinist features, complete with a good deal of anti-Arab racialism. 'International morality' arguments counted for little, for who, except possibly the virtuous Swiss and Swedes, was in a position to preach morality and 'human rights' to France?

The feeling of defiance was widespread, and, by and large, the French conscripts who were called up in large numbers after February 1956 to 'defend Algeria' went there without a murmur. They were defending a 'part of France'; and they were defending French lives—over a million of them.

In provincial France, in the Dordogne, for instance (a part of the country known in the past for its pro-Munich pacifism) people were now in a fire-eating mood. The local carpenter, a notorious Communist *résistant* during the war, and still a Party member, was now praising Poujade for at least having a 'constructive' policy in Algeria: which was to kill off two or three million Arabs, 'so that we may have peace . . .' And my Paris charlady, a kindly squint-eyed old woman living in proletarian Belleville, full of memories of the Commune of 1871, often said that the war in Algeria was a terrible thing; 'but what can you do if the Russians and the Americans want to take Algeria away from us?'

Mendès was made increasingly conscious of these moods during his more and more frequent clashes with Lacoste, the Socialist, the Strong Man of Algiers who believed in the stick, and not in the carrot —at least not yet. And so blunt, Ernest Bevin-like Lacoste, Lacoste with roots deep in the soil of his native Périgord, and Frenchman first and Socialist only second—was built up as the 'Clemenceau of Algiers'. And in June ,1956, at the National Assembly, he received an ovation which went all the way from the Poujadists to the Socialists; and only the Communists and a small group of men around Mendès did not rise to their feet and cheer. Mendès, aware of the long-term realities of Algeria, refused to be carried away by this strange outburst of earthy, primitive nationalism.

He tried sweet reasonableness in other fields too—and again he miscalculated the real mood. He tried to conquer the Radical Party; but except for a few thousand young enthusiasts, Mendès had no real following—not, at any rate, on a long-term basis. Herriot, with his extraordinary flair, and despite the failings of his old age, was among the first to become aware of it

Mendès-France is a man who never quite played the game. The conflict between him and Edgar Faure was fundamental in this respect. Faure had a genius for compromise and believed in doing things 'gradually', and Faure made no enemies. Mendès, even if he com-

B

promised, always did it with bad grace. At heart, he despised his fellow-men, and had an authoritarian streak that went down badly.

In the case of Algeria, Mendès reacted with proverbial 'French logic', while the bulk of his countrymen were guided by sentiment—and resentment.

Temperamentally, Mendès is strangely like de Gaulle, for though totally different in upbringing and appearance, and less capable of inspiring mass enthusiasm for any length of time, he has certain intellectual qualities similar to de Gaulle's. Also, like de Gaulle—though in a different way—he dislikes his fellow-countrymen, but loves France. Is that the fault of France? Is it the fault of Mendès? Between France and Mendès there is a strange love-hate relationship. Mendès both loves and hates France; while France both respects and dislikes him and, except on rare occasions, would rather do without him.

Yet his influence, though not always apparent, is considerable even during those long periods when little is heard of him. Other men —often more adaptable men—have closely studied Mendès-France's ideas and methods and have been able, in various fields, to follow Mendès-France's lines of thought, and to do so with more public support and more organised party support than he could do.

Take, for instance, that famous 'reappraisal of France's position *vis-à-vis* the West' speech that Christian Pineau delivered in March, 1956—a speech which caused such alarm to Sir Anthony Eden. Looking at the world, and at France's position in it, with reference to the 'atomic equilibrium' of 1956 and to the new trends in Soviet foreign policy, Pineau boldly expressed thoughts which Mendès might just as easily have expressed—but not with the same impunity. In January, 1956 Mendès-France had been promised the Quai d'Orsay by Mollet; but it was Pineau who was given the post of Foreign Minister. Why? Again, partly because public opinion in France was likely to be less perturbed if the 'dangerous thoughts' came from Pineau—a good Atlantic Pact, Marshall Aid, and 'Europe' man in the past—than if they came from the 'disquieting' Mendès-France. Pineau was, moreover, a man with the backing of a large Party behind him. He belonged to the 'system'; Mendès did not.

And so, in May, 1956, after numerous clashes with Lacoste, Mendès resigned. It is said that he will come to the fore again if there is a catastrophe in North Africa; even that is not certain. Perhaps too much has already been done to create an anti-Mendès-France prejudice in the country.

In the last analysis, the French reaction against Mendès-France—who since 1954 had come to symbolize *retreat*—was like part of a more general irrational revolt against *national humiliation*, a humiliation which went back to the Pyrrhic victory of 1918, to 1940, and to the loss of Indo-China, Syria, Tunisia and Morocco. Numerous British reactions to Suez—and not only on the Right—were akin to this sentiment in France.

The greater part of this book deals—directly or indirectly—with the crisis of the French North-African Empire, the most critical of all French problems during the recent past and during the immediate future, whereas a long chapter is devoted to a first-hand examination of the three countries of French North Africa in the course of the summer and autumn of 1956—a period during which the Suez Crisis added further acuteness to France's relations with her Arab partners and citizens. I wish to express my particular gratitude to the Editor of *Reynolds News* for having sent me on this memorable journey.

As for the bulk of this book, my thanks go, first and foremost, to M. Pierre Mendès-France himself, not least for our numerous illuminating conversations in the course of the last two or three years. I trust he will not hold it against me if, for all my genuine admiration for his great qualities, I have also dwelt on certain of his errors and weaknesses and on his frequent bad luck, which explains, more perhaps than his failings, why this book is not an undiluted Success Story.

Perhaps Mendès-France has always aimed too high. And the most difficult thing in politics—especially in French politics—is to swim against the current of (often irrational) public sentiment. Yet it often happens that such currents suddenly change their course. Thus, in 1924-25, the wave of French nationalism over the Ruhr occupation was succeeded by an era of Briandism, pacifism and reconciliation with Germany. Could not the same happen again in the case of Algeria?

A. W.

July 1957.

P.S. There are some inevitable points of resemblance between Part IV of this book (*The Mendès-France Government of 1954-55*) and the three chapters on the same subject in my earlier book, *France 1940-55*. But while many of the bare facts are, naturally, the same, the episode is treated in a somewhat different perspective, after the lapse of three or four years; and, more important, I have, in the present book reduced to a minimum the discussion on Indo-China, EDC and German rearmament, and have dealt in much greater detail than in *France 1940-55* with the Algerian and North-African issues as they already existed in France in 1954-55.

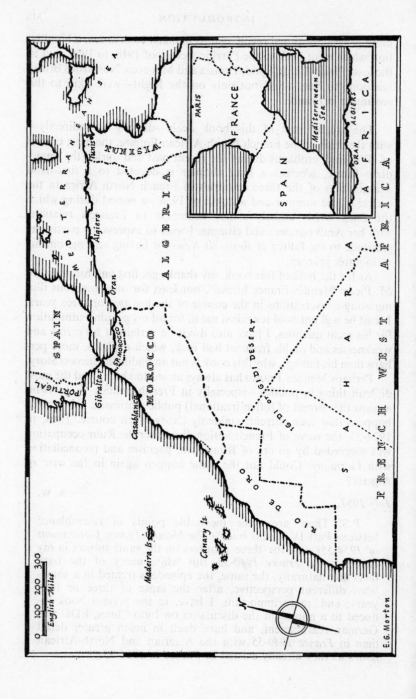

E.G. Morton

PART I
PRE-WAR

CHAPTER 1

LE BENJAMIN

AFTER the 1956 election, a popular Paris magazine published a picture of Pierre Poujade at the age of two, holding his right foot with his left hand, and, beside it, another picture of Pierre Poujade, aged thirty-five, also holding his right foot with his left hand. 'Already at the age of two he had the same mannerisms as now,' said the caption.

There seems nothing more inane than such attempts to 'personalize' great men from the day of their birth, though, heaven knows, it is part of a sentimentalization technique, which is particularly popular in the build-up of any dictator or prospective dictator. One only has to remember the sentimental pictures of Hitler, which the Germans loved. Little Adolf, aged three, or *'Der Führer als Tierfreund'* (Hitler feeding a goat), or *'Ein kleiner Besuch in Berchtesgaden'* (Hitler treating two three-year-olds to chocolate éclairs). A similar propaganda technique was applied to other budding dictators; many in France remember the 'album' of sloppy photographs illustrating the private life of Jacques Doriot, including a separate picture of his bedroom slippers! The slippers that had the honour of being worn by the great man, after his hard day's work—for *your* good, of course.

There are no such pictures of Pierre Mendès-France, aged six months, or two years, or five years; and even if there were, it is doubtful whether they would be of the slightest interest. The only picture of the kind published is one of Little Pierre, aged eight, wearing a 'sailor suit' and holding a hoop in his hand, from which one may assume that (*a*) he played in some public garden with his hoop; though what garden is hard to say: there isn't any in the *quartier du Sentier* or the *quartier du Temple*, except for one or two small squares, and (*b*) that his parents were sufficiently well-off to buy a 'sailor suit'. The only striking thing about the picture is the child's face: tight-lipped, earnest, and already remarkably like the face of the grown-up PMF.

There is a striking difference between the legend of the *'petit Juif du Sentier'*, as he is often described by his enemies, and the real story of Mendès's family background. The *Sentier* is the 'soft-goods' district of Paris, largely composed of old and shabby warehouses, and,

3

roughly, the Whitechapel of Paris (though much more central than Whitechapel). The implication of the nasty phrase: *'petit Juif du Sentier'* is that his family must have come from Poland or Galicia about 1905, in the great exodus of uncouth and patriarchally-talmudic Jews from the ghettoes of Eastern Europe to England, France and the United States. Mendès-France is, on the contrary, very conscious of having deep roots in the soil of France. And it is perfectly true that he belongs to one of the three or four oldest Jewish families in the country.

'Our family is a *marrane* family, that is, of Jewish-Portuguese origin,' he said one day. 'They left Portugal some time between 1500 and 1600, and have been established at Bordeaux ever since. At times they have played a small, but still rather brilliant part in French colonial history—notably in the colonization of San Domingo. That was one of the most glorious periods of my family's history.

'Thus, for over three centuries my family have lived in Bordeaux, which my own father was the first to leave for Paris.

'My grandfather was the first in the family not to have married a *marrane*. My father, who is still alive, has been running a medium-sized business in Paris—*confections pour dames*, with a fairly big export trade, and is thus the first Parisian in our family.'

Mendès-France then spoke of his mother, and of her family, which was Alsatian. Like so many other patriotic French families (whether Gentile or Jew), his mother's family, who had been established at Strasbourg, emigrated to France after the defeat of 1870. *'Une famille assez active,'* he added.

Mendès-France clearly felt strongly on the subject. His father's family had been French for generations; so had his mother's family. *'Mes ancêtres'* was how he proudly referred to them.

There was, some years ago, a public meeting at which a titled gentleman made an offensive allusion to Mendès not being 'properly French'. *'Monsieur le Comte,'* Mendès snapped back. 'Allow me to point out that whereas *my* family left Alsace after the 1870 war out of loyalty to France, *your* ancestors joined the Duke of Brunswick in 1792 in order to fight against France.'

'The name Mendès-France,' he said, 'was adopted by my ancestors around 1600. It was merely a *sobriquet*, a nickname, as you say in English; perhaps the corruption of the name of somebody one of them had married, so as to distinguish him from the other Mendèses. But there is nothing to show that the word "France" appended to the Mendès had any arrogant motive, as has sometimes been suggested by my critics. Anyway,' he smiled, 'it wasn't I who added the "France", but some unknown ancestor of mine! Maybe it was a corruption of Franco, Francis, or François. I just don't know.'

In short, Pierre Mendès-France was born in the 'soft-goods' district of Paris in 1907, the only son of a fairly prosperous family in the *confections pour dames* business. Precisely like Léon Blum, whose family had a big ribbon business in the same part of Paris.

However Jewish their background, Mendès-France's parents were determined that their son, whose unusual intelligence was obvious, would make a French career, and not be burdened with the *confections pour dames* shop, which could look after itself. He was sent to an elementary French school first, then to the Ecole Turgot in the rue Turbigo, and started right-away on his famous career as a *benjamin:* the youngest boy of all to take his *baccalaureat,* then the youngest graduate at the *Ecole des Sciences Politiques* and the *Faculté de Droit,* the youngest *Docteur en Droit,* the youngest lawyer of the Paris bar, and finally, in 1932, the youngest deputy in the Chamber of Deputies. *Ecole laique:* from his early youth Mendès-France was a great believer in the French system of non-religious State education.

There is not much that can be said about Mendès-France's years of training, and it would be idle to look laboriously for picturesque anecdotes.

Neither then nor later was he a 'picturesque' figure. He had a happy and orderly family background, and an orderly family life is something in the importance of which he has always believed. He became a law student around 1925, and his most important formative years coincided (apart from the monetary crisis of 1926 and the collapse of the *Cartel des Gauches*[1]) with the happiest and most peaceful of the France between the two wars. Poincaré was the great man who, in 1926, had 'saved the franc'; few questioned parliamentary democracy as it existed in the days of Poincaré and of the hugely fat M. Henry Chéron, the only finance minister in the whole history of France since 1914 to have accumulated enormous budget surpluses (which were, alas! to be spent on building the Maginot Line), and to have sincerely believed in the virtues of the proverbial *bas de laine,* the woollen stocking where you tucked away your savings. M. Chéron had all the virtues of the thrifty Norman farmer, and France seemed the richest and most prosperous country in Europe, far more prosperous than Britain with its chronic unemployment and its approaching sterling crisis.

[1] The moderate Left-wing coalition which, under the leadership of Herriot, had emerged from the 1924 Election.

No doubt, all was not well in France either. The cost of living was going up and the *Canard Enchaîné* had coined the phrase '*la vie Chéron*'. But by 1926 the Riff war was over; in Europe, the Briand-Stresemann idyll was in full swing, and, except for Russia and Italy, democracy seemed to be working satisfactorily in the greater part of post-Versailles Europe. When matters threatened to get out of hand, there were still sincere democrats like Raymond Poincaré to put things right. During those years a great part of Europe—and of France—liked to take the League Covenant and—around 1928-29—even the Kellogg Pact 'outlawing war', seriously.

No doubt there was, in France, a good deal of doctrinaire talk about the *mur d'argent*, the power of the vested interests, which had 'imposed' Poincaré on the Chamber of Deputies; but, compared with later years, life still seemed remarkably pleasant and easy. At Radical Congresses (especially when they met, not in Paris, but in some provincial city, these were like a four-days' talking and banqueting orgy) many speakers thundered against the *mur d'argent*—which was held responsible for that artificially-created financial panic which led to the collapse of Herriot's *Cartel des Gauches* in 1926. But the greatest issue by far was still *laïcité*, and the dangers of a clerical offensive against education. At such Congresses, Herriot and Daladier would talk for hours about the *école laïque*, and speak with reverence of Great Ancestors like Jules Ferry and Camille Pelletan and *le petit père* Combes, and of the Radical Party's sacred duty to save the *école laïque* from all ill. . . . At several such Congresses, *laïcité* and the closely allied problem of 'participation' in a government like Poincaré's were the main issues. This was the *milieu* in which Mendès-France first became politically active.

Politically, one of the few disturbing elements in France at that time was the *Action Française*. The Latin Quarter had many Maurras adepts among the students, and it seems that Mendès-France was made conscious of this before very long. Among his fellow-students were many 'reactionaries' and anti-semites.

In the 1920's, the Socialists were essentially an Opposition Party; also they were guilty of a sort of scholastic approach to world affairs. It was a time when Léon Blum was still preaching unilateral disarmament as the remedy for all ills. The Radicals, on the other hand, were a government party, steeped in the everyday affairs of running the State; they were defenders of that *laïcité*, the virtues of which Mendès had already learned to appreciate at school; they stood for progress, for *les grands principes républicains*, for racial tolerance, free enterprise, international friendship, and a kind of optimistic outlook on both home and foreign affairs, which, by and large, suited young Mendès perfectly.

1928-29 marked the height of prosperity in France between the two wars.

At the 1928 Congress at Angers, the Radicals decided to drop out of the Poincaré Government, and the Party—though then, as always, a very mixed crew—decided to go into Opposition. In 1929 came the Wall Street crash; but for quite some time the repercussions were hardly felt in France; and in 1930 the new French Premier, M. André Tardieu thought fit to boast that France, whose currency was one of the soundest in Europe, would somehow remain an island of prosperity in a sea of depression. It was an absurd illusion that did not last, and in 1931-32, not only was the budget deficit assuming alarming proportions, after three years of 'Chéron prosperity', but the fall in wholesale prices and production as well as the steep increase in unemployment were rapidly putting an end to the euphoria of the Poincaré-Chéron period. True, the position in France in 1932, with 500,000 unemployed, was not as disastrous as in Britain, with 3 million, or in Germany with 6 million unemployed; nevertheless, the deterioration of economic conditions was sufficiently marked to justify many cries of alarm on the Left, and to help the Left to gain substantial successes in the 1932 election—that very election in which Mendès-France, then just over 25, succeeded in winning Louviers for the Radicals by a ludicrously small majority of about 150 votes over the Right-wing candidate.

As a student, Mendès-France had been active in the AURS, the *Association Universitaire Républicaine-Socialiste;* before long, he became associated with the Radical Party, and, soon after graduating, he set up a lawyer's practice, not in Paris, as he could have done, but at Louviers, in the Eure. That was in 1928, when he was barely 21 years old. For four years he nursed Louviers for the Radicals, even though the chances for a Radical to be elected in so conservative and Catholic a Norman constituency must have seemed very remote at the time.

I remember once asking Mendès how he ever got to Louviers in the first place. 'Well,' he said, 'it was a bit of a fluke—a lucky fluke, as it turned out. I was then a young *militant* of the Radical Party, having joined it while active in the AURS. The Party headquarters would send me to various places in France to give talks. The first time I went to Louviers, where the people on the spot had invited me to give a talk, was at the beginning of 1928. You no doubt know that a

newly graduated young lawyer has practically no chance at all of
making a living in Paris for quite a number of years. So I thought I
had better try some provincial town. I had some good friends at
Louviers, and I liked the place; and one day I made up my mind to
settle there, and to join the Louviers Bar. The town, as you know, has
a little law court ...

'It's really hard going in Paris for a young lawyer,' he continued.
'Professionally it was greatly preferable to start in a provincial town.
It's not that my people were hard up and could not have supported
me. They were comfortably off, and were now living in the 16th
arrondissement, but I did not like the idea of being dependent on them.
So during the first year at Louviers I earned 40,000 francs—which
would have been inconceivable in Paris. 40,000 francs then—well,
that was, after all, about a million francs at the present rate—not bad
at all for a *petit avocat* in his very first year!

'From 1928 on I became increasingly active in the Radical Party.
I must say that I was still something of an idealist in those days, full
of illusions about a bright future, and full of reformist zeal. There
were many "bright" young people in the Radical Party—or on its outskirts—in those days, who soon came to be nicknamed the Young
Turks, *les jeunes Turcs*. It was never to become a coherent body; and
the way these Young Turks were to disperse in subsequent years is
both comic and tragic when you come to think of it. We were, if you
like, iconoclasts, who were critical in our attitude to the older men—
the Herriots, the Sarrauts, the Caillaux.

'Among these Young Turks were men of very different types; all
that we really had in common was our youth and our more or less
critical attitude to the "authority" of the leaders. Perhaps the most
prominent of the Young Turks was my friend Jean Zay, who was to
become a remarkable Minister of Education under the Popular Front
Governments from 1936 on. As an anti-clerical and as a Jew he was
bitterly hated by Vichy, and finally murdered by Darnand's *milice*. In
1940 we were together in prison, first at Casablanca, and later at
Clermont-Ferrand. Among other prominent Young Turks there was
Jacques Kayser, who had been active as a bit of a "rebel" in the
Radical Party since 1923; he more or less dropped out of politics in
1945, after a brief flirtation with the *progressistes;* other prominent
Young Turks were Pierre Cot, who, during the war, became practically a Communist; at the other extreme was a man like Bergery whose
influence was great in 1934, as the originator of the *Front Commun*
movement and Editor of *La Flèche;* it was he, indeed, who was one
of the first ideologists of an anti-Fascist counter-offensive after the

6 *Février* riots of 1934; but he did not get on with the Communists and, being both cynical and ambitious, he later went to the other extreme and became a ghost-writer of Pétain's broadcasts and subsequently, Vichy Ambassador, first in Moscow and then in Ankara.

'Yes, we scattered in strange ways; but all of us represented, around 1933-34, that ferment of ideas, and that search for new ideas and new solutions that was so typical of the tormented France of that period. Some of us went Fascist, others went Communist. I was one of the very few to have consistently stuck to the Radical Party—though my position in it is, as you know, a little unusual . . .

'In 1930, 1931, 1932 I was still a young man full of illusions of a happy future; what shook me very badly for the first time was, of course, the 6 *Février* rioting in the Place de la Concorde. And after that, of course, things went from bad to worse: the Spanish War, and the growing aggressiveness of Nazi Germany, and finally Munich *et la suite* . . . True, the Popular Front was a salutary reaction to the 6 *Février*, and I was, in spite of everything, one of its most whole-hearted supporters in the Radical Party; all the same, from 1937 on, I became more and more convinced that we were heading for disaster . . .

'True, it was no use just aimlessly wringing one's hands. In 1938 I was Under-Secretary of Finance in the short-lived second Blum Government. As an economist I found that period of the greatest interest, and I regret to say that I was so absorbed in economic problems that I even tended to neglect questions like national defence. Think, all the same, how rich economics were, during those years, in new theories and new ideas! the New Deal in America, and the Schacht experiment in Germany; and the whole sum-total of Keynesian economics. In 1938 I had a group of friends who closely studied all these phenomena and, although for some years, we had groped in the dark, we began to see all sorts of links between the New Deal, and Keynes, and Schacht, and were finding out new things for ourselves. I was largely responsible for the preamble—the *exposé des motifs*—of the famous Blum Finance Bill of 1938—which came to grief at the Senate; but here was really, for the first time in France, something coming fairly close to the Circuit Theory, this very important aspect of the New Deal and of the monetary aspect of the Keynesian theories. Among my friends I particularly ought to mention Georges Boris, who, at that time, had indeed, made a very profound study of New Deal economics . . .

'Of course, our orthodox financiers, men like Rueff and Caillaux, were ironical about it all; and altogether the Senate was violently hostile to the Second Blum Government, and thought it impertinent that Blum should even have dared to think of a National Government based on the Left, two years after the election—when, in the past, all "National Governments" with a "saving mission" were invariably based on the Right! And yet,' Mendès reflected, 'Caillaux *c'était tout de même un grand monsieur.*'

It was a curious reflection, considering that Caillaux had ignominiously driven the Blum Government out of office in April, 1938, after a three weeks' inglorious existence, and had treated with derision the suggestion made by *The Times* correspondent at the time that the Blum-Mendès Financial Plan was the first coherent plan produced in France since Poincaré. '*Diable!*' Caillaux had snarled. And he had sneered about this 'Rooseveltism for Lilliput'. But Mendès admired a man like Caillaux, just as he had admired Poincaré, because both were public figures of great weight and authority, and were head-and-shoulders above the ordinary run of French politicians, whether one agreed with them or not . . . And they were men who added to the prestige of France. This also explains his lasting attachment to de Gaulle in later years.

CHAPTER 2

DEPUTY AT 25

THE 1932 Election, in which Mendès-France was first elected to Parliament, was, for reasons already explained, a substantial victory for the Socialists and the Radicals—though a sterile victory since the Socialists, led by the extremely doctrinaire Léon Blum, would on no account enter into a government coalition with the Radicals. And in October, 1933, they turned out the Daladier government, thus opening an era of acute unrest and parliamentary instability in France.

A comparison of the 1928 and 1932 election returns shows, nevertheless how important an election victory it was:

	Votes in 1932 election	SEATS 1932	SEATS 1928	Under PR they would have had in 1932
RIGHT:				
Conserv.	83,000	5	8 ⎫	
URD	1,234,000	76	90 ⎬	118
Indépendants	499,000	28	26 ⎭	
CENTRE:				
Dém.-Pop.	309,000	16	19 ⎫	
Rép. de Gauche	1,300,000	72	101 ⎬	162
Rad. Ind.	956,000	62	90 ⎭	
LEFT CENTRE:				
Rad.-Soc.	1,837,000	157	109 ⎫	
Rép.-Soc.	515,000	37	32 ⎭	148
LEFT:				
Socialists (SFIO)	1,964,000	129	112	122
Soc-Com.	78,000	11	5	5
Communists	797,000	12	10	50
	9,575,000			

The election was, of course, conducted under the *scrutin d'arrondissement* system, i.e., the single-member-constituency system under which there was a second round whenever no candidate had obtained an absolute majority in the first round. The general gang-up against

11

the Communists in 1932 resulted in their being grossly under-represented—ten seats, instead of 50. *Cette vieille pourriture de scrutin d'arrondissement*, Jacques Duclos was to call it in November, 1955, when Mendès-France tried to reintroduce the system, in opposition to M. Edgar Faure. The Communists had, indeed, every reason to distrust the *scrutin d'arrondissement*: the only time it had not harmed them was in 1936, under the Popular Front, when 72 Communists were returned, with the help of the Radicals and Socialists. In all other *scrutin d'arrondissement* elections before the war they saw the other parties enter into the oddest alliances to keep them out.

It is perhaps worth noting that if, in 1932, young Mendès-France was elected at Louviers—it was thanks to Communist votes in the second round. The figures were as follows:

LOUVIERS (EURE)

Electorate 13,937

	1st Round	2nd Round
Votes cast	12,268	12,578
Duval (URD)	5,973	6,108
Mendès-France (Rad.)	5,824	6,347
Vimard (Comm.)	471	106
Others	—	17

In short, by giving some votes to Mendès-France in the second round, the Communist voters secured his victory and Duval's defeat! In 1936 they were, under the Popular Front, to secure his return even more effectively, by raising his majority from 150 to nearly 800.

Mendès-France made his first major impression on the whole of the Radical Party at the Congress that was held at the end of 1932 at Toulouse. He was the youngest Deputy elected to the Chamber in the election, and that, in itself, aroused interest in the seemingly timid and reserved young man. He took no part in some of the stormy discussions at that Congress, particularly in the head-on collision between Bergery and Herriot on German reparations and disarmament. After the abortive Tardieu Plan that Britain in particular had rejected at the League, France had now produced for the League a new Plan, complete with national units earmarked for an international 'League' army, which bore the name of the Paul-Boncour Plan. Bergery argued that the whole problem of reparations had been mishandled by Herriot who, in the end, had surrendered all along the line at the Lausanne Conference that had followed Hoover's moratorium proposal. He had thus gained nothing, and had merely lost the benefit of responding favourably to Hoover's proposal from the start. He also argued in favour of French disarmament down to the 1928 level—so long as Germany had not yet started rearming. But Herriot would take no chances on this score; all the more so as the Weimar Republic had already as good as been killed by von Papen, and the Nazis had become a major menace. Hitler was, indeed, to become Chancellor only two months later.

Mendès-France took no part in these discussions. But after Georges Bonnet, the Minister of Finance, had spoken, he made a long speech on the French financial situation. The two most striking features of this speech were the absence of any orthodox financial fetishism, and a profound study of the inequalities and injustices from which the French fiscal system was suffering. Without being strictly 'Keynesian', his speech already showed a reluctance to accept as gospel truth the classical deflationist remedies and the sanctity of a carefully balanced budget.

For three years, he said, France had seen a return of a budget deficit. There was one of $2\frac{1}{2}$ milliard francs in 1930-31, one of $4\frac{1}{2}$ milliards in 1931-32 and an estimated deficit of 12 milliards in 1932-33.

'But,' said Mendès-France, 'I know the classical theory according to which one cannot cover a permanently established budget deficit by borrowing. And yet, insofar as this deficit is something occasional, resulting from special circumstances, such as the fall in the yield of taxes, a fall due to the present economic crisis, it is permissible to resort to borrowing and so to spread over several years the consequences of such a crisis. . . . In short, *no financial measures must be taken which would weaken us economically.*'

This approach was bold and, according to French 1932 standards, fresh and new—and very different from both the financial orthodoxy of the Poincaré-Chéron period and that even less justifiable deflationist policy that was to be pursued by Laval in 1935, the whole fallacy of which was to be demonstrated by Mendès many years later in his book, *Economics and Action.*[1]

In the course of his long speech he touched on numerous subjects:

Military expenditure, which he did not propose to reduce as such, but which, he said, left room for economies, in view of the fall in the price of so many commodities bought by the Army;

The abnormally low wages of the French *fonctionnaires;* he

[1] P. Mendès-France and G. Ardant, *Economics and Action* (Paris, Unesco, 1954).

C

considered that government servants, if they were to be efficient and incorruptible, should be well paid;

The grossly unfair distribution of taxation in France, where the greater part of the peasantry, including some of its most prosperous elements, were paying no direct taxes to speak of; the same was true of the 'non-commercial' income tax schedule, under which doctors and lawyers, for instance, dodged taxes with complete impunity;

The countless ways by which taxation was evaded in the case of 'unearned' incomes; here Mendès-France cited, as in many other cases, the example of England, where taxation at source was much more wide-spread than in France.

He also protested against certain 'abuses' by the various monopolies, such as the electricity firms and the insurance companies—rather suggesting that if these were not to be nationalized, they should, at any rate, be closely controlled by the State.

'In accordance with the wishes of the electorate, we must impose on these people—whatever their strength and their power *vis-à-vis* the State, and on those who want the State to be weak, and who are enjoying all kinds of immunities which have lasted far too long—that indispensable discipline which alone can bring about an economic revival, and that *social Republic* which we alone can bring into being.' (*Loud and unanimous cheers.*)

No doubt, some of this resembled the old well-meaning Radical verbiage that had been heard before; but much in Mendès-France's speech was relatively new: a reaction against orthodox finance, a fairer distribution of taxation, which should also extend to privileged and electorally powerful bodies like the peasantry, the curbing of certain anti-social vested interests, and so on. And already he significantly raised some awkward questions—for example, about the extravagant subsidies that the State was paying to the *betteraviers* for their vast quantities of unwanted alcohol.

Curious and unusual were the reactions of the Congress to this 'maiden speech' of the young 25-year-old deputy.

M. Théodore Steeg, the Chairman, and one of the 'old beards' of the Radical Party remarked:

Your applause has well expressed the gratitude we owe Citizen Mendès-France. I should also like to take this opportunity to thank him for having won one of the hardest, and consequently, most deserved victories in the last general election. It should also like to recall that Pierre Mendès-France is the *secrétaire d'âge* [i.e.

the youngest secretary] of the Chamber of Deputies. He is only 25 years old, but he already shows how he can combine faith, conviction and courage with knowledge, science and erudition. He does honour to a Party which can attract men of such merit and talent. (*Unanimous approval and prolonged applause*.)

But the best was yet to come—and makes ironical reading in the light of the subsequent hatred between Mendès-France and Martinaud-Déplat, the future head of the 'McCarthyite' fringe of the Radical Party, and one of the pillars of the North Africa Lobby. Young Martinaud-Déplat jumped to his feet and exclaimed:

I have cheered the magnificent and exhaustive speech of that great Minister of Finance which my friend and colleague Mendès-France is certain to be one day.[1]

* * *

At the time of that Toulouse Congress, France stood on the threshold of an era of trouble. Hitler was preparing to become Germany's Chancellor; and the Disarmament Conference at Geneva was muddling along aimlessly. Britain was in the grip of a sort of 'disarmament *mystique*', and France was, as usual, having a poisonously bad press in Britain. Something of the feeling of grievance widely felt in France at the time was reflected in Herriot's emotional speech at that Toulouse Congress:

I who speak to you now am the same man who, in 1924, had certain colleagues whom he has not forgotten—Leon Bourgeois and Aristide Briand. . . . To-day their shadows follow and encourage me, and I have been trying to draw courage from their example. Once again France has conceived and proposed a new plan. In the presence of the whole world, France has made proposals which show that if she wants peace for herself, she also wants peace for others. May those be cursed who continue to accuse us of imperialism! I shall be the first to drive them out! (*Loud cheers*.) Who can accuse us of hegemony? Who in France wants hegemony? And it is also said that we are a militarist country! Oh, go and ask our workers, our peasants, our employees if any of them wants war again. Go and ask those who have spent four years in the mud and blood of the trenches! (*Loud cheers*.) France is well above this slander. Following the traditions of 1789 and 1848, our country is offering peace to Europe and to the world. I repeat it, I swear it, France has no ambition other than

[1] 29e *Congrès du Parti Républicain Radical et Radical-Socialiste*, Toulouse, November 3–6, 1932 (Paris, 1932), pp. 164–195.

to bring up her children, that painfully curtailed treasure that we still have, and to bring them up in an atmosphere of work, peace and freedom. (*Prolonged cheers, ovation.*)

A resolution, drawn up by Emile Roche, Jacques Kayser, and Edouard Pfeffer said, among other things, that the failure of the Disarmament Conference could only lead to the rearmament of Germany. It congratulated the Government on having tabled at the Disarmament Conference a Plan which, if applied, would secure equal rights, security and general controlled disarmament for all.

Alas, two months later Adolf Hitler was in power. Mendès-France had entered the political arena in a big way at a moment when the League of Nations was almost on its death-bed, and when, in France itself, parliamentary democracy was about to be challenged as never before in the anti-parliamentary riots of February, 1934. 1933, at the beginning of which Hitler came to power, still seemed a 'normal' year in France; but it did not take long before new forces came to the surface, the movement being led by the *Action Française* to the anti-parliamentary cry of 'Down with the thieves'—*A bas les voleurs!*

CHAPTER 3

1934-39: ERA OF ANGUISH

THE 1934 RIOTS

I T is essential to recall, at least briefly, a few of the principal landmarks between the French crisis of 1934 (which was the real prelude to 'Vichy'), and the outbreak of the war five years later.

A combined parliamentary and economic crisis had been brewing in France, particularly since the fall of the Daladier government in October, 1933. This crisis came to a head with the 'bombshell' of the *affaire Stavisky* in January, 1934. The disclosures (some true, others false) of the close links between this adventurer—who was conveniently 'suicided' by the police on January 8—and a number of (chiefly Radical) politicians, and of large-scale corruption extending to Parliament, the judiciary and the police led to anti-parliamentary rioting in Paris throughout January, until the fall of the Chautemps government, whose rôle in minimizing the Stavisky scandal appeared particularly suspect.

There followed the appointment of a 'strong men' government under M. Daladier, who, believing Jean Chiappe, the Prefect of Police, to be largely responsible for the anti-parliamentary agitation by the *Action Française*, and a number of 'leagues'—the *Croix de Feu*, the *Jeunesses Patriotes*, the *Solidarité Française* and others—dismissed him, after offering him the post of Resident-General in Morocco, which Chiappe refused.

This 'provocation' of the 'Fascist leagues' by the Daladier Government led to mass demonstrations in the Place de la Concorde on the evening of February 6. 100,000 persons assembled in the Place de la Concorde, and a pitched battle broke out between the demonstrators and the police. On two occasions the demonstrators tried to break through the police cordons across the Concorde Bridge and invade the Chamber of Deputies. They would have broken through, had not the police been ordered to open fire. In the two attacks some twenty people were killed; and there were, moreover, several hundred wounded among both the police and the demonstrators.

On the following day, despite the Socialists' warning that it was dangerous for the government to 'surrender to street pressure' the Daladier Government resigned. There followed in Paris a night of chaos and large-scale looting. President Lebrun had

17

meantime summoned ex-President Doumergue to Paris to form a 'national government'.

On February 9, the Communists (whose attitude on February 6 had been, to say the least, ambiguous), staged the first 'anti-Fascist' demonstration around the Place de la République. There were numerous clashes with the police, and several casualties.

On February 12, the CGT, the Communists and Socialists held what were meant to be separate 'anti-Fascist' demonstrations, but these, together with the general strike called by the trade unions, developed into what was in effect a gigantic joint demonstration, foreshadowing the Popular Front. The day revealed a genuine desire for a united anti-Fascist front among the rank-and-file, though there were many doubts on the subject among both the Socialist and the Communist leadership.[1]

The '6th of February' and the '12th of February' became symbols of that conflict between the 'two Frances' which was to continue, in various forms, during the next few years.

Although the 6th of February was an extremely confused affair in many ways, it had, nevertheless, played into the hands of all the Right-wing and anti-parliamentary forces in the country, and marked, in a sense, a revival of the 'anti-Dreyfus' spirit, but, even more so, the beginning of something which, six years later, became crystallized at Vichy.[2]

Between '6th of February' Fascism and '12th of February' anti-Fascism there was a large body of French opinion that hesitated, and still liked to believe in the possibility of a 'third way'. But the attraction to either one extreme or the other was very strong. The case of Daladier is significant in this respect; having first been hurled to the 'Left' by the menace of Fascism, and having joined the Popular Front of 1935, he then went to the other extreme and, especially after Munich, proceeded to build up something of an authoritarian regime, which was fanatically anti-Communist, and already provided a foretaste of 'Vichy'.

The events of February, 1934, certainly shook France, and gave rise to some very hard thinking in many quarters. The ferment of ideas had, indeed, already set in before 1934; for example, in the French

[1] For full details of this turning-point in France's pre-war history see the author's *France in Ferment* (Jarrolds, London, 1934).

[2] Cf. the author's *France and Munich: Before and After the Surrender* (Hamilton, London, 1939).

Socialist Party where, in 1933, an 'authoritarian' rebellion—which 'horrified' Léon Blum (as he put it)—was led by a 'neo-Socialist' group with Marcel Déat, the future Nazi, and Adrien Marquet, a future Vichyite at their head. Their slogan was 'Order, Authority, Nation', and Déat became the principal ideologist of this group. The impact of Hitler's victory in Germany was unmistakable.

The Radical Party, for its part, was sharply divided: there were those who considered the 6th of February a salutary warning, and thought the 'National Government' under Doumergue, and with Herriot included in this ministry of 'truce', to be a lesser evil. It was not until Doumergue, strongly supported by Tardieu and the *Croix de Feu* (which by now had become the most powerful of the 'Fascist Leagues'), had threatened to revise the Constitution in an authoritarian manner, and had declared war, not only on the Communists, but also on the Socialists, that the Radicals decided to take the risk (despite much 'street intimidation') of breaking up the Doumergue Government in October.

Provincial France was, at that time, severely shaken by the 'phantom of Fascism', and nearly all Radicals were conscious of this: not only the Young Turks like Zay, Mendès-France and Pierre Cot, but also some of the Radicals inside the Government, especially Herriot, 'France's republican conscience'. As for Daladier, the prospect of a Popular Front which was beginning to take shape at that time, seemed to him like a short cut to his own rehabilitation.

But this interest in the Popular Front was not, in fact, shared by the 'governmental' Radicals, even despite their decision to break up the Doumergue Government, and to replace it by a 'normal' Centre coalition under Flandin.

The Popular Front, which became a reality in the middle of 1935, received full support from Daladier and from the younger Radicals, but only half-hearted support (if that) from the older men. To these, the election alliance with the Socialists and Communists in 1936 was little more than a tactical manœuvre, and it was not long, in 1936, especially after the stay-in strikes of June that year, before they began to look the other way.

Although Mendès-France was not in great evidence in 1934, 1935 and 1936, a period during which he worked hard on various Chamber Committees, notably on the technical Customs Committee as well as at the *mairie* of Louviers (he was elected mayor of Louviers in 1935)— he was certainly among the young Radicals most sympathetic to the Popular Front—though probably not quite as whole-heartedly as, say, Pierre Cot, whom many still remember perched on the hood of a taxi and waving a tricolour flag in the Place de la Bastille at the first great Popular Front demonstration on July 14, 1935.

Between the fall of the Doumergue Government in October, 1934, and the general election of May, 1936, the French Governments were headed first by M. Flandin (who liked to impersonate a sort of return to 'republican normality'); then by Laval, who conducted a sharp deflationist policy at home and a pro-Italian policy abroad (Rome agreements, Stresa, Free Hand in Abyssinia, Hoare-Laval Plan), and lastly, by the ill-fated Albert Sarraut, one of the Old Men of the Radical Party, under whose government, in March, 1936, Hitler reoccupied the Rhineland—which was the first step towards the smashing of France's whole system of alliances in Europe.

Then came the 1936 election which marked a substantial victory for the Popular Front.

The 'National Front'—which received an eve-of-the-poll boost from Marshal Pétain—was defeated. The figures were:

				Under Proportional Representation there would have been:
NATIONAL FRONT	..	..	222 Seats	259 Seats
POPULAR FRONT:				
Radicals ..	109 Seats			89
Rep. Soc., etc.	56			46
Socialists	149			121
Communists	72			93
		—		
		386		
	Total ..		608 Seats	608 Seats

THE POPULAR FRONT WORRIES THE RADICALS

The Communists supported the Blum Government, but refused to enter it; and the two principal government parties were the Socialists and the Radicals. The Communists preferred to 'lead the masses', and claimed the greater share of the credit for the great Popular Front reforms of June–July, 1936, that were agreed to under the pressure of the vast strike movement of June, 1936: the Matignon Agreements on higher wages, collective bargaining, holidays with pay, 40-hour week, etc. There is no doubt that these agreements, and, above all, the stay-in strikes had rattled many of the Radicals who, in 1934, had become so alarmed by 'Fascism'. Also, as time went on, they were more and more worried about the Spanish War, and the Communist agitation in favour of 'Aeroplanes for Spain', and against the non-intervention to which Blum and his Radical Foreign Minister, M. Delbos, had subscribed; Blum with some qualms, Delbos much more wholeheartedly . . .

The post-election Congress of the Radical Party met at Biarritz on October 22 in a stormy and uneasy atmosphere.

The opening speech by Daladier, the Minister of Defence, already produced some significant arguments and reactions.

Last year in Paris, at the Salle Wagram, our Party unanimously decided to collaborate with all the popular forces in the country. (*Protests.*) Against the manœuvres and ambitions of Fascism, all democrats united, in order to defend the Republic. (*More protests.*)

Then came the election argument:

We lost 400,000 votes in the election. But in view of the enormous discontent that existed in the country, we would have lost many more votes, if we hadn't joined the Popular Front . . . In 1934 there were one million wage earners in this country who were earning less than 15 francs a day. Who can condemn the collective agreements? Who can condemn the holidays with pay, or the increase in wages?

On the whole, the Congress was in a nervous state, and showed a great deal of hostility to the Popular Front. Among its left-wing members, it is true, there was, for example, M. Albert Bayet, who, unwilling to close his eyes to the Fascist menace that had not been eliminated entirely (far from it), argued in favour of a purge in the civil service where, he said, there were 'far too many high officials who are hostile to the régime and to the republican institutions, of which they ought to be the servants . . .'

Vichy, in short, was already in the air. But, on the other hand, nothing was done to put an end to the 'non-intervention' policy in Spain, and M. Delbos, the Foreign Minister, was wholly non-interventionist, and 'hoped' that the London talks under the chairmanship of Lord Perth would result in non-intervention becoming a reality . . . As for the military situation of France, General Brissaud-Desmaillet, who was the *rapporteur* on Defence, expressed great optimism at the thought that the defence of France was 'in able Radical hands'—with Daladier at the Ministry of Defence, Cot at the Air Ministry, and Gasnier-Duparc at the Ministry of Marine . . . 'They have taken the necessary measures so that our frontiers should be effectively and

energetically defended . . .' He added that, thanks to Daladier, the
Maginot Line was being effectively extended all along the Belgian
border . . . He even indicated that 'good progress' was being made in
the motorization and mechanization of the French Army.

It all makes pretty grim and ironical reading today. There were
some economic discussions. A certain M. Potut violently criticized the
economics and finance of the Popular Front Government. And it was,
significantly, Mendès-France who took the defence of the Popular
Front in financial and economic matters. In particular, he defended
the devaluation which came into force in the autumn of 1936.

As distinct from his Toulouse report four years earlier, Mendès-
France was on highly controversial ground, and this time his speech
was very far from producing unanimous applause.

MENDÈS DEFENDS THE POPULAR FRONT

This time he was being more unorthodox than was good for anyone
wishing to be popular with the *vieilles barbes* of the Radical Party, that
party where, it was said, there were more beards to the square yard
than anywhere else in France.

'The four years that have elapsed since my report to the
Toulouse Congress,' he said, 'were marked by immense economic
and financial difficulties in France . . . The last parliament practised
what is known as "deflation". Some of you sincerely believed that
it could solve our troubles. Others knew that it was a thoroughly
anti-democratic device, and wholly incapable of putting an end to
the slump. This policy of deflation has been condemned by the
electorate . . .

'Our production index dropped from 107 in 1933 to 94 in 1935;
and in some branches—such as building and textiles—the slump
was much worse still. In October, 1933, we had 275,000 unemployed; two years later, there were 426,000. In 1935, 35 per cent of
investments produced no dividends; there was a catastrophic fall
in agricultural prices, with wheat touching rock-bottom at 35
frs. a quintal. Wages dropped by 30 per cent in a few years.

'1934-35 were years of systematic deflation in France—and
that at a time when the rest of the world was beginning to con-
valesce; in May, 1936, USA production was back to 91, and British
production back to 116.'

At first, Mendès-France said, the Blum Government had tried to
avoid devaluation. Blum had accepted as his slogan 'neither deflation,
nor devaluation, but reflation'.

A voice came from the hall: 'Reflation—it doesn't mean a damn
thing.'

Mendès-France: Yes, it does. Its purpose was to make up for the effects of the deflation of the previous years, and even to go beyond that by acting on the country's economy—not, indeed, in order to make it anaemic, but to make it stronger. It was a case of stimulating purchasing power. In the case of the workers, that was the purpose of the Matignon agreements, which added 12 milliard francs to the purchasing power of the working class. In the case of the peasants, a rise in agricultural prices was provided for.

Only, Mendès continued, amidst loud booing, it was, of course, important that, in the circumstances, there should be no rise in retail prices. Unfortunately, the hoarded capital in this country refused to help. Of the loan of 4 milliard francs that was raised, Big Business subscribed only 180 millions ...

He went on, however, to demonstrate that since the inevitable devaluation of October, 1936, there were signs of a marked improvement in France's economic prospects; also, law and order were coming into their own again. The end of his speech was loudly cheered.

'Loud cheers' perhaps. But with a large part of the Radical Congress of 1936, Mendès-France had made himself unpopular; it was this part of the Congress which also gave 'loud cheers' to the orthodox M. Potut when he abused Vincent Auriol, the Finance Minister, and declared that devaluation was 'contrary to the Party's doctrine and, indeed, contrary to plain honesty'.

The clock of history went on ticking ominously. If at Toulouse, four years before, some alarm was expressed over the doings of Von Papen in Germany, the Biarritz Congress paid vague compliments to the Radical Foreign Minister M. Delbos who, poor man, had come into office only to find 'Locarno' in ruins, who was now being urged to do what he could 'to strengthen the League Covenant', and was congratulated on having subscribed to the Non-Intervention policy in Spain.

Of course it was no good; but the Radicals at Biarritz preferred not to think too much of what was going on—only a few miles south of Biarritz, in the Spanish part of that same Basque country. ... Then came 1937, without any major disaster having occurred in the world. In France, the Popular Front had been watered down—with Blum proclaiming the 'pause', and with Georges Bonnet being brought back from the Washington Embassy to take the finances of France in hand. Bonnet, who was much more orthodox than Vincent Auriol, and whose name never produced any booing among the *bien-pensants* at Radical Congresses. ...

BLUM 'DISCOVERS' MENDÈS

At the end of 1937, Delbos, the Foreign Minister, had gone on his tour through Central and Eastern Europe, only to find France's system of alliances virtually in ruins. After Hitler's 1936 Rhineland *coup*, Delbos found that, of all her allies, the Czechs alone still believed in the virtues of the French Alliance.

And then, in 1938, the big trouble started.

In March, Hitler marched into Austria. On that day France was without a Government. The cautious M. Chautemps, who had understood the full significance of Mr. Eden's resignation and of Mr. Chamberlain's Pontius Pilate gesture in respect of Austria just over a fortnight before, knew that Austria was doomed, and preferred to resign before he had to face the music. . . . Chautemps—*le ténébreux*, the *Action Française* used to call him—had, throughout 1937, played the leading rôle in breaking up the Popular Front from inside. Together with Bonnet—whom he had appointed Finance Minister after the fall of the first Popular Front Government in the spring of 1937—he made relations increasingly difficult between Radicals and Socialists.

Sandwiched between the Chautemps-Bonnet Government (which nearly lasted till the Anschluss) and the Daladier-Bonnet Government (which extended to Munich and beyond) was the brief interlude of the second Blum Government, which, extraordinarily enough, tried to put the clock back—back to the *Front Populaire* conceptions of 1936—with a substantial degree of planning, a camouflaged type of exchange control, a rebellion against the Bank of France, the stimulation of purchasing power, and, in the foreign field, a sudden breakaway from Chamberlainism, and a refusal to support any longer the non-intervention farce in Spain. Blum and his Foreign Minister Paul-Boncour decided to throw open the frontier into Republican Spain, and send arms to the Republicans.

'Rooseveltism for Lilliput', Caillaux had already snarled at the first Front Populaire Government; and he was even more vicious this time. As for Blum's and Paul Boncour's new policy *vis-à-vis* Spain, it caused alarm and despondency at Downing Street, and Mr. Chamberlain was praying for an early downfall of this anachronistic monster. . . .

Already in January, 1938, Blum had tried to form a broad 'national coalition' stretching 'from Reynaud to Thorez'; but he received no support from the Right, and the Radicals, too, were reluctant to enter into a government including the Communists. So the plan failed, and instead, M. Chautemps formed his second government which lasted from January to March 8, 1938.

Three days later, the Germans marched into Austria, and Blum now thought that the time was *really* ripe for a genuine National Government, 'not like the Poincaré and Doumergue governments based on the Right, but a National Government around the working class, directed by the Socialists, and with the brotherly support of the CGT'. But it came to nothing. The Right would not hear of Blum's proposal, despite the pathetic appeal he addressed to them on March 12, the day after the *Anschluss*. He argued that, much as he disliked the Communists, it was impossible to keep them out in such a national emergency; for, in case of war, they would fight for France like all others. He even offered to let the Right choose the Finance Minister. But it was no good. The Right knew that the *Front Populaire*, if left to itself, would soon die a natural death; and Flandin and other Right-wing leaders were determined to drive not only the Communists, but also the Socialists into opposition.

So Blum formed a government of Socialists and Radicals, almost the very image of the *Front Populaire* government of June, 1936. It was an anachronism, and Blum himself felt it keenly, and repeated a little too often that this was the wrong kind of government in the circumstances, but that it would gladly resign if a more representative government could take its place. These reflections only played into the hands of its enemies.

All the same, Blum decided to die fighting, and was determined to present his ambitious plenary powers Bill to the Senate, after it had been passed by a small majority at the Chamber. As I wrote at the time:

> Some of the Socialists had the mistaken idea that the over-throw of yet another Left-wing government by the Senate could become the basis of a great anti-Senate campaign in the country... Blum's plenary powers Bill was a bold enterprise, and was intended, among other things, as a great financial sermon to the country. It went on the assumption that France could not go on living from hand to mouth, as she had done in the last seven years, with a little inflation here, and a little borrowing there... The reliance on 'confidence' had been overdone; Blum argued that, even in the best of circumstances, the repatriation of exported capital, estimated at 80 milliard francs, and the 'unfreezing' of hoarded capital, could meet only a small part of the Treasury's borrowing needs... In fact, Blum was proposing to put France on what he called a semi-war basis, complete with a small capital levy, a camouflaged form of exchange control, a large variety of taxes, and—this was to be labour's contribution to the 'all-round sacrifices'—a readjustment of the 40-hour week. Trade and production must be revived by a wide expansion of credit. Here was planned

economy, an economy reminiscent in some ways of German and Italian methods.[1]

Who had been working on this Plan—a plan which had stirred the imagination of the Paris correspondent of *The Times*, who had declared it to be the first coherent plan since Poincaré? It was, though few people knew it at the time, largely the work of an obscure Under-Secretary of Finance, a young man called Mendès-France.

I have already quoted a conversation with Mendès-France, in the course of which he recalled how he had worked on this Blum Plan, and was largely responsible for its *exposé des motifs*. In his quiet way, Mendès had, during previous years (as was already apparent from his two Radical Congress Reports) looked at the world around him: at the New Deal, at Schacht, at Keynes, and had tried to apply some of this theory and practice to France.

Georges Boris, one of his oldest friends, once described to me as follows the early days of Mendès-France:

I've known Mendès since 1932, especially since 1938, but it is not true, as has been alleged, that I 'inflicted' him on Blum. Although Mendès was active on the economic committees of the Chamber and was president of the Customs Committee, he was little known, and Blum asked me whether he knew much about fiscal reform. I said I thought so. So Blum invited him to his flat on the Ile St. Louis, and there he was tremendously impressed by Mendès's dazzling *exposé*, and its extreme simplicity and clarity. Blum took a great liking to him. It was, of course, a great moment in Mendès's career. He was not then the Mendès-France of today; he was still a junior, who tended to be overawed by Blum, very much a *vieux monsieur*. However, as you know, that Government didn't last, and was mercilessly turned out at the Senate by Caillaux . . .

Little is known of what young Mendès-France really felt about it all in those days. No doubt it was flattering for him to be made Under-Secretary of Finance at the age of 31; but did he have any illusions that the Blum Government could last? Blum personally impressed him; but it seems that his ideas on the Popular Front were extremely divided. He was not carried away by the Popular Front *mystique* of 1936, with its stay-in strikes—any more than he was going to be carried away by the CNR Charter of 1944; he was no pro-Communist, and although he condemned the deflationist policy of Laval of 1935 as a failure, and as

[1] Alexander Werth, *France and Munich: Before and After the Surrender* (London, 1939), pp 127–128.

a perfect demonstration of the fallacy of the 'un-Keynesian' and classical methods, he was reticent on the economic and financial aspects of the Popular Front. Everything, for instance, shows that, although he welcomed the Matignon Agreements of 1936, which held out a promise of more normal relations between capital and labour on the basis of collective bargaining, he cannot have done other than deplore the effects on French production of the newly-introduced 40-hour week.

He did not formally become a 'Blum man' until 1938, He was, in the last analysis, persuaded to do so by the appalling dangers of the international situation.

'In March–April, 1938,' he later wrote, 'I worked with Blum in elaborating a financial Bill the purpose of which was to mobilize all the means of production and all the wealth of the nation in order to raise our defence to the very highest degree of efficiency. For political reasons, our Bill was rejected by the Senate.'[1]

And so it came to nothing.

MENDÈS SILENCED BY MUNICH

After his brief under-secretaryship of April 1938, Mendès faded from public view. He continued with his various 'technical' jobs, and with his *mairie* at Louviers, but preferred not to dabble in high politics. He was in the depths of gloom.

'My study of the economic realities of the dreadful years of 1937, '38 and '39 (he wrote in 1943) convinced me only too clearly what was in store . . . We were rapidly advancing towards war, which Germany would start very soon. She was determined to make a maximum effort to fight a short victorious war, while the democracies were much slower in mobilizing their resources, and were only preparing for a defensive war. The highest military authorities—Weygand, Pétain, Gamelin—were saying that our territory could never be invaded and that, protected by the Maginot Line, we could forge our weapons and take the offensive later, after the enemy had been weakened by the frittering away of his reserves . . .'

Occasionally he was included by the supporters of 'appeasement', and by pro-Fascist and anti-semitic papers among the 'warmongers'; and subsequently, during the war, he himself liked to refer to himself as a 'notorious anti-Munichite'. In reality, his attitude was not as emphatic as it might have been. Like 535 other deputies (including all

[1] *Liberté, liberté chérie* (New York, 1943), p. 5.

the Radicals but one) he voted for the Daladier Government in the famous vote of October 4, 1938, thus implicitly approving the Munich Settlement. The only ones to vote against it were the 73 Communists, one obscure Radical, and a nationalist, M. de Kerillis. Subsequently, when the Daladier Government declared the Popular Front to be officially at an end, and when it asked for its Plenary Powers of October, 1938, and demanded that its general policy—both home and foreign—complete with its drive against the trade unions—be approved, Mendès-France was among the 25 or 30 Radical deputies to abstain. He was obviously out of sympathy both with Bonnet's post-Munich foreign policy, complete with the Franco-German apotheosis of the Ribbentrop visit to Paris in December, 1938, and its free-hand-in-the-East implications, and with Daladier's authoritarian way of governing the country with the full support of the Right, and against both the Communists and the Socialists.

Daladier, already then supported in his reactionary policy by Radicals like Emile Roche and Martinaud-Déplat, fancied himself the 'strong man of France' or, rather, tried to persuade himself that he was one, though, at heart, he had grave doubts on the subject. Although Munich had made him suffer, he allowed himself to be fêted as the 'saviour of peace'. When, at the Marseille Congress of the Radical Party at the end of October, the small left-wing minority (with which Mendès-France was in sympathy, though he did not officially identify himself with it) proposed to support Albert Bayet's motion which said: 'We let Ethiopia down; we handed Spain over to Franco, and we allowed Czechoslovakia to be disembered', Daladier, supported by the vast majority of the Congress, would have none of it. Even when Herriot proposed that the final motion include some reference to France's 'fidelity to the League of Nations', Daladier said that France, of course, loved the League of Nations, but in view of Italy's and Germany's attitude to it, he asked that Herriot refrain from pressing the point. Herriot, who had 'sat dreamily through the speeches exalting the virtues of Munich',[1] walked out. How, indeed, could Herriot be anything but 'dreamy' when he listened to Daladier proclaiming, amid roars of approval from the provincial delegates, that 'the Munich settlement was in absolutely no sense whatsoever a capitulation for France'?

'Dreadful years—1937—1938—1939', Mendès wrote in 1943, as he looked back on this period; the years of the collapse of the League, the years of Austria, Munich, and of that pre-Vichy atmosphere which already came into being in France at the time of the Ribbentrop visit to Paris in December, 1938. He was unhappy, he knew that

[1] *Le Temps*, October 29, 1938.

was imminent, but while feebly protesting in all sorts of small ways—for instance by not supporting Daladier—he did not feel in a sufficiently strong position to take a strikingly independent stand. He was cautious, for instance, not to identify himself too closely with Bayet when, in the midst of booing, the latter refused, unlike the majority of the Radical Congress

to congratulate Premier Daladier and Georges Bonnet on their clearsightedness, the courage and the energy with which, during the perilous weeks of September, they safeguarded the preservation of peace

or when Bayet declared in the midst of an uproar:

'Many of you are rejoicing because the Popular Front has broken up. I deplore it, because it means the divorce between the Radical Party and the working class of this country.'

Or, better still, when he proposed a vote condemning the behaviour of Flandin who, during the pre-Munich call-up of reservists, tried to sabotage this mobilization by means of posters, and later sent an enthusiastic telegram to Hitler, congratulating him on the Munich settlement.

Mendès-France was in sympathy with all this, but did not say much. He was certainly not impressed by Daladier's antics. When, on November 19, Daladier proclaimed: 'France can count on me to act as a Jacobin', Margaine, Mendès-France, Pierre Cot and six other Radicals abstained from approving Daladier's 'strong-man' stuff. For one thing, the 'Jacobin' was in remarkably un-Jacobin company. . . .

Then came Daladier's victory over that General Strike of November 30—a strike which was, indirectly, a belated protest against Munich, as well as against Daladier's *pleins pouvoirs*. Daladier's line was approved by 315 votes to 214, and there were 54 abstentions, including 30 Radical abstentions, Margaine, André Albert, Pierre Cot, Mendès-France, and even Delbos being among them.

It was, after all, psychologically impossible for a man like Mendès-France to vote for a Government whose Foreign Minister had just been hobnobbing with Ribbentrop in the most suspect manner imaginable, and who was encouraging a fantastic press campaign in the *Matin* and even the *Temps* in favour of an independent 'Greater Ukraine' under German suzerainty!

The whole international atmosphere during that post-Munich

period was 'phoney' in more ways than one—with its 'Greater Ukraine' campaign, its Ribbentrop visit, in the course of which the two Jewish members of the French Government—Georges Mandel and Jean Zay—were not invited to official receptions in deference to the Guest; with the *Temps* articles describing the happy state of post-Munich Czechoslovakia, and with Chamberlain and Halifax still pretending, during their visit to Paris, that Munich was a great act of statesmanship. And the majority of the Radical Party was as pro-Munich as was the extreme Right. If Herriot and Delbos felt at least a little uneasy, most of the leaders, including Caillaux (who, only a few months before, had overthrown at the Senate the Blum Government, in which Mendès had held his first government post) paid tribute after tribute to the 'wisdom' and the 'statesmanship' of Daladier and Bonnet.[1] Temperamentally and personally, Mendès-France would have been more at home in the Socialist Party, where there were men whom he admired, and from whom he had received his first major encouragement, such as Léon Blum.

Why he persisted in staying in the Radical Party, where there were few men, apart from Herriot, with whom he was in sympathy at all, is a minor mystery in the life of Mendès-France. Perhaps the real answer is 'Louviers'—that Louviers where, on the village-pump scale, he had proved an outstanding success as its Mayor, and where he had also succeeded in building up one of the more important Radical Federations in the country. To leave the Party was to hand over the local Radical Federation to others.

He had his country house at Louviers; when, while in prison, he thought of his family, it was always with Louviers as their background. Louviers, to him, symbolized his first election victory, his activity as a local administrator, his roots in the French soil. Louviers was his home, and, with Louviers went the Radical Federation of the Eure. . . . Moreover, he was not, in any doctrinaire sense, a Socialist.

Little need be said of Mendès-France during the months that preceded the outbreak of war. 1939, as he later wrote, was as 'horrible' as had been 1938 and 1937. The atmosphere in Europe had become intolerable, and the outbreak of World War II brought him an uncanny feeling of relief, as to so many others. The humiliating era of kowtowing to Ribbentrop and of hanging on Hitler's lips was over at last; also, for the first time since Munich, did a man like Mendès-France feel that he had at last been fully restored to the status of a full-fledged French citizen.

As Chairman of the Customs Committee of the Chamber (one of

[1] e.g., Caillaux' speech at Tours. *Le Temps*, December 9, 1938.

the most technical and least exciting and controversial committees) he had done his work conscientiously, but without enthusiasm.

'During those last ten years, parliamentary government had shown deficiencies, which alarmed all true believers in democracy,'[1] he wrote in 1943. And the last ten or twelve months of this democracy, with Daladier trying to ape Hitler and Mussolini, had been even less stimulating to watch than before.

Liberté, liberté chérie, p. 5.

PART II
WAR

WAR

From Defeat to Liberation

YOUNG Mendès-France's experience of Vichy France had a profound effect on his outlook. Although, in the book he wrote in 1943, after his escape, he uttered many of the usual remarks, almost compulsory in wartime, about the sound instincts of 'the French people', there is undoubtedly something that left a deep mark on his character: the nauseating feeling that there was a terrifying amount of sycophancy in France, and a puzzling amount of cruelty and *méchanceté*. In his book he tried to convince his readers, and convince himself that 'Vichy' was not 'typical' of France, and that its hundreds of thousands of policemen, servile judges, spies, gaolers, and the pompous asses of Pétain's Legion (whom he met after his escape from the Clermont-Ferrand military prison) were not as 'typical' as the many friendly and loyal people he had known; but the impression given by his book is that he felt, even after his escape, a hunted man, who could trust almost nobody.

I remember his reflecting, many years later, on the strange anomaly of the French civil service. The trouble with them, he said, was that they had been demoralized by Vichy. They had been obliged to serve Vichy; and how was one to expect all of them, or even most of them, to be devoted servants of the Fourth Republic? To them, a job was a job, whoever was boss, and how, in the circumstances, was it possible to expect from these people any sort of republican *mystique?*

Although in the course of his narrative he speaks with admiration of many decent and loyal men he met—particularly the officers under whom he had served, and who, ignoring the wishes of the Vichy Government and of its judges and public prosecutor, denied the charges of desertion brought against him, and declared him to have been 'absolutely incapable of desertion'—the men who left the deepest impression on Mendès-France were the 'villains'. For instance, the policemen, the gaolers, a *juge d'instruction* like the utterly cynical Colonel Leprêtre, or the sycophantic Colonel Bailly, who had bowed Mendès-France, though only a lieutenant, into the lift during his visit to the Air Ministry on May 10, 1940, and had peppered his speech with *Monsieur le Ministre* this and *Monsieur le Ministre* that, but who, in 1941, as Darlan's ADC, was prepared to give against Mendès-France the most dubious evidence at the latter's trial.

35

When the war broke out in September, 1939, Mendès-France, who was only 32, reflected that there would not be much for a deputy to do. He seems also to have taken the word of the Gamelins, Pétains and Weygands that the war in Europe would be a long and dreary affair, based on the British hope that, after several years of blockade and bombing, Germany would be broken economically.

It seems to have been a point of honour with him, as a politician who had, for a long time, been treated as one of the 'warmongers', to do some actual fighting. He started therefore looking for an 'active' front; and as a lieutenant of the French air force, he had himself sent to the Middle East. He arrived at Beyrouth in September 1939 and stayed there till the following spring.

> I wanted to become a navigator. I met with the objection that, in theory, men of 33 were not accepted as airmen. However, without being an athlete, I was strong and healthy. So I persisted, and finally received satisfaction. On April 22, 1940, I was posted observer, with congratulations from the examining commission . . . A few days later, Colonel Alamichel, commander of the French air forces in the Middle East, granted me a long leave, so that I could go to France to deal with my constituency, and to take a rest, which I badly needed, after the strenuous course of training I had undergone in a climate that did not suit me . . .[1]

Arriving in Paris on May 4, 1940, less than a week before the great German offensive, Mendès-France found the state of morale in the country extremely low.

> Everybody was talking of Recreation in the Army, Sports in the Army, Art in the Army, Theatre in the Army . . . On May 7 or 8, I came across a truly fantastic example of the fools' paradise which the 'phoney war' had created in France, and not least among important persons, with an influence on the press, and even among members of the Government. I saw in a paper an Appeal for 'Rosebushes on the Maginot Line'. A number of very distinguished ladies had formed a committee, under the chairmanship, I believe, of Mme. H. de Carbuccia, wife of the editor of *Gringoire*, which had by this time become a flag-waving sort of publication . . . These well-meaning ladies had been distressed at the thought that so many soldiers should be living in the dugouts of the Maginot Line, without any loveliness and poetry to adorn their lives. So they had the idea of planting rose-bushes all along the Maginot Line; several hundred thousand francs were collected, and even the City of Paris had contributed to this worthy undertaking . . .

[1] *Liberté, liberté chérie*, p. 6. An abridged version of this book was published in English in 1956 under the title *The Pursuit of Freedom* (Longmans, Green).

Nobody in the government or at the head of the army had reacted in any way against this kind of dangerous lunacy. For it *was* dangerous . . .

A few men like Reynaud, Blum and Mandel saw the danger; but the French High Command lacked imagination and a lively mind, and this, as it happened, suited the British, who were still depending on the blockade to 'exhaust' Germany.

Mendès-France found Daladier, the Minister of Defence, about whom he had already developed many doubts during the Munich period, more than disappointing.

Unfortunately, he said, the generals were in favour of 'waiting'. Daladier, who had a great faith in his 'specialists' and 'experts', let them take the decisions. He seemed to know, at the back of his mind, that France was following the wrong road, or, at any rate, a road that was dangerous in many ways; but as a civilian, he did not have the courage to dictate a different policy to the soldiers. . . . Also, he attached too much importance to political and parliamentary intrigues and wirepulling.

Thus, under pressure from rural deputies, he would grant long leave to peasant recruits in the Army, some of whom were actually allowed to go home on May 10, the very day of the German invasion!

It does not appear from Mendès-France's narrative of the few days he spent in Paris just before the German invasion that he was aware of some much deeper plotting that was going on around men like Deat and Laval; nor did he (writing, as he did, in 1943) have any comments to make on the Communist position. The Communist party had been disbanded, and many of its leaders were in gaol. But he was struck by the general state of demoralization and irresponsibility into which France had sunk during the eight months of the 'phoney war'.

He learned of the German invasion on the morning of May 10, during a visit he paid to M. Laurent-Eynac, the Minister of Air. Laurent-Eynac received him 'very amiably', but when Mendès-France asked to be sent to Norway, the Minister said: 'Good heavens! Haven't you heard? . . .'

I was lucky to be in France, where they were fighting now. I asked the Minister to incorporate me in a fighting unit . . . He thereupon sent me to see Colonel Lucien, head of Military Personnel . . .

This Colonel had to admit to Mendès-France that there were quite enough airmen in France . . . but not enough planes. And he suggested that Mendès take another course of training—which did not suit him at all. He thought he would try again.

That day he had lunch with his wife, with Emil Ludwig and Henri de Kerillis, the right-wing deputy (and the only one to have voted against the Munich settlement), and he listened with some scepticism to Kerillis's prophecy that the Germans would be in Paris 'within a month'. . . .

What happened to Lieutenant Mendès-France between May 10 and the collapse of the French resistance on June 17? In his book, *Liberté, liberté chérie* he tells in great detail about the various interviews he had at the Air Ministry, where he tried to be drafted into a fighting unit—but without success—again because of the large number of trained airmen and the wholly inadequate number of planes. This part of the story, though it mattered to Mendès-France (who did his utmost to prove that he had *not* deserted—not by the widest stretch of the imagination)—is of little interest today. It was conclusively proved at his trial at Clermont-Ferrand in 1941 (despite the verdict) that he had not deserted, and that the action taken against him was a crude political machination. That is all there is to it. But, psychologically, it is curious that Mendès-France should have gone to such endless trouble to convince his readers that he was no deserter; it is typical perhaps of the man's defensive reflexes, and of his acute consciousness of the hostility that was surrounding him in Vichy France.

At the Air Ministry he saw the slimy Captain Bailly, who, as already said, had treated him with the greatest deference as '*Monsieur le Ministre*' and was later to be the only one to testify against him at the Clermont trial; and Colonel Lucien who, in the end, instructed him not to return to Syria but to join the air force unit, into which he had been drafted, at Merignac-Bordeaux airport. But Lucien had not reached this decision until June 10, when everything in Paris was already in a state of chaos, with the population on the run, and with all the government offices on the point of being evacuated. The Germans were, indeed, to enter Paris four days later. In his book Mendès describes the panic in Paris on May 16, but thinks that, on the whole, morale in Paris was reasonably good:

'These magnificent people foresee everything, are prepared for everything, except treason. . . .'

Perhaps allowances should be made for the fact that his book was written during the war, partly, at any rate, for American and British consumption, and that he should have tried to play down the atmosphere of gloom and doom that was typical of the Paris of May–June,

1940. The most curious episode Mendès describes in his book is his flying visit to Louviers, the Norman town, of which he had been mayor for the last five years.

> On June 9, I tried to pay a brief visit to Louviers, which was in process of being evacuated. Much to my surprise, when I arrived at Vernon, I found the town in flames. Being unable to cross the Seine, I tried to by-pass the town along the left bank of the river. The Germans were on the other side of the Seine, and my car, riddled with bullets, suddenly stopped. I got out and hid behind it for about half an hour, until the firing had ceased. On the other side of the river, there were about 20 German tanks. The bridge had been blown up. Just outside Vernon, a handful of French soldiers, armed with a few machine-guns, were resisting as best they could. I managed to join them, and they explained that they were all alone there, without officers, or any instructions, and total-ly cut off from their unit. They were trying to prevent the Germans from crossing the Seine . . . I stayed with these fine fellows who were fighting a losing battle, knowing full well that, after night-fall, they would not be able to stop the Germans from crossing the river . . . They were not afraid. They were brave and full of deter-mination. They rightly said that if only a couple of planes or a 75 mm battery had been sent, as they had asked, they could have stopped the Germans. But since nothing had been sent, they were doing what they could with the miserable means at their disposal... But they felt furious at having been thus abandoned.

The German shelling increased in intensity, and Mendès-France was slightly wounded by a shell splinter.

> What I saw at Vernon happened, unfortunately, in many other places . . . There were many acts of individual heroism. There would have been many more, and much more effective acts of heroism, if only the responsible army chiefs had taken the neces-sary measures . . . Unfortunately, the 'technicians' had never visualized this kind of war. And that is why, practically everywhere between Belgium and the Loire, French soldiers found themselves face-to-face with an enemy endowed with vastly superior strength . . . The example of Vernon is only one among a thousand similar examples during those two tragic months . . .

Wounded, and with his car wrecked, he made no attempt to go on to Louviers, but after much difficulty, succeeded in getting a lift back to Paris. It was here, on June 10, that he at last obtained from Colonel Lucien his instructions to go to Mérignac-Bordeaux.

It is unnecessary to quote Mendès-France's description of his

journey, first to Jarnac in the Charente-Maritime where he had a
country house to which his family had been evacuated, and his subsequent journey to Bordeaux. The story of the panic exodus from Paris
has been told by others, and more graphically. But his 'farewell to
Paris' is worth quoting:

> And now I was going to leave Paris. Paris where I was born,
> and where I had spent my youth. For the last time, I went to
> spend an hour at my home, my home where I had lived (alas! for
> only such a short time) since my marriage. Already the nursery
> and my wife's studio had had an abandoned feel since the begin-
> ning of the war. Here also was my office, with its large desk, and
> its library with its books collected one by one . . . What stranger
> was now going to defile these rooms and these familiar objects?
> And when would I be back here again?

After a stop at Jarnac, he went on to Bordeaux where those whom
he called 'the traitors' were already active.

At Mérignac he learned that the air force unit in which he was now
incorporated, had left for Morocco. By an extraordinary coincidence,
he learned that same day that an auxiliary cruiser, the *Massilia*, had
been placed at the disposal of any members of parliament who intended
to sail to North Africa. To him, it was not a case of taking part in any
political operation, but simply of joining his unit. The sailing of the
Massilia was 'providential' in his case for this, and no other reason. It
is true that practically all of the deputies and senators who sailed on
the *Massilia* were men who were determined to 'continue the fight in
North Africa'. The double operation engineered by Laval and others
in letting them go aimed at showing that they were either (*a*) warmongers or (*b*) 'bad Frenchmen' or deserters, unwilling to stay with
France in her hour of need. . . .

Mendès-France's chapter on the 'traitors' and on the machinations
that went on at Bordeaux on the eve of Pétain's appeal for an armistice
was written in 1943, when there was still a tendency to oversimplify
matters, and sharply divide the French leaders into fight-to-a-finish
patriots and 'traitors'. One even feels that his account of the impression
made in France by Pétain's armistice broadcast of June 17, had an
element of war propaganda about it, and there is, for instance, a false
ring about this paragraph:

> I listened to this broadcast in a café, in the midst of a crowd
> that was completely shattered and dumbfounded . . . Everybody
> had, indeed, believed that a Pétain Government could only stand

for war, for a fight-to-the-finish . . . When the Marshal had explained his intentions, I watched the men and women around me. This was yet the hardest blow they had received during the terrible past six weeks. In a corner, an old man was silently sobbing. No one said anything. There were no comments, but only a feeling of immense despair and of that feeling of shame, which was to spread wider and wider in the following months and years . . .

At the same time, he noted that many people did not believe in the possibility of the war being successfully continued by Britain.

All the soldiers claim that Britain will be invaded and beaten in three weeks; if the French army, the finest army in the world was broken in a few days, what could be expected from the British army which had scarcely been created? . . .

As Mendès tells the story, he spent the 18th in a state of great despondency, listening to the defeatist talk at Bordeaux: it was then that, almost by accident, he heard de Gaulle's famous broadcast from London:

'*Quoi qu'il arrive, la flamme de la résistance française ne doit pas s'éteindre et ne s'éteindra pas.*'

THE 'MASSILIA'

The *Massilia*, with some 40 deputies and senators (some with their families) on board sailed from the estuary of the Gironde on June 20. She was an auxiliary cruiser, which had recently taken part in the Narvik operation. A good deal of confusion surrounded this voyage. It began, as said, on June 20, that is, three days after Pétain's armistice broadcast, but before the Armistice had been signed. In other words, it was still uncertain (at least in theory) whether the French Government would not have to continue the fight in North Africa, if the German conditions proved unacceptable.

There is no point in recalling all the confusing episodes that preceded the sailing of the *Massilia*: the attempt by President Lebrun to sail for North Africa; the hesitations of Herriot and Jeanneney, presidents of the Chamber and Senate; the intrigues of Laval, the purpose of which was to stop Lebrun from leaving, and to induce only those to leave who were known to be opposed to the Armistice. Practically all the parliamentarians on the *Massilia* had, indeed, been, more or less, 'warmongers' in the past: or were, at any rate, out of sympathy with the Armistice: Mandel, Marin, Campinchi, Viénot, Daladier, Zay, Le Troquer, Jammy-Schmidt, Tony Révillon, Denais, Lazurick, Grumbach, Mendès-France, and a few others. Some, like Jammy-

Schmidt, were notorious freemasons; some others—Lazurick, Zay, Mandel, Grumbach and Mendès-France—were Jews.

The crew of the *Massilia*, and especially its officers, were hostile to the distinguished passengers.

However, at Casablanca, Mendès found morale among the French excellent. 'The French in Morocco,' he wrote, 'are living in a state of imperial pride', and his first impression was that General Noguès, the Resident-General, was prepared to fight the Germans to a finish. But no sooner was the Armistice signed than the tune began to change. Noguès was being flooded with instructions from Bordeaux. Lord Gort and Mr. Duff-Cooper, who had specially come to Morocco in a sea-plane, were not allowed to meet the French parliamentarians. These were living on board the *Massilia*; and to prevent any contacts between them and the British (especially after Mandel had succeeded in seeing the British Consul-General at Rabat), the *Massilia* was taken out to sea and anchored a mile off Casablanca, until Gort and Duff-Cooper had gone!

The parliamentarians had, in fact, been interned for two days, while the British representatives were trying to establish contact with them.

> Personally (Mendès wrote), I began to doubt the success of any North-African initiative against the Bordeaux Government, Noguès, who at first proclaimed his intention to resist, was becoming more and more evasive. Our internment on the *Massilia* showed that the naval authorities, and perhaps the military authorities too, had decided to submit to the instructions that had come from Bordeaux . . .[1]

On the 27th, with the British safely out of the way, the *Massilia* was brought back to port, and all the parliamentarians were allowed to go freely ashore, with the exception of Mandel, who was driven off in a police van. Already on June 23 a press campaign of vilification had been started against the 'cowards who had deserted their country on board the *Massilia*.' This campaign was let loose by M. Prouvost, High Commissioner for Information in the Pétain Government, textile king, owner of *Paris-Soir*, and, subsequently the proprietor of *Paris-Match*. It was Prouvost, too, who became one of the most violent anti-British propagandists in Vichy France.

Noguès, Boisson, and so many of the French Governors and Resident-Generals in Africa, as well as all admirals and practically all generals , hastened to rally to the Marshal.

[1] *Liberté, liberté chérie*, p. 76.

All these men (Mendès wrote), betrayed France to save their positions and privileges . . . No doubt Noguès did not like the idea of seeing North Africa included in the armistice. But every day he was receiving imperative telegrams from Pétain and Weygand, who kept on appealing to his sense of discipline. As a sop to his own conscience (and to show, as it were, that he would have preferred North Africa to resist), Noguès published Weygand's telegrams in the local press. What finally decided him to accept Bordeaux as the legal government of France, what gave his attitude a juridical basis, as it were, was the recognition of the Bordeaux Government by the United States . . .[1]

It was no good. The North African French were accepting Vichy. Mendès attended the National Mourning ceremony in the Place Lyautey at Casablanca on June 25, after the signing of the Armistice. People's nerves were on edge. 'It would have been enough for one man, for one leader to say the right word . . . but nobody said anything.' Yet there were at that time in North Africa, according to Mendès, 1,800 military planes and a large standing army.

The planes were later to be sent back to France, or handed over to the Germans, or dismantled.

What had Mendès been doing during this time? On the 27th he went to Rabat to receive orders from General d'Astier de la Vigerie, the regional air commander.

He greeted me in a friendly manner, and informed me that my unit had been sent to Meknes, but it was no use my going there since all air activity had been stopped. 'In a few days you will probably be demobilized like the rest of your comrades. Meantime, I should like you to stay on my General Staff, where I shall need you . . .'

Mendès's troubles started from the moment General d'Astier was moved from Rabat only a few weeks later.

PRISONER OF VICHY

Indeed, on July 25, soon after the Third Republic had been liquidated at Vichy, a French cabinet meeting decided to take action against the 'deserters' of the *Massilia*. A Havas note appeared in the press saying that Viénot, Zay, Wiltzer and Mendès-France were going to be tried by a military tribunal on charges of desertion. The obvious purpose of the operation was to cast further discredit on the Third Republic deputies who had 'fled' on the *Massilia*.

[1] Op. cit., p. 84.

General d'Astier—who was still at Rabat—called in Mendès and, after examining his case, declared that there must have been a mistake. He forwarded to Noguès the memorandum Mendès had prepared, in which he explained the exact circumstances in which he had sailed on the *Massilia*, and protested against the publicity given to the wild charges brought against him by Vichy. Noguès 'bravely' (as Mendès put it) preferred not to forward the memorandum to Vichy himself, but returned it to General d'Astier, saying that it was 'a matter for the Air Ministry'. This was the beginning of the frame-up. The Air Ministry at Vichy refused to answer the memorandum; the press continued, with complete impunity, to publish photographs of Mendès, with his name and 'deserter' as their only caption; and it looked as if he might be arrested at any moment. The question that arose in his mind was this: Should he fight it out to a finish with the Vichy authorities, or should he, like so many others, try to escape to Gibraltar? General d'Astier insisted that Mendès stay.

'Whatever the risks,' he said, 'you must stay here, defend your honour and face all the attacks. You have no right to run away. You have no rights to cast doubts on the fairness of the military courts, and of the officers who may be called upon to try you.'

And the General asked him to give him his word of honour that he would not escape.

Looking back on it, Mendès reflected that, in spite of everything that happened afterwards, d'Astier was right; but, in August 1940, 'it was an agonizing decision to take'.

His first task now was to organize his defence. He found a lawyer —Maître Sombsthay, a war veteran of 1914-18 and a man with a high reputation of integrity. What happened a few days later was typical. Sombsthay informed Mendès that he had received a visit from Major Vial of the *2e Bureau*. 'He asked me, in the name of the authorities, not to accept your brief.'

The witch-hunt was now in full swing. Jean Zay, the former Minister of Education in the Blum Government, had even a stranger experience. His wife at Rabat was about to give birth to a child, when the midwife she had engaged was also instructed by the authorities not to 'work' for her.

Such incidents pointed to such a degree of malice and to such inflamed political passions that they demoralized us completely. We tried to hide these insults from our wives, while they tried to hide from us the insults that they also had to suffer . . .

Zay was arrested on August 12 and transferred to Clermont-Ferrand. For a time nothing happened to Mendès-France; but on August 22 General d'Astier was transferred from Rabat—and that was precisely what Vichy had been waiting for to strike at Mendès-France. D'Astier was succeeded by a Colonel Janin,

> a notorious freemason in the past, but one who was now de-
> termined to live down his political past, so that he could keep his
> job . . . One day he called me in and begged me on no account to
> try to escape to Gibraltar, as it would do him terrible harm.

No doubt much to Janin's relief, Mendès-France was duly arrested on August 31 and locked up in Casablanca military prison. In his cell—specially cleaned for the occasion—he spent about a month till the day when Admiral Darlan—who was, at that time, among other things, Acting Minister of Air—quite arbitrarily ordered his transfer to Clermont-Ferrand. The chief reason for this was that the examining magistrate, Colonel Voiturier, was proving more and more helpless in dealing with the cooked-up charges brought against Mendès-France. At Clermont, there was Colonel Leprêtre, who was a real genius at dealing with a case like this.

Mendès's family stayed on in Morocco.

Mendès-France arrived at Clermont-Ferrand on October 12, 1940, after an interminable sea voyage along the Spanish coast and a weary railway journey through Vichy France. This part of his story is re-markable for two reasons. He became more convinced than ever of the terrifying malice, the *méchanceté*, and the meanness and servility of a very large proportion of his fellow-humans, especially under the influence of an authoritarian regime. Secondly, the story of his escape from prison which is one of the most exciting escape stories ever written, illustrates to a remarkable degree the man's power of con-centration, and his capacity for organizing everything down to the finest detail.

The military prison of Clermont-Ferrand had none of the amenities and facilities of Casablanca gaol. The food was horrible, and hygienic conditions appalling.

> Especially those who had been there for some months were
> thin and worn-out and pathetically helpless to look at. The prison
> doctor once told me that the incidence of T.B. among them was
> exceptionally high . . . There was no sanitation in the prison.
> There was a cesspool which was never emptied, so that part of the
> building and the whole yard were in a constant stink . . . On the

E

ground floor there were seven or eight W.C's. But when prisoners
were in their cells they had to be content with a horrible pail which
was emptied only once a day, and, while in the yard, they had to
use a large tank in a corner, unprotected from their fellow-
prisoners' eyes by any screen or partition . . .

This was one of the prisons of Vichy France where the Vichy
government was systematically trying to break the spirit of its victims.

Even so, Mendès-France, being still an officer, was in a relatively
privileged position. He was allowed to receive occasional food parcels,
and was allowed a small stove in his cell at the height of winter; others
were not even allowed that.

For two months he received nobody; but there were at least three
other fellow-passengers from the *Massilia* whom he saw occasionally:
Vienot, Wiltzer and Zay; but after Zay had been sentenced, and the
other two transferred somewhere else, there were no kindred souls left
inside the prison. Of the prison staff, only one gendarme behaved
decently.

After a while, however, Mendès was able to receive a few visitors,
among them his aged father, who had managed to come all the way
from occupied Paris.

The visitors of officers are allowed to see them in their cells.
My father looked with unspeakable horror at the tiny space to
which I was confined. Every time a warder passed, or there was a
rattle of keys, my father went pale. Already he had been upset by
the coarse and insulting manner with which a prison warder had
treated him on his arrival. There are many ugly things during that
period which I shall not forget; but one of the worst was the case
of the gendarme called Montagne, who had been cruel and insulting to an old man whose son was in prison, and who deserved
pity and respect.

There was no case at all against Mendès-France; so much so that
even so servile and cynical an examining magistrate as Colonel
Leprêtre remarked more than once that his case would probably have
to be dismissed. The reason why, despite Mendès's own toughness
and the genuine care and devotion of his two lawyers, Maitre Rochat,
of Clermont-Ferrand, and Maitre Fonlupt of Strasbourg, he was still
sentenced to six years' imprisonment as a deserter is that Colonel de
Margueritte, the army commander at Clermont-Ferrand, General
Bergeret, the Air Minister, and Admiral Darlan were determined that
the case must on no account be dismissed.

A very curious portrait, marked by an almost Balzac-like quality, is to be found in Mendès's account of his closest Vichy 'contact', the examining magistrate who had been entrusted with his case and who, in the eyes of Vichy, was ever so much more 'competent' to deal with it than the well-meaning but muddle-headed Colonel Voiturier of Casablanca.

Every ten days or every fortnight Colonel Leprêtre would come to the Prison. He liked to have long talks with the prisoners with whose cases he was dealing. These talks were very free and not at all formal, compared with our official interviews with him. He found these private talks an amusing pastime, typical of the man's spiteful nature, and of the morbid joy he took in playing with a prisoner like a cat with a mouse . . . Sitting at the edge of my bed, he would spend several hours talking to me . . . Often I talked to him with the greatest candour and insolence. Since there were no witnesses, he didn't mind . . . One day I said to him: 'Of course I would gladly have deserted in June, 1940, to join de Gaulle, if only I had known that Pétain was going to sign the Armistice. But on June 19 and 20 Pétain was saying he would continue the fight in North Africa. That's why I went there, all the more so as my unit was in North Africa. Really a bit of bad luck for you! To sentence me in the circumstances, you will just have to fake the whole case. I am going to make this trial a public scandal, so that you'll be really sorry one day . . .'
On another occasion I told him that I would have him tried later on, and that I hoped he would be duly hanged. He took it better than one might have expected . . .

Mendès attached considerable importance to the personality of Leprêtre, who, to him, personified a whole French class. Leprêtre was 'a slender little man, discreet, slightly timid, and distinguished in his manner and speech, with greying hair and a little grey moustache. And yet—

Leprêtre is one of the most important men of the Military Justice machinery of Vichy. In most cases, it is he who takes the decisions himself; in some particularly important cases, Vichy decides, on the strength of his reports. He has dealt with practically all the most important cases: he has questioned Mandel and Reynaud, Lecal and Devaux (Reynaud's assistants), Zay, Viénot, Wiltzer, Philippe de Rothschild, and many others. It was also he who conducted the proceedings against Colonel d'Ornano, General Leclerc, General Mittelhauser, etc. To all cases he applied the same cruelty, the same taste for repression . . .
What largely accounts for his character is the feeling of having been a 'failure'. It has made him bitter. He is worth much more

than the work he has to do; and he knows it. As a graduate of the *École Normale Supérieure*, and having several diplomas in Letters and Law, he feels that he could have done much better ... After the 1914-18 war, in which he was wounded, he decided to stay in the Army; he had hoped to make a grand career; instead, this morbidly ambitious man merely became a military judge.

Apart from that, the man was full of meanness and avarice. ... In the course of an undistinguished, but carefully conducted career, he had succeeded in putting aside a little fortune; just enough to give him the feeling of belonging to the *owner class*; hence his hatred for a man like Mendès-France who believed in far-reaching fiscal reform....

Several times Leprêtre tried to improve his prospects and speed up his own promotion. He looked for political support, and was not squeamish even if there was a chance of getting something from the Left. He did a lot of wire-pulling in an endeavour to be taken on as an adviser to Paul-Boncour, when the latter was Minister of War. But it came to nothing ... His disappointment developed into acute resentment against a régime which had not fully appreciated his qualities and was, moreover, plotting to introduce taxation which might well prevent him from greatly increasing his nest-egg ...

Although Leprêtre denied that he belonged to any political party, he on one occasion admitted to be much in sympathy with the *Action Française*, and to hate 'all these bad Frenchmen belonging to the Popular Front, the Masonic Lodges, and Jewry. . . .'

Needless to say with this background, and with this mentality, a man like Leprêtre could only be highly malevolent to the prisoners of the *Massilia* . . . He particularly hated Jean Zay, the former Minister of Education: 'That fellow', he said, 'has been corrupting the minds of French youth for four years . . .'

I have dwelt at some length on the case of Colonel Leprêtre, not only because Mendès-France was particularly interested in him as a 'social type', but also because, throughout his career, Mendès-France was constantly confronted with coalitions of an endless variety of Leprêtres. These people belonged to that *ancien régime* which, in Mendès-France's view, has never ceased, in the last 150 years, to manifest itself, more or less virulently. Under Vichy, the *ancien régime* had triumphed completely for a time; during the Liberation, it went underground; but it was going to manifest itself again, in a variety of ways, during the subsequent years of the Fourth Republic—and to sabotage, as best it could, the efforts of Republicans like Mendès-France. Under

Vichy these men came closest to destroying him not only politically, but also physically. The famous *affaire des fuites* in 1956 was like a major come-back of the Leprêtres.

Leprêtre was not the only Balzacian 'monster' Mendès-France met during those months at Clermont prison. There were the other magistrates who conducted his trial; for instance, Colonel Perré, the Permanent President of the Military Tribunal of Clermont-Ferrand.

He was a young colonel, tall and broad-shouldered, and full of his own importance. With his chin always sticking out a mile, he looked rather like a caricature of Mussolini, whose mimicry, gestures and grandiloquence he loved imitating.
... Contrary to all previous rules, his function as President of the Military Tribunal had been repeatedly renewed every six months. He had certainly done his utmost to pass all the sentences that Vichy wanted to see passed ...
He was responsible for centuries of imprisonment and hard labour. He had also passed many death sentences ... Most of the sentences passed on alleged Gaullists were accomapnied by a subsidiary sentence confiscating the accused man's property: thus Perré, more than any one else, has on his conscience the destruction of homes, the women and children thrown out into the street ... All of this he did with the utmost cynicism and lack of sensibility. Any arguments on the subject left him completely cold. He did not believe in acquittals. During the eight months I spent at Clermont, several hundred cases were dealt with by Perré; out of the whole lot, there were only three acquittals ...
He sentenced to 20 years' hard labour a boy of 19 alleged to be a Communist ... Perré played the part of 'a soldier, nothing-but-a-soldier'. All the same, he hung about Ministers' anterooms in the past, and was attached at one time to the staff of Painlevé, the Minister of War. But this, of course, he was careful never to mention.

This is another revealing remark: Mendès-France does not doubt that the Republican régime in France, both under the Third Republic and under the Fourth has always been 'colonized' by men wholly lacking in a republican *mystique* and belonging, temperamentally, to the *ancien régime*. In the case of Colonel Perré this was particularly blatant: he went so far as to write accounts in the *Action Française* of the trials over which he had himself presided!

To cut the story short, on May 9, 1941, after he had been in prison at Clermont since October, Mendès-France was at last brought up for trial.

The case against him was so non-existent that even Colonel Leprêtre had, on several occasions, expressed the view that it should be dismissed. But Admiral Darlan and General Bergeret, the Minister of Air, would not hear of it. Even before the trial, Darlan had him dismissed as Mayor of Louviers, and a violent press campaign against the 'deserter' and *le député juif* Mendès-France was launched by *Gringoire*. Already in February, 1941, a circular was sent to Mendès-France by the Presidents of the Chamber of Deputies and the Senate informing him of the Act of October 2, 1940, under which Jews could not be elected to any public functions. Mendès thereupon wrote a significant letter to Pétain, in which he not only protested against the racial laws, but also stressed the 'Frenchness' of his family:

> In this letter I said . . . that although I was not claiming any credit for what my ancestors had done, I did not hesitate to point out to the Marshal all that my family had done for the country for centuries and centuries, and how much blood they had shed for it. In the circumstances I had the right to emphasize the pride I took in my family as a French family . . . As for my personal case, I briefly pointed out to the Marshal . . . that the fantastic charges brought against me had had to be abandoned, but that the examining magistrate was now trying to think up something else . . . I asked that my case be speeded up. To make quite sure that the letter reached the Marshal, I sent it to his *chef de cabinet*, M. Du Moulin de Labarthète, whom I had known for a long time, and whom I considered a loyal political adversary. A few days later, my lawyer received a reply from Labarthète; in it he said that the Marshal had read my letter and had asked that I be informed that this letter had 'deeply moved him' . . .

This was the kind of hypocrisy that a man like Mendès-France was up against. The Marshal had been 'deeply moved'; and even Leprêtre thought the case had better be dismissed. And yet, when he found that this suggestion met with no favour at Vichy, he tried to think up something else.

At the trial Mendès had, from the very start, the uncomfortable feeling that the public in court had been carefully selected, and that the audience was overwhelmingly hostile to him.

> I am used to public meetings. I know how to distinguish between friendly and hostile audiences . . . To the left of me, in particular, there were two rows of seats occupied by a lot of smart ladies who had obviously no liking for me. Some of them were wives of the very magistrates who were trying me. One of the most excited of these ladies was Madame Andrée Corthis who, throughout the day, was making offensive remarks . . .

He made a long statement to the court, omitting no detail whatsoever. Every minute or two Colonel Perré would interrupt him and ask
some wholly irrelevant question; firmly, Mendès (who had the advantage of being an experienced lawyer) pointed out that he had a
perfect right to deal with each question separately.

Despite all these angry interruptions, I finished my statement
on the 'affair' on the 10th of May, then on the 'affair' of the 10th
of June, and felt that I had really impressed the audience . . . The
sharp words I used in conclusion to denounce the odious machination against me went down better than I might have expected.

In the afternoon the witnesses were heard: Colonel Alamichel,
who had been Mendès's commanding officer in Syria.

Defence Counsel: You have known Mendès-France since he
served under you. Do you think him capable of
deserting?
Col. Alamichel: Quite out of the question.

The same opinion was given by Lieut.-Col. Fay, who had also
known Mendès in Syria. Same with General d'Astier, under whom
Mendès had served in Morocco. And finally, there were two important
witnesses who were able to clear up completely the 'affair' of June 10:
Colonel Lucien and Colonel Le Coq de Kerland. Le Coq de Kerland
was, like d'Astier, one of the aces of the French air force in the 1914-18
war, and 'no one in this Court could give him any lessons in military
honour'.

Completely self-confident, he told the Court how he had known
me in the Middle East, where I had been training as an observer.
He recalled that I was first among my colleagues who had followed
the same course, and that I had shown the greatest eagerness to
go and fight in Norway, or else at the French front. Le Coq de
Kerland was well-informed about my whole case.
'Everything', he concluded, 'is perfectly clear. Never did
Mendès make the slightest mistake, or take the slightest liberty
with his military duties. I vouch for his character: he is not the
kind of man who deserts . . .'
The president of the Court, not at all pleased, merely grunted:
'Have you anything more to add?'
Le Coq de Kerland: 'Just this. Whatever happens tonight, I
wish to state it publicly: I shall always have the greatest regard
for Mendès-France.'

A strange thing then happened. The public, so hostile at first, burst
into applause.

Perré was furious, and threatened to clear the Court. Since the cheering continued, he hastened to suspend the hearing and adjourned it till 9 p.m.

The only witness for the prosecution had been Colonel Bailly, who had fumbled and mumbled something about an alleged conversation at Bordeaux, and who then hastened, under shellfire from the defence, to withdraw, on the plea that 'Admiral Darlan was waiting for him'.

What finally the prosecution thought up was that, having received orders on June 10 to go to Mérignac-Bordeaux, Mendès had taken longer than three days to get there. Assuming that—even within the chaotic state of the exodus—three days was enough to travel from Paris to Bordeaux, Mendès had still been only a few hours late in reaching his destination. The whole thing was a fantastic quibble; but the allegation that Mendès had been a few hours late in joining his base was considered sufficient by the prosecution to ask that he be sentenced to eight years' imprisonment for desertion!

During the passionate speeches for the defence by Maîtres Rochat and Fonlupt, the public prosecutor and the judges 'all displayed a sort of insolent determination to ignore the defence and all its arguments'.

After a brief statement by the accused, who maintained that he had not committed the slightest offence, the court withdrew, and, only a few minutes later returned the verdict: *Guilty of desertion.*

Mendès interrupted: 'The Court has lied.'

The Clerk of the Court, who was reading out the verdict, disconcerted by my interruption, and expecting the Court to react, stopped for a second. Then he proceeded:
"6 years' imprisonment. Military degradation." 10 years' loss of civil and civic rights. . . .
At last he finished reading the verdict. I turned to the guard. The soldiers were looking pale. I said to them: 'They have just sentenced an innocent man out of political hatred. This is not French justice. This is Hitler's justice. Don't despair of France . . .'
I then turned to Colonel Degache who had his eyes firmly fixed on the ground: '*M. le Commissaire du Gouvernment,* I hope you have an easy conscience. You have done a good job—for Hitler —and for your own promotion.'

He appealed against the sentence, and it took several more months before his appeal was rejected.

In the meantime he was in prison, knowing in advance that his appeal would be rejected, and planning to escape as soon as this rejection was official. He was determined not to remain longer than necessary at the mercy of the Vichy authorities. He could not help reflecting

that Vichy was an essentially French invention, and that it was no use
putting all the blame on the Germans:

> Public opinion in France knew that the Government was
> persecuting all those it suspected of Gaullist or Communist sym-
> pathies; but it did not know in what horrible conditions the sen-
> tences were being served. It is no use saying that it was all the fault
> of the Germans. The Germans expected Vichy to be ruthless; but
> the Germans were not responsible for the shamefully low rations
> in the Vichy prisons, for the appalling filth, for the lack of water,
> for the constant victimization of prisoners and the neglect of their
> health by the medical services . . .[1]

So, after months and months of preparation, and while he had been
temporarily transferred to a cell attached to the military hospital at
Clermont-Ferrand, he escaped from this cell, after filing away, over a
period of several weeks, the steel bars of the small window. Shortly
before midnight, after giving sleeping tablets to his cell mate, he
slid down the 25 feet of the prison wall. This escape was a truly
scientific job, in which the tiniest details had been worked out in
advance.

It is outside the scope of this book to recount this story of Pierre
Mendès-France in the rôle of Monte Cristo; it is sufficient to say that
the whole adventure was an astonishing example of ingenuity combined with a cool head and outstanding physical and moral endurance.
Nothing was left to chance. The small and rusty saw he picked up in
a prison workshop (before using it he made quite sure that nobody
was aware of its disappearance); the noise of filing the bars, which he
made coincide with the snores of the warders next door; the box of
mascara he took from a lady visitor, not knowing at first what he
wanted it for, but then using it, together with a paste made of ashes
and soap to camouflage the cuts he had already made in the steel bars;
all the false clues he created while still in prison—such as the map he
left in his cell, a map from which he cut out a section which was a part
of the country to which he was *not* going; the clues he left in a street
leading *away* from the railway station, while in reality he went *to* the
station to catch a train for Grenoble; and, finally, the pipe he bartered
from a fellow-prisoner—a pipe which enabled him to cover part of his
face with his hand, and to give his mouth an expression (*un rictus*—a
sort of sneer) that was difficult to create without the help of a pipe;
all these, and many other details, had been worked out through sheer
power of concentration.

[1] Op. cit., p. 205.

A CHAPLINESQUE FIGURE

Mendès escaped from Clermont jail on the night of June 21, 1941 —the historic night on which the Germans invaded Russia. It took him eight months to reach London. . . .

Writing in 1943, Mendès camouflaged and 'arranged' the next part of his narrative, for obvious security reasons; very few names or places in the story that follows can be easily identified. But the story is a good story as it is. All the time he had to avoid familiar faces; but once, at Grenoble, he met in the market a lady who had lived in great luxury before the war, but who now looked extremely down-at-heel.

I was very tempted to talk to her. It was very hard to be as isolated as I was, never to have a friendly talk with anybody I could trust, never to meet anyone who knew who I was, and with whom I didn't have to keep up this sickening farce. But I made it an absolute rule not to yield to such temptation . . . So I turned my back on Mme. G.B. . . . Anyway, for all I knew, she might have received me very badly. Later I met some other people I had known. Twice, in the street, I ran into François Poncet, our former Ambassador in Berlin and Rome. I quickly took to my heels . . .

A truly Chaplinesque figure, with his hunted look, his pipe, his beret, his glasses and his moustache. . . . One can just see him taking to his heels at the sight of a representative of that *other* France, the pompous self-satisfied François Poncet, who, in 1946, was going to re-emerge in the Fourth Republic once again as *Ambassadeur de France*. . .

Equally Chaplinesque is the story of how Mendès took part in a great outdoor rally, organized by Pétain's Legion, and of how, sandwiched between two legionnaires in a motor coach, he bellowed as loudly as any of them: *Maréchal, nous voilà!*

By a stroke of luck—which he does not quite explain—the search for him ceased after it was announced on the BBC (while he was still in France) that he had duly arrived in London.

He says very little about the Resistance; but he was certainly in contact with some of the Resistance leaders during those eight months in Vichy France. (He also went on a short visit to the Occupied Zone.) His impression of the morale of the country was a rather confused one. It was, on the whole, better in the occupied zone than in the 'free' zone, and was particularly bad at Marseilles and on the Riviera, with its black-marketing and its endless rackets . . . Not to mention North Africa which was almost entirely Vichyite or *Doriotiste*.

One day, while he was having dinner with a French family—who did not know who he was—there arrived a man who had just come from Paris:

> Among other things, D. told us how he had visited the anti-Jewish exhibition the *Illustration* had organized at the Palais Berlitz in Paris. He produced an illustrated catalogue, various propaganda leaflets, and a copy of *L'Illustration* with an important article on this exhibition. Great was my surprise when I discovered from the catalogue that my humble person had been given a place of honour at this show! At the exhibition there was a sort of vestibule crowded with wax figures of the most representative and nefarious Jews—one per country. Basil Zaharoff represented Greece; Hore-Belisha, England; Litvinov, Russia; while France was represented by—me! ... D. then remarked that, together with some other commercial travellers, he had visited this exhibition, and one of the visitors had remarked, as he looked at the Mendès-France wax figure: 'Why did they pick on Mendès-France as so specially typical? He never played a major rôle. Surely, they should have chosen Blum or Mandel ... In this way I heard my name uttered—for the first time in several weeks. I was delighted to hear from D. the good news that I had escaped to England, and had already enlisted in de Gaulle's forces. All the same, I was slightly vexed to hear people say that I had never played a major part in the political life of my country! It is one of those truths one would rather not hear said ...[1]

And so, after eight months' wandering, or rather hiding, in Vichy France, Mendès finally reached London. After a visit to the United States, whither his family had succeeded in going from Morocco, he returned to London, and there joined the Free French air force.

AIRMAN IN BRITAIN

7.15 a.m. on Sunday, October 3, 1943. Through the thin partitions of the army hut I could hear the batman coming and going, carrying shaving water, or pretending to brush our shoes.

'Lovely day, sir', he said, entering my room. Every morning he said 'Lovely day, sir', even when it was raining ... Classical English breakfast. It's become a firm habit with me now; it'll be hard to shake off after the war.

What a different world from the world of the Radical Congresses, or that other world of the Clermont-Ferrand prison, or of the hunted man's wanderings through Vichy France only a year before! Mendès

[1] Op. cit., p. 438.

was now an airman of the Lorraine Squadron of the Free French air force based in Britain. In a sense, every day to him *was* a 'lovely day, sir'.

October, 1943: already countless politicians who had been in London since the early stages of the war, and others who had gone to North Africa at some stage, were now busy swarming and buzzing round de Gaulle at Algiers. By October, 1943, de Gaulle had virtually eliminated Giraud from the 'dual leadership' of the Free French Committee; there were jobs going at Algiers, jobs which would have the *Monsieur le Ministre* appellation attached to them before long.

Mendès was in no hurry to go to Algiers. He wanted to be *different* from the politicians; there were deep psychological reasons, which can be well imagined, why, after the humiliations of Vichy France, he was determined, while the war was in progress, to do the one thing that could never be questioned: which was to fight. Algiers did not attract him at that stage; he preferred to be surrounded by other men who *also* were fighting the Germans, and daily risking their lives.

In the October, 1952, issue of *Forces Aériennes Françaises*, the official monthly of the French Air Force, we find a surprising article written by Mendès-France, and called *Roissy-en-France*. It is the account of a bombing mission over the Paris area, in which, on October 3, 1943, Mendès took part as a navigator on board a Boston, with the Cross of Lorraine painted on the fuselage, as well as the words 'Lieutenant Sandre'—'this was the name of one of the comrades of our Lorraine Squadron who had been killed during the campaign in Libya'.

Curious how in this account of a bombing mission over France, Mendès tells his story in a manner that almost verges on the sentimental.

> For months we had discussed the question whether it was right for French airmen to bomb France. We all agreed that it was right; and yet on every occasion we resumed the argument; our minds and our hearts were not in full agreement . . . But then, if we did not go on bombing missions over France, others would go instead, and they might not aim with the same minute care as we were doing. However careful they might be, we still had an extra argument for being specially careful in our endeavour not to destroy French lives . . . We had developed a technique of bombing from a very low height; it made us more vulnerable to certain forms of anti-aircraft defence, but enabled us to practise quite exceptional precision bombing . . . and not to drop our bombs outside the target, no matter how small . . .

That day their mission was to bomb an electric power station at Chevilly-Larue, near Orly, just south of Paris.

So we were going to fly over Paris, where so many of us had lived, where some of us had been born! A Paris occupied by the Boche. We were going to breathe the air of Paris, see again its houses, its streets, its bridges, its domes . . .

And so the twelve Bostons set off on their mission.
As he flew over the Channel, he caught sight of the French coastline.

That blurred dark line, just above the horizon is France—my country. As on other occasions, so now again I could feel my heart beating at this always new, always so touching sight of my country, of which I had been robbed for so long. There, to the left, was Tréport, and the estuary of the Bresle; a long way to the right was Dieppe . . .

And then they crossed the coast.

This country that was now racing past below me, why was it so much more beautiful than any other? There was no real difference between it and the English countryside we had crossed a few minutes before. And yet, among a hundred other landscapes I would always recognize France. It had an aspect, an atmosphere peculiar to itself . . . And now we are between Gournay and Lyons, in the *département* of the Eure, my *département*. A few miles from my home. If only we could rise 1500 or 2000 feet, I would see, beyond the Seine, Louviers and the little village of Les Monts, with my house, my garden, my apple trees . . .

What follows is much more technical and matter-of-fact: the story of how they reached their target, how Mendès pressed four times the button of the bomb release; how one of the planes was hit and was beginning to lose height, till finally (as was later learned) it made a forced landing near Compiègne, where the crew, some of them wounded, were taken prisoner and two of them escaped and found their way to England a month later.

After dropping their bombs, they flew over Paris, but they were flying so low that the streets and public buildings and monuments 'of which I had thought so much that morning' were hard to distinguish:

Only, as I raised my eyes, I was overcome by a great emotion: over there, dominating the houses and the roofs, and emerging from the mist was the Sacré-Cœur, shining in all its white splendour in the sun . . . But then I looked to the right; below us was the football ground of Vincennes, with a football match in progress and a lot of spectators. Were they Germans or French? As we were in doubt, we did not machine-gun them; but then we

noticed a car park : with hundreds of cars ; so they must have been
Germans after all. Well, it was too late now. Couldn't be helped . . .

And then he recorded two experiences : of a crowded village square,
where nobody reacted to the Free French planes : he was disappointed
at first, but then remembered that, in public, with Germans or spies
around, it was impossible for anyone to welcome the Free French.
But a few minutes later they flew over a road, and on the road was a
cart driven by an old man in a straw hat and a boy :

> They saw us. And suddenly the cart stopped, and the old man
> and the boy, standing up, gave us a military salute. I felt my eyes
> filling with tears . . .

MENDÈS AND DE GAULLE

How was it that a prominent politician like Mendès-France, who
had come to London after his fantastic escape from a Vichy prison,
and with a long experience of Vichy France, should not have chosen to
play any political rôle at Carlton Gardens? With Mendès, fighting was
more important at the time, and he did not apparently care very much
for the people around de Gaulle, and, while admiring de Gaulle, he
had no ambition to join in the political rivalries surrounding him.
There is nothing gregarious about Mendès : he is a lonely man, and he,
somehow, prefers to be lonely.

I once asked Mendès about his relations with de Gaulle.

'It's a great pity,' he said, 'I had not met de Gaulle before the
war. The trouble is that I had specialized so much in economic
and financial problems that I rather overlooked the military side
—and, rather foolishly, took for granted that a man like Daladier
knew what he was talking about. I wish I had met de Gaulle before the war, but I just didn't. I met him for the first time in
London in 1942. He had, I am glad to say, a good deal of regard
for me ; and that for two reasons. For one thing, I never asked
him for anything, whereas, most of the time, he was surrounded
by people wanting jobs and appointments. I, for my part, was
perfectly content to serve in the air-force, and ask for no favours.
That's why he liked me. Also, he has a respect for people who
speak frankly to him. He can get very nasty when you contradict
him ; but if, on thinking it over, he finally agrees with you, then
he becomes very reasonable, and is glad to continue the discussion.

'While I was still in the air-force, the Consultative Assembly
was set up at Algiers, and de Gaulle proposed to me that I become
one of its members. I said I was sorry, but I preferred to stay in
the air-force, since I didn't attach much importance to this assembly. It was not until several months later, after he had finally

got rid of Giraud, that I received a telegram from de Gaulle at Algiers which was something like this:

'I know you won't be pleased with this, but I am your chief, so look upon this as an order. I want you to be my Commissioner for Finance, because you will be the right man in the right place.' The chaps at the air-base were amused to find that one of their comrades had suddenly become *Monsieur le Ministre*. We had a very cordial, very friendly farewell. In many ways I was sorry to leave England.'

MENDÈS'S FINANCIAL SALVATION PLAN REJECTED

At Algiers, Mendès worked hard on an economic and financial Plan, which he hoped would be applied to France, just after the Liberation. But it was after the Liberation that the trouble really started. De Gaulle, obsessed by *grandeur française*, was not greatly interested in either economics or finance; and rather casually, he appointed Mendès Minister of Economic Affairs in the first post-Liberation government, and Lepercq Minister of Finance. 'It did not make much sense,' Mendès said, 'but, since I had always talked about economic affairs, de Gaulle thought the Ministry of Economic Affairs was the obvious post for me, and the Ministry of Finance something incidental. He never really gave much thought to it.

'But you no doubt remember that Lepercq was killed in a motor accident in November, 1944, soon after the Liberation; and it was then that de Gaulle had to make a grave decision: who was to succeed Lepercq as Minister of Finance? At this stage something strange and rather mysterious happened; and the mystery has not been fully cleared up yet. But, in short, as you know, the choice lay between what used to be called at the time a 'Crippsian' policy of austerity and severe controls all over the place, and a more 'liberal' policy, based on the cultivation of 'confidence'—including the 'confidence' of the war profiteers and black-market sharks. And here is an important question which may some day be fully cleared up. Just before de Gaulle made his final choice of Pleven as Minister of Finance (and that was really a fateful decision), he had been seeing a good deal of Churchill, with whom he travelled to the East. I honestly don't think that Pleven had been pulling any wires. My impression was that he was perfectly content to be Minister of Colonies, and was interested in his work. But Churchill, alarmed at the development of 'Socialist' tendencies in Europe, and afraid that an increasingly Socialist Europe would only stimulate a Labour victory in England, probably thought it would be better if, in France, there wasn't a Minister of Finance who would be much too 'Socialist' to his taste . . . And I think it's quite possible that Churchill advised de Gaulle to appoint Pleven Minister of Finance instead of me. De Gaulle did not always follow Churchill's advice—far from it; but he knew next to nothing about economic and financial matters, and if he could be agreeable to Churchill in a field in which he did not feel strongly one way or the other, so much the better. He might get out of Churchill something in exchange—in some field in which de Gaulle was vitally interested . . .'

'Yes,' Mendès reflected, 'small causes often have big effects in this world.'

Not, of course, that Churchill's advice alone counted. With the exception of some of the Socialists—notably André Philip—nobody was really favourable to the Mendès-France Plan of monetary reform; there was some opposition to it among the CGT, and among the Communists, too. Partly because the whole thing was above most people's heads; and partly because, with municipal and, before long, a General Election in the offing, there were too many people among *all* sections of the population who, on a short-term basis, stood to lose something from a currency conversion, and who were, in any case, reluctant to submit to the inevitable checks and controls that such an operation would involve. The peasantry, in particular, had stored away enormous quantities of French banknotes, 'earned' during the war, and preferred not to declare them, as they would have had to do under the Mendès-France Plan. Opposition also came from the Bank of France and from the experts of the Ministry of Finance. So Mendès-France found himself almost completely alone.

Before the Liberation, Mendès-France, as *Commissaire* of Finance in de Gaulle's National Committee at Algiers, had drawn up a plan of drastic financial reform, to be applied to France after the Liberation. In France, at the same time, the Resistance had drawn up the famous CNR Charter, in which there were some somewhat vague references to monetary reform, and to the necessity of a stable currency. But Mendès-France and the authors of the CNR Charter (though this was officially the charter of the New France) did not see entirely eye-to-eye. In Mendès-France's view, the CNR Charter lacked novelty and originality, and was little more than a rehash of the *Front Populaire* programme of 1936. Nor did it, in a sufficient degree, propose specific measures of a financial nature, which were, to Mendès-France, the real corner-stone of France's economic welfare for many years to come. If the finances were not put in order, Mendès reflected, France would be building on sand, and the country would continue to be at the mercy of the black market.

As I wrote in *France 1940-1955:*

Little or nothing, in his view, could be done about the black market and the 'illicit profits' accumulated during the war years, without a drastic monetary reform. Only a few weeks later, Belgium carried out a monetary reform rather on the lines of the Mendès Plan, complete with the exchange of notes, the freezing of accounts and an instructive, if not perfect, inventory of wartime profits. One of Mendès-France's principal ideas was that the black market would necessarily be paralysed, if not come to a complete standstill, if the mountains of currency in the possession of the *trafiquants* were frozen, or exchanged for new notes only progressively, and subject to various controls and checks, as in Belgium. This monetary reform should, in Mendès's view, be accompanied by appropriate measures to balance the budget, and to draw goods on to the official, instead of the black market. But monetary reform was the cornerstone of the whole structure.

But from the start Mendès came up against opposition—from the permanent officials of the Ministry of Finance; from the Bank of France and from the political parties—or most of them. And also (though this was scarcely suspected at the time) from Churchill.

Since Mendès has often been described as 'France's Stafford Cripps', it is very important to clear up a misunderstanding that widely exists abroad. The phrase has caught on to such an extent, that it has been applied quite indiscriminately to Mendès-France in almost any context. In reality, Mendès-France was no Stafford Cripps either in 1938 or, still less, in the 1950's. But he *was* a Stafford Cripps in 1944-45, when austerity seemed to him the only solution in a France that was short of everything, and which presented a demoralizing spectacle of shocking inequalities in income and consumption.

But the fact remains that Mendès received very little support. For then, as on so many other occasions, he was unwilling to make concessions to certain peculiarities of the French character—to the French lack of economic discipline, to the French innate hostility to that 'fiscal inquisition' which was an inevitable part of his whole scheme—one of the purposes of which was to discover, as accurately as possible, into what pockets the 600 milliards of notes had gone which the Germans had spent, by way of occupation costs, in the French towns and villages.

To interfere with the hoards of banknotes, was to raise a major political issue. M. Gutt, the Belgian Finance Minister, who had carried out the financial reform in Belgium, himself agreed that Belgium and France did not present identical problems:

For France, as for all other liberated countries, monetary reform is problem No. 1. If this isn't solved, you will have devaluation and a constant rise in prices . . . Only, in France, the assault against the 600 milliards of hoarded notes affects 18 million peasants—and that, of course, is a major political problem.[1]

Already in January, 1945, Mendès-France sent his resignation to de Gaulle, but de Gaulle asked him to stay on, so as not to create more alarm in the country than necessary. Nevertheless, Mendès sent de Gaulle an 'irrevocable' resignation three months later, a few weeks before VE day.

What was the last straw, from Mendès's point of view, was the 'Plan' announced by M. Pleven: this 'plan' provided for all the bank-notes in circulation to be exchanged on a one-for-one basis, 'without freezing or retention', a small capital levy of sorts, and another issue of bonds for 'small holders'. These last two items were chicken-feed, but the first item meant the final rejection of the Mendès-France plan. It meant complete surrender to the Black Market. After resigning, Mendès-France held a 'farewell' press conference, in which he said:

It was necessary to build the foundations without delay. This was not done; now inflation is in full swing, and the black market is triumphing all along the line. There can be no order in the food supply if there is no normal currency . . . The working class is being starved, and the middle class with fixed incomes is being ruined.

He spoke bitterly of the need to draw up an inventory of French fortunes; 600 milliards had been extorted by the Germans from France, and all this money had been spent in France; yet all M. Pleven was hoping to recover under the 1945 budget by way of illicit profits was 12 milliards! With Pleven's 'capital levy' spread out over four years, and with notes exchanged at par without any checks or controls, all the illicit profits would have time to go into hiding.

So Mendès retired into relative obscurity. On VE day De Gaulle sent him an inscribed photograph, in which he treated him as one of the men who deserved the greatest credit for France's victory. 'It was a nice thought,' Mendès commented later, 'and I was rather touched, because I greatly admired de Gaulle, despite all his denseness in economic and financial matters . . . But it didn't get France out of the financial bog. Under Pleven things were bound to go from bad to worse.'

---

[1] *Combat*, December 26, 1944.

PART III
THE NINE YEARS' ECLIPSE

CHAPTER 1

VOLUNTARY WITHDRAWAL

MENDÈS is one of the very rare major political figures in any country who consciously and deliberately retired into the background of public affairs for nearly ten years. Ten years—1945 to 1954! Psychologically, this is a strange phenomenon. As the *Monde* wrote on one occasion: 'It is hard to make out—is he extraordinarily ambitious—or not ambitious at all?' Anyone who is neither one nor the other would, in the course of these ten years, have found some reason—or some excuse—for being content with a secondary government rôle. It seems that he was not interested: that it was, to him, everything or nothing.

I am not going to recall in detail the history of 1945—with its de Gaulle regime, which was so different from anything France had seen either before or after: a personalist régime under which the person of de Gaulle held together the uneasy post-Liberation coalition of Socialists, Communists, and members of the Catholic MRP. A number of nationalizations were carried out; but it cannot be said that the New France, which had been provided for in the Charter of the *Conseil National de la Résistance* had come into being. Worse still, every chance of giving this Charter a sound basis had already been missed under Pleven's mismanagement in 1944-45.

Even so, Mendès-France was given one more chance of putting France on its feet financially. After de Gaulle's resignation in January, 1946, M. Félix Gouin, the Socialist leader, was called upon to form a tripartite government; and it was then that he approached Mendès-France. Gouin's ambition was to form a 'grand ministry' combining national economy, finance, production, agriculture and food—and he offered this Ministry to Mendès-France. Already, great damage had been done by Pleven's mismanagement of the currency problem; nevertheless, Mendès was still willing to consider Gouin's offer: but he laid down the following conditions:

No more banknotes to be printed;
Drastic cuts in military expenditure;
Drastic cuts in civil expenditure, with reduction in the number of officials;
The abolition of subsidies;
A steep increase in taxes on wealth;

65

Draconic measures against food speculation;
Freezing of wages and prices.

All this was rather too much for the three government parties to
swallow. The MRP wanted a big military budget; the Socialists and
Communists were chary about tampering with wages; and, in any case,
the Radical Party, which had been left out in the cold for so long, and
which was still suffering from the disdain with which the 'Resistential-
ists' in the Government—as they spitefully called them—had been
treating it, vetoed Mendès's acceptance of the post. Whether he would
have done any better than M. André Philip, the rather unsuccessful
Minister of Economy and Finance in 1946, is impossible to say: much
of the damage had already been done; and the experience of Yves
Farge, who tried to wage a holy war on the Black Market during the
last five months of 1946, indicates that Mendès would quite likely have
met with the same kind of stifling opposition.

Instead, Mendès was to become, for quite a long time, a mere
'technician'. Already in 1944, he had been head of the French delegation at the monetary conference of Bretton Woods; now, in March,
1946, he went to the financial conference of Savannah; after that, he
was appointed French administrator of the International Monetary
Fund, and French Executive Director of the International Bank of Reconstruction in Washington—two posts which he abandoned after a
few months. In May, 1947, he was appointed Permanent French Delegate to the Economic and Social Council of UN; and subsequently
attended, as principal French representative, a number of other international monetary and financial conferences.

In 1945 he had failed to be elected to the First Constituent Assembly; but he was duly elected Radical Deputy of the Eure in the June,
1946, election to the Second Constituent Assembly, and again re-
elected in November, 1946, and in 1951 to the National Assembly.

But since he was busy, during a large part of the time, with the UN
Economic and Social Council, he played only a relatively small part
in the parliamentary life of France until about 1950. His most memorable vote was his abstention at the end of the ratification debate on
the Atlantic Pact in the summer of 1949. But since he was absent from
Paris at the time, he later always protested against any political significance being attached to this vote. Nevertheless, it was this vote which,
for quite a time, was to give him something of a 'neutralist' reputation,
which he later did his utmost to live down... Actually, it was not until
1950 that he came into sudden prominence again, thanks to the rôle
he assumed as the sharpest and most constructive critic of the various
ineptitudes of the '*immobiliste*' period of 1950-53.

CHAPTER 2

MENDÈS AND FRENCH RADICALISM

R ADICAL, Radical ... What did the word mean in 1945, 1949, 1950? The Radical Party,[1] very badly discredited during the Occupation and under Vichy, had now become one of the most conservative groups in France. The Young Turks had all scattered in different directions; some had gone Fascist; some had gone Communist; Jean Zay had been murdered by Vichy; although Daladier had put up a good defence at the Riom Trial in 1942, and had behaved with personal courage, he had not lived down either his megalomaniac airs of 1939 or his fumbling, mumbling behaviour as Premier during the 'phoney war'. Marc Rucard, Paul Bastid, editor of the post-Liberation *Aurore* and a few other Radical parliamentarians had played a minor—a very minor—part in the Resistance; but, by and large, the Radical Deputies and Senators of the pre-war days had voted in large numbers for Pétain, and some of them, in the words of the *Canard Enchaîné*, 'represented several centuries of *indignité nationale*'. Bonnet, Mistler, and countless others had been either Vichyite or *collabo;* and even the record of the g.o.m., Edouard Herriot, was not outstandingly heroic. He had called on France to 'rally round the Marshal' in July, 1940; and later, in 1944, he had his strange meeting in Paris with Laval, only a few days before the Liberation, when Laval had hoped to use Herriot for recalling the old 1940 Parliament—with Herriot then taking his place at the head of the Government. This scheme was obviously directed against the Resistance and de Gaulle, and might have succeeded if only the Germans, and Déat and Doriot hadn't interfered. Herriot later suggested that the idea had been suggested to Laval by the United States Government. Herriot, a great believer in the restoration, purely and simply, of the Third Republic, was not necessarily hostile to the Laval plan; he simply wasn't given a chance to put it into practice, and was packed off to Germany, despite Laval's protests. When I saw Herriot in Moscow, after he had been liberated by the Red Army, he gave some extremely involved (and somewhat embarrassed) explanations on all the ins and outs of his negotiations with Laval in August, 1944.

[1] For a detailed description of the extraordinarily complex organization—or rather, lack of organization—of the Radical Party, see Philip Williams' *Politics in Post-War France*, pp. 94–102.

Some of the other older men, like Delbos, had an honourable, but somewhat passive record; but the rôle of Chautemps had been as shady as ever (with Pétain's blessing, this Prince of Freemasonry went off to America to conduct Vichy propaganda) and the two Sarrauts, who had continued to publish the *Dépêche de Toulouse* under Vichy, had little to be proud of; but then by now Albert Sarraut (Léon Daudet's '*gorille*') was a very old man, while Maurice was mysteriously murdered towards the end of the war—some say by the Vichy *Milice*, others say by the Resistance. Another old man of the Radical Party, Joseph Caillaux, had died in 1945, aged 82, in his country house at Mamers, in the Sarthe. It is said that the old Germanophil was truculent to the Germans when a few of them called on him in 1940 or 1941 to pay their respects, and declared himself convinced of a British victory. A pleasant legend, but with little proof that it was true.

In short, there was little for the Radicals, 'the flesh and blood of France', to be proud of. If they were not Vichyites and *collabos*, they were nearly all *attentistes*—except for some of the former *jeunes Turcs*—who had sailed on the *Massilia*, among them Campinchi, Zay, Mendès, Jammy-Schmidt, and a few more. Mendès was one of the very few Radical 'resisters' who actually survived, and found their way back into Parliament. The 1945 Congress at which the Radical Party was reconstituted was a pretty morose affair, as the survivors looked around.

And yet, as time went on, and as *tripartisme* broke down, the Radicals felt that they still had a chance. After all, at Algiers, the somnolent M. Queuille—one of the few old Radical politicians to have joined de Gaulle even at that late stage—still had the distinction—as Emmanuel d'Astier noted in his book, *Sept fois sept jours*—of not behaving like an amateur at Cabinet meetings. The Radicals had a government tradition, and they were determined to revive it under the Fourth Republic. This revival of the Radical Party—though more than ever a 'Party of Committees', with no rank-and-file *militants* to speak of—dates back to the *immobiliste* era of 1948-50. Only a few—a very few—young people were tempted to join the Radical Party in the early days of the Fourth Republic: among the few, who guessed at an early stage that the Radicals had perhaps a bigger future than the MRP, were Edgar Faure and Bourgès-Maunoury.

What a mixed crew they still were, these Radicals of 1949-50! A McCarthyite fringe, composed of men like Martinaud-Déplat and Charles Brune; a large part of the North Africa Lobby inside Parliament: for instance, René Mayer, deputy for Constantine (Algeria), and Senator Borgeaud, the 'uncrowned king of Algeria'; and, outside

Parliament, M. Emile Roche, the *de facto* head of the Settlers' Organization, *Présence Française*, in Morocco. Alongside these, there were the respectable 'old parliamentarians', men like Herriot, Queuille and Delbos; another group flirted with de Gaulle and went in, in a big way, for the unholy practice of 'bigamy'—which meant belonging both to the Radical Party and to the RPF; and, quite isolated from any of these groups, was Mendès-France, with a growing prestige in Parliament generally, but with practically no personal following at all among the Radical Party . . . If he had any friends at that time, it was among the small UDSR group[1] and among the Socialists and—before very long, among some of the Gaullists.[2] Looking back on it, it seems clear that if Mendès-France stayed inside the Radical Party, especially during those years when the Radical Party was either under a cloud, as after the Liberation, or more identified than any other with the whole concept of *immobilisme*, it was partly because he wanted to *belong* to this 'flesh-and-blood-of-France' formation, and partly perhaps because he felt that, some day, he might 'waken' the Radical Party, and turn it into a dynamic force. That is, indeed, what he attempted to do in 1955—with such disappointing results. This error of judgment was due to an irrational attachment, on Mendès's part, to the Radical Party, where, in spite of everything, he felt more at home than elsewhere.

A singular characteristic of the Radicals since the war was the decline of their old anti-clericalism (in the past provincial Radicals often closely resembled M. Homais, the priest-devouring apothecary from *Madame Bovary*), and their willingness to compromise even on the sacrosanct principle of *laïcité;* in the famous vote on the *Loi Barangé* in August, 1951 (granting state subsidies to religious schools), a substantial proportion of Radicals supported the Catholic MRP; and although Mendès-France personally voted against the *Loi Barangé*, he never took a strong doctrinaire line on *laïcité*, as was very apparent from his election campaign in December, 1955. Under the Fourth Republic, the champions of *laïcité* are no longer the Radicals, but the Socialists and Communists—despite Herriot's oft-repeated slogan to the effect that he who was not *laïque* was not a good Republican.

It might be added that Freemasonry was dissolved by Vichy. Since

---

[1] This group, formed after the Liberation as an ally of the Socialists, later became a mixed parliamentary body comprising men as different as M. Pleven, constant ally of the MRP, and Mitterrand, one of Mendès's closest allies.

[2] When de Gaulle started his mass movement, the RPF, he asked Mendès to join it; Mendès thought it 'a lot of foolishness', and preferred to remain a 'pure' Radical.

their revival after the war, the Lodges have not regained anything like their past influence; the total number of Freemasons in France is believed to be only about 30,000, i.e., several times smaller than before the war; and if the Lodges have any influence left at all, it is with the Socialists rather than with the Radicals.

CHAPTER 3

'THE FINEST BRAIN IN PARLIAMENT'

FROM 1950 to 1953 Mendès-France built himself the reputation of the most brilliant intellect in Parliament. His not very frequent speeches gradually came to be regarded as political events of major importance. He was a formidable leader of the Opposition—almost in the British sense. He had a gift for stating eloquently and concisely all that was wrong with France, and with the methods of government employed by his old enemy Pleven (who was Premier during the greater part of 1950 and 1951) and by Pinay, René Mayer and Laniel in 1952 and 1953. The extravagant expenditure on the war in Indo-China, its futility, and all the corruption surrounding it were an *idée fixe* with Mendès-France. So long as that hopeless war continued, and France was dragged deeper and deeper into the bog, there was no prospect of her concentrating her energies on home reconstruction. Similarly, he was greatly disturbed by the tough and short-sighted policy adopted by France in relation to Tunisia in December, 1951, after the abortive attempt made by the Chenik Government to obtain a number of concessions from the French. The money spent on Indo-China would, he thought, be much better employed in developing both France and North Africa economically.

On France's own economic backwardness he had the strongest views, and considered it insane for France to waste her energies on Indo-China and large-scale rearmament if her economic development continued, as it did, to lag behind all the other major industrial countries of the world. Most significant was his big programme speech on December 30, 1951, in which he sharply criticized Pleven's subservience to the United States, and his total dependence on American aid. These were the main points he made:

French production in 1951 was no higher than it had been in 1929, while all other European countries had shown a substantial increase over the 1929 level. Ten times since the Liberation had wages been 'adjusted' to the cost of living, but the balance had never been maintained. There could be no question of scrapping any major item of expenditure: social services, military expenditure, the standard of living, or reconstruction. But priorities should be set up in each category of expenses, and the working

71

class, to improve its standard of living, should work longer hours, or more productively.

On the other hand, an effective taxation system should be introduced. There were greater inequalities of income in England, but no such great inequalities in private spending.

Indirect taxation represented 69 per cent of France's revenue, as against 55 per cent before the war.

There was much 'fancy' spending, and the nationalization of the banks, for instance, had not been followed by any rationalization measures, which would have saved a lot of money.

French railways were running at a heavy loss, because motor transport was represented by powerful pressure groups.

The Monnet Plan had been a relative failure, because money had been spent irrationally since the war; not nearly enough had been put into capital investments. And things had gone from bad to worse. If, in 1949, these investments were still twice as much as military expenditure, in 1952 they would be equal to only half the military expenditure.

The successive governments had been relying too much on American aid, *espoir suprême et suprême pensée*. Pleven's and René Mayer's speeches all seemed to be addressed to America, and not to France. No doubt, Marshall Aid had been a godsend to France, which had received food and raw materials and some equipment; but during the Marshall Aid euphoria, France had failed to prepare herself industrially for the future. Now Marshall Aid was at an end, and all France could now expect from America was military aid. France was allowing the USA to fix her war budget for her; and the Government of the last two years had acquired the bad habit of assuring the Americans that France would do this and that, and then assuring the French that America would pay. All sorts of lunatic promises had been made to the USA at the outbreak of the Korean war; but in reality the divisions France was to produce were still largely on paper.

It was these irresponsible promises made at international conferences that were undermining France's credit abroad. French ministers went to these conferences now, never knowing exactly what they wanted, or what they could, or could not, promise. All this was largely due to that inflation which he (Mendès-France) had tried to prevent in 1945. In 1951 prices had risen 30 per cent, while the government had estimated only a 5 per cent rise; what kind of healthy budgeting was possible in such conditions?

This attack on Bidault's and Pleven's behaviour at international conferences was typical of Mendès-France; the man believed in precision and careful planning and 'book-keeping', while Pleven and Bidault merely muddled along, hoping, like so many Mr. Micawbers, for something to turn up. Yet what *could* turn up? They were allowing the Indo-China war to drag on, hoping that, in the end, America would pay for most of it—but since France would still do most of the fighting, she would continue to enjoy the advantage of ranking as one of the Great Anti-Communist Powers.

Mendès-France did not mince his words. There was, he said, only one obvious thing for France to do—and that was to change her Indo-China policy. It was not a question of abandoning Indo-China, or of capitulating, but of starting talks with Vietminh.

> Some think it is wicked to negotiate with Communists; but then what are the Americans doing in Korea? The French Government is instead talking of internationalizing the war, or of embarking on 'multilateral' talks, in which France can only be the loser.

And he concluded:

> By some incredible paradox we have given priority to Asia, thus siding with MacArthur and with the American anti-Europeans. In such conditions, the Germans are bound to gain crushing superiority in the European Army you are planning . . .

Public opinion in France became highly conscious, after this speech, of the fact that here was a man—and a man of the French bourgeoisie at that—who had an alternative policy to propose, and who had not hesitated to declare that the Indo-China war must be stopped. No doubt, Bidault had uttered an angry, defiant ' *Non* ' But had not the Bidault policy lasted far too long? The war in Indo-China had already continued for five years; and there was no prospect of its ever ending.

Probably for the first time, after that speech of December 30, 1951, did France become fully 'Mendès-conscious'. His name began to appear more and more often in the press. Papers like *L'Aurore*, *Le Figaro* and many others were uncompromisingly hostile; but all the left-wing intellectuals in France took him up as 'their man'; the Socialists became increasingly sympathetic towards him, and even the Communists thought his line on Indo-China 'promising'. If Mendès did not say much about North Africa in his speech, it was because the disastrous effects of the French Note of December 15, 1951, putting an end to the negotiations with the Tunisian Government, had not yet become fully obvious. But less than a fortnight later, trouble flared up in Tunisia. We shall examine this case in connection with Mendès's historic flight to Tunis three years later.

CHAPTER 4

MENDÈS NEARLY SUCCEEDS IN 1953

THE Pinay Government, which had ruled France during most of 1952, and whose most memorable achievement was the stabilization of the cost of living, was replaced by one under René Mayer, which lasted from January to May. The fight over EDC had now reached an active stage, and it looked as though the time for decisions was close at hand. The atmosphere in France was unhealthy. The Bordeaux trial of the SS-men who had taken part in the Oradour massacre of June, 1944, stirred up anti-German feeling as nothing had done for a long time. Financial difficulties, too, were piling up, and when, in May, Mayer tried to increase various taxes, and to challenge the privileges of road transport monopolies and of the *bouilleurs de cru* (the 3½ million tax-free distillers) the grievances aroused by these proposals added themselves to the widespread dislike of Mayer's pro-EDC policy, and his government was overthrown. This cabinet crisis, which opened on May 21, was to last right through June, and it was in the course of it that Mendès-France attempted for the first time to be invested by the National Assembly for the premiership.

It was unfortunate for France that Mendès-France should have been short of 13 votes—without which he did not obtain that 'constitutional majority' which, at that time, was still required by any prospective premier before he could go ahead with his cabinet-making. It is impossible to say what exactly would have happened if Mendès had succeeded in forming his government; but it seems probable that an attempt would have been made to put an end to the Indo-China war without waiting for the disaster of Dien Bien Phu. Also, it seems unlikely that if Mendès had been premier in the summer of 1953, the Moroccan diehards would have dared overthrow the Sultan, which, after all, was done, if not with the direct complicity, at any rate with the tacit approval of M. Bidault, M. Laniel's Foreign Minister.

For already at that time Mendès had certainly many clear ideas on both Indo-China and North Africa. On June 16 he wrote a preface to a remarkable book by François Mitterrand, in which the latter argued in favour of winding up the war in Indo-China at almost any price, and in favour of concentrating as many of France's resources as possible on developing North Africa.

Since Stalin's death, Mendès wrote, things had clearly changed for the better. There were signs of a *détente* everywhere—in Korea, in Austria, in Yugoslavia, with which Russia had just resumed diplomatic relations;

> There is only one place in the world (he wrote) where there is no question of truce, peace, *détente* or anything, and where it looks as if the war would have to go on for ever. Why do the Soviet leaders and their friends make an exception for Indo-China? But surely, it is for us to launch a peace offensive in the one place where the Russians have not launched it ... It all looks as if the war in Indo-China was a frightful trap into which we had fallen, so that we should exhaust all our strength in it, so that we should lose our men and our equipment there, and be reduced to helplessness in Europe. It is unforgivable that we should never have tried to extricate ourselves from that trap; and that we should go on with a war in which, in any case, we have nothing to gain ... Even at its very best, even if we win a resounding victory in the Far East, all it will entitle us to will be to go home ... Already, the concessions we have made to Bao Dai greatly exceed all that Ho Chi Minh asked from us in 1946. Our concessions to Bao Dai have set up a precedent which the Tunisian nationalists have been quick to take advantage of ...[1]

The investiture speech of Mendès-France only a few days later was one of the major landmarks in the history of the Fourth Republic. It aroused interest in the country, as no other investiture speech had done. 'Like a breath of fresh air', a Socialist speaker remarked; and the same phrase (or similar phrases) were used by a large part of the press. Here at last was somebody *different* from the 'old gang'—from the Mayers, and Bidaults and Schumans and Queuilles and Plevens. The general public was impressed by the self-confidence of the little man, who juggled with figures which, unlike Pleven's figures, *meant* something, who did not mince his words, and whose speech seemed to bring to the surface all kinds of thoughts that had been lying hidden in the country's consciousness, without any responsible person on the government bench daring to utter them.

He spoke of the 'decline of France', of the appalling budget deficit of 1,000 milliard francs in 1953; of the production that had increased by only 8 per cent since 1929, whereas it had doubled in the USA; of the 50,000 houses France had built in 1952, while Western Germany had built 437,000.

[1] François Mitterrand. *Aux frontières de l'Union Française*. Préface de P. Mendès-France (Paris, 1953), pp. 12–14.

He said he had a plan for Indo-China, which he would submit to the British and the Americans at Bermuda—which was to take place later in the year. But he did not say enough: and this was a psychological mistake; for as a result of his reticence, the Right and the MRP suspected him of 'capitulationism', and the Left of wanting to 'internationalize' the war. Similarly, he was insufficiently precise on EDC; for when he said that EDC represented a conflict 'within every French heart', and suggested that a compromise was desirable which would satisfy everybody in France, he again steered a middle course which satisfied neither the pro-EDC nor the anti-EDC people. Further, he suggested that he would like to engage in reasonable negotiations with Tunisia 'on the basis of internal autonomy'—which did not fail to scare the Right and, above all, the men of the North Africa Lobby.

The Socialists were, however, wholly enthusiastic about Mendès's performance, so much so that the Right began to wonder whether there was not a danger of a new and predominantly Left majority crystallizing at the Assembly. The Gaullists, for their part, were divided; General de Bénouville 'phoned de Gaulle himself at Colombey-les-Deux-Eglises and asked for 'guidance'—even though, shortly before (in connection with the Gaullist *débâcle* in the local elections), de Gaulle had dissociated himself from the Gaullist deputies in Parliament.

According to the *Monde*, Bénouville was told by de Gaulle that he thought Mendès 'unsuitable', in view of his 'disquieting' ideas on Indo-China and North Africa. Also, it was later reported that de Gaulle thought Mendès unsuitable, as he 'wouldn't have the guts to stand up to the Americans over EDC'. De Gaulle was one of the most passionate opponents of the 'supra-national' army. Nor had he abandoned his old-time ideas on the French 'Empire'.

As for the MRP, the leaders (though not the rank-and-file), were almost unanimously hostile; M. Teitgen, expressed his 'intuitive anxiety' over many of the things that Mendès had said; and the others were scarcely any more favourable. 'Intuitive anxiety' had, indeed, been widely aroused among the 'old gang', who suspected Mendès of planning a far-reaching reversal of France's foreign and colonial policy—and perhaps her home policy, too. They felt that even if many of his words were wrapped up in all kinds of precautions, his mind was sharp and precise ; and, once in office, he might do many dangerous things: such as stopping the war in Indo-China, abandoning the tough North-African policy of the last two years, and undermining the 'European' idea, by tampering with EDC.

The final vote of the principal parties was significant:

	For	Against	Abstained
Communists	—	101	—
Socialists	105	—	—
MRP	52	2	29
UDSR	19	—	3
Radicals	68	—	6
Right (Independents, Peasants and dissident Gaullists) ..	16	14	99
Gaullists	25	2	52

Including various splinter groups, the total of votes cast for Mendès was 301, and against him, 119; but there were 191 abstentions, and he thus failed by 13 votes to secure the 'constitutional majority' required. There was, however, a crazy kind of logic about this vote: it reflected the indecision—as it still existed in 1953—on a large number of issues.

In the end, after a long-drawn-out cabinet crisis, the National Assembly—exhausted by all these unsuccessful investiture speeches—finally voted for an obscure right-wing politician, M. Joseph Laniel—the Laniel under whose government—which lasted nearly a year—one mistake after another was made. It was under this government that the Sultan of Morocco was deposed, And, in the end, it was the Laniel Government that was buried under the burning wreckage of Dien Bien Phu, which marked the disastrous end of the war in Indo-China—a catastrophe which Mendès-France might have avoided had he received those extra 13 votes.

The reception given to his investiture speech in the country at large was so favourable that Mendès-France could now afford to sit back and wait for his next opportunity—which, clearly, was not far off. He, however, watched the antics of the Laniel Government with growing dismay; the complete loss of authority, as displayed by Laniel and Bidault at the Bermuda conference; the various tricks Bidault tried to play at the Berlin conference in February, 1954, and so on. On EDC, however, Mendès gained the clear conviction that, even before Bermuda, in the November, 1953, debate, parliamentary opinion in France was not less, but more hostile to it than ever. It was with this conviction that he tackled the EDC problem when he came into office six months later . . .

But what brought on the government crisis of June, 1954, was not EDC, but Indo-China.

CHAPTER 5

PERSONAL CLOSE-UP

NOW that the time has come to deal with Mendès-France as an outstanding international figure—the man who ended the war in Indo-China, pacified Tunisia by giving her internal autonomy, killed EDC and got France, soon afterwards, to ratify German rearmament—it may be useful to have a close look at Mendès-France the man.

I have heard Mendès speak at least a hundred times; he has an admirable voice—a deep baritone is, I believe, the right word for it—he uses well-rounded phrases, often packed with facts, figures and information which he rattles off with great ease. He is like a great lawyer with a perfect knowledge of his brief. He never stumbles or stutters. Most expressive is the restrained, and yet vigorous, use of his small white hands. He can be formidable in a debate, has a gift of quick repartee, but although, occasionally, he produces some happy 'formulae', as they say in French—for instance, *gouverner, c'est choisir*, his mind is analytical rather than epigrammatical. He will hammer in a fact with great force, when necessary: for instance when, looking back on his Indo-China 'deadline', he later declared: 'People thought it ridiculous that I should set myself a 30-day time limit; but now I can tell you: the French generals in Indo-China were prepared to give me only a fortnight, after which they refused to take responsibility for what might happen.' But he does not strive to dazzle his audience by any felicitous *bon mot*, or by Churchillian purple patches that capture and fire the imagination. If he arouses keen interest, it is less through any rhetoric in his speeches or through the magnetism of personality than through what he stands for—a greater tidiness in the conduct of public affairs, the impression he gives of having a better and clearer vision of France and her problems than most people, and that air of intellectual superiority and high mental quality which always impresses a French audience.

He arouses respect and admiration rather than enthusiasm and affection. Back in 1953-54 he used to demonstrate brilliantly the shortcomings and the follies of the Bidaults and Plevens, and could make out a convincing case against alcoholism even in front of an audience of *bouilleurs de cru;* he used to impress people by his mental agility in dodging awkward questions and, at the same time, by his courage in telling unpopular truths. He impressed them also by his intellectual and dialectical virtuosity, as well as by his profound sense of purpose.

It is qualities like these which, for a time, endeared him to some young Radicals, for instance, of the '*Jacobin*' group, who thought that Mendès had the secret of a 'cleaner, better, more efficient France'. In a few—as in François Mauriac, the great Catholic novelist and liberal crusader for the colonial peoples—he used, for a long time, to arouse feelings bordering on reverence, hero-worship and adoration; to Mauriac, Mendès was like the answer to France's prayer for a major statesman. Mauriac accepted him almost mystically, as a Providential Figure.

Yet few people look less cut out than he for any 'mystical' rôle; he has an attractive voice and beautiful and expressive hands; he is solidly built, but small; pasty-faced, heavy-lidded, tight-lipped; he has neither the Plutarchian physical beauty of a Saint-Just nor the fanatical austerity of a Robespierre. When some particularly stupid question is asked, he cannot suppress a sardonic and contemptuous expression. He can snap sharply at a heckler, and can brilliantly demolish an opponent's argument; but he is not known ever to have made a joke—let alone a salty joke—in the style of Clemenceau.

Like Poincaré, he has a tremendous working capacity and a sense of purpose, indeed, a sense of mission, but he lacks the lachrymose warmth of an Herriot, the wit of a Clemenceau or a Jacques Duclos, the rhetorical dazzle of a Pierre Cot or a Pierre-Henri Teitgen. And, above all, he lacks—or seems to lack—warmth. Like Poincaré, he surrounds himself with a chilly little circle; he avoids *camaraderie*, and is on terms of familiar *tutoyage* with extremely few people. He seldom smiles and hardly ever laughs. In the 1955 election campaign, his most ardent admirers—mostly young people—liked to think him warm and friendly; but, at heart, they were still conscious of an air of forbidding intellectual austerity surrounding him. He loves France in an abstract kind of way; but it is not certain that he loves many of his fellow-countrymen: he has *this* in common with de Gaulle.

In addition—and why deny it?—he feels handicapped by the unfair fact that he is not considered 'entirely French'.

And then there are the Cicurel millions over which tongues have never stopped wagging. The fact that in 1933 the young deputy married Lily Cicurel, one of Cairo's wealthiest heiresses, did not fail to cause a whispering campaign about the department store and the *Uniprix* type of shops—so detested by small shopkeepers—from which Mme. Mendès-France was supposed to have 'got her money'.

Little need be said of his private life, and anyone interested in his eating and drinking habits, can do no better than study the work of Mr. McCormick.[1] Here he will learn that 'work occupies so much of his time that he frequently misses meals altogether'; but that, for breakfast—shared by the whole family—he eats porridge, eggs and bacon, and for dinner a grilled steak'. Also, that he takes calcium and vitamin pills and 'has a schoolboy's passion for sweets, cakes and puddings, probably because he is a non-smoker'. And, further, that if he prefers milk or orange juice to wine, it is not because he is a fanatical teetotaller, but because he has a weak liver.

He doesn't dance, rarely visits the theatre or hears a concert, and dislikes the cinema. On the other hand, he loves to play the piano and has a great admiration for the works of Bach, essentially the choice of a mathematical mind.

And again, a page later: 'Piano playing is almost his sole relaxation.'

To tell the truth, I never checked whether Mendès-France always had porridge for breakfast; but the playing of Bach as a regular form of relaxation intrigued me, and one day I ventured to ask: 'Tell me, *Monsieur le Président*, do you really spend a lot of time playing the piano, and Bach in particular?'

It was one of those rare occasions when Mendès laughed. And his answer was very typical.

'I did play the piano till about the age of twenty. But now—good heavens, no!' And then, very earnestly: '*In order to play the piano properly, one has to practice between five and six hours every day;* otherwise it's not worth doing.'

As for his houses, Mr. McCormick mentions La Logie Pascale, a country villa 'in the mountains near Louviers', and 'the modest apartment in a pleasant district of Passy-Muette, on the fourth floor of a suburban house'.

No, no! The 'mountain' is only 200 feet high, and as for the 'modest' apartment, it is a large one in a *de-luxe* block of flats, a stone's throw from the Bois de Boulogne . . . As for being 'suburban', how would you like Knightsbridge or Kensington to be included in 'suburbia'?

[1] *Mr. France* by Donald McCormick (London, Jarrolds, 1955).

CHAPTER 6

THE ROAD TO THE PREMIERSHIP

IN June, 1953, after Mendès-France failed, by 13 votes, to be appointed premier, and after several unsuccessful attempts by other candidates to be 'invested', the Assembly finally gave its approval to M. Laniel, one of the most absurd figures of the Fourth Republic. He was slow and bovine to look at, and not at all the 'cunning Norman' he was thought to be. He allowed himself to be guided and manœuvred by the 'old gang' with whom he had surrounded himself in his cabinet. Bidault was his Foreign Minister; Pleven his Minister of Defence, Reynaud and Teitgen his Vice-premiers, Martinaud-Déplat his Minister of the Interior. Among the brighter and younger people were M. Edgar Faure, the Minister of Finance, who alone had a creditable record in the Laniel Government—to which he stuck till the end; and M. Mitterrand, who resigned as a protest against the deposition of the Sultan of Morocco in August, 1953—barely two months after the government was formed.

The Laniel Government is associated with several important events:

(1) The plot to depose the Sultan of Morocco—a plot hatched by the French and Moslem *ultras* in Morocco (notably El Glaoui and M. Boniface) and supported by the Resident-General, General Guillaume, and by Marshal Juin, and condoned by M. Bidault, the Foreign Minister; after that things went from bad to worse in Morocco.

(2) The Bermuda Conference, where M. Laniel and M. Bidault were very roughly treated by both Eisenhower and especially by Churchill for still having failed to get EDC ratified, even though it was clear from the Assembly debate only a fortnight before that France was less keen than ever on doing so. The Bermuda Conference was followed by the Berlin Conference of Foreign Ministers in January–February 1954; here the discussions with Molotov on the future of Germany were wholly fruitless, but it was finally agreed that a nine-power conference be held at Geneva to deal with Indo-China and Korea.

(3) And finally, Dien Bien Phu, where 15,000 French troops were trapped by Vietminh, who then captured this stronghold (wholly cut off from the French bases in Tongking) after several weeks' fighting. The impression created in France by this disaster

was overwhelming; and a quarrel started between those wanting
to drag America into the Indo-China war and to 'internationalize' it, and those who thought that the sooner the
cease-fire was negotiated in Indo-China, the better. Public
opinion in France was almost wholeheartedly in favour of
winding up the war at almost any price. This gave Mendés-
France his supreme chance.

Nothing was more crazy than the weeks that preceded the fall of
Dien Bien Phu: General Navarre's insane venture of establishing an
'impregnable' fortress far inside the enemy line, in order to 'disorganize
Vietminh's communications'; the surprise caused by the powerful onslaught of the Vietminh forces, complete with artillery, on Dien Bien
Phu; the kicks in the pants received at the Etoile by Laniel and Pleven
from a crowd of Indo-China veterans; the ban on the Moscow ballet
at the Paris opera; and, on the other hand, the attempt made by
Bidault, the Foreign Minister, to 'internationalize' the war—an attempt encouraged by certain American 'roll-back' generals and admirals and favoured by Mr. Dulles, but discouraged by Eisenhower
and especially by Eden and Churchill. Bidault meantime played for
time at the Geneva Conference, and took good care to have as little
contact as possible with the Russian, Chinese and Vietminh delegates,
still hoping that the USA would intervene with 500-plane raids on the
Vietminh forces besieging Dien Bien Phu; or, after the fall of the fortress, still 'do something'. The Laniel Government went so far, on
June 1, as to replace M. Jacquet, Minister for Indo-China—who,
heartily disagreeing with Bidault, had resigned—by M. Frédéric-
Dupont, an Indo-China diehard, if ever there was one. To the MRP,
in particular, it was a point of honour to go on with the Indo-China
war on almost any terms: it was they who had taken responsibility
for it for the last seven years ...

However, in the first week in June, three weeks after the fall of
Dien Bien Phu, and with the French Expeditionary Force in danger
of being thrown into the sea, the Laniel Government was now clearly
on its last legs.

The *coup de grâce* was delivered by Mendès-France, who angrily
ridiculed Bidault's attempt to suggest that he had secured China's
neutrality in Vietnam in return for US recognition of the Chinese
Government—a course to which Bidault had been in no position at all
to commit the USA. He accused Bidault of playing a waiting game at
Geneva, and avoiding all contact with 'the enemy'. Worse still, Bidault
had, Mendès said, nearly started World War III:

You had a plan which was revealed at the beginning of May:
the large-scale intervention of the American airforce at the risk

of provoking Chinese intervention and starting a general war. Parliament had adjourned on April 10, but M. Laniel had undertaken to call it if there was anything new and important. The American intervention plan had been prepared, and was about to come into action—at your request, too. The attack was to be launched on April 28, and the ships with the aircraft and the atom bombs were on the way. President Eisenhower was going to ask Congress on April 26 for the necessary authority. The French parliament was going to be faced with a *fait accompli* . . . Fortunately, the plan was rejected by Britain and by public opinion in the USA—at least for the time being.

He called for entirely new methods at Geneva, and suggested that there was no time to lose. If, he concluded, a new government was formed that was like the Laniel Government, then it was not worth while having a cabinet crisis; but if Parliament was willing to listen to the clamour coming from the French towns and villages, then it was high time to turn over a new leaf.

Three days after this speech the Laniel Government was overthrown.

PART IV
MENDÈS-FRANCE'S 1954-55 GOVERNMENT

CHAPTER 1

INDO-CHINA

TODAY, in 1957, with the storm-centre having moved to French North Africa, one looks back to the disaster of Dien Bien Phu and the winding-up of the Indo-China war in 1954 as almost a secondary episode in the great crisis of the French colonial empire.

It should, however, be remembered that, for several years, the whole political and economic life of France had been poisoned by this running sore of Indo-China. And when Mendès-France took it upon himself to put an end to that war, he became, for a short time, the most popular man in France.

The Indo-China war had cost France £3,000 millions and even though, by the end of 1953, the United States had begun to pay the greater part of the cost of this war, there was a new danger of which the whole of France was becoming increasingly conscious. If, up till 1954, only 19,000 Frenchmen had lost their lives in the Indo-China war, while the rest of the 76,000 men killed were mostly men of the Foreign Legion and 'coloured' troops, the fact was beginning to be more and more frequently mentioned that if the war in Indo-China continued, it would soon be necessary to send parts of the French conscript army (*le contingent*) there. There was a grave danger of a 'colonial' expedition, fought chiefly by 'mercenaries' (though also by a large number of French professional officers—whose absence was badly weakening France's military and diplomatic position in Europe) becoming a 'national' war—which nobody in France wanted. The fear of ordinary conscripts being sent to Indo-China enormously increased the clamour in the country for a rapid winding-up of the war.

June–July 1954: in all the history of France during the past ten years, there was hardly another moment to equal it for the kind of nation-wide elation, nation-wide optimism that was suddenly created on June 18 by Mendès-France, when he fixed himself a time-limit of 30 days to stop the fighting in Indo-China. Optimism: for years it had been drummed into France that Indo-China was at the root of all her troubles; and, after the humiliating tragedy of Dien Bien Phu, the urgency of this 'liquidation' had become obvious to everybody. It almost seemed that if only Indo-China was cleared out of the way,

everything else would be easy; and there was, in the country, an astonishing faith in this little man, who had shunned office for over nine
years and who was now promising to end the war in Indo-China, settle
the problem of Germany, put France on her feet economically, and
reach a settlement in North Africa.

No doubt, in Parliament they liked him less than they liked him
in the country at large. The MRP refused to be associated with his
experiment. His whole manner was like a series of slaps in the face for
M. Bidault. The Socialists, though sympathetic to Mendès, preferred
to stay clear of his government. They were uncertain about his
economic programme, and cared little for his Minister of Finance,
M. Edgar Faure.

Also, there was something 'disquieting' about the man. He was not
quite playing the parliamentary game. There was something more
'personalist' about his whole manner in dealing with people than anything France had seen since the days of de Gaulle. He did not negotiate
with the groups and parties; he picked his ministers individually; he
said he would have nothing to do with the old practice of *dosage*—that
system of cabinet-making based on buying the support of this or that
party in return for 2, 3 or 4 ministerial posts, and 2, 3 or 4 under-
secretaryships. What helped him enormously in the eyes of the Western
world was the fact that he had refused to 'count' the Communist votes
cast in his favour. He was invested by 419 votes; but, before the vote,
he had said that he would not take any account of the Communist
votes, since the Communists had supported the enemy in Indo-China.
Angrily, Jacques Duclos exclaimed: 'This is unconstitutional.' So, in a
sense, it was, and set up a dangerous precedent. But, in the circumstances, Mendès-France thought the gamble worth while; all the more
so, as his anti-Communist stand earned him a large number of right-
wing votes. So much so that, even after deducting the Communist
votes, he was still invested by a 'constitutional majority' of 324 votes,
that is, ten votes above the required minimum. 'Coldfooted little Jew,'
Duclos later angrily commented in the lobbies, much to the delight of
the Jewish press in America, which picked up the remark with great
relish. Later, Duclos was rapped over the knuckles for it by the Communist Central Committee.

No doubt, this refusal of the Communist votes was a dangerous
gamble: for if only a handful of people had voted the other way, the
whole Mendès-France plan would have collapsed, just as it did a year
before. But he thought the risk worth taking; and this risk, like the
risk of the July 20 deadline, justified itself.

It should be added that although the Communists were furious,
they still voted for him; but they were voting neither for the

government programme as a whole, still less for the person of M. Mendès France, but for the one and only item contained in his government programme—which was peace in Indo-China.

Abroad, reactions to Mendès-France was mixed at first. In Britain he had an almost universally good press. He came to be referred to as 'Mr. France'. In the USA his appointment at first alarmed the State Department; President Coty had to reassure the US Ambassador, Mr. Dillon, that the Mendès-France appointment did not mean the 'Popular Front'; nor did it mean—as had been suggested by the State Department—that France would now 'sabotage' Europe. (That, indeed, was the first German reaction to his appointment.) All the same, his 'Communist-votes-don't-count' produced the right impression in America.

Western Germany was much more sceptical, and indeed alarmed; here it was thought that EDC might well be wrecked, perhaps all the more so as, in the words of the *Frankfurter Allgemeine*, here, for the first time in many years, there was a striking personality at the head of the French Government. Other 'Europeans' like Spaak also got alarmed, and Spaak rushed to Paris only a few days after Mendès had taken over, and urged an immediate conference on EDC, only to be sharply told that the Indo-China settlement must come first.

At the Geneva Conference, which had been dragging on for two months, more dead than alive, the Mendès appointment caused a sensation: it looked as if now at last some progress might be made. Some no doubt realized that in France he was being used for just this one particular job: peace in Indo-China; and after that, once he started tackling economic and financial matters, he might well be thrown out before long. But in Geneva at that moment he seemed indispensable, if the Conference was to get anywhere. The truth was that Russia, China, India, Vietminh and the other Asian powers all distrusted Bidault. As André Fontaine wrote in the *Monde* of June 29, all these powers were convinced that Bidault was merely playing for time, and working for a purely provisional settlement, which would then give him time to drag the United States into war.

It would, of course, be a mistake to think that during those '30 days' Mendès did nothing but negotiate at Geneva. He spent only a relatively small proportion of his time in Switzerland. He worked with tremendous energy on a whole range of problems: EDC, Indo-China, North Africa, economic plans. He started, of course, with long talks with Eden and Bedell Smith; he rushed down to Berne to see Chou En Lai, the Chinese Foreign Minister (he did not take long to discover that there wasn't a word of truth in Bedault's earlier idea that

China had decided to remain 'neutral' in Indo-China), and agreed with him on simultaneous negotiations on a cease-fire and a political settlement: he also established his first contact with Pham Van Dong, that Vietminh delegate with whom Bidault refused to have anything to do. But much of the time was spent in Paris. Mendès knew, from his conferences with Voizard, the French Resident-General in Tunisia, and M. Francis Lacoste, the French Resident-General in Morocco that, before long, far-reaching decisions would have to be taken in respect of North Africa.

At the same time, Mendès also kept an eye on that Brains Trust, presided over by M. Gruson at the Ministry of Finance, which was said to be working on a spectacular recasting of the whole economic structure of France. Or so it seemed at the time.

Also, Adenauer was in a state of alarm. He thought EDC was in grave danger now of not being ratified. Mendès, anxious to reassure him, was about to send to Bonn M. Guérin de Beaumont, one of the pro-EDC members of his government; but after some particularly unfortunate and unfriendly remarks made by Adenauer, this mission was cancelled.

Indo-China, despite all these pressing demands coming from all sides and concerning a variety of other matters, continued to be Mendès's biggest worry. Conditions there were rapidly deteriorating. There was a danger of Vietminh striking out and throwing the French expeditionary force into the sea. In the last days of June, the French troops began to evacuate the whole southern part of the Red River Delta, 'to shorten their front', as the phrase went; and thousands of refugees began to pour into Haiphong and Hanoi—that very Hanoi from which French civilians were preparing to move out. All the news from Geneva was now, indeed, suggesting that, whatever concessions Vietminh made, they were determined to establish themselves firmly in Tongking. So alarming did the situation become for the French forces in Indo-China, that Mendès—who had merely alluded to this danger before—felt obliged on July 7 to announce that he was preparing a Bill authorizing the Government to send units of the regular French Army in Europe to Indo-China.

It created the right impression at Geneva. For if, during the first week of the Mendès régime, things at Geneva seemed to be improving, the second week was much less satisfactory. But now that only 10 or 12 days were left until the deadline expired, something had to be done to speed things up. Mendès's warning proved useful.

Molotov returned to Geneva a few days later, and Mendès dined with him, and things went 'much better than could have been expected'.

AFP published some appetizing details of the dinner Molotov had given Mendès-France, complete with caviare and countless other *zakuski, riabchiki* (woodcocks specially flown from Russia), *bombe glacée*, and bottles of Tsinandali and Napareuli, Georgian white and red wines.

And then, on the 16th, there was what the *Monde* called a 'capital' meeting between Molotov, Mendès and Eden. On the same day, it was reported from Delhi that Nehru was 'optimistic', and thought Mendès would 'make it' by July 20th.

At last, after the 'crazy night' of July 20 to 21, after everything already seemed in the bag, a last-minute hitch arose over Cambodia. As André Fontaine wrote in the *Monde* on July 21:

> Before the *dénouement* of this conference, Geneva was destined to experience the craziest, most agitated night. It was thought that the problem of Cambodia had been settled: but not at all. It compelled the Nine to embark on a further discussion which delayed till 3.50 a.m. the signing of the armistice agreements with Vietnam and Laos; and the agreement with Cambodia was not signed until 12.38 this afternoon . . .
>
> And yet, yesterday's meetings had started in an atmosphere of euphoria. The lunch given by M. Mendès-France to Mr. Chou En Lai was marked by an atmosphere of charm and cordiality, and everybody talked about everything except politics. The problems over which the delegates had squabbled for weeks were settled in a few minutes now . . . Even Mr. Trang-Van-Dong, Bao Dai's representative, while telling Mendès-France that he considered the agreement iniquitous—and he said this with genuine sadness and dignity—agreed, all the same, to accept the agreement. And then, suddenly, in the afternoon, there was a hitch over Cambodia; the Cambodian delegate refused to sign . . . However, in the end he obtained partial satisfaction. It was agreed that in case of a 'threat', Cambodia could call for the help of foreign troops. It was not clear who would be qualified to decide on the existence of such a 'threat'. All the same, the principle of the thing was accepted, and somebody had the idea of extending these Communist concessions to the Laos armistice too.

Thus, at 4 a.m. on July 21, the Laos and Vietnam armistice agreements were signed, followed later by the Cambodia agreement. All the agreements were dated July 20; and the Cambodian one specified: '24 o'clock'.

It is not necessary here to summarize the Geneva agreements—the demarcation line along the 17th parallel, the evacuation of the French —within 300 days—from Tongking; the evacuation of Vietminh forces from Cambodia, Laos and South Vietnam; the exchange of prisoners, etc. What is certain is that if, during the first 15 days of the Mendès experiment (while the deputies were still in charge at Geneva), nothing was achieved, spectacular progress was made during the last 10 or 12 days, in the course of the talks between Mendès-France, Chou En Lai, Pham Van Dong, Bedell Smith, Eden and Molotov.

Looking back on it, Mendès commented on those last days at Geneva:

'They were infernally tough, especially Molotov and Pham Van Dong. Pham Van Dong, Ho Chi Minh's foreign minister (who had already been his spokesman at Fontainebleau in 1946) was a fanatic—and extremely hard to move. Brilliant chap, all the same, with French culture. Molotov was as tough as nails: I often really had the impression that he did not want an agreement. It was only when that providential Cambodian hitch cropped up that I realized how utterly scared he was of the agreement not being signed. It was quite illuminating to see how Molotov's bluff suddenly broke down: he could not conceal his worry any longer. Eden, of course, was wonderful, and he was an immense help throughout. *And I honestly believe that if it hadn't been for the British Government, we might really have had World War III at the time when Bidault and Dulles and Radford were planning their mass raid on the Vietminh forces round Dien Bien Phu . . .*'

The fact that Mendès had 'won his bet' made a tremendous impression in the world, and not least in France itself.

Not that it meant the end of all trouble in Indo-China. There were grave doubts on what was going to happen in South Vietnam. Here there was no organization comparable even to Syngman Rhee's in South Korea. Bao Dai had no authority left. Would the USA try to take over the Diem régime? And if so, what about those elections in July, 1956, provided for in the agreement? The future of *la présence française* in Vietnam seemed highly precarious—whatever happened.

All the same, the news of the Geneva agreement was received with practically unanimous satisfaction in France; the danger of *le contingent* being sent there had disappeared. In the USA and Britain Mendès-France's prestige had reached heights unattained by any other leader of the Fourth Republic; the *New York Times* described him as France's national hero:

He can now return to Paris with all the authority of a national hero, in order to tackle his programme of the political, economic and military revival of his country . . .

In Britain the press and the radio built up Mendès-France as no French leader had been built up for years.

'Thanks to Mendès-France,' Jean Wetz, the London correspondent of the *Monde* wrote, 'France has acquired a new glamour on the diplomatic stage, it is felt in London. The Entente Cordiale has been strengthened by the close co-operation at Geneva of Eden and Mendès-France.'

It was a triumphal homecoming for Mendès-France. The whole government had gone out to Villacoublay to meet him. Pushing his way through the crowd, he went to embrace his wife and his parents, who had also come to meet him—his mother and his 82-year-old father.

At the National Assembly he was at the top of his form. The public galleries were packed, as seldom before. As he appeared in the Assembly, he was loudly cheered by the Socialists, Communists, Gaullists, most of the Radicals and some members of the Right. The MRP alone remained glumly silent.

After paying a tribute to the French soldiers in Vietnam, and discussing in some detail the conditions in which the agreements had been reached, Mendès dealt with the Expeditionary Corps' future:

We have agreed to withdraw it when the governments in question ask for it. The question does not arise in Cambodia and Laos, whose governments wish the present treaty with France to remain in force. In Vietnam, the Expeditionary Corps will be regrouped in the South, will be maintained at its present level, will enjoy full freedom of movement . . . and will be able to be replaced progressively . . .

He stressed that France's 'cultural and economic' links with Vietnam—both parts of it—would be maintained; he had been given assurances by Pham Van Dong that French property and enterprises in North Vietnam would be safeguarded, and that, in cases of requisition or expropriation, the 'legitimate interests of French nationals would be taken into consideration'.

Mendès was glad to say that while France had, so far, not taken part in the SEATO talks between the British and Americans, General Bedell Smith had stated on behalf of the US Government that it would not interfere with the application of the Geneva settlement, 'but that it would consider any new aggression as a violation of this settlement'. 'This,' said Mendès-France, 'consolidated the system built up at Geneva.'

H

After referring to the July, 1956, election which would unify Vietnam, Mendès-France concluded that France's rôle in the Far East had not been ended; that it was her mission to pursue a generous and realistic policy which would increase the well-being of the nations to which she had granted independence.

> I never said that the end of hostilities would remove the burden resting on our shoulders; but the settlement means that our youth will be preserved; and we shall also be in a better position to reinforce our military position in Europe and Africa.

True, there was one snag: American aid for the Indo-China war would stop; and this would mean the need for certain economic and financial readjustments in France itself.

But he ended on an optimistic note: the Indo-China settlement showed that France was capable of great achievements if there was a general will of the people behind them, as was the case with the liquidation of the Indo-China war.

That same day and the following day witnessed a procession of ghosts—Bidault, Frédéric-Dupont, Letourneau and some other Indo-China diehards, who either argued that they would have obtained better terms, had they been allowed to 'continue' the negotiations at Geneva, or darkly prophesied (as Frédéric-Dupont did in particular) that Indo-China would be 'lost to Communism' in three stages—the first of which had been consecrated at Geneva.

As for Bidault, who spoke with a good deal of bitterness, he tended to take a 'philosophical' view of the whole thing:

> On this question of Indo-China, there have always been two schools of thought. There was my school, which was not very assiduously frequented, and which considered it essential that France's word be sacred, and that the presence of France in Indo-China, within the framework of the Free World, required a long and patient effort, until such time as we could be certain that the young State of Vietnam would not fall into Communist hands. To the other school, of which you, M. Mendès-France, are the brilliant and undisputed chief, the alpha and omega of any kind of French revival was the liquidation of the Indo-China war. Not, of course, at any price, but, all the same, at a very high price, since you daily proclaimed what we were doing to be a hopeless and absurd venture without any future . . .

But the critics did not have their hearts in it; obviously, it was the wrong moment for criticizing Mendès-France who was at the height of his popularity in the country; he was loudly cheered by the greater

part of the Assembly, and, in the end, a motion was carried by an
overwhelming majority approving the Geneva settlement and congratulating Mendès-France in particular.

The Indo-China settlement was, as far as it went, a complete
(though negative) success. The bloodshed in Indo-China, which had
gone on for eight years, had at last been stopped. There were, indeed,
not many illusions in the country that '*la présence française*' in the Far
East would be maintained in any real sense. Indo-China could be
written off as a good riddance.

CHAPTER 2

MENDÈS VERSUS THE SYSTEM

UNDER his government programme, Mendès-France had announced that he would deal with the main problems in the following order: Indo-China cease-fire; economic programme; EDC. But in reality this programme was upset, almost from the moment the Geneva agreement in Indo-China had been signed.

For one thing, the fact that no more dollars were likely to be earmarked for Indo-China—dollars which were of the greatest value to the French Treasury, which, for the purposes of Indo-China, converted the dollars into francs, and used the dollars elsewhere—made it necessary to develop export markets and also to embark on a variety of other economic reforms.

However, it was not until the end of July that the main outline of the plenary powers Bill that the Mendès-France Government was shortly to submit to Parliament was drawn up.

The main features of the Plan were quarterly wage increases, in accordance with a growth in productivity; such increases to be agreed upon by the *Conseil Economique* on which both the trade unions and the employers were represented. Further, provisions were made for the reconversion of redundant industries and for the 'readaptation' of labour; moreover, by encouraging foreign trade, including imports, the Government intended to lower home prices, and eliminate, as far as possible, 'marginal' businesses; provisions would be made for giving substantial financial support in cases of unemployment resulting from the elimination of such marginal businesses; also, training centres would be set up to 're-adapt' workers to a new trade and to encourage them to move to more productive industrial centres. On the other hand, credits would be made available to any businesses capable of a 'rational' conversion.

Other measures were also agreed upon: a new distribution of taxation in the case of rail and road transport, so as to transfer to road transport the work done by 'secondary' railway lines; on the other hand, some of the main-line traffic was to go back to the railways. A special fund, independent of social security, was to be created for old-age pensions; some new capital investments were to be made, especially in respect of the Post Office, the State Railways, etc.

It is, however, impossible to deal with all these economic measures without going into a mass of details concerning credit, tax exemption, import duty adjustments in this or that sector, the variety of measures contemplated for 'reconverting' this or that industry, for readjusting labour in cases of conversion, etc.

It would, moreover, be a mistake to assume that Mendès-France was starting from scratch, as it were. Earlier in 1954 the details had been elaborated for the Second Modernization and Equipment Plan, under which the national income was to be increased by 25 per cent in the next four years (1954–57). With this plan was also linked another plan—the Edgar Faure Plan—covering the next 18 months, and providing for cheap money, more housing, a 'revaluation' of purchasing power, a 10 per cent increase in the national income in these 18 months, etc.

Faure, as he never failed to recall, had strengthened France economically in 1953—during which period he was Finance Minister—and the antagonism between Faure and Mendès probably dates back to 1954—a year during which Faure was continuing to run the finances and economic affairs of France in his own 'liberal' way, without taking much notice of the more *dirigiste* solutions Mendès was proposing—even though being himself almost entirely preoccupied with foreign and colonial affairs.

As the very conservative *Année Politique* wrote:

Mendès-France had reiterated over and over again, his desire to renovate the economic structure of France, and to practise a planned economy; this clearly upset many people. However, the fact that he maintained M. Edgar Faure at the Ministry of Finance safeguarded the continuity of the previous economic and financial policy. With tenacity and subtlety, M. Faure was thus able to pursue a policy favourable both to stability and to expansion, and so achieve the objectives fixed by his 18-Months Plan.[1]

That, in a way, was Mendès's main trouble. His Finance Minister had laid down certain plans, which, he considered, had worked satisfactorily in 1953, and which he saw no reason for scrapping, even despite the outcry among certain papers of the Left against what they called his *immobilisme*. After all, production *was* steadily increasing throughout 1953 and 1954; wages were slightly higher than they had been; there was no serious economic discontent in the country; and in 1953, for the first time since the Liberation, it could be said that

[1] *Année Politique*, 1954, p. 129.

industrial shares had become attractive even to the most timid of investors, and that gold—that refuge of the timid investor—had reached the lowest level since the war. Reconversion, decentralization of industry—which were among Mendès's favourite remedies—were all very well, but Faure did not think they had to be treated as something quite so urgent or revolutionary.

There were many important innovations that Mendès-France introduced into the technique of governing France. He governed with greater 'drive', with a greater sense of 'time' than any of his predecessors; with a well-organized publicity machinery which made everybody aware that not for a single day had *immobilisme* come into its own again. In a little over seven months he ended the war in Indo-China; he flew in spectacular style to Tunis, to lay the foundations for 'internal autonomy', i.e., for a new relationship between France and Tunisia (eventually to be followed by a similar settlement with Morocco); no sooner was he back from Tunis than he obtained plenary powers for a variety of financial and economic reforms; immediately afterwards he proceeded to carry out his promise to settle the problem of EDC in one way or another, so as to put an end to the three years' hesitations and shilly-shallying over the question of 'Europe' and German rearmament; when EDC was defeated by the National Assembly after the compromise solution he had submitted to the Brussels Conference had failed, he did not take long to 'choose' between the 'isolation' which, he was now convinced, was threatening France, and those London-Paris agreements which enabled France to remain a member of the Atlantic Pact on a different basis. Under very strong personal pressure from Mendès-France himself, the National Assembly yielded to his arguments on the dangers of 'isolation' and, before 1954 had ended, approved the Paris Agreements by a small majority. All the time, during those seven and half months Mendès-France was on the move. As somebody remarked: 'This isn't a government; it's a newsreel!'

And yet the whole experiment was largely being built on sand.

All the time, except perhaps during the first few weeks, Mendès was being plotted against. Already at the end of July the *Canard Enchaîné* published a cartoon showing Maurice Schumann, with his arms raised to heaven, exclaiming: 'This is the 38th day of our Battle for the Liberation of the Quai d'Orsay'—that Quai d'Orsay which had been the stronghold of the Catholic MRP for nearly ten years . . . And then, in October, just as the Mendès Government was showing the first serious cracks, owing to the Premier's *volte-face* in favour of German rearmament, the *Affaire Dides* blew up. Or rather, it did not blow up, but began to smoulder, and fill the air with a poisonous stench, and it started a whispering campaign, in which both Mitterrand, Mendès's Minister of the Interior, and even Mendès himself were implicated. The whispering was to the effect that France had not been defeated in Indo-China, but betrayed . . . stabbed in the back by Communists and fellow-travellers, and that people now in the government had either condoned these manœuvres, or had actually taken part in them . . .

It was the beginning of the end. In October, 1954—at the very time of Herriot's glowing tribute to Mendès-France as the new Leader— the government was already condemned. There was the Dides Affair; there was a general mobilization of the vested interests which Mendès was threatening: the *betteraviers*, and the *bouilleurs de cru;* and Mendès's enemies were merely waiting for the moment when it would be most advantageous to get rid of him: for one thing, it was to their advantage to let Mendès make himself unpopular with the Left by getting the Paris agreements ratified . . .

And what finally sealed his fate was the Aurés rebellion that broke out in Algeria on November 1, 1954. Now the North Africa Lobby were up in arms against him. But they were also willing to *wait*—wait till he had lost many of his friends by getting Germany rearmed. It is ironical to think that at the time Mr. Dulles referred to Mendès as a 'Superman', the latter had already been sentenced to death by the National Assembly . . .

On the day after his fall, André Chênebenoît wrote in the *Monde:*

What a strange political destiny—the destiny of this man who after having for so long evaded office in the absence of the proper means for carrying out his policy, finally accepted office at a moment when so much clearing away had to be done before any building could be started . . .

He was thought to be capable of revising France's system of alliances—yet if he did it in the end, it was only to introduce Germany into the Atlantic Alliance. He was supposed to be a man of the Left; yet, since he did not have a solid Left to support him, he kept stretching out his hand to those who were against him . . .

Was this strange contradiction part of his personal character? Or was it an outcome of the whole system?

Mendès is a man who believes in efficient action, and often ignores human susceptibilities . . . After all, every statesman has to pick and choose among three policies: that which others want him to pursue; that which he would like to pursue himself; and that which the hard realities of the moment will allow him to pursue . . .

And these realities, from the very outset, were Indo-China,

the rearmament of Germany, and North Africa. In moving from one problem to the other, he had to *last* in order to be able to *act* at all.

For, when all is said and done, what did the Mendès-France experiment amount to? He ended the war in Indo-China with the minimum of damage, and it was *that*, and nothing else, that made him immensely popular throughout the country. His economic experiment was still in the future: there was nothing world-shaking in the Edgar Faure decrees, and even if the beginning of a major campaign against alcohol rackets and against alcoholism gave many a foretaste of a 'better and more virtuous France', the fact remained so (as many people observed) that, in order to recast the whole internal economy and 'way of life' of France, Mendès would need *four years of uninterrupted rule*—and a working majority in parliament—which just wasn't there.

I remember the day when I put this question to Mendès:

What reforms would you have carried through had you remained in office?

He made an impatient gesture, as if I had asked a silly question.

There is no answer to your question. There can't be. I never at any moment had a sincere majority. Therefore there could be no question of carrying out any far-reaching reforms. What I *might* have done is mere idle speculation. It's just not worth discussing . . .

And then, Germany. That was something outside France's control. Again I must quote Mendès himself:

'You look upon Dulles's visit to Bonn after the Assembly rejected EDC as a gesture of hostility towards France. Especially when he said he hadn't time to come to Paris. Well, in a sense it *was* that. But there was a much, much more serious side to it. Dulles was fully prepared to agree unilaterally to the rearmament of Germany: a straight German-American deal, a deal between himself and Adenauer which, he thought, England would accept, more or less willingly, as a *fait accompli*. Eden and I had to do some very quick and hard thinking to avert this danger. I shall be eternally grateful to Eden for having taken that line at the time when it was really touch-and-go. He was of immense help to me at Geneva, when we tried to get the best possible settlement in Indo-China; and it was thanks to him again that we avoided the uncontrolled kind of German rearmament that Dulles was prepared to agree to . . .'

'But then', I remarked, 'Dulles called you a Superman'. Mendès smiled, a little wistfully.

'Yes, I became a "superman" after Eden and I had agreed on the Paris settlement in October—not before. Anyway, the phrase has been taken out of its context: he merely paid a tribute to my physical endurance, my toughness, as you say in English. He said it needed a "superman" to be both Prime Minister and Foreign Minister, and to rush about the world, without collapsing, as I was doing at the time . . .

'Germany: after all, had not France's part in the German settlement been a passive one? Germany *was* going to be rearmed: Dulles had made this amply plain. And Churchill—Churchill was determined that France should ratify EDC; and since she did not do so, he was determined that she should at least ratify the Paris agreements.

'When I went to Chartwell that day, after the Brussels Conference (what a *beastly* Conference that was!)', Mendès once said, 'I found Churchill in a very nervous and anxious state of mind. He had sent that famous cable to Adenauer—which caused me so much trouble at Brussels—in a moment of great nervous agitation, I am sure. Churchill had an *idée fixe*, a real obsession. And that was the idea that, God forbid, America might get so fed-up with France that it might well pull out of Europe and adopt "peripheral strategy", which was favoured by at least some of its generals. And Churchill already saw the Iron Curtain moving further West, if that were to happen . . .'

And yet, in analysing the main phases and features of the Mendès-France experiment, we must always bear in mind that what ultimately mattered was neither Indo-China, nor Germany, but North Africa. It has been argued that if Mendès-France was, technically, overthrown on the North African issue, this was merely an excuse: the growing opposition in Parliament was determined to get rid of him anyway; and there would not have been such an overwhelming vote against him if so many (the MRP for instance) had not borne him a grudge for his 'murder' of EDC; and if others (the Communists) did not hate him for having agreed to the rearmament of Western Germany. But whether North Africa was, at the time, merely a technical excuse for his overthrow, it is highly symbolic that his government should have fallen over the North African issue. For this was to be the great issue in France for the next two years—the issue on which the whole future of France ultimately depended . . . It was the revolt of the partisans of a tough policy in North Africa against the man who had tried to negotiate with the 'murderers' mobilized by Arab nationalism . .

The whole of Mendès-France's subsequent career—in 1955, '56 and '57—which includes his election campaign, the *Express* experiment, and the rôle of 'sleeping partner' assigned to him in the Mollet Government after the general election of January 2, 1956—is wholly inseparable from the nightmare of North Africa. . . .

CHAPTER 3

TUNIS: 'LIKE AN ANGEL FROM HEAVEN'

O N July 31, barely a week after his Indo-China 'apotheosis', readers of evening papers rubbed their eyes as they read:

Accompanied by Marshal Juin and M. Christian Fouchet,
M. MENDÈS-FRANCE HAS GONE TO TUNIS.
HE ASKS THE BEY TO AGREE TO REFORMS WHICH WILL SAFE-GUARD THE PERMANENT PRESENCE OF FRANCE IN TUNISIA.

'The internal autonomy of Tunisia is recognised and proclaimed by France without mental reservations or ulterior motives,' says M. Mendès-France to the Bey.

It may be useful to recall the principal phases of the Tunisian crisis over the few previous years. It was in 1950 that M. Robert Schuman, the then Foreign Minister, agreed to discuss a programme of progressive reforms with Tunisia, with the granting of 'internal autonomy' as their ultimate object. A relatively progressive government (though subject like all previous governments to the part-French-part-Tunisian principle) was formed under the premiership of a mild Tunisian nationalist, Mr. Chenik. The negotiations dragged on for several months. The '7 points' of Bourguiba, the leader of the Neo-Destour, having been turned down by the French, Chenik proposed in October, 1951, a 'minimum programme' of 3 points. But the opposition even to this very mild programme was so violent from the men of the Africa Lobby and from the *Présence Française*, the Settlers' organization in Tunisia, that, after numerous negotiations, the Quai d'Orsay, on the initiative of M. Maurice Schumann, M. Robert Schuman's right-hand man, sent a Note to Chenik on December 15, 1951, which amounted to a breaking-off of the negotiations that had gone on for over a year. Although the Note did not use the word 'co-sovereignty', abhorred by the Tunisians, it was, in fact, interpreted both by the Tunisians and by the French to mean that the French Government had decided to perpetuate Franco-Tunisian co-sovereignty (complete with the French Resident-General and French members of the Cabinet). It was soon afterwards that two members of the Chenik Government, and both members of the more extreme nationalist party, the Neo-Destour—M. Barda and M. Salah Ben Yussef—unexpectedly arrived at the UN at the Palais Chaillot in Paris, to lodge a complaint against France. Their visit coincided with the arrival in Tunis, in the midst of a great military and naval parade, of the new, and extremely tough Resident-General, M. de Hauteclocque, who had been appointed to replace the liberal M. Périllier. The consequences of the French Note of December 15, 1951, and of the appointment of Hauteclocque soon became apparent. Rioting broke out in various parts of Tunisia; the Neo-Destour Congress, which was to be held on January 18, was prohibited, and the Tunisian nationalist leaders, among them Bourguiba, besides hundreds of others, were arrested on orders from M. de Hauteclocque.

The shortlived Edgar Faure Government (Jan.–Feb. 1952) was still in office; and although both Faure and some of his Ministers, notably M. François Mitterrand were liberally inclined, M. de Hauteclocque and General Garbay, the Commander of the French forces in Tunisia, were going to stand no nonsense. The Tunisian appeal to UN was taken particularly badly, and the rioting in the Cap Bon area led to the famous *ratissages* (i.e., punitive expedition) organized by General Garbay (who had already distinguished himself as the leader of much larger-scale punitive expeditions in Madagascar in 1947— where 80,000 people were believed to have been killed).

Among the liberal-minded people in Paris this *ratissage* produced a violent reaction; an MRP deputy, M. Fonlupt-Espéraber, went to Tunisia to investigate, and brought back some harrowing details of the various outrages committed by the Foreign Legion. M. Faure then entrusted M. Mitterrand with the task of drawing up a programme of liberal reforms, which came to be known as the Mitterrand Plan; and there is no doubt that this Plan would have been gladly accepted by the Chenik Government, and accepted, at least in the main, even by the Neo-Destour leaders. But at the end of February the Faure Government was overthrown, and replaced a few days later, by the Pinay government, which shelved the Mitterrand Plan, and gave the Resident-General in Tunisia, M. de Hauteclocque, a free hand. After a few peremptory demands addressed to the Bey, M. de Hauteclocque simply arrested Chenik and several other Tunisian Ministers, and appointed in his place a *beni-oui-oui*, a French stooge, M. Baccouche, one of the wealthiest men in Tunisia, and principal shareholder of the Tunisian branch of Coca Cola.

Terrorism and counter-terrorism continued for some months; but by the summer there was a lull. A large proportion of the arrested people had been released, but the French were not willing to grant anything more than a few fragmentary reforms to Tunisia, and were determined to cling to 'co-sovereignty'. Opposition came chiefly from two sources: the Beylical Palace, and the UGTT, the Tunisian Trade Union Federation, the head of which was Ferhat Hashed. Ferhat Hashed was in close contact with the CIO and the AF of L, and his federation, numbering 100,000 members, was a member of the ICFTU (the International Federation of Free Trade Unions). The French Residence looked upon the Trade Unions, and especially their leader, as 'American stooges', and as weapons of American Imperialism. As for the Bey, he infuriated the French in September by appointing a sort of unofficial Tunisian parliament—a Council of Forty.

However, the French waited before striking. After the Presidential Election in the USA in November, 1952, which replaced the Truman Administration by the Eisenhower Administration, the French *colons* became much more confident, and it seems that they persuaded the new American leaders that it was in the interests of the Free World that they should be given a free hand to 'keep North Africa in order'.

On December 4, 1952, Ferhat Hashed was assassinated—probably by that 'Red Hand' ('red with the blood of the enemies of France') which had already warned him on several occasions that he was considered an American agent, and would soon have to suffer for it. This murder had far-reaching repercussions both in Tunisia and especially in Morocco. In Casablanca, a protest strike, organized by the Moroccan trade unions on December 8, was used as a pretext by the French extremists for striking at the trade unions, and the 'riots' developed into a general lynching of Moroccan trade unionists by the Europeans of Casablanca. 500 Moroccans lost their lives, as against 4 or 5 Europeans.

These Casablanca riots led to an outcry in France, but the He-men of Morocco were not to be put off. Inspired by M. Boniface, the Prefect of Casablanca, and the top He-man of the French in Morocco, the French diehards undertook, during the spring and summer of 1953, that famous operation which finally led to the overthrow of the Sultan, Sidi Mohammed Ben Yussef.

In Tunisia, encouraged by the toughness of the French in Morocco and the non-interference of the United States, M. de Hauteclocque extracted from the Bey a number of decrees which were calculated, as it were, to consecrate the principle of co-sovereignty.

Compared with Morocco, Tunisia was relatively quiet during the greater part of 1953; but towards the end of the year a partisan war was started by the fellaghas, guerilla units that had been formed over a period of several months.

By the summer of 1954 this guerilla activity had assumed alarming proportions. Not a day passed without acts of terrorism or counter-terrorism being perpetrated. One day, French gunmen would shoot down several Tunisians in a café; the next day several Europeans would be murdered in similar conditions. Tunisia, with its 250,000 Europeans (of whom some 150,000 were of French descent) and its 3 million Moslems was sinking deeper and deeper into chaos.

What further complicated matters in the summer of 1954 was the British decision to evacuate Suez. This was bound to have immediate repercussions in French North Africa.

As the *Monde* wrote on the day of Mendès-France's visit to Tunis:

> It is much more than an administrative matter. The whole question of France's relations with the Arab world, and of her relations with the peoples of North Africa is involved . . . The decisions taken by the Government (to grant internal autonomy to Tunisia) have been announced barely a few days after the announcement that British troops will evacuate the Suez Canal Zone. The Anglo-Egyptian Treaty opens up a new era in the life of the Arab world. The last obstacle to Egypt's collaboration with the West has now disappeared; but, at the same time, propaganda in French North Africa has become its primary objective . . .
>
> America's pan-Arab policy has borne fruit. It has encouraged all the Arab capitals around the Mediterranean. As for the British, they have, after a spell of bad humour, returned to their original conception of Anglo-Arab friendship, which was symbolised in the past by Mr. Eden becoming the god-father of the Arab League, and Mr. Churchill the inventor of the kingdoms of Jordan and Libya.
>
> Trapped between the Arab bloc determined to support the independence of French Morocco and allies who are keen to see French North Africa sink into a state of chaos, France had no choice but to act quickly. Our relations with the Moslem world were in danger of gravely deteriorating; and terrorism was threatening the position of the French in Tunisia itself . . . In the past, our governments took only an intermittent interest in Tunisia and Morocco, which were offered some sketchy reforms without any serious basis. In the present circumstances, both internal and international, a psychological shock was indispensable. M. Mendès-France understood this . . . There is nothing new in his promise of internal autonomy. What is new is his assurance that the promise is made without ulterior motives and without mental reservations.[1]

It added, however, that there was, apart from the above considerations, no connection between the British in Egypt and the French in French North Africa. In one case, it was a matter of recalling soldiers

Le Monde, August 1, 1954.

and officials and handing the country over to its native population.
In the case of French North Africa it was different:

> Up till now the struggle in North Africa has been a struggle
> between two minorities: the European diehards who want to
> give nothing away, and the Moslem extremists who want to grab
> everything. But between these two there is a mass of millions of
> people: Europeans, Arabs, Berbers, Jews. M. Mendès-France's
> task is obvious: he must not allow himself to be intimated by
> either the European diehards or the Moslem extremists.

Mendès, however, took no chances on this occasion. To 'appease'
the French in Tunisia, he went to Tunis accompanied by Marshal Juin,
notorious as a North African diehard, and also M. Christian Fouchet,
the Gaullist Minister for Tunisia and Morocco, as well as by General
Boyer de La Tour, who was, at the same time, appointed Resident-
General in place of the 'ineffectual' M. Voizard, who was heartily disliked by the French community in Tunisia . . . The party arrived at
Tunis airfield at 10 o'clock in the morning, and, almost immediately
afterwards, M. Mendès-France drove to the Bey's palace at Carthage
where he read out his address to the Sovereign:

> *Monseigneur,* (it began) I have come here as your friend, as a
> friend of your Highness and as a friend of your country . . .

There followed the 'loyal promise, loyal and without mental reservations', of internal autonomy. He proposed that a new Tunisian
government be formed, which would negotiate new conventions with
France. He added, of course, that it was the right of the French living
in Tunisia to go on living there—and not only they but also their
children and grandchildren. Defence and diplomacy would continue
to be in the hands of the French.

In conclusion, he appealed for an immediate end to violence:

> Let everybody with any influence appeal for peace . . . During
> the last few weeks there has been constant growth in violence.
> If any more outrages are committed, and I say it in all loyalty, we
> shall take severe sanctions, because it is our duty to hasten the
> hour of reconciliation . . .

Présence Française, the French settlers' organization in Tunis, refused to see Mendès-France, but they saw Marshal Juin, who assured
them that no conventions would be signed with the Tunisian government, unless the rights of the French in Tunisia were safeguarded.

Meantime M. Fouchet had several meetings with 'moderate' Tunisian leaders; and, a day or two after Mendès's visit, it was confirmed that M. Tahar Ben Ammar would form the next Government, in place of the 'puppet' premier, M. M'Zali.

Rather more alarming was the fact that there seemed some connection between the Tunis visit and a new outbreak of rioting in Morocco, after a comparatively quiet spell. Already on August 2, several people were killed in rioting at Fez, where the rumour had been spread that the deposed Sultan had been brought back to France from Madagascar, after nearly a year's exile, and that his son, Moulay Hassan had actually arrived at Rabat. There were more riots in Fez and other towns on the following day, and several more people were killed. At Petitjean four Jews were murdered. Hundreds of letters, addressed to M. Francis Lacoste, the Resident-General, 'placed their trust' in Mendès-France and M. Fouchet, and urged them to bring back to Morocco the Sultan Ben Yussef . . .

In the days that followed things went from bad to worse. At Port Lyautey nine Europeans were murdered (including a Frenchwoman and her two daughters), and there were new clashes at Fez between Arab supporters of the old Sultan and Berber 'pilgrims' who had come to welcome the 'new' Sultan, Ben Arafa. M. Lemaigre-Dubreuil, the liberal-minded editor of *Maroc-Presse*, wrote that there would be no peace in Morocco until Ben Yussef returned.

The reactions to the unrest in Morocco were sharpest of all in Paris, where the Africa Lobby and the Right in general proceeded to blame Mendès-France for having 'endangered' the whole of North Africa by his ill-considered visit to Tunis.

CHAPTER 4

THE 'EMPIRE WRECKER' CAMPAIGN STARTS

G REAT was the impatience among the Right to cause trouble over North Africa. Only a week after Mendès had returned from Tunis, they demanded a full-dress debate on North Africa; and the 'date-fixing' debate on August 10 developed almost into a dress-rehearsal of the subsequent two-day debate of August 27 and 28. Speaker after speaker urged Mendès-France to commit himself firmly to this date of August 27—no matter what happened in the interval in the international or any other field. For it should be remembered that Mendès-France was just about to leave for Brussels to lay his compromise proposals before the other five EDC Powers. Also, the Assembly had just—during the morning session on that same August 10—granted Mendès plenary powers for carrying out an economic programme during the next three months, with its emphasis on 'expansion'.

While the discussion on the Government's economic plans was short and of no great interest, a large part of the Assembly was greatly excited over North Africa; the key-note of most of the Right-wing speeches was that everybody was plotting against France: Libya and British Agents in Libya; the Arab League and Cairo Radio; the United States and its Irving Browns who, in the name of international trade union solidarity, were, in reality, playing an American imperialist game against France, and planning to steal all her potential oil resources in North Africa. And, a little further in the background there was Moscow.

In a scholarly speech, M. Jacques Bardoux, officially an historian and a Member of the Institute, but unofficially also a member of the North Africa Lobby, opened the attack by asking Mendès-France whether he considered it regular for the Libyan Government to 'intervene in Tunisian affairs'.

As I already informed the Queuille Government in 1951, a "vigilance committee" of 24 members was set up in London at the time, presided over by a Pakistani colonel, Aqbel Zefar Cureshi. He had already been active in Palestine and Kashmir and was, at that time, about to leave for Cairo to establish contact with Tunisian emigrés, who were planning to raise a volunteer army.

M. Bardoux then recalled the visit to London of Habib Bourguiba, who had spoken to a Committee of the House of Lords and another Committee of the House of Commons, and had argued in favour of establishing closer contacts between British agents in Libya and the British consular services in Tunisia, as well as between the King of Libya and the Bey of Tunisia. He was also in favour of basing Tunisian economy on sterling, rather than on the French franc.

Bardoux then spoke of 'brigands' who, later in the year, had raided Tunisia from Libya; only, it so happened that these 'brigands' were wearing British battle-dress, were armed with brand-new tommyguns, and had been trained in a special camp in Tripolitania.

Another Right-wing deputy and Algerian Lobby man, General Aumeran, sounded a warning which was to be repeated, in one form or another, a thousand times after that. Referring to Mendès's visit to Tunis, he said:

> I wish you would realise that any mistake made in Tunis will have disastrous repercussions throughout the whole of North Africa, especially in Algeria and Morocco, because the seditious men to whom you are about to hand over Tunisia are carrying out precisely the same policy as the equally seditious leaders in the two other countries . . . Only the solemn reaffirmation that France intends to exercise her authority over the whole of North Africa can allay fears, restore order and reassure our friends . . . You must say clearly where you stand: we stay in Africa or we go. We can't stay and go away at the same time.

M. Quilici, the vehement Corsican deputy for Oran, said that Mendès's Tunis trip was 'not a turning point, but a breaking point'—an end of France's 'policy of integration'. Only, it was unnecessary to look upon North Africa in the same light as it had become customary to look upon Indo-China; and it was not necessary to make the same mistakes in both places.

He demanded firmness in Tunisia. What Mendès had done in Tunis would start off a chain reaction; the unrest in Morocco and Tunisia in the last two years had not yet affected Algeria; but now the contagion was sure to spread.

North Africa, Quilici exclaimed, represented France's last chance of remaining a Great Power: but now it looked as though, for the second time in her history, France was going to lose her colonial empire. In the 18th century France could afford to lose it; she could not afford to lose it now.

Several other Right-wing deputies pursued the attack. M. Joseph Halleguen made a particularly virulent onslaught on the 'Anglo-Saxons'.

> Your visit to Tunis, where you descended like an angel from heaven (he said) has earned you the unanimous approval of the British and American press; but that is the kind of approval that cannot help worrying me.

No doubt, he continued, the growing terrorism in Tunisia was the chief reason for Mendès's decision. No doubt, the Premier was convinced that his visit would bring peace and quiet to Tunisia. But what if he proved wrong?

> Is not, after all, the Neo-Destour, which will now be the most influential part of the Tunisian Government, behind all these outrages? When Salah Ben Yussef was Minister of Justice, it was notorious that none of the terrorists was ever discovered. The Arab League is, of course, jubilant at present: for what Mendès has done is merely the first step towards the complete eviction of the French from North Africa—and this is the ultimate object of all the Arab League's activity.

It was most unfortunate, he said, that the French radio should have represented the armistice agreement in Indo-China as a sort of French apotheosis, and the Mendès visit to Tunis as a victory of France's prestige, a victory that had gained the applause of the whole world. The people on the French radio would be well advised to listen in to the *Voice of the Arabs* radio. But there wasn't only Cairo. He hoped Mendès-France would be able to deny the story that had appeared in numerous papers, according to which Arab prisoners, captured by Vietminh in Indo-China, were being trained in Russia as paratroop commandos, for service in North Africa.

But apart from Moscow and Cairo, there was also London. M. Halleguen said that he was not anti-British. Like Mendès-France himself, he had served in the Free French air force based in England during the war. He was not anti-American; *amica America*, by all means; *sed magis amica veritas* . . .

The British had turned the French out of Syria in 1945. Was there not a similar plot to oust the French from North Africa? Marshal Juin had been very precise on the subject. He had spoken of 'that foreign conspiracy that was being concentrated round French North Africa ever since the Liberation'. And he quoted Juin as writing as follows in 1952:

> Both at Rabat and in Washington, I did not fail to say to our American friends that it was most regrettable that, in the case of North Africa, they talked the same language as Moscow. It hurts our feelings, and it also makes us wonder whether we have not been taking the wrong view of international solidarity . . .

UN, the same speaker said, was being used as a 'humanitarian' screen for pushing the French out of North Africa.

> There is an international plot against France's authority in North Africa. I wonder whether it was fully realised in England what an insult it was to us to see Bourguiba being invited to talk on the BBC—which we had always associated with a different kind of broadcasts . . . So he spoke on the BBC, he was received at the Lords and at the Commons, at Chatham House and even at the Foreign Office . . . He was a trump card in the hands of a country that had established itself in Tripolitania and Cyrenaica . . . And why, may I ask, does England keep whole garrisons of officials on the border of Libya and Tunisia—officials who, with all their experience in the Levant, are specialists in anti-French action? Why also has England allowed a 'vigilance committee' to be set up in London, the sole purpose of which is to turn the French out of North Africa?

In conclusion M. Halleguen said that the Neo-Destour and the Istiqlal were being generously subsidised from abroad, and that foreign powers were extremely interested in the 'petrol possibilities of French North Africa'.

M. Christian Fouchet, Mendès's Minister for Tunisia and Morocco, argued that on the day the Mendès Government was formed, the situation in Tunisia was truly tragic. The whole machinery of the country had been paralysed; neither its government, nor its Prime Minister, M. M'Zali, had any authority left. All transport was at the mercy of the fellagha bands, who specialized in murdering any Tunisians known to be friendly to France.

He defended the internal autonomy proposals made by Mendès-France, for these proposals alone, if adopted, would guarantee a peaceful co-existence between France and Tunisia. The proposals did not consist merely of concessions to Tunisia; they also provided for certain clearly defined duties by Tunisia *vis-à-vis* France.

But the attack from the Right did not cease. No sooner had Fouchet stopped than another speaker of the Right, General de Monsabert, spoke:

You think this agreement with Tunisia will be a final agreement? Not at all. Habib Bourguiba, reminding us of his presence, has just announced: 'These proposals . . . are merely a big step towards complete independence . . .' Already this resurrection of Bourguiba has had dangerous repercussions; at the other end of North Africa, in Morocco, the outcry for the restoration of the deposed Sultan has grown in violence.

General de Monsabert made another point: the Africa Army was a mixed army, and the best symbol of Franco-Moslem co-operation; there must be no possible compromise on this score. The Beylical Guard must be the only purely Tunisian force in Tunisia; on the question of the Africa Army, France must be very firm: she must exercise sole control over this mixed army.

And General de Monsabert said in conclusion:

The future of North Africa involves the whole future of France. If we fail to form united Franco-African states under our aegis, we will be reduced to the status of Switzerland, without even enjoying the advantages of a long-established neutrality.

But the most ferocious attack on Mendès-France was yet to come —from his 'fellow-Radical', M. Martinaud-Déplat.

Although you and I (he said to Mendès) have many ideas in common, we have never seen eye to eye on North Africa.

Had Mendès overlooked the fact, he asked, that under the Bardo Treaty of 1881, 'His Highness the Bey undertakes to carry out any administrative, judicial and financial reforms which the French Government considers useful'? This, he said, meant that the Bardo Treaty clearly implied for France certain rights of 'direct administration'. Therefore, it was no use sneering at the reforms carried out, on French initiative, and under the Beylical Seal, between 1951 and 1954.

However, 'direct administration' was admittedly a thing of the past; what was in force now was 'co-sovereignty'. The third stage had been initiated by Mendès-France: 'internal autonomy'—that internal autonomy which had already been promised to the Tunisians by M. Robert Schuman.

For the time being, therefore, I cannot accuse you of having surrendered anything . . . But the new Tunisian Government is, in fact, the outcome of an agreement between (a) the French Government, (b) the Bey, and (c) the Neo-Destour.

And the Neo-Destour (Martinaud-Déplat said) meant Bourguiba. Under the last Resident-General, M. Voizard, even the Bey thought it was a good thing that Bourguiba should be kept interned in France. But Mendès had yielded to the blackmail of the terrorists; and the results could already be observed.

> *M. Martinaud-Déplat:* The day after your visit to Tunis there was an immediate increase in the terrorism in Morocco . . . Although Tunisia and Morocco are different in many ways, there is an obvious link between your visit to Tunis and the murders at Fez and Petitjean. (*Loud protests on the Left. Cheers on Right and on several benches on Extreme Right.*)
> *M. Mendès-France:* This is absolutely intolerable. Not only is this a lie, but the former Minister of the Interior knows it perfectly well. (*Cheers on Left and on some benches on extreme Left and extreme Right.*)

Martinaud snapped back. He charged Mendès-France with naiveté and an unjustifiable degree of 'good faith'. What was the good of treating these people with good faith when no one could honestly believe in the good faith of men like Bourguiba and Salah Ben Yussef? And he proceeded to make allegations about Bourguiba's wartime record, when he spoke on Rome radio in 1943 and allegedly declared that 'the defeat of France must lead to the independence of Tunisia'. He went on to quote a variety of other seditious remarks Bourguiba was supposed to have made, in speaking or in writing . .

At last Mendès spoke:

> With all due respect to M. Martinaud-Déplat, he said, the basis of France's relations with Tunisia had been unsound. France was not yielding to the blackmail of the terrorists; but the activity of these were no reason why France should not go on with reforms which were in her great emancipatory tradition, and which were essential in the middle of the 20th century. Internal autonomy had been promised to Tunisia by a large number of French Governments; was it really necessary to go on repeating these promises without any intention of carrying them out? The basis of the agreement he (Mendès) had proposed to Tunisia was (1) internal autonomy, (2) diplomatic union, and (3) military union. But in order that the new Tunisian Government should be representative, it was impossible to keep the Neo-Destour out of it.

Then came a typical head-on collision between Mendès and Martinaud-Déplat: it was when Mendès remarked that Martinaud-Déplat was now using against Bourguiba certain documents (some of very doubtful quality) which he had acquired while Minister of Justice in the previous Government.

> *M. Martinaud-Déplat:* I did not extract any document out of any *dossier.* The documents are in the possession of the examining magistrate. You only have to write to the Public Prosecutor at Tunis, who will send you copies. You can then study these at your leisure. Excuse me if I happen to have a good memory, and have kept copies. (*Cheers on Right. Uproar on Left.*)
> *M. Mendès-France:* So M. Martinaud-Déplat confirms that he has acquainted us with documents which were extracted from the *dossier* in the possession of the examining magistrate at Tunis . . . Will you allow me to make very serious reservations as to such a highly unusual procedure, which enables a Minister of Justice to hand over his post, but still keep for future reference— just in case—any documents that might prove useful to him. (*Cheers on Left and extreme Right. Protests on Right.*)

It went on like this for several minutes, and was a nice illustration of the way Mendès-France dealt with the 'grubbier' type of French politicians—and, incidentally, his enemy No. 1 in the Radical Party.

Mendès then passed on to Bourguiba. Of course, he said, Bourguiba was the ideological guide of the Neo-Destour.

> If I negotiate with the Neo-Destour, it is not because I am in agreement with it—if I were, there would be nothing to negotiate about—but because I am in disagreement with it. I should like to know what other constructive policy you have to propose. M. Martinaud-Déplat has been associated with the policy of repression during the past few years; and look at the results! (*Loud cheers on Left.*)

And then came his famous statement on Morocco, which was to upset his best friends so much—above all François Mauriac, who wrote that week that Mendès had failed to say the one word which he had hoped to hear.

He did not propose that the deposed Sultan be reinstated. On the contrary, he declared that while he agreed with M. Christian Pineau's statement, earlier in the debate, that the dynastic question was at the root of most of the trouble in Morocco,

> France must, as in the past, try to pacify this people, so often torn by internal strife, by seeking an agreement with His Majesty Sidi Moulay Ben Arafa . . .

A year before, when questioned on Morocco, he had frankly stated that he had not had time to study the question, and therefore wished to express no opinion. Now Mendès had clearly decided that it was too much for him to take on both Tunisia and Morocco. Juin, for one thing, had strongly advised him against it. And so Morocco was allowed to live in that state of ever-growing chaos into which it had been cast by the Juin-Glaoui-Boniface conspiracy of August, 1953. His Majesty Sidi Moulay Ben Arafa was the stooge they had put on the throne, and the old man had practically no support in the country. But Mendès —and after him, Edgar Faure—still hoped for some miracle to happen; and it was not until the summer of 1955—after the murder of Lemaigre-Dubreuil by French gunmen—that Faure embarked on the eleventh-hour 'Grandval experiment'. But by this time it was too late. . .

Regardless of all the hullaballoo over EDC and the Brussels Conference—complete with flying visit to Chartwell—that had started in the interval, the Assembly was determined to get on with the North Africa debate on the fixed date, August 27.

This debate followed much the same lines as the date-fixing one, except for some new interesting points that arose. For one thing, Tahar Ben Ammar, the Tunisian Premier had come to France in the interval, and the French Government had placed a car at his disposal—in which (much to the indignation of several diehards) he had gone to Montargis to visit Bourguiba. Bourguiba was in the centre of this discussion.

Again it started with a speech by M. Bardoux, who this time stressed the disastrous effect on the Arab world of the French débâcle of Dien Bien Phu. Also, he spoke of the importance of Cairo propaganda—in three different fields: North African students in Paris, Montpellier and Clermont-Ferrand were completely under the spell of this propaganda. Secondly, there was, in Cairo, a training centre for North African saboteurs and terrorists. Finally, there was *The Voice of the Arabs* of Cairo radio, which was having a disastrous effect on the native populations of French North Africa.

Very different was the speech of M. Christian Pineau (Socialist), one of the few pro-government speakers. He described the deposition of the Sultan of Morocco in August, 1953, as 'a very grave mistake', and while he realized that it was difficult to bring the old Sultan back, it was useless keeping on the new one: he had no desire to stay, anyway. There were intermediate solutions which were worth considering.

As for Tunisia, Pineau praised the 'Mendès-France solution'; if, he said, Martinaud-Déplat could not stomach Bourguiba, he should remember, all the same, that Tahar Ben Ammar would never have formed the government without the express approval of Bourguiba and the Neo-Destour. Martinaud-Déplat was one of those people in France who believed in the 'stooge' policy, which had already proved a disastrous failure on so many occasions, notably in Indo-China, with the unfortunate Bao Dai experiment.

Bourguiba seemed like an obsession with the Right. M. Jacques Vassor angrily exclaimed that the government were in fact negotiating with Bourguiba, and that Tahar Ben Ammar, who had visited him, had declared that he and Bourguiba had always worked 'hand in hand'. There should, he said, be no such thing as 'Tunisian internal autonomy', but a 'Franco-Tunisian internal autonomy'.

M. Halleguen took up again the anti-American and anti-British theme, saying that the Americans had not only encouraged every form of Arab nationalism in the name of their 'anti-colonialism', but were also showing an unhealthy interest in the oil resources of French North Africa.

> Moreover, since your visit to Tunis, Mr. Prime Minister (he said) i.e., since July 2, not only Radio Cairo, but also Radio Tetuan is being relayed by Radio Budapest.

There were further references to the Neo-Destour headquarters in New York, to the Maghreb Committee which had received a first instalment of £E15,000, and so on. It was quite obvious, he concluded, that Mendès-France was going to be duped by the Tunisians.

General de Monsabert (Right) was willing to agree that it might be possible to come to terms with Bourguiba; 'but behind Bourguiba there are Salah Ben Yussef and the blackmail of Cairo'. And already, Monsabert prophesied that the 'Bourguiba phase' would be succeeded by a 'Salah Ben Yussef phase'. He then said that France's prestige was low because there were only 34,000 French troops in Morocco, as against 68,000 in 1938. In the whole of North Africa, M. de Monsabert said, it was essential to form big armies under French command, in which the Arab conscripts would be in a privileged position, and would act as a link between France and the native populations.

There were several more speeches, notably by M. Clostermann (Gaullist), France's great fighter ace of the last war, who thought the reinstatement of the old Sultan alone could stop the rot in Morocco; by M. Quilici, who sharply attacked Labour M.P's and particularly Mr. Fenner Brockway for encouraging chaos in French North Africa; and by M. Cadi Abdelkader, the Algerian deputy, who compared the Sultan Arafa to 'a hairy dummy whom you want to introduce to us as your wife' (*loud protests on Right:* 'You are insulting a Sovereign who is a friend of France'). After that, M. René Mayer, the future 'killer' of the Mendès-France Government, spoke. He regretted that although M. Mendès-France's statement to the Bey was 'perfectly precise', the statements made since then by Tahar Ben Ammar and Bourguiba were far from precise.

And then came the 'Free World' argument—which was to become so familiar again in 1956:

> Algeria is covered by the Atlantic Pact. In future negotiations with Tunisia and Morocco, one should try to extend the Atlantic Pact to them, too. In other words, no matter what kind of autonomy you give these countries, you must on no account give them independence . . . Moreover, the British understand this perfectly well. One of the British government spokesmen recently declared that there were certain parts of the British Commonwealth, such as Cyprus, which, in view of their special position, could never be made entirely independent.

Not without a touch of mental jugglery, M. Mayer added that, under the Protectorate Treaty with Tunisia, France had undertaken to protect the Husseite dynasty of the Bey; in the circumstances, France could not possibly approve the establishment of a Tunisian Assembly which might, some day, wish to scrap the Bey . . . Therefore the Tunisian Assembly should be consultative at first, then legislative, but, on no account, constituent.

At last, after many more speeches (including one by Mme. Sportisse, the Algerian Communist deputy who deplored that Algeria had, throughout, been ignored in this debate), Mendès-France spoke.

He declared that the situation in Tunisia, following his visit to Tunis, was highly promising; the Tunisian Government that had been formed was willing to negotiate new Conventions with France which would include a form of internal autonomy acceptable to France.

An atmosphere of mutual confidence in Tunisia had been created once again. By and large, the French in Tunisia had taken the Government's policy well, and General Boyer de La Tour, during his recent tour of Tunisia, had been very well received everywhere.

As for Morocco, Mendès still wouldn't budge. He was still in favour of coming to an agreement with 'His Majesty Sidi Mohammed Moulay Ben Arafa'. He vaguely referred—thus foreshadowing Faure's Aix-les-Bains meeting a year later—to a sort of 'round-table' conference in which representatives of the various Moroccan interests would take part; no representative body of opinion would be excluded. He said trade unionism among the Moroccans should be encouraged, and young Moroccans should have more and more outlets for employment in the Moroccan administration. He then paid a tribute to 'the French of Morocco, whose creative activity was a magnificent model'; and he added:

> The successful evolution of Moroccan institutions is inconceivable without the permanent presence and permanent action of the French; for Morocco needs them, and it would be wicked of us to discourage them.

In conclusion he expressed deep faith in that Great Solidarity stretching 'all the way from Flanders and Alsace to the Equator'. Only, this solidarity must be 'more true, more conscious, more active'.

> This solidarity requires from us not a conservative and defensive attitude, but a continuous effort of creation and animation; a great friendly upsurge which, in North Africa, will be treated with interest, confidence and faith; for the fate of the people of North Africa will remain closely linked with the future of France.

It was on this well-meaning rhetorical note that the first great North African debate ended. The Government's policy was approved by 451 votes to 122.

CHAPTER 5

THE PERSONAL BUILD-UP

ARIS-MATCH, with its one-million circulation, and consistently hostile to Mendès-France, nevertheless devoted an enormous amount of space to his various expeditions—to Geneva, to Tunis, to Brussels, to Chartwell, to London, to the United States, and so on, right down to his final downfall on February 4, 1955. Once he had fallen, it said lots of nasty things about him, but explained, indirectly, why it had given him so much space. It was, it said, because the man could never keep quiet; he always managed to keep the public entertained: *C'était du cinéma*. There never had been such a French Premier under the Fourth Republic.

C'était du cinéma. And, true enough, under Mendès-France everything he touched somehow managed to acquire a dramatic quality. Not, needless to say, without the help of the press, including *Paris-Match*, which did more perhaps than any other paper to *personalize* Mendès, by printing whole pages of photographs of the Premier embracing his old father at the airfield on his return from Geneva; yawning; sleeping in his armchair in the plane from (or to) Geneva; drinking milk on 101 occasions; drinking a *vin d'honneur* at the *Hotel de Ville* at Marseilles, with a slightly squeamish wrinkle in a corner of his mouth; being patted on the back by Herriot; looking furious after the defeat of his government, looking slightly overawed in the presence of a tremendously severe, and cigar-chewing Churchill. 'A good-natured featherweight boxer' one paper described him. And it is true that, all the time, there was an emphasis on the physical side of Mendès-France, on his physical power of endurance. Every paper, friendly or hostile, stressed this side of the 'cinema': how did he manage to do so many things all at once? There never had been such a crowded seven months in the whole history of the Fourth Republic.

Mendès, who had shunned office for nine years, proved a great master of self-advertising when he became Premier. But self-advertising cuts both ways in France. More than most French leaders, Mendès relied on the support of public opinion, and relied on it independently of Parliament. He was a parliamentary man: he had been deputy since 1932. But in his heart of hearts he despised parliament. His cabinet-making was unorthodox. As already said, he despised the practice of *dosage:* he did not negotiate with the parties whose support he needed. He called upon *men* to join his team. The parties could take it or leave it. When his popularity was at its height—and *it was at a very high level for exactly two months*—he had nothing to fear from the press. Between his famous 'bet' to make peace in Indo-China within 30 days and his announcement that he was going to Brussels to have a showdown with the others on EDC he was invulnerable. Except for a few rabid Vichyite and anti-semitic papers like *Aspects de la France* and *Rivarol*, the whole press was more or less pro-Mendès. Even the *Aurore* of M. Boussac, with an eye on circulation, unearthed Mendès's war-time reminiscences (including his escape from Vichy!) and published them as a serial. The *Figaro*, which had been hostile at the beginning, now became remarkably polite. Some of the most influential papers like *France-Soir* and *Le Monde* were plainly *mendésiste;* so were all the Left-wing papers which had campaigned for years for peace in Indo-China—*Esprit, France-Observateur, Témoignage Chrétien*, etc. The weekly *Express*, to which Mendès had often contributed articles since its foundation in the spring of 1953, had become his personal mouthpiece.

The *Express* was impressive as a *mendésiste* propaganda weapon : for its contributors included Albert Camus, who wrote 'philosophical' articles on the future of France ; Alfred Sauvy, who analysed merciless-ly—and in an ostensibly *mendésiste* spirit—the anomalies of the French economy and such flaws as low production, heavy drinking, insufficient housing, and the distortion of parliamentary life through what he called 'lobbification' ; and, most important of all perhaps, François Mauriac, to whom Mendès became almost like a mystical symbol of Hope for France.

The *Canard Enchaîné*—that great French institution which had played so important a part in the life of the Third Republic, and which had been resurrected under the Fourth—took a hand in the build-up of Mendès. For one thing, it was traditionally anti-clerical and anti-colonialist, and therefore had the time of its life showing up the petty intriguing that went on against Mendès on the part of the MRP. It ridiculed Bidault, who, it alleged, had left his 'agents' at the Quai d'Orsay, to keep an eye on Mendès; it wrote up the mutual *petit chantage* that went on between the two warring teams of officials at the Quai d'Orsay—the Mendès team who went through the archives in search of evidence that the MRP had missed numerous opportunities to end the war in Indo-China in much better conditions; and the anti-*mendésistes*, who looked for documents to show that Mendès had, at various times, been in contact with Ho Chi Minh . . . It even wrote up Madame Bidault and Madame Mendès-France snarling at each other on one occasion. A 'sketch' by Tréno showed Mendès arriving at the

National Assembly and calling a surprise meeting at which, after his Tunis visit, he tabled a Bill giving Internal Autonomy to the French— freedom from pressure groups, freedom from Party caucuses, freedom from tax-dodgers among the peasants . . . In the end only three or four negro deputies from Equatorial Africa agreed to grant France the internal autonomy Mendès was proposing.

Another point which the *Canard* (and the *Express* for that matter) never failed to stress was the fundamental disagreement between Mendès and Edgar Faure, his Finance Minister, who believed in limited planning, but had no use for Mendès's spectacular solutions. As *Paris-Match* explained the relationship:

> Mendès took Faure on as Finance Minister because he thought Faure was the best man for carrying out the Mendès policy; Faure entered the Mendès Government because he believed that Mendès was the most likely Premier to allow Faure's own 18-months' programme to be applied in practice. It was Faure who had guessed right in the end . .

No less important than the press was, in Mendès's view, the radio. His Saturday talks were intended to create a close bond between him (Mendès) and 'public opinion'. There had been a dangerous precedent to such regular talks: Doumergue, in 1934, had tried, time and again, to talk to the people over the heads of Parliament, and often in a sharply anti-parliamentary vein. There had also been Pétain with his broadcasts. 'Fireside chats' in which a politician 'took the people into his confidence' therefore had a bad name in France. Nevertheless, Mendès felt, in June, 1954, that he could well afford to cash in on the popularity he had aroused in the country by the bet he had taken on to end the war in Indo-China. In a sense, he tried to mobilize the *pays réel* against the Assembly, regardless of the risks involved and the resentment caused. He did not even, in the circumstances, refrain from some of the mannerisms Doumergue had gone in for. In his very first broadcast on June 26 he said:

> It would be comforting and encouraging and promising for both sides if there became established between the Government and the representatives of the people, on the one hand, and public opinion, on the other, a sort of affectionate intimacy . . . The principal object of this talk is to tell you that I intend to address you at regular intervals, and to speak to you in all simplicity, as I am doing tonight, and to keep you informed of what the Government—your Government—is doing and thinking.

On this occasion he spoke of the attempt to end the Indo-China war. He tried to put confidence into the French—confidence in France and, incidentally, in Mendès-France. 'France is a good and sound ship', he proclaimed in his second broadcast; in the third one, even before the Geneva settlement had been reached, he announced that France had 'entered a new and decisive stage, which would lead to peace'.

Typical was the conclusion of this talk:

Every day in the last three weeks, I have longed to speak to the youth of France. But assailed as I have been by my hard daily tasks, of which you have read in the press, I have not yet had a chance of speaking to them.

Yet now I want to take this opportunity of speaking to you, young women, young girls, young men of France, all you who work in an atmosphere of uncertainty, and sometimes of worry over your future. And how can you not worry when, for years now, your future has been overshadowed by that war in Indo-China, a war which has made it impossible for you to look ahead, to plan and to build?

Once peace has been restored it will open for everybody, and especially for you, a more fruitful future, and more promising perspectives. I tell you this tonight: I am putting in every ounce of my energy to achieve this result. Your plans, your ambitions, your hopes—of which I never stop thinking—will give me the strength to go ahead with my task, and to succeed in it, if that is humanly possible.

And while we work at Geneva, think with deeper faith than before of the rôle you will have to play in the life of the nation: if, tomorrow, we succeed in this first and arduous task, be ready to harness yourselves for the immense work of reconstruction awaiting us all . . .

Young people: yes, there is no doubt that Mendès was thinking of himself as the leader of the young generation. In his election campaign at the end of 1955, it was the young, above all, whom he expected to support him, and to raise him to national leadership. And it is true that it was the young people in the Radical Party and the young people among the electorate who were most impressed by Mendès-France. Where his personal magnetism worked—because he was bodily present there, as, for instance, at the Radical Congresses in 1955 and again in a well-worked constituency like the Eure Department—he had an impressive following. Where they knew Mendès only at second-hand—he did not succeed so well.

There is no doubt that Mendès was extremely conscious of the immense importance of the *personal* contact and it is not surprising that, during his premiership, he should not have neglected the possibilities provided by radio—despite the long-standing French prejudice against this form of 'personal publicity'. Both he and some of his friends had closely studied the technique of FDR and other American leaders in this matter and there is, indeed, no doubt that for several weeks, at any rate, the Mendès broadcasts were extremely popular.

CHAPTER 6

THE FIGHT OVER GERMANY

B ACK in 1950—soon after the outbreak of the Korean War—the USA decided that Germany must be rearmed. Bevin did not take long to surrender to the Truman-Acheson pressure. Schuman, who was a great believer in Franco-German 'reconciliation', was finally also forced to accept the principle of the thing. He, however, hoped that, by hitching German rearmament to the supra-national Schuman Plan, which was just then in process of elaboration, he could use it for strengthening 'Europe'. The German rearmament under the French scheme (which took the form of the 'Pleven Plan') was, however, to be very limited in both quantity and quality. There followed years of squabbling among Paris, London, Washington and Bonn; and one of the few things that were quite obvious was the extreme reluctance of French public and parliamentary opinion to subscribe to any form of German rearmament. There was clearly only a minority in the country in favour of 'merging' the French army in a supra-national army, under which, it was always suspected, France would become a junior partner, while her army would lose its 'identity'.

Throughout 1951, 1952 and 1953, the French continued to resort to delaying tactics. The chief reason for this was that, although men like Bidault, Schuman and René Mayer, who were pro-EDC men, kept on promising the USA an early ratification of EDC, they at heart knew that there was no majority for it in the French National Assembly. So they kept asking for 'additional protocols' and 'interpretive protocols', but still hesitated to put the EDC Treaty before the Assembly.

By the end of 1953, Churchill and Eisenhower had had enough of these delaying tactics, and treated the unfortunate M. Laniel with extreme roughness at the Bermuda Conference, ignoring the fact that, only a fortnight before, the National Assembly had (as Mendès noted at the time) shown itself not more eager, but *less eager than ever before* to commit itself to EDC—at least without a good many new 'safeguards'. Churchill, though determined not to involve Britain in EDC, was particularly hard on the French.

At the Berlin Conference in February, 1954, Bidault still used EDC as a bargaining counter, hoping to secure the internationalization of the war in Indo-China in return for a 'promise' that EDC would soon be ratified—even though he was in no position to make any such promise, in view of the violent opposition coming to EDC not only from the Communists, many Socialists, many Radicals, but also from de Gaulle, and many of his followers. Even many members of the classical Right were hostile, and the only Party that was wholeheartedly pro-EDC was the MRP. And even here there were *nuances*, not to mention a few 'rebels' like Senator Hamon.

Both in his investiture speech in June, 1953, and in that of June, 1954, Mendès made it clear that he considered it essential to have the EDC question settled one way or the other. Between these two speeches, British and American pressure had taken on a tone that was little short of menacing; and in 1954 Mendès was determined not to delay a decision any longer, once Indo-China had been cleared out of the way.

While the Geneva Conference was still in progress, a hot-and-bothered Spaak came to Paris, to urge an immediate meeting of the Six. Mendès, who had other fish to fry, asked for a few weeks' grace, and it was decided that the Six meet in Brussels on July 19. He believed it his duty to propose a compromise acceptable to most Frenchmen. Hence the Brussels draft protocols which, by 'discriminating' against Germany, by allowing members to withdraw from EDC if Germany became reunited, and by associating Britain more closely with EDC, and generally weakening the supra-national nature of the agreement, infuriated the EDC 'purists', not only in Belgium and Holland and Germany, but also in France.

Mendès, who, from the very outset, had considered EDC unacceptable in its 'pure' state, had formed his government in such a way that about half its members were pro-EDC men, and the other half anti-EDC men. To the anti-EDC men, even the Mendès protocols were too much, and after some heated discussions inside the Cabinet, General Koenig, M. Chaban-Delmas and M. Lemaire—i.e., three of the Gaullists—resigned, rather than run the risk of a compromise being reached at Brussels under which many of the essential features of the original EDC would survive.

Mendès's Brussels proposals were among his least happy ventures, and annoyed both the pro-EDC people in France and the anti-EDC people. However, the latter heaved a sigh of relief when what they dreaded most—compromise between 'pure' EDC and the Mendès protocols—did not come off. Only, the glamour of Mendès-France had suffered greatly in their eyes. As for the pro-EDC people, they stopped at nothing in their endeavour to discourage Mendès's Brussels partners against making any concessions to him. Robert Schuman directly communicated with Adenauer, telling him that EDC would be passed by the National Assembly, if only the EDC ministers at the Brussels Conference proved adamant in their attitude to Mendès. Similarly a number of Socialists (André Philip among them) let it be known to Spaak that there was no need to yield to Mendès's 'preposterous' demands.

The outside pressures were blatant. The opening of the Brussels Conference coincided with a telegram from Churchill to Adenauer clearly indicating that whatever happened at Brussels, Germany would be rearmed. Worst of all, Mr. Bruce, the US Ambassador, suddenly turned up at the Brussels Conference to encourage Spaak to be uncompromising.

This direct interference by Churchill and the US Government caused the greatest annoyance of all to Mendès. The US visit took place only a few hours before the break-up of the Conference, a break-up which (as *Paris-Match* put it) Spaak announced in a firm voice, but with his glasses moist with tears.

Ten days after the breakdown of the Brussels Conference and Mendès's abortive attempt to 'drag' Britain into EDC at the very last moment, EDC was defeated at the French Assembly by 319 votes to 264.

The breakdown of EDC left the MRP leaders livid with rage, while grand old man Herriot declared, in a voice that seemed to boom from the depths of French history, that 'a country that was not master of its army was not master of its destiny'. Shades of Danton, shades of Kléber! Mendès, who had been treated in cavalier manner at Brussels by Spaak and Beyen (while Adenauer, rather than take part in the discussion, had gone on a sightseeing trip to Bruges), showed no sign of favouring the ratification of EDC in its original form. He decided that the Government would not vote, one way or another. He was not going to go out of his way to have EDC ratified in the form which he had already himself condemned before going to Brussels.

But then a strange thing happened. After a few days of elation—for, in spite of all the pressure and intimidation to which France had been subjected over EDC, she had still said *merde* to the outside world by turning EDC down—many Frenchmen, and Mendès among them, began to wonder, as they saw themselves faced with the most serious dilemma. Angry comments were coming from London, Washington and Bonn, where Adenauer made statement after statement in which he declared Mendès-France personally responsible for the 'breakdown of Europe'.

Mendès's mood before Brussels, during Brussels and after the rejection of EDC was well explained by himself in his Saturday broadcasts. On August 14, he said:

> It is about three years since the negotiators elaborated the EDC Treaty. Four out of five of our European partners have already ratified it. All eyes are turned on France . . . They are beginning to doubt our good faith . . . We must say yes or no; we cannot drag it on any longer . . . These delays are undermining our prestige and authority . . . Nor is that everything: our British and American allies are preparing to recognise the sovereignty of Western Germany—partially for the present, but *only* for the present.

And then, on August 24, after the breakdown of Brussels:

> Since returning to Paris, I wanted to re-establish contact with you, and to tell you that, throughout this difficult period, I had not ceased for a moment to think of you, that is, of the country in whose name I was speaking. That was why, after making all reasonable concessions, I decided that I could not accept proposals that would have shocked the conscience of so many Frenchmen, and which were likely to be disavowed by their deputies.

In an 'interim' broadcast, just before the EDC debate, Mendès said that, as distinct from Geneva, where he had the 'irresistible force of French public opinion' behind him, he was not conscious of the same support at Brussels.

The most interesting point of Mendès's broadcast after the defeat of EDC by the National Assembly on August 30 was his assertion that EDC was implicitly defeated on a vote of procedure by a majority of 55; if, he said, it had been an explicit vote on whether the Assembly approved, or not, of EDC, the majority against EDC would have been, not 55, but 110.

Anyway, EDC had been turned down, and now France was threatened with 'the empty chair'. Eden and Dulles started on their respective European tours; one behaved 'sympathetically' to the French; the other less so. Clearly, the rejection of EDC had created a vacuum, which both Britain and the United States were in a hurry to fill. Barely ten days after the rejection of EDC Mendès-France spoke of the 'constructive solutions' he would examine with Mr. Eden. What was indispensable, he said, was that France and 'our old friend England, should act together and see eye-to-eye'.

What followed the rejection of EDC is an extremely complicated story, as far as its details are concerned, but also a very simple one as regards the outcome of the interminable discussions, first in London and then in Paris.

Mendès-France, fundamentally anglophil, and also afraid of seeing France isolated (he had always gone out of his way to protest against the suggestion that he held 'neutralist' views—even though he was not entirely out of sympathy with them at one time—not that he ever thought them practical), announced barely a few days after the collapse of EDC that, 'before the end of the year' he was expecting another agreement to take its place . . .

There followed the discussions in London, the discussions in Paris, preceded by Mendès's interim report on the international situation to the National Assembly at the beginning of October, then his triumphal visit to Canada and the United States, and, finally, from December 21 to 30, the full-dress debate at the National Assembly on the Paris Agreements.

Mendès was scared of France's isolation. Hence the extreme haste with which he concluded the new agreements, and the haste with which he tried to get them ratified, despite numerous gaps and loopholes. Thus, the armaments pool—on which the French had been very insistent—was left over for later discussion, and in reality never came to anything, while the Saar settlement between Mendès and Adenauer on October 23, 1954, was given at Bonn an entirely different interpretation from that which the French had given it.

Indeed, Mendès was in a desperate hurry to get the Paris agreements through Parliament, so that he could 'keep the promise' he had given both to Churchill and to Dulles. Some of his critics insisted on 'suspensive' clauses being attached to the 'armaments pool' (which the Allies had, more or less, 'promised' France—thus showing a willingness to revive in a small way a piece of supra-nationality—in a field where it might *really* matter) as well as to the Saar agreement, until a large number of points had been clarified. The gap between the official French interpretation of the Saar agreements and the no less official German interpretation was far too wide. But Mendès would not hear of it. Rather than see the ratification of the Paris agreements delayed, he merely said that the Assembly was voting on 'the text' signed by himself and Adenauer, and not on the 'Bonn interpretation'!

Anyone who saw Mendès during the weeks following the rejection of EDC, was struck by the man's extremely tired and worn-out look. He was not the Mendès of Geneva or of Tunis. He was being treated rough by Churchill, Dulles, and his former anti-EDC friends, not to speak of the champions of EDC; and he was having trouble inside his cabinet. Several of the pro-EDC ministers resigned after its rejection;

and the new cabinet that was formed in September was incoherent. The resignation of Bourgès-Maunoury, Hugues and Claudius-Petit upset what little political equilibrium the government still had left after the resignation in August of three of the anti-EDC Gaullist Ministers.

At the beginning of September the new Government was composed as follows:

Premier and Foreign Affairs ..	P. Mendès-France (Rad.)
Indo-China	Guy La Chambre (Right)
Justice	Guérin de Beaumont (Right)
Defence	E. Temple (Right)
Interior	F. Mitterrand (UDSR)
Finance	E. Faure (Rad.)
Education	Berthoin (Rad. sen.)
Public Works	Chaban-Dalmas (Gaull.)
Industry and Commerce ..	H. Ulver (Gaull.)
Agriculture	Houdet (Right Senator)
Labour	Aujulat (Overseas Right)
Overseas France	R. Buron (MRP)
Health	A. Monteil (ex-MRP)
War Veterans	J. Masson (Rad.)
Morocco and Tunisia	C. Fouchet (Gaull.)

There were also twelve 'Secretaries of State', representing the Parties in roughly the same proportions.

It was an unsatisfactory team; and Mendès was hoping to widen the basis of his government by persuading the Socialists to join it. In this he failed, though in September and October he still had some illusions on the subject. At their Asnières Congress the Socialists laid down economic conditions which Mendès refused to accept.

Nevertheless, shortly before, in the Nevers speech, he had painted a glowing picture of an increasingly rich and prosperous France ... if only it were run on more-or-less *mendésiste* lines ... It was also in October that he had enjoyed his greatest triumph at home: at the Radical Congress at Marseilles, for the first time in his life, he had been acclaimed as the universally accepted and acknowledged leader of the Radical Party. The impression was, of course, deceptive. Already the red ants of the *affaire des fuites* were trying to undermine the government from inside; and the Lobbies—though anxious that he should take upon himself the discredit of the Paris agreements—were waiting for the time to strike.

Mendès was terrified of the threatened isolation of France. Already in his speech at Nevers, soon after the defeat of EDC, he had spoken

of the necessity of a 'Franco-German reconciliation', and on the following day, at a meeting of the Council of Europe, he made a further
speech in which he largely attributed the rejection of EDC by France
to an excess of supra-nationality; now he proposed as a basis for a
wider alliance, comprising Germany, the old Brussels Treaty, with
certain supra-national features attached, which would control the
amount of armament allocated to each member. This Strasbourg
speech, which infuriated the MRP members present, was partly the
outcome of Mendès's talks with Eden only a few days before; and the
whole approach—complete with Mendès's forecast that, by the end of
the year, there would be another European Treaty—foreshadowed the
future Paris Agreements. It was, indeed, only a week after Mendès's
Strasbourg speech that the Nine-Power Conference started in London
(Sept. 28-Oct. 3), to be followed three weeks later by the Paris Conference.

By the end of October everything was in the bag. It only remained
for the National Assembly to pass the Paris Agreements. Mendès had
reached the summits of popularity in the United States, and had become extremely disappointing to a vast number of Frenchmen, despite
the man's apparent virtuosity in dealing with very sticky international
situations, and his ever-repeated intention to make a better and stronger
France. But, for one thing, did everybody in France believe in France's
greatness? A curious remark was made by one of Mendès's bitterest
enemies, the MRP leader, P. H. Teitgen:

Why do we not take part in the Mendès-France Government,
when we supported the Laniel and Pinay Governments? The
answer is this. In supporting Pinay and Laniel and in opposing
Mendès we were guided by this fact. The first two did not arouse
any excessive hopes. But Mendès raised hopes that were so
enormous that they could only be disappointed . . .

The phrase aroused deep indignation in Mauriac . . . and also in
the *Canard Enchaîné* which recalled that it was, alas! the fate of France
to be *le pays de la mesure*, that is to say, *le pays de la médiocrité*: in the
end it was always Thiers who appealed to the French more than the
Commune did; and Deschanel more than Clemenceau. It did not
believe in *grands espoirs;* it liked its *petits espoirs*—tummy at 40 and
an old-age pension at 60. And this was the spirit that the enemies of
Mendès were constantly encouraging.

So even if a bold and unorthodox new policy was conceivable after
the rejection of EDC, Mendès preferred not to be tempted by it too

far, all the more so as the Russians, at that time, were not in the least helpful. So he hastened to sign the Paris Agreements, and, after being patted on the back by Herriot at Marseilles, and after being called a few names over the *affaire des fuites*—which began to hot up in October —Mendès, accompanied by his wife, went off to Canada and the United States.

CHAPTER 7

P.M.F. KEEPS HIS PROMISE TO CHURCHILL

THE whole publicity of his visit had been organized by Mr. Sonnenberg, considered by many as the greatest public-relations man in the United States. The result was spectacular. As Raymond Cartier, *Paris-Match*'s star reporter wrote:

The tangle of cables, in which you got caught as in a net, and which they had brought to the airfield pointed to the importance of his visit. Television networks don't transport all their material at heavy cost like this unless they are sure the guy will 'sell' . . . The milk-drinking Frenchman, the Premier who always seemed in a hurry, the Mystery Man of Europe had raised so many questions in the minds of Americans, that he had indubitably become a 'star'. According to old press hands, the coverage of his arrival in Washington was bigger than that of any European statesman since the war . . .

There followed a glowing account of his first visit to Eisenhower, in the course of which Indo-China and Tunis were discussed. *Paris-Match* reported that the Tunis visit had been by far the most popular thing Mendès-France had done, only to add grudgingly that, unfortunately, the Americans were under the spell of a childish sort of anti-colonialism, and didn't understand the first thing about French North Africa . . .!

Anyway . . .

Mendès-France (Cartier wrote with a touch of reluctance and bad grace) has never had to complain about his treatment by the Americans. His reputation, his entourage, his friendship for the neutralists, his hostile vote in the case of the Atlantic Pact, justified, on the part of Americans, the greatest reserve *vis-à-vis* this man. And yet, during his long years of waiting, there already emerged a number of American writers and journalists, who were speaking of him as the man who could get France out of the rut . . .

And then, when he had become Premier, in particularly dramatic conditions—

133

It became immediately obvious to Americans that Mendès-France was completely different from the conformist silhouettes . . . of the French political scene. This enterprising and strong-willed man was certainly going to lead France somewhere —but where to? The question put by one journal 'Kerensky or Roosevelt?' just about summed it up . . .

But he was respected for his economic competence:

One reason why American opinion has always had a soft spot for Mendès was his constant criticism of the French economic system . . . Mendès's diagnosis of France's troubles closely coincided for years with certain diagnoses made by American experts. A rich country, but vitiated and sterilized by the fear of risk, the search for big profits in place of big production, the alignment of industry and agriculture in accordance with the capacity of its weakest members . . .

And then came this wonderful bit of naiveté from *Match*:

Many American government experts are also in agreement with Mendès's views on alcoholism in France. But their documents are carefully hidden, because nothing would be more damaging than if the Communists got to learn that the State Department disapproved of the drinking habits of the French.

True, his stock had reached rock-bottom after the Brussels Conference. But then, unlike many of his colleagues, Dulles had still believed that EDC would be ratified, despite Mendès. And there followed a comic description of how the 'fatal flash' had affected Dulles:

For a quarter of an hour he was left stunned and completely speechless. One has to be a cynical diplomat of the *ancien régime* to take calmly the breakdown of a policy, and nothing is less cynical in the world than the mighty Protestant conscience of John Foster Dulles.

However, Cartier added that the breach had been 'partly healed' by the Paris Agreements which were giving Germany some kind of independent army; and there were no serious regrets over the death of EDC any more. . . Nevertheless, suspicions remained, and it was still feared lest Mendès ('influenced by his entourage') yielded to the siren voices of Moscow before committing himself 'unequivocally' to the ratification of the Paris Agreements.

James Reston, in the *New York Times* wrote that whereas, a few weeks before, the US Government would have welcomed the fall of Mendès-France, it was afraid of it now. Some observers, it is true,

Cartier noted with some satisfaction, were aware of the fact that Mendès had little use for 'Europe', and was more representative of a refurbished sort of French nationalism. And he noted, with a touch of peevishness, that the press had a 'somewhat *simpliste*' way of describing him as 'the most dynamic French public figure since Clemenceau', or 'the most serious French statesman since Poincaré'. And the whole Cartier story ended with some rather waspish remarks on Mendès's genius as a self-publicity fiend: he certainly knew how to 'put himself across' the press, radio and TV ... And then, of course, there was Madame Mendès-France, whose 'smartness and charm' had been unanimously acknowledged by an enthusiastic press ...

The American visit put a finishing touch to Mendès's 'conversion to the West'. But there were snags. Being popular in the USA has never been a guarantee of success in France. As the *Canard Enchaîné* wrote:

> When he returns he will find the road on which he treads well paved with banana skins and orange peel ... Because both at the Palais Bourbon and at the Radical headquarters there was an awful lot of coming and going during the US Tour.

There were those who had been 'left out' in the Cabinet reshuffle of November, and decided that even though they were more concerned about the *bouilleurs de cru* and the *betteraviers*, Tunisia and Algeria were the sticks with which it would still be easiest to beat Mendès ... Among the chief intriguers against Mendès were René Mayer and ... his own Finance Minister, Edgar Faure ...

Altogether, the whole period that followed Mendès's 'triumphal' homecoming from the USA was anything but pleasant. There was the *affaire des fuites*, which came up for discussion at the National Assembly on December 4. There was Algeria. There was the ratification of the Paris Agreements.

As regards these, there was widespread anxiety that nothing seemed to have been definitely settled about the Saar and the 'armaments pool'. On the other hand, the Political Council provided in the Paris Agreements would, as General Billotte, the *rapporteur* of the Foreign Affairs Committee put it, 'enable Europe to act coherently'. The British contribution, he also said, was important in the sense that 'a certain minimum of British forces' available on the Continent would conform to a majority vote taken on this Council.

But there was much opposition to the creation of a German General Staff, while M. Jacques Bardoux (Right), 'speaking as an historian and as a student of diplomatic documents', said that never in his life had he seen 'such a jumble of incoherent documents as these Paris Agreements'; they pointed to 'a decline of general culture and to a decay in the art of diplomacy'.

Soustelle, for the Gaullists, while saying that the Paris Agreements were 'less bad' than EDC—since they did not drown the French army in 'a cosmopolitan puddle'—still thought the agreements would consecrate German military superiority in Europe, with France relegated to the background.

Altogether, the criticisms coming from nearly all sides were so sharp that Paul Reynaud was no doubt right when he said that 'if this debate were allowed to continue for another fortnight, there wouldn't be a soul in the whole place to vote for the Agreements'!

On one occasion, on December 24, the Assembly actually rejected the first paragraph of the Ratification Bill, by 280 votes to 259. The discussions continued for several more days; throughout, Mendès-France's main argument was that France could not afford to drop out of the Atlantic Alliance. 'If only every deputy would read, as I do, the critical and often malevolent comments coming from every foreign capital'!

The truth is that Mendès had *promised* Churchill the ratification of the Paris Agreements, and, finally, on December 29, the Agreements were passed by 287 votes to 260, without the Assembly having received any serious assurances from Mendès about either the Saar or the Armaments Pool. London and Washington had, throughout, been violent in their criticisms of the Assembly, disregarding the fact that men of such varying opinions as Reynaud, Daladier, Maurice Schumann, Robert Schuman, Coste-Floret, Herriot, Moch, Soustelle and many other responsible leaders had made many vital criticisms of the Agreements.

The EDC leaders, among them Pinay, Schuman, Reynaud and Bidault abstained, and Mendès got the Bill through the Assembly thanks to the following he was still enjoying among the Gaullists, the Radicals and some other Centre groups, but above all, thanks to the 'discipline' Guy Mollet had imposed on the Socialist deputies, of whom only 18 disobeyed.

The result of the vote was announced in complete silence, followed by an uproar from the Communists who proceeded to abuse Mendès-France and Mollet. The predominant feeling was that France had been bullied into it. Never was Mendès less popular, and it was now widely felt that, having got the awkward 'German problem' out of the way, the Assembly could well afford, before long, to get rid of him.

CHAPTER 8

SMEAR CAMPAIGN STARTS

ALREADY since October, Mendès's enemies had been sharpening their knives in real earnest. After his return from the United States, and despite the unquestionable propaganda success of his visit, all the ground on which he trod was paved, as the *Canard* had put it, with orange peel and banana skins.

True, he still had some supporters; de Gaulle was, on the whole, favourable to him, though he expressed the wish, early in December, that the ratification of the Paris Agreements be delayed until another attempt had been made to reach an agreement with the Russians.

But these Paris Agreements were not an all-embracing issue. To get rid of Mendès had become almost an obsession with the Right and the MRP. Hence their unholy alliance over the *affaire des fuites* which had come to the surface in October, and had come up for discussion in Parliament on December 3, just after Mendès's return from the U.S.A.

That there had been 'leakages' of military secrets was true enough; but the emphasis was not on these leakages, but on the 'rôle' either Mendès, or some of his Ministers or personal friends had played in them. Actually, it was not till the trial of Mons, Baranès, Labrousse and Turpin in 1956 that the general public began, even vaguely, to understand what it was all about, and what, roughly, had happened; also, it was not until 1956 that Mendès made a long statement on the part he had—or rather, had not—played in this *affaire*. But as in 1956, so in 1954, one thing was crystal-clear; there was a well-planned attempt to show that the 'progressive Left' was, in some way, guilty of 'treason', and was, somehow, to blame for the loss of the war in Indo-China.

The parliamentary onslaught in 1954 was directed chiefly against the Mendès Government: it was an attempt to blow it up from inside, as it were, by directly implicating M. Mitterrand, the Minister of the Interior. In 1956, the juridical onslaught (significantly conducted by Tixier-Vignancour, a lawyer who had been, before the war, an all-out Fascist, had been one of the most violent extremists at Vichy, and who, having become eligible again in 1956, now came to head the Fascist-Poujadist opposition in the National Assembly), was directed, along a broader front, against the whole of the 'progressive Left'—with

137

which an earnest attempt was made to identify Mendès. All the more so because Mendès had never made a secret of his desire to see the war in Indo-China end much sooner than it actually did.

When the *affaire des fuites* came up for discussion on December 3, it was obvious that no hard facts would emerge from it; for these were still in the hands of the examining magistrate. It all started with a virulent (but clumsy) attack by M. Legendre, Right-wing deputy of the Oise (and one of the pillars of the *betterave* lobby), who said that if France lost the war in Indo-China, it was because of treason at home

> First, he said, there was a 'leak' which resulted in *L'Observateur* publishing information that it could only have obtained from the minutes of the National Defence Committee of July 24, 1953, at which General Navarre said that he hadn't enough troops to defend Laos . . .

He went on, and on, and on, insinuating in the process of his speech that M. Mitterrand had been treated as a 'traitor' by President Auriol; that there was a network of treason with which the editor of *Libération*, M. d'Astier de la Vigerie, was closely associated: that d'Astier was in personal touch with Mendès-France; for his part, Mendès-France had secret Communists among his closest collaborators, notably Georges Boris and Simon Nora; if, in the course of the Mendès-France régime Baylot was dismissed from his post of Prefect of Police, and the *commissaire* Dides sacked, it was because these were the moving spirits of a great anti-Communist network.

Mitterrand, the Minister of the Interior, showed that Legendre had been working on forged documents, and that he was trying to implicate members of the government by using them. Then he explained the reasons why he had left the Laniel Government in September, 1953: not because of the 'leakage', but because he was in disagreement with its colonial policy, and particularly with the deposition of the Sultan of Morocco.

M. Bidault, when challenged on this score, very reluctantly had to admit that these, indeed, were the reasons for M. Mitterrand's resignation; but, said he, 'I wish to pay you no further compliments', and added that he was not going to repeat at this stage what he had already said, in the course of a 20-minute session, to the examining magistrate . . .

M. Mitterrand, while noting that Bidault had confirmed the reasons for his (Mitterrand's) resignation, nevertheless thought there were some nasty innuendoes in the rest of his statement.

M. Edgar Faure, coming to Mitterrand's rescue, stressed the circumstances in which the latter had resigned from the Laniel Government. At Laniel's request, he said, he had gone to see Mitterrand and had specially urged him to withdraw his resignation.

> *Mitterrand:* It is high time an end was put to all these 'parallel' police services grafted on to the regular republican police; this knows its job quite well enough to fight treason whenever the latter tries to penetrate into the public services . . . When all the motives of this present agitation become known, we shall show that there are Frenchmen who are willing to serve foreign powers in an attempt to undermine the Republic. We shall then have another *rendez-vous*, Monsieur Legendre. (*Cheers on Left.*)

In short, Mitterrand had alluded to what Mendès-France, in later months, often liked to refer to as *le Gang*: a Gang which was linked up with certain Lobbies, with American espionage services, with a variety of neo-Fascists, who, in 1955-56 came to be more and more identified with two names—Tixier-Vignancour and Dides—the *commissaire* who had been sacked by the Mendès Government but who became a deputy in 1956, affiliated with the Poujade movement . . .

It is curious, looking back on 1954, how some of these political phenomena were already alluded to, and foreshadowed, in the course of that December debate.

Thus, Louis Vallon, the ex-Gaullist, said that the Government should not hesitate to tackle certain foreign intelligence agencies and the 'action groups' running parallel to certain public administrations. There was, for instance, a group called *Groupement pour la sauvegarde de l'Union Française*, composed of Indo-China war veterans and used by Dides and his agents. They had already organized a number of demonstrations (such as the attack on Laniel and Pleven at the Etoile in April, 1954), and a number of explosions. It was alarming to see the names of Dides and Tixier-Vignancour reunited again. Also, it seemed odd that Baranès, only quite recently a member of the Communist Party, should choose Tixier-Vignancour, a member of the Action Française, as his lawyer. It was only possible if Dides had advised him to do so.

Vallon went on to say that Dides had been playing a very important part in *Paix et Liberté*,[1] where he had an office, along with a man called Delarue, a jailbird with a hideous Occupation record. Vallon alleged that numerous meetings had been held at *Paix et Liberté*, meetings attended by representatives of NATO, and sometimes presided over by M. Baylot. *Paix et Liberté* was heavily subsidized by the USA.

[1] An extremely wealthy anti-Communist propaganda organization.

Jean Paul David (Radical), president of *Paix et Liberté*, protested against attempts to implicate his organization in the *affaire des fuites* . . .

Vallon, more and more violently interrupted by the Right, nevertheless concluded by saying it was high time an end was put to these police activities by rival gangs, some working in the name of Vodka-Volga, others in the name of Coca-Cola. (*Laughter.*)

Earlier in the debate, M. Loustaunau-Lacau (who, though nominally on the Right, liked to take a detached view of things) said that unfortunately there were already four major intelligence services working in France: Soviet, American, British and, latterly, German. The Americans were the wealthiest of all, and they paid for practically every spy in France!

The debate was wound up by Mendès-France. He spoke with an air of weary disgust. He deplored the method of M. Legendre and of some others which consisted in resorting to slander and insinuations as part of a 'debating' technique. He recalled slander campaigns in the past—against Jaurès, against Clemenceau, against Salengro, Blum's Minister of the Interior, who, in 1936, was driven to suicide. He thought it abominable that the idea should be put across with such persistence that the war in Indo-China had not been lost, but that the French Government had stabbed the French army in the back . . . Moreover, said Mendès emphatically, it should, after all, be recognized that although the leakages had gone on for years, it was this government which was the first to take action, and to unmask the traitors . . .

And now (said Mendès) I want to speak of another, very serious aspect of the whole affair. When, in September, I was negotiating in London a number of agreements on which the whole future of Europe depends, I decided to tell you some day about the intolerable humiliation that I suffered at the sight of fellow-Frenchmen warning my foreign partners against me, with the help of documents fabricated in France . . . It was abominable to know that our partners were accusing us, behind our backs, of divulging military secrets . . . I am not sure that our negotiations would have succeeded but for the energetic action taken, and the discoveries made, by the Minister of the Interior . . .

And I must ask you to stop this kind of thing. This is a government which has done a great deal in the last six months. (*Interruptions on Right.*) But not a day has passed without our having come up against a wall of distrust and slander, of which this *affaire des fuites* is the most striking, but by no means the only, example . . .

And then Mendès denounced the practice of picking quarrels with, and conducting campaigns against, the government for the *wrong* reasons : those most worried about the alcohol restrictions, said nothing about alcohol, but screamed loudest about North Africa ; or those hostile to the Paris Agreements, would attack the government over the *fuites*. And so on. He (Mendès) thought there was a constant attempt to wear down the government ; but he would not yield. He wanted a clear-cut answer in this debate, as in the coming debate on the Paris Agreements ; and after that, he said, the Government would reach its second stage :

> As from January 15, I have resolved to devote myself entirely to the premiership, and concentrate on economic and financial matters. That was why I asked for the plenary powers to last, not merely until December 31, but until March 31. The time that has already gone has not been wasted ; but there are still many other things to be done.

In other words, Edgar Faure had carried out a sort of minimum programme, based on his own 18-months' plan ; but the great economic reforms would be tackled by Mendès-France himself, once he took over the economic and financial affairs of the country on January 15 ...

For his enemies, there was no time to lose. Once the Paris Agreements had been cleared out of the way, the time would be ripe for putting an end to the Mendès experiment . . .

In the vote on the *affaire des fuites* the Government secured only a small majority of 287 to 240, and 88 abstentions. The Communists voted against ; Waldeck Rochet explained on their behalf that 'although, in the main, the Communists approved of the action taken against the Baranès gang', they disapproved of the Government's anti-Communist manoeuvres and the general trend of its policy, both in respect of German rearmament and North Africa.

K

CHAPTER 9

THE ANTI-ALCOHOL DRIVE

BARELY a few weeks after he had taken office, photographs began to appear in the daily press (usually accompanied by somewhat facetious captions) showing Mendès-France at an official banquet with a glass of milk in front of him. There is no doubt that, by declaring war on alcoholism in France, Mendès made a big impression. Not that he was the first one to attempt such a campaign. René Mayer and Pinay had already attempted to limit the drinking of hard liquor in France by increasing the taxation of alcohol. They had met with considerable opposition, and the overthrow of their Governments was at least partly attributable to the opposition they had aroused among the various 'alcohol lobbies' in the National Assembly.

There were several such lobbies, the most important of which were those representing the interests of the *betteraviers* (the growers of sugar beet) and of the *bouilleurs de cru* (the 3½ million tax-free distillers). The problem of alcohol in France is a question of extreme complexity, and it is possible here only to enumerate the main points.

First of all, there is the question of *per capita* consumption which, according to all statistics compiled on the subject, is certainly considerably higher than in all other countries for which similar statistics are available. According to the French Institute of Demographic Studies, the average consumption among adults is about 28 litres of pure alcohol per year, which is twice as high as in Italy and more than three times as high as in Britain. But hard liquor is not alone responsible for this. Especially in the southern half of France, wine-drinking is as much responsible for alcoholism as hard liquor. Wine produces what medical experts have called *alcoolisme vinique*, different in its effects from the alcoholism caused by spirits, but just as damaging—especially in the case of the numerous persons drinking two, three or more litres of wine a day—usually in the firm belief that 'it's good for you'.

It must be said right away that Mendès-France did not even attempt to tackle wine-drinking; this would have been too intolerably 'un-French'. But he declared war on two old French institutions: the *betteraviers* and the *bouilleurs de cru*. The *betteraviers*—the growers of

142

sugar beet—presented, in a sense, a chronic financial scandal, rather than a major social scandal. In virtue of legislation passed during the first world war, the growers of sugar beet (notably in the North of France) had been turning a large part of their crop, not into sugar, but into alcohol—which the State had originally agreed to buy up at a remunerative price. Whether it needed the stuff or not, the State continued, ever since 1917, to buy up this alcohol—ostensibly as a 'subsidy' to agriculture, but in reality in order to keep a powerful parliamentary lobby quiet. In this way, about 10 milliard francs of public money latterly went into the pockets of the *betteraviers*—and of their friends in parliament—every year. The reason why the beet was converted into almost useless alcohol, rather than into sugar was that it was much cheaper to run a distillery than a sugar refinery, especially with the state-fixed price of beet earmarked for sugar and of that earmarked for alcohol being the same.

Among the decrees issued by Mendès-France were several tending to encourage the conversion of beet into sugar, instead of into alcohol; to meet the objection that there was an overproduction of sugar in the country, Mendès even decided in favour of giving free milk and sugar to all school-children.

On whether the measures taken against the *betteraviers* had any effect on alcoholism in France no agreement has ever been reached; some, like M. Paul Reynaud, argued at the National Assembly that it was all a mere propaganda stunt, since no beet alcohol was drunk by anybody. Others, on the contrary, argued that a good deal of beet alcohol went—at least unofficially—into the manufacture of various liqueurs and *apéritifs*. Be that as it may, a large part of the surplus beet alcohol was converted into motor fuel, on the dubious ground that it cut down dollar imports. In reality this was a futile argument used by the *betteraviers*, since the alcohol used in this way by the State cost about ten times more than imported petrol.

Mendès-France's attack on the *betteraviers* was, in the main, intended to put an end to a scandalous financial racket which had gone on far too long, rather than as a measure against alcoholism.

More important from the point of view of alcoholism was the great problem of the *bouilleurs de cru*. Originally, a *bouilleur de cru* was a *bona fide* farmer who was allowed the privilege of distilling ten litres of pure alcohol a year for his private use, and free of tax. Before 1914 there were 800,000 *bouilleurs de cru* in France; but the number constantly grew, and by 1954 there were 3½ million persons who claimed the privilege of *bouilleurs de cru*, many of them merely on the ground that they had one or two fruit trees in their back garden. I remember the indignation with which Mendès-France talked about the 10,000

bouilleurs de cru in the *Département* of the Seine alone (i.e., in Paris
and its immediate neighbourhood)—'not a notoriously agricultural
part of the country, as you know'.

The institution of the *bouilleurs de cru* was—and still is—responsible for much of the alcoholism in France. Not only did the official
ten tax-free litres of pure alcohol produced by the $3\frac{1}{2}$ million *bouilleurs
de cru* represent some 70 or 80 million bottles of tax-free hard liquor,
but many of the *bouilleurs de cru* were known to produce twice, three
times, sometimes ten, or even a hundred times more tax-free liquor
than they were supposed to do. Not only was *bouilleur de cru* liquor
very largely responsible for widespread alcoholism in the countryside,
especially in the apple-growing areas of Brittany and Normandy, but
it was also held responsible for a vast clandestine market in alcohol
sold either directly in the rural 'black market', or to an army of more
or less fraudulent manufacturers of 'commercial' liquor.

Mendès-France's anti-alcohol decree aimed at limiting the number
of persons enjoying the *bouilleurs de cru* privilege to *bona fide* farmers
and at controlling more severely than before the numbers and activities
of the ambulating distillers. Also, the taxes on commercial hard liquor
were raised by 25 per cent, the alcoholic content of certain drinks was
lowered; automats distributing hard liquor were practically prohibited,
and their replacement by automats distributing soft drinks was encouraged; a variety of restrictions were placed on the issue of licences,
and cafés were forbidden to serve hard liquor between 5 and 10 a.m.
(a point which produced a good number of ironical comments in the
British press). The manufacture and serving of soft drinks was, on the
other hand encouraged.[1]

All these measures were, in a sense, important; but they met with
resistance while Mendès-France was in office; and some—like certain
measures concerning the *bouilleurs de cru* privilege—were 'suspended'
after the fall of the Mendès Government. It must also be said that even
while Mendès-France was in office, the new taxes applied to hard
liquor were less stringent than what he had originally planned.

On balance, what did the Mendès-France anti-alcohol drive amount
to? It is hard to assess its results with any accuracy. The drinking of
wine has continued, as usual; but there is little doubt that the psychological effect of Mendès-France's anti-alcohol drive has been considerable, and that he 'started something'. Among the younger people in
particular, soft drinks have largely replaced *apéritifs* and hard liquor;
the very high figures of the consumption of various 'fruit drinks' made
by firms like Perrier, Vittel and many others (as well as Coca Cola)

[1] For full details of these decrees, see *La lutte antialcoolique sous le Gouvernement
de M. Mendès-France*. Preface de P. Legatte (Paris, February, 1955).

during the last two years are highly indicative of a change in French drinking habits.

Altogether, Mendès-France's deliberately noisy anti-alcohol campaign has not been wasted; it made an impression on the young generation, and also induced certain government departments, like the Ministry of Health, to pursue some significantly anti-alcohol campaigns, as may, for instance, be seen from the thousands of posters all over France (for instance in the carriages of the Paris *métro*) urging people to 'stay sober', not to drink more than half-a-bottle of wine a day, and not to make *apéritif*-drinking a regular habit.

The anti-alcohol campaign, started by Mendès, is probably the most important thing he did inside France—and one with a far-reaching and beneficial effect on the nation's health, at least in the urban areas. His propaganda in this respect was even more effective than his legislation.

CHAPTER 10

TROUBLE STARTS IN ALGERIA

DURING those last three months of the Mendès-France régime, its early end was, somehow, taken for granted.
All that, in the eyes of his enemies, he had to do was to get the Paris Agreements through the National Assembly. After that he should go. But there was also much disappointment among Mendès's friends. Thus, the *Monde* wrote on December 12, just after the Assembly had 'approved' his North-African policy by a narrow majority:

> Many people (wrote P. H. Simon in the *Monde*) who expected Mendès-France to bring about a democratic revival of France's policy, are now anxious and even embittered at the results . . . Three things were expected: in foreign affairs, certain steps that would seriously improve East-West relations; . . . in the colonial field, the abandonment of colonial methods and loyal talks with the various nationalist parties; in home affairs a substantial improvement in the wage-earners' lot. On this three-cornered basis, it was hoped, a policy, which would be both generous and realistic, could be built; this would be a sort of *travaillisme française* . . . which would deprive French Communism of its *raison d'être*.[1]

But there were two terrible obstacles which Mendès's critics overlooked: the need to deal with problems one by one, and the time factor.

> Politics (Simon wrote) is an art of timing. Nothing can be achieved in a short time. No matter how dynamic and 'superman' a man may be, he cannot solve all problems immediately and simultaneously. All the more so when, as is the case today, all questions are more or less interdependent . . .
> A statesman worthy of the name—that is, one who wants to impress an idea on the course of history, has these two obstacles before him: the very *order* in which problems must be dealt with, and the time factor . . .

---

[1] *Travaillisme français*—French 'Labourism' seems about the only correct translation, with its implications of full employment, fairer wages, welfare state, and healthier relations with the colonial territories.

The time factor—in a different sense—was also a terrible obstacle in any attempt to revise colonial problems: for here a statesman, no matter how good his intentions, was burdened by the after-effects of all the errors of the past:

If, after a century of colonialist mistakes, such a statesman tries to establish a fairer relationship between the metropolis and the natives, it will not be sufficient to have good intentions. Such intentions will not remove the psychological and other difficulties; nor will a 'new style' immediately take the place of the old . . . The fellagha insurrection in Tunisia and the Aurès riots in Algeria are derived from a long process of colonial relations, for which the present Government is in no way responsible . . .

And P. H. Simon's conclusion was very significant: it would be unfair to dismiss the Mendès-France Government merely because at a certain phase of its career it had 'disappointed':

Giving confidence to a government should mean that the country gives this government *time*, and is not prepared to turn it out because it is disappointed, at a given moment, with this or that result of its policy . . .[1]

Obviously, the Mendès Government was creaking—especially after the Socialists, in November, had refused to join it. The Simon article in the *Monde* was typical of the desire on the part of Mendès's admirers to fight that disappointment which was becoming so noticeable everywhere. As for the Government's enemies, they had no difficulty in cashing in on its loss of popularity.

The first big attack was launched on account of Algeria. Already on November 12, Mendès-France and Mitterrand, his Minister of the Interior, were hauled over the coals in the National Assembly over what came to be known as the 'Aurès Rebellion' which had broken out in the Aurès mountains in the Constantinois on the night of October 31 to November 1. Actually, the total number of French lives lost was only seven; but there had also been some rioting 'of an insurrectional kind' (as M. Mitterrand put it) in various other parts of Algeria. No doubt, both he and Mendès agreed that the propaganda of Cairo radio had much to do with it; and they promised to deal 'with the utmost rigour' with the real culprits; but they already then protested against the argument that had been used by so many Right-wing speakers (and was to be used over and over again in subsequent debates) that Mendès's

[1] *Le Monde*, December 12, 1954.

famous Tunis trip had encouraged this outbreak of 'banditry' in Algeria.

It was difficult, however, to deliver an all-out attack on Mendès at that stage: the rioting was on a relatively small scale; the Government had acted promptly; and had also taken a highly doubtful measure which, nevertheless, greatly pleased the Opposition: it had outlawed the MTLD, Messali Hadj's nationalist party in Algeria, and had taken measures to prevent Messali himself (who had been interned in France for years) from making any statement to the press. From an internee he had become a prisoner.

There were at the Assembly two further North-African episodes on November 22 and 24, in connection with the budget—episodes which the irrepressible M. Quilici again tried to turn into a major political debate; however, with Mendès-France in the USA at the time, it was decided to wait for his return.

On December 9 the first big attack was launched, the debate being opened by M. Bidault, who warned the Government against bringing the ex-Sultan of Morocco 'nearer home'; who denounced Bourguiba as an arch-enemy of France, and concluded by expressing his anxiety over the 'mysteriousness' of Mendès-France's aims in the colonial field. 'What *do* you want? Where *are* you going?'

Members of the North Africa lobby and a variety of Vichyites were more outspoken. M. Jean Grousseaud declared that there had never been 'a more disastrous Government in France'. It had, within a few months, lost Hanoi, Haiphong, Pondicherry and other French colonies in India (on which, at last, an amicable settlement had been reached for their return to India), and, if it went on like this, it would lose Tunis, Casablanca, Oran and Algiers. Venomously he addressed Mendès:

> You will be abhorred by future generations of Frenchmen; for the time may come when schoolchildren will be taught: 'There was a Prime Minister, whose name was Mendès, and he also had another name, but he was much too small for so big a name. (*Loud protests on Left*.) It was he who made France lose enormous territories. (*More protests*.)

After being called upon by the President to be 'more moderate' in his language, M. Grousseaud concluded:

> He made France lose immense territories, as I already said, over which flew, before he arrived, the tricolour flag of France . . . May Providence protect us, and may Providence drive you out, *Monsieur le Président du Conseil*, so that France may live!

It was to go on like this for hours.

With René Mayer the debate took on a more serious turn.

He was glad Mendès had told Washington that Algeria was 'covered by the Atlantic Pact'. But he was not satisfied with the way the fellagha problem had been 'settled' in Tunisia. It was the business of the French command to make the fellaghas lay down their arms; it was not something that should have been 'negotiated' between the French Government, the Tunisian Government and the rebels . . . The whole procedure had disconcerted the Europeans in Algeria. During the winter season the fellaghas could now quietly go home; but would they not become a weapon in the hands of the Neo-Destour in spring if, by any chance, there was disagreement between the French and Tunisian Governments?

All the coming and going of armed bands between Tunisia and Algeria must be prevented; yet the Tunisian Government had refused to place any restrictions on such movements. In any case, said M. Mayer, it was important to have more numerous French garrisons in the Aurès country.

M. Mayer stressed that North Africa presented a very difficult problem: except for French North Africa, all Moslem countries in the world were independent. For France to lose North Africa would, however, mean the end of France. The bonds with Tunisia and Morocco must not be loosened any more, and, as for Algeria, there were solutions other than independence (which France could not allow) or assimilation (which was an out-of-date conception). He therefore advocated a 'reasonable evolution' for Algeria.

René Mayer still pulled his punches; but he was obviously not satisfied with Mendès's 'over-generous' handling of Tunisia; and it was he, indeed, who delivered the final blow to the Mendès Government only six weeks later—on this very issue of Algeria.

But this time he was not ready yet to help to overthrow the Government, even though the MRP hoped that René Mayer would 'bring' them 20 votes. By a narrow majority the Government scraped through.

Before the vote M. Mitterrand had spoken of the 'deep causes' of the trouble in Algeria. The 1947 *Statut d'Algérie*, he said, had remained a dead letter, and it was high time it was applied.

Mendès, for his part, had recalled that ten Governments had promised Tunisia internal autonomy, and it was high time France fulfilled her promise. The fellagha operation had proved a complete success since, thanks to the co-operation of the Tunisian and French authorities, order had been restored in Tunisia—for the first time in years. Economic discontent was, he said, at the root of the trouble in North Africa, and especially in Algeria:

> Our greatest preoccupation—for that is the real cause of what disaffection there is towards France—is the economic and social situation in North Africa. On the one hand, a strong population pressure, on the other hand, underemployment, undernourishment and appalling poverty—though not as appalling as in some other Mediterranean countries. (*Cries of:* 'Egypt—which is trying to teach us!')

And then came this conclusion—with its melancholy undertones:

> If there is a field in which—if only French political customs would allow it—there should be complete national unanimity, it is surely this question of North Africa. The destiny of France and the destiny of North Africa are bound up forever. Let us forget secondary problems and our petty quarrels. Let us be united at last on this question—a question on which the future of France, of a Greater France depends. (*Prolonged cheers on Radical, Socialist and Gaullist benches.*)

M. Fayet, a Communist speaker, remarked that this was all very well, but it was not true, as the Government had asserted, that Algeria was composed of three French *départements;* Algeria was, in reality, a colony, and was treated as such.

With the ratification of the Paris Agreements in the offing, the Communists were not feeling in the least charitable to Mendès-France.

CHAPTER 11

*THE MALRAUX-MAURIAC 'PLOT', OR MENDÈS
AS THE TORCH-BEARER OF A NEW LIBERALISM*

A FEW days later the long debate began on the ratification of
the Paris Agreements; and then came the New Year of 1955.
Mendès went for a holiday—or rather, a busman's holiday—
to Italy, in the course of which he was received in audience by the
Pope—a curious episode which will be dealt with later.

What perhaps characterized more than anything else the atmosphere of the Mendès experiment during the last few weeks of 1954 was
the growing disillusionment on the part of Mendès and his admirers
in the accepted French forms of parliamentary government and parliamentary procedure. Mendès probably knew as well as anybody that
his days were numbered; but he was hoping for a come-back, and it
was towards the end of 1954 that one observes two ideas taking shape:
his proposal for a return to the *scrutin d'arrondissement* and the conception of a *Nouvelle Gauche*. With this was to be linked up, early in
the new year, the appointment of Jacques Soustelle as Governor-
General of Algeria.

It is difficult to deal with this stage of Mendès-France's career
without saying something about *L'Express*. Although, in a conversation with me later in 1955 or 1956, Mendès said he hated the terms
'*mendésiste*' or '*mendésisme*' (which, somehow, implied that the thinking was done by one man, and the rest merely followed sheepishly)
L'Express was, for lack of a better word, considered a '*mendésiste*'
paper, almost since its first appearance in May, 1953—barely a month
before Mendès made his famous first investiture speech, after which
he just missed being appointed Premier. It was this failure which finally
resulted in the disastrous formation of the Laniel Government.

The main feature of the first number of *L'Express*, published on
May 16, was a long interview by Mendès, called 'France Can Stand
the Truth', and was almost a pre-view of his subsequent investiture
speech. The main points of the interview were splashed by the *Express*.

No More Piecemeal Remedies.
Indo-China: We Must Negotiate.
Reduce The Defence Budget.
Modernize Industry.

151

Great Housing Programme.
Large-Scale Investments in Africa.

These were, as it were, the six commandments which *L'Express* closely followed during the next couple of years.

What following Mendès had in the country had not properly crystallized at any time in 1954; while, in 1955, it was not given enough time to crystallize, except on a small scale, notably in the Paris area and in the Eure Department. So Mendès had neither a proper mass following, nor a proper political following at any time of his premiership; all he had was a *group* of supporters; and the centre of their activity was *L'Express*. The circulation of this important weekly steeply rose throughout 1953 and 1954 to about 150,000 copies. Closely connected with it were some of Mendès's personal friends and 'political associates', such as the young editor of the paper, Jean-Jacques Servan-Schreiber. Belonging to the Servan-Schreiber family, who owned the financial paper, *Les Echos*, and some of whose members had been closely associated in the past with the Radical leadership, Jean-Jacques made a very rapid, and varied, career in French journalism. In 1949, he wrote some near-neutralist articles in the *Monde*, which aroused considerable attention. However, before long, he quarrelled with the *Monde*, and is even said to have sworn to 'sink' it, by turning *Paris-Presse* into a dangerous rival of the *Monde*. *Paris-Presse*, of which Servan-Schreiber became foreign editor, was anything but 'neutralist', but, on the contrary, extremely Atlantic; and Servan-Schreiber also became 'Atlantic' at that stage (1950-51). However, times change; and, by 1953, Servan-Schreiber was again active on *Le Monde*, whence he conducted a crusade against M. Bidault and his Indo-Chinese policy.

Soon afterwards, Servan-Schreiber decided to devote himself wholly to his new weekly, *L'Express*. The Laniel Government was, of course, fair game. It lent itself to criticism like no other Government. Its Indo-China policy was suicidal. So was its policy in North Africa.

One of the greatest assets of the new weekly was François Mauriac who, in his weekly *Bloc Notes* proceeded to let off steam—which he was finding increasingly difficult to do in the pro-Government *Figaro*. His campaign against the colonial policy of repression, which had reached its climax in the Casablanca massacres of December, 1952, when several hundred Moroccan workers were killed, had made him Enemy No. 1 of the North Africa Lobby and of the French diehards in North Africa.

Is the key to the Moroccan enigma (he wrote on one occasion) really to be found in the functioning of the Moroccan 'lobby'? It is this dark side of contemporary history which one should explore. The bright side of history is composed of the story of the *effects*, but the true *causes* remain obscure. The lives of illustrious men teach us nothing that we did not know before. It is the lives of men who are not illustrious that would be interesting if they could be studied in broad daylight . . . Wouldn't the life of M. Emile Roche be interesting! Or that of M. François-Charles Roux, or of M. Martinaud-Déplat, and of so many others whose biographies would form part of a general history of the relationship between politics, business activities and private fortunes under both the Third and the Fourth Republic!

Mauriac developed, over a period of a few months, an almost mystical faith in Mendès-France as the saviour of the country. Mendès was to him the enemy of the forces of evil. His influence among wide circles of readers was unquestionable. As for the *Express* itself, it liked to stress the *novelty* of what Mendès-France represented in French public life. After the Indo-China settlement, it wrote that two new elements had entered French public life with Mendès-France : first, the end of the Indo-China war, with its paralysing effect on the economy and armed strength of the country. And secondly—

> Secondly, in the last four weeks, the whole political 'style' in the conduct of the country's affairs has been changed. Pierre Mendès-France has not discovered any new formula of genius ; nor has he thought up any 'stunt' which nobody had thought of before. His method has simply consisted in stating with complete clarity what he intended to do, and then to go ahead with the maximum of precision, and never to say one thing to some people and something else to others, but always to say the same thing to everybody. This common-sense method marked a complete departure from previous methods.

This 'build-up' of Mendès and what came to be known as '*mendésisme*' went on in the *Express* throughout the seven months of the Mendès-France Government. But towards the end of this period— and indeed before—it looked as though the imminent fall of Mendès might not necessarily guarantee the survival of the things and methods he stood for. Not unless certain steps were taken.

It is significant that on December 25, 1954, i.e., while the debate on the ratification of the Paris Agreements was in full swing, and the subsequent overthrow of Mendès by the National Assembly easy to foresee, the *Express* should have started a spectacular campaign for a *Nouvelle Gauche*, a new 'non-Marxist' Left, centred round Mendès. And the first two 'big' names it enlisted in this new movement were— Mauriac and Malraux.

Their 'first conversation' with Malraux—which was, in fact, like a manifesto of the *Nouvelle Gauche*—published in the *Express* of December 25—had a preamble which said:

> May we be allowed to stress the extraordinary fact of a new political axis which marks the encounter of Pierre Mendès-France, the liberal statesman; François Mauriac, the inspirer of the Catholic Left; and André Malraux, the revolutionary guide, who has renounced none of the things that link him with General de Gaulle.

And this is what Malraux, great novelist, ardent political torch-bearer, de Gaulle's Minister of Information in 1946, and de Gaulle's chief election propagandist in 1951 had to say:

> I believe we are witnessing the beginning of a new phenomenon . . . Since the Liberation France has, on the whole, conceived both the Right and the Left only in Marxist terms. The French Left identified itself with the proletariat, and the French Right expressed the anti-proletarian attitude.
>
> Yet for over a century France has known a Left which corresponded to a state of mind, rather than to an economic reality. This Left seems to be in process of reviving. *The new and unexpected thing is the revival of French liberalism.*
>
> This liberalism (Malraux continued) is symbolised by Mendès-France. It is, however, in the nature of the French Liberal Left not to be fully aware of itself, *except in opposition.* If Mendès-France falls, the crystallization process may come on with astonishing speed. *I do not exclude the possibility of Mendès being overthrown in a month or two, and then being returned in the next general election with a plebiscite-like sweep.* All the more so as France likes liberalism, but does not like it too soft. Mendès has the necessary energetic style.

And then Malraux came to one of his favourite ideas, and one which Mendès also liked to put forward—especially in his interviews with the American press:

> There are only 400,000 wholehearted Communist voters in France; well, let's add to them 1 million more hangers-on; yet in the last election 5 million people voted Communist. That leaves us a margin of $3\frac{1}{2}$ million votes.

These, Malraux argued, could be 'won over' by a New Left formation. This would not be Marxist or even pre-Marxist; it would be 'New Deal'.

It is unnecessary here to enter into all the historical, psychological and moral considerations which, in Malraux's view, made this crystallization of a new French *mystique* of social justice, and justice *tout court* ('The Socialist Party would not be what it is if Jaurès had not taken Dreyfus's side in his time') promising and probable. It would not be anti-Christian: it would be supported by the Catholic Left, headed by Mauriac, which was in opposition to the false Christianity of the MRP. And France, he once again argued, was great when she had a *mission*—as at the time of St. Louis, or at the time of the Revolution.

When one came to think of it, as one read the rhetorical prose of Malraux's 'First Conversation', it was singularly reminiscent of the election speeches he had already made for de Gaulle's RPF in May, 1951: only now his Hero No. 1 was no longer de Gaulle but—by implication—de Gaulle's successor, Mendès-France.

Mauriac, in the same issue of *L'Express*, was pleased with the Malraux piece ... but could not help doubting whether Mendès, after his fall, really *would* appeal to the country ... Would he not rather retire like Clemenceau and de Gaulle? Moreover (and this was where Mauriac put an awkward question to Malraux) what would de Gaulle's rôle be?

He is still there. His latest interventions in our national life have shown that he has lost nothing of his old prestige and that the liquidation of the RPF has indeed put him back in his right place. In the presence of the *mendésiste* phenomenon, after the fall of the Mendès Government, will de Gaulle remain neutral, or merely benevolent? Or will he, on the contrary, agree that his mission shall continue, but personified now by his most prodigious spiritual son, whose vocation is politics?

Mauriac, who, already before the war, had taken the defence of the Spanish republicans against Franco, Hitler and Mussolini, and the defence of Abyssinia against the Duce; who was one of the rare French writers of the older generation—and practically the only *académicien*—to have been anti-Vichyite and to have played an honourable part in the Resistance; and who, especially since 1952, had fought, more effectively than any other man, against the follies of the French colonialists in Tunisia and Morocco, convinced himself, during 1954, that Mendès-France came closest to that ideal of a statesman who would lead France along the road of social justice and a fair deal for the Arabs.

The hero-worship that Mauriac, the Catholic, developed, more and more, for Mendès-France, the Jew and agnostic, is one of the strangest psychological cases in recent French history. Mauriac admired de Gaulle; but de Gaulle, to him, was what I have called elsewhere 'a noble anachronism'—'like a cold wind of French greatness, blowing from very high and very far'. Somehow, Mauriac convinced himself that although the two men were dissimilar, Mendès-France could, thanks to his qualities of mind and character, and his realistic assessment of the possibilities of the present time, restore France to greatness . . . It was not quite the mystical greatness of de Gaulle's imagination; but a similar greatness adapted to the present-day world . . .

How seriously did Mendès-France take this campaign in his favour on the part of Mauriac, Malraux and—indirectly—de Gaulle himself? There were moments, before the fall of his Government on February 4, 1955, when he perhaps believed in the possibility of a *Regroupement* around himself—with the Gaullists, the Socialists and some of the Radicals as his principal supporters. It seems that his appointment of Jacques Soustelle as Governor-General of Algeria was decided upon at a time when Mendès believed in the possibility of a *Nouvelle Gauche* coming into being. But the illusion did not last. During the last days of his Government, he was made increasingly conscious of the bitter hatreds he had aroused; and of the fact that he had at that time, far more enemies than friends in the country, and especially at the National Assembly.

When asked, a long time afterwards, what he thought of the Mauriac-Malraux 'campaign', he winced and said, with a vague gesture of discouragement: 'Oh, nothing in it . . .'

CHAPTER 12

THE HALF-HEARTED MITTERRAND PLAN FOR ALGERIA

ALTHOUGH, after the ratification of the Paris Agreements, everything suggested that the opposition to Mendès-France had grown, and that the MRP and the Right would not miss any convenient opportunity for overthrowing his Government before long, Mendès continued to act, throughout January, as though he and his Government might last indefinitely. The ratification debate, which had lasted for over a week, had given him a greater feeling of solitude than anything else. Although the ratification was passed in the end by a small majority, literally nobody actively supported Mendès in his struggle for 'Western Unity', except one man, Guy Mollet, the Socialist Leader. But none of the others: neither the former EDC men, like Pinay, Schuman, Bidault, René Mayer, nor the anti-EDC men like Herriot, Soustelle or Palewski. He fought his battle single-handed, and all the time, at the back of his mind, were the 'promise' he had made to Churchill, and the warnings he had received from London and Washington.

Mendès's dramatic and exhausting fight for this ratification had, nevertheless, not damped his energies. He was (or seemed to be) full of plans for the future. He was thinking hard of East-West relations, and asked Mr. Hammarskjold, the Director-General of UN to stop in Paris on January 1 on his way to China, so that he could have a long talk with him at Orly airfield. He saw M. Sainteny, the French representative in North Vietnam on the following day, discussed with him Franco-Vietnamese relations and the gradual withdrawal from Vietnam of the remaining French troops. He worked on big plans for a new kind of European Community, and decided to discuss this (and much else) with the Italian and German Governments.

The plans for a visit to Italy had been settled some time before, but now he decided to visit Adenauer in Baden-Baden. He announced, early in January, that there would be a cabinet reshuffle, that he would hand the Quai d'Orsay over to Edgar Faure, and would largely devote himself to economic problems, together with the new Finance Minister, M. Buron. There were the Tunisian agreements to be finally elaborated during the next few weeks; he also wanted to achieve results on the projected European Armaments Agency, complete with a supranational machinery, at which the USA and the UK had been looking askance, ever since the even more ambitious French project for a supranational Armaments Pool had been launched. (By the beginning of January, with the Paris Agreements duly ratified, this ambitious scheme had already assumed much more modest proportions.) He had also promised the Assembly to clear up certain points concerning the Saar, the Assembly having approved the Mendès-France—Adenauer agreements of October 23 only with the greatest reluctance.

And then there was Algeria—that Algeria where the situation was becoming increasingly dangerous, with the Aurès rebellion threatening to spread to densely-populated Kabylia. Mendès's Minister of the Interior, François Mitterrand, had been working hard on a series of reforms which meant, in effect, the revival of the *Statut d'Algérie*, which had been passed in 1947, but never been properly applied,

It should be recalled here that the law called '*Statut organique de l'Algérie*' was passed by the National Assembly on September 20, 1947. This provided, *inter alia*, for a two-college Algerian Assembly, but although, in terms of the Statute, 'every Algerian is a French citizen, irrespective of origin, race, language or religion', the very structure of the Algerian Assembly showed that there were, in reality, two categories of French citizens in Algeria—those voting for the first college, and whose civil status was French, and those voting for the second college, and whose civil status was 'local'. In other words, 500,000 French voters, plus some 70,000 'select' Moslems (distinguished war record, decorations, etc.), were represented by the first college, and, on the other hand, 1,450,000 non-privileged Moslem voters were represented by the second college. The Moslem voters did not include women, and since the two colleges of sixty members each were equal, the 'weight' of a Moslem voter was, even on paper, six times smaller than that of a European voter.

Moreover, to be completely on the safe side, the Assembly took the precaution of providing, by Article 39 of the *Statut d'Algérie*, that

> The Assembly takes its decisions by a majority vote. However, at the demand of the Governor-General, or of the Committee of Finance, or of one-quarter of the members, a vote may not be valid except if taken by a two-third majority . . . unless there is a simple majority in each of the colleges.

There are two striking aspects of the *Statut d'Algérie*: one is that all the 'democratic' reforms—which looked good on paper—were subordinated from the outset to their actual *application* by—the

Algerian Assembly itself! As a result of this, practically none of the major reforms provided by the Statute was applied. Thus, nothing was done about the abolition of the *communes mixtes* (large administrative units under the sole authority of a French administrator appointed by the Governor-General) and their replacement by a more democratic form of local government; or the extension of voting rights to Algerian women; or the independence of the Moslem religion *vis-à-vis* the State, or the teaching of Arabic in all schools; or the promotion of Arabic to the status of a second official language in Algeria, or the large-scale admission of Arabs to administrative posts.

Secondly, to be completely on the safe side, the French administration in Algeria instituted its system of proverbial 'Algerian elections' to the said Assembly, as a result of which the election 'results' had no connection at all with the actual voting. Thus, the sixty representatives of the second (Moslem) College to the first Algerian Assembly were—

'Independents' (i.e., administrative candidates)			..	..	43
MTLD (Messali Hadj)	..	..	..	..	9
UDMA (Ferhat Abbas)	..	..	..	..	8
Communists ..	..	..	..	..	0

M. Naegelen, the Socialist Governor-General of 1948, who was supposed to 'bring about the application of the Statute', had the effrontery to 'congratulate' the Algerian people on the 'calm and dignity' with which they had carried out their 'electoral duties'.[1]

It was not until 1955 that the 'administrative representatives'—who formed the great majority of the Second College—mostly ignorant and illiterate men who had been tempted by the French to play the part of obedient stooges—joined, as it were, in the general rebellion against the French.

As if foreseeing this danger, the Mendès-France Government hastened after a delay of seven years to 'start applying' the *Statut d'Algérie*. It was against this background of lost opportunities that Mitterrand proposed—

A programme for great public works, notably in the hydraulic field, with a consequent 'reclaiming' of arid soils;

A reduction in the huge difference between Algerian wages and French wages;

The admission of Algerians to responsible posts and even positions of authority in the Algerian administration, and the creation of an Administrative School for that purpose at Algiers;

[1] C. et F. Jeanson, *L'Algérie hors la loi* (Paris, 1956), p. 82.

the application of the Statute, implying 'equality of right and duties', and the extension of voting rights to certain categories of Algerian women;
Administrative reforms through the modification of the present régime of mixed communes, now under the orders of a civil administrator; and a decentralization of Algeria through the creation of new *départements*. The over-centralization had resulted in a loss of contact, in certain areas, such as the Aurès (where the rebellion had started in November) between the administration and the population.

A 'cultural effort', including the creation of a centre of Islamic studies attached to the University of Paris, which would attract many Moslem students.

These, and various other reforms, concerning the 'democratization' of local government (such as the plan for deliberations by local councils without the *caïd* having to be present), were, in reality, very small stuff; nevertheless they were sufficient to arouse the hostility of the settlers; at the same time they did not satisfy the Algerian nationalists by any means. Too much water had already flowed under the bridges since 1947.

Despite the scrappiness of the Mitterrand proposals, all based on the principle of 'Algeria, an integral part of France', it was on this issue that the Mendès-France Government was to fall less than a month later.

But it was not quite sure yet that this would happen, and Mendès-France still had at least one card up his sleeve—the appointment of Soustelle as Governor-General of Algeria. But this card he was not to play until a few days before the final debate.

Another of his projects to which Mendès attached great importance was electoral reform—complete with a return to the *scrutin d'arrondissement*. This was an issue on which all parties were divided, except the Communists. These were totally opposed to *cette vieille pourriture* (as Duclos called the *scrutin d'arrondissement*) which, if adopted, would mean the virtual elimination of the Communists from the National Assembly.

Nothing was going to be decided on this issue immediately; but Mendès had made up his mind that, whether in the Government, or out of it, he was going to devote much of his time before the next general election to getting the *scrutin d'arrondissement* adopted. He hoped, in this way, to create a strong 'democratic, anti-Communist' Left, of which he would be the leader.

CHAPTER 13

MENDES GOES EUROPEAN AND SEES THE POPE

M. AND MME. MENDES-FRANCE went for a short holiday to Positano, near Naples. The 'horny-handed fishermen of the town council'[1] made Mendès the first honorary citizen of Positano, while Madame Mendès-France was presented with 'a tablecloth embroidered by the inmates of the local orphanage'.

A few days later, at his villa near Naples, President Einaudi treated the Mendès-Frances to lunch; and then they went to Rome, where a very crowded programme was awaiting the French Premier. Though he had been pestered even more than usual by sightseers and autograph-hunters during his short holiday (for Mendès was still one of the most famous men in Europe), he arrived in Rome 'at the top of his form', as all the papers reported.

Besides a variety of protocol visits, Mendès had long talks with Premier Scelba, Foreign Minister Martino and Finance Minister Vanoni. He talked with them about a 'consolidation of Western Europe', about East-West relations, and about his own three-point programme for the Armaments Agency: standardization of equipment; co-ordination of arms production; and the joint production of certain items. All this was obviously small stuff to put before the Armaments Conference a few days later, compared with the original plan for a real 'armaments pool', complete with a supra-national organism which would have distributed American military aid, elaborated joint production and investment plans, and placed orders among the members of the European Defence Union. But all this 'supra-national' planning was obviously more than the USA and Britain were willing to consider. It is significant that although Mendès was very lukewarm in his attitude to the European Army, with its supra-national organism, he considered such an organism highly desirable in the case of armaments production, and especially distribution. The Italians politely agreed with many of his arguments, but knew as well as—a hostile—Adenauer did, that the Armaments pool stood no chance of being considered, and that even the modest French proposals that had taken its place were unlikely to be approved by Britain and the USA.

At the press conference he gave at the end of his Rome visit,

[1] *Le Monde*, January 8, 1955.

Mendès said that the French and Italian Governments had, in respect of the European Armaments agency, 'reached a general agreement on doctrine and methods of approach'; which was perhaps a little thin. He stressed the need of a 4-power conference with the Russians, as soon as possible after the ratification of the Paris Agreements by the Senate, and then made some general remarks on the need for closer economic bonds between France and Italy. Some precise preliminary agreements were reached concerning cultural exchanges, transport co-ordination, and, above all, the emigration of Italian labour to France; an increase was agreed to in the building-trade quota, and Mendès hoped that improved economic conditions in France would make it possible for Italian labour in France to be increased.

Above all, Mendès tried to make the most of his revival, on a somewhat different basis, of the 'European idea'; this greatly pleased not only the Italian Government but, even more so, the Vatican.

For the highlight of Mendès's Italian journey was his visit to the Pope. As the *Monde* described the visit:

> Wearing tails and a black waistcoat, in accordance with the protocol, and accompanied by Mme. Mendès-France in a high-necked black dress and cape, as well as by M. Boris, M. Seydoux and M. de Margerie, and conducted by Count Wladimir d'Ormesson, French Ambassador to the Holy See, the Premier arrived at the Vatican at 11 o'clock for the audience granted to him by Pius XII.

After describing the whole ritual through which Mendès went before seeing the Pope in his private library, the *Monde* correspondent said that, after speaking to the Pope by himself for over 20 minutes, he then presented to His Holiness his wife and assistants. After the audience with the Pope, Mendès had a long conversation with the pro-secretary, Mgr. Tardini. There followed a visit to the Sistine Chapel and the Raphael loggias, 'after which M. d'Ormesson gave a luncheon in honour of M. Mendès-France, a luncheon which was attended by six cardinals, all Grand Crosses of the Legion of Honour...'

> This visit to the Vatican has been in the centre of all attention here. It cannot be too strongly stressed that when the audience was asked for, the Pope was still in a very enfeebled state after his serious illness; but overlooking the counsels of caution, His Holiness nevertheless expressed the desire to receive the French Premier, the first civilian foreigner to have been received in audience by the Pope since his illness. This must be considered as a precious and significant expression of his friendship and solicitude for France ...

Needless to say, there was some hee-hawing over it in France. The anti-clerical *Canard Enchaîné* published a cartoon showing Mendès asking the Pope to pray for him next time he (Mendès) faced the National Assembly. It is also said that many of the MRP were furious at the special regard shown for Mendès by the Pope.

Mendès, sounding 'more European' than ever before, seemed to be taking the wind out of the sails of the MRP.

> The extreme cordiality surrounding Mendès-France during his visit to the Vatican shows that it was no simple formality ... The strong prejudice felt against him at the Vatican seems to have finally disappeared. Much of this prejudice was due to Mendès's alleged hostility to European integration. In his Christmas message, Pius XII criticised the Paris Agreements on this score. But the Rome *communiqués*, with their numerous references to the building of a united Europe, show that there is no reason at all for accusing Mendès-France of being hostile to that Europe which the Vatican unquestionably regards as the last rampart against Communism.[1]

However, the old pro-EDC men still continued to claim, whatever Mendès did, that they were better Europeans than he.

To him, little Europe was not a 'mystical' conception by any means; also, he had grave doubts about supra-national agencies; he believed, however, that there were still some unexplored trade possibilities even within the narrow framework of Little Europe. He was extremely vague, in his broadcast of January 15, as to what he had achieved during his meeting with Adenauer the day before; the Saar had been discussed—but how successfully was not at all clear. But he made the most of his German visit with reference to inter-European trade: a new commercial agreement between France and Western Germany had been signed: Germany would buy 500,000 tons of wheat from France, which was twice as much as last year, and she would also buy some butter and—for the first time—sugar. A new draft agreement for a 3-year trade plan had been discussed, and Mendès made the most of this, saying that this was part of a much wider plan

> the purpose of which is to increase France's rôle as an exporter country; by opening up regular markets, such a policy will safe-guard our producers, notably of agricultural produce against overproduction and unstable prices ... Without fear, they can then expand their production ...

[1] *Le Monde*, January 14, 1955.

Mendès's reference to sugar was significant: it suggested that in encouraging surplus beet to be turned into sugar, instead of alcohol, his
government was contributing to the development of a rational trade
system within West-European limits. But he was very far from advo-
cating anything in the nature of a Common Market—a conception to
which he was to show the most uncompromising hostility two years
later.

CHAPTER 14

THE SOUSTELLE APPOINTMENT

ALTHOUGH he was building on sand, Mendès never ceased to act in a dramatic, swift and spectacular way. After the visit to the Vatican and the Cabinet reshuffle a few days later (a reshuffle which suggested that the Government intended to last), came another spectacular move: despite some opposition from his colleagues (particularly M. Mitterrand, who proposed the appointment of M. Dubois, the Paris Prefect of Police) Mendès on January 26, appointed M. Jacques Soustelle Governor-General of Algeria. Soustelle, a brilliant speaker and scholar, had been one of de Gaulle's closest associates ever since 1940, and was considered as the leader of the 'progressive' wing of the RPF and, later, of what was left of the Gaullist movement. He had closely followed de Gaulle's policy of opposition to EDC and the Paris Agreements, and, worse still, the Right-wing press thought him dangerously Left-wing. Needless to say, the moment the Soustelle appointment was announced, Mendès's enemies jumped to the conclusion that Mendès had thought up an extremely tricky—and cunning —parliamentary manœuvre, as a result of which he might secure a new majority to support him—a majority composed of Socialists, the greater part of the Radicals, the UDSR and most of the Gaullists. The move seemed like a further development, in parliamentary terms, of that *Nouvelle Gauche*, of which Malraux, de Gaulle's former propaganda chief, had laid the foundation in the famous *Express* interview a month before.

Mendès strongly denied this in the course of the subsequent Assembly debate; but there is no doubt that the MRP, some of the Radicals and the Right saw a major danger signal in the appointment of Soustelle—the danger being the perpetuation of the Mendès Government. To some of the Radicals and to the MRP it became imperative to get rid of Mendès as quickly as possible, before he had time to consolidate the new majority.

The Soustelle episode is a landmark in more ways than one. His appointment precipitated the fall of the Mendès-France Government. In Algiers it was very badly received at first. The Right-wing press in France was extremely critical: 'Soustelle is a neutralist', the *Figaro* wrote.

His recent journey to Poland, his agreement with the Communists over EDC and the Paris Agreements cannot but worry his colleagues. They do not think these are good qualifications for the post of Governor-General of Algeria.

And the *Aurore*, going even further, conjured up terrible visions of this '*crypto-progressiste*', though wearing Gaullist plumes, embarking on some dangerous experiments in Algeria which could only end in disaster! The *Humanité*, on the other hand, simply said that the Soustelle appointment represented another desperate attempt by Mendès-France to save his government by every conceivable trick.

Be that as it may, the case of Soustelle is an extremely significant one in the history of North Africa in the last two years. Very coolly received at first by the *colons* as a 'Mendès-France nominee', Soustelle was gradually won over by them and became, within less than a year, one of the staunchest supporters of a tough native policy in Algeria.

When, after the 1956 election, Soustelle was recalled by the Republican Front Government of M. Mollet, the French of Algiers organized violent demonstrations against Soustelle's departure; only with the greatest difficulty did he succeed in boarding the ship that was to take him back to France. Soustelle thereupon became the most powerful champion of the no-surrender-to-the-Arabs policy.

Combat's prophecy on January 27, 1955, that he 'would not allow himself to be diverted from his mission' proved singularly erroneous, though it is only fair to say that if this Liberal of January, 1955, became a discouraged man six months later, he seems genuinely to have lost faith in a Franco-Algerian settlement acceptable to both sides. After the August massacres and the collapse of France's policy in Morocco, Soustelle came to the conclusion that the gloves were off, and that France was destined to wage a ruthless war against the Arab League and Islam generally.

As regards Soustelle's own views on Algeria at the time of his appointment in January, 1955, the following statement shows that he was then thinking in terms of a 'federal' solution—a solution which had been considered at Brazzaville during the war, but had since been shelved. This solution, he thought, should be revived.

The present organization of the French Republic (he said) was a lopsided compromise, which could not last. French institutions at present were a combination of three systems; first, the old colonial regime of which there were more traces than was generally admitted—both in the administrative *moeurs* on the spot, and in the behaviour of Europeans. Secondly, there was the system of 'assimilation', which, though inspired by generous motives in the first place, was wholly out-of-date now; and finally, the federal system, which was reflected in 'assemblies', 'grand councils', etc., but these organisms were only rudimentary and fragmentary ...

Hence the astonishing situation in which the Paris Parliament included a certain number of African deputies—too numerous when Bills were discussed which concerned only the Metropolis, and not sufficiently numerous when purely colonial questions arose ... In this way, the Assembly was neither that of a unitary state, nor that of a federal state; also, the fact that, numerically, the Africans were under-represented savoured of the colonial past ... 'Local' Assemblies—which would include the Metropolitan Assembly—must legislate with reference to their own territorial entity; whereas a *Federal Parliament* must legislate for the whole of the French Union. Similarly, there must be no confusion between the Metropolitan Government and the Federal Government; and certain federal ministries must be created with attributions extending to the whole of Europe-Africa ... (*Le Monde*, January 29, 1955)

We shall see later what came of these 'federalist' ideas of Jacques Soustelle. The 'federalist' theory gave way, before long, to the theory of 'integration', not to be followed by a revival of the 'federalist' idea until August, 1956—this time by Marshal Juin! All of which shows how unmanageable a problem Algeria was to anyone afraid of 'giving too much away'.

It was on the day following the Soustelle appointment to Algiers that the Executive Committee of the Radical Party met, and here René Mayer launched his first major attack on Mendès-France's North African policy. The Soustelle appointment, for one thing, enabled Mayer and other old parliamentary hands to accuse Mendès of resorting to the kind of parliamentary operations which he had always condemned in the past. Was it not a typical piece of *dosage*, for the purpose of winning over some Gaullist votes, to have appointed Soustelle Governor-General of Algeria?

The cabinet reshuffle only a few days before was also attributed by René Mayer to parliamentary considerations of the same sort. Although the rank-and-file *militants* of the Radical Party were favourable to Mendès and indignant over René Mayer's attitude, it was clear that, among the parliamentary group, many were now ready to abandon Mendès-France. René Mayer already made it plain that he was going to have a showdown with Mendès over North Africa.

CHAPTER 15

NORTH AFRICA KILLS
MENDÈS-FRANCE GOVERNMENT

DURING those few days before his overthrow, Mendès-France was in a fighting mood. He was conscious of still enjoying a good deal of support among the *young* people in France; the attitude of the *militants* of the Radical Party, who remembered Mendès's dazzling start, was still favourable.

Nevertheless, his stock had slumped heavily since the Geneva Conference and even since his short-lived apotheosis at the Radical Congress in October, when Herriot had bestowed on him his fatherly blessing.

For various reasons, some beyond his control, he had annoyed too many people and had disappointed others. Herriot himself had turned against him—or rather, against his policy—on the German rearmament issue. So had many others. He had lifted up a few stones, and had uncovered swarms of maggots underneath: he had, for example, been the first to start, not a discreet (as others had done) but a noisy campaign against the drink racket in France.

Since he was planning to reorganize French economy, he was now also likely to do many other things which would annoy important groups of voters, and to encroach on the preserves of potentially powerful and highly organized vested interests. Shopkeepers and peasants and café proprietors had already, by this time, begun to listen with the greatest attention to the demagogy of Pierre Poujade, the 'good Frenchman' with the little stationery shop at St. Céré in the Lot. To Poujade, Mendès was Enemy No. 1. He was the enemy of the shopkeepers, the enemy of the *bouilleurs de cru*, the enemy of the café proprietors, and member of that evil race who owned 'all' those department stores and Monoprix and Uniprix shops which were cutting the throats of the *petits commerçants*.

Mendès's majority had badly dwindled. The Communists, to whom he was 'the Man who had rearmed Germany' were going to vote against him, whether he 'counted' their votes or not. The men of the African Lobby and, in fact, the whole of the Right, were up in arms against his North African policy; or, at any rate, thought it the best stick with which to beat him; and, in the circumstances, the MRP were delighted to have this opportunity of wreaking vengeance on the man who had made such fools of them over Indo-China. His attempt to win over a sufficient number of Gaullist votes to make up for probable Radical desertions—desertions of which Martinaud-Déplat and René Mayer would take good care—did not succeed.

And lastly, his belated 'Europeanism', complete with his visit to the Pope incensed the Little-Europe Catholics more perhaps than anything else. The most violent among them, P. H. Teitgen, uttered the phrase, before Mendès was overthrown, which gave one a better insight than anything else into the dread among the MRP of Mendès succeeding, after all, in turning the corner. 'It is now or never', Teitgen exclaimed.

But 'Revenge for Indo-China' was, to the MRP, the deepest motive of all. This was stressed, even before the debate opened, by M. Maurice Duverger in a remarkable article in the *Monde* on February 3:

> The MRP and their Right-wing allies will make Mendès's life a misery over North Africa, just as he made their life a misery over Indo-China . . . It seems utter nonsense—but there it is! When Mendès attacked Laniel and his Ministers, he was attacking the men who were responsible for the eight-years war in Indo-China . . . When these people now attack Mendès for our present difficulties in North Africa, they are, in fact, attacking a man who is trying to break away from the disastrous policy they started there, particularly on December 15, 1951. It was an MRP Minister that day who broke off negotiations with Tunisia. It was an MRP Minister who appointed M. de Hauteclocque to Tunisia—the man who started the civil war there. It was Bidault, supported by Laniel, who condoned the deposition of the Sultan of Morocco, since when Morocco has been in a state of chaos . . . It is also these people who are responsible for the lack of social progress in Algeria, for the violation of the *Statut d'Algérie*, for the faked elections.

He went on to say that, in theory, the MRP had a generous policy for North Africa; but this never went beyond speeches and motions.

> When Mendès overthrew Laniel in June, it was to put an end to a war and to make peace. When Laniel and his friends want to overthrow Mendès now, it is to return to the policy of repression in North Africa. Delicate negotiations are in progress with Tunisia, and the signing of the conventions is close at hand, despite many difficulties . . . Once these conventions are signed, conditions will be favourable for seeking peaceful solutions in Morocco . . . and Algeria. A reconciliation of France and Islam

will at last be in sight . . . Our influence in the Middle East will be restored.

But this policy can only succeed if Mendès-France remains in office. Others can make promises . . . but the truth is that Mendès-France (thanks to his Tunis visit) is the only man in whom the North African spokesmen have any confidence. His eventual successors are all people who have lied to them in the past . . . Let there be no mistake about it: the fall of Mendès will put an end to the fruitful experiment he has started in North Africa.

For all that, Mendès was overthrown at the end of a two-days' debate on North Africa.

The debate started rather tamely. Only a month had passed since the last North African debate, and many of the speeches—mostly by the same 'specialists'—were a mere rehash of their December speeches. The learned M. Bardoux again attached the greatest importance to the sinister machinations of the British in Libya, 'where they practise the religion of Oil'; the British were responsible for the arming of the Tunisian fellaghas, and also for the Libyan demand that France hand over the Fezzan to Libya, that 'artificial monstrosity'. The apoplectic-looking M. Dronne was furious because the Quai d'Orsay had agreed, under British pressure, to negotiate with Libya over the Fezzan country. There was every reason to expect a new French capitulation, if the Mendès Government remained in office.

M. de Villeneuve, another Right-wing deputy, said that if France abandoned the Fezzan territory to Libya, it would mean that she could no longer use the one track (Track No. 5) connecting Tunisia with the Chad territory, and would have to restore Track No. 4, which would take years.

Any agreement with Libya must give us full access to Track No. 5, as well as to the Ghadamès and Sabha Tracks . . . If you sign away anything more, we shall demand that you be tried by the High Court. You say, M. Mendès-France, that your pre-decessors obeyed orders from Washington. But are not you a flunkey of London? (*Cheers on Right.*)

With remarkably bad faith, one of the North Africa Lobby men, M. François Quilici, said that Algeria was becoming gradually and peacefully integrated in the French community; but then came the Tunis visit, and since then 'the whole North African edifice has been crumbling'.

M. Quilici: You realized what you had done, and you there-upon offered the post of supreme chief over all three territories to Marshal Juin.

M. Mendès-France: Never was an offer of this kind made to Marshal Juin.

M. Quilici: So you now say. I must take your word for it. But you are using that great soldier as a strange sort of screen in all your doings in North Africa. You made him go to Tunis with you. Since then, troops have been sent to Algeria, but with instructions which completely paralysed their powers of repression. Thirty policemen with a little money with which they could untie many native tongues would be more effective than 3,000 soldiers without any authority . . .

But these were still only initial skirmishes. The decisive attack on Mendès was launched by his fellow-Radical, M. René Mayer. This was the long-awaited bomb that turned twenty Radical votes and a number of 'wobblers' in other parties against the Government, and so sealed its fate.

Pompous and well-groomed, as usual, René Mayer, speaking with unusual sharpness and precision, was fully conscious of the 'historical' speech he was making. He had taken days to prepare it. He started with Tunisia:

Bourguiba and Salah Ben Yussef are making speeches which clearly show that they want independence for Tunisia, and are no longer content with the internal autonomy you [Mendès-France] have offered them. Is your Tunis statement still the basis on which negotiations with Tunisia are being conducted?

Mendès-France: Yes, unquestionably.

René Mayer: All these slow negotiations with Tunisia are having a very bad effect on Algeria. The atmosphere in Algeria is getting worse every day. There is, in the country, a general feeling of insecurity, especially in the rural areas. A kind of intoxication can be observed among both Europeans and Moslems. For the first time in eight years is there a tendency among both communities to have nothing to do with each other. For the first time since the creation of the Algerian Assembly has it happened for its Second [Moslem] College to meet separately and pass separate motions . . . They have, of course, a right to do this; but the fact remains that the Tunisian talks have had a strange effect on their mentality.

Mayer then made some ironical remarks on the Soustelle appointment, and wondered whether 'parliamentary motives' had now taken the place of Mendès's dazzling 'deadline' technique of the past.

Returning to the question of the 'outrageous' behaviour of the Second College, M. Mayer noted that they had passed a motion demanding that 'repression' in Algeria be stopped. No doubt, he said, repression was always nasty, but it had not been indiscriminate lately, and when there were outrages in so many places, repression was inevitable. Moslems loyal to France were being terrorized and victimized, and it was France's duty to protect them.

It was all very well treating him (Mayer) as a 'reactionary'; but when he read that Azzam Pasha, head of the Arab League, was demanding that France 'adapt herself to the conditions of the modern world', his answer was No. He did not wish France to 'adapt' herself in North Africa, as she had already 'adapted' herself in Vietnam, in India and the Fezzan. (*Loud cheers.*)

And then came the final blows:

I shall vote against the Government, undeterred by the press and even by *L'Express*. (*Laughter on Right.*) I am sure, *monsieur le président du conseil*, that you have measured all the harm done you by certain weekly columns and *bloc-notes*, from which there seem to emerge the black horns of Don Basilio's hat . . . (*Prolonged cheers from Right, Centre and some Gaullist benches.*)

That was one for M. François Mauriac, who, for weeks, had conducted a passionate campaign for Mendès-France, and had said many unkind things of his opponents in his weekly *bloc-notes* on the back page of *L'Express*. René Mayer added that he would vote against Mendès, not only because of his African policy, but because of his international policy as well. And he concluded:

I do not know where you are going, and I refuse to believe that a policy of 'movement' cannot find a happy medium between what is called *immobilisme* on the one hand, and reckless adventure on the other.

The words were greeted by an ovation that went half-way across the Assembly. Many Radicals joined in the cheering of the 'executioner'. It was as if Laniel's execution by Mendès eight months before had been avenged.

Yet M. René Mayer's triumph was not complete; how could it be? Only a few minutes after he had ended his 'indictment', a speech was made by a Moslem deputy, belonging to the Socialist Party. He did not speak in general terms, as Mayer had done; he spoke of something Mayer had not mentioned: of the tortures practised by the French police in Algeria.

He said that the delegation of the Second College that had come to Paris was not proposing any Algerian separatism, but had merely come to protest against police methods in Algeria.

My fellow-Moslems [M. Benhamed said] know what is meant by 'the bath-tub torture'. They also know what is meant by the 'water-pipe' trick. It is a way of pumping water into the stomach of people who are not even guilty but who have often simply been denounced anonymously by somebody . . . Moslems living in the *bled* know at last what electricity means—they know it not from electric bulbs, but from the electric gadgets that are inserted into various parts of their body. I might also mention the 'bottle torture'; it consists in forcing quarter-bottles of Perrier you know where. I maintain that all these tortures are regularly practised in Algeria today. I do not think there is anybody in this House who is not as indignant about it as I am . . . (*Loud cheers.*)

I have irrefutable evidence of an old man of 70 or 75 being made to perform a dance in the nude in front of his wife, his children and grandchildren. Such methods are unworthy of France. And France has nothing to gain from them . . .

M. Mitterrand, Minister of the Interior, admitted that this sort of thing unfortunately continued to happen in Algeria, despite an attempt to discipline the police.

The Algerian deputy concluded that if the insurrection in Algeria had not yet taken on wider proportions, it was precisely *because* the negotiations with Tunisia were continuing. If the Mendès Government was overthrown, he said, it would make a very bad impression among the Moslems; it would be considered as a repudiation of the liberal policy of the last few months.

It was clear from this speech, that even the hand-picked 'Second College' Algerians were becoming desperate.

After various other speakers, Mendès-France at last rose to speak. He was visibly angry, and did not mince his words in dealing with René Mayer and his 'donkey's kick'—*coup de pied de l'âne*. He remarked that Mayer had supported the Government for six months; with a six months' delay he suddenly discovered that the Government had been liquidating French North Africa and 'betraying France'.

And then came a reference to something with which France was to become even more familiar—on February 6, 1956—the 'pressure of the street', exercised on the French Government by the French of Algeria.

M. René Mayer [Mendès-France said] has referred to foreign telegrams foretelling the kind of disorders in North Africa,

M

which might exercise an influence on our debate here. It is quite true that alarming news reached us; and we promptly took measures to deal with the matter.

And then, with superb irony, Mendès said:

> M. René Mayer then told us that he had advised against these demonstrations (advised whom? he didn't tell us). Anyway, I am grateful to M. René Mayer for having advised against them.

After dealing with the question of the Fezzan, the negotiations with Libya, the protests made by the French Government against camps in Libya where the Tunisian and Algerian fellaghas were being trained; and against the anti-French propaganda on Cairo radio, Mendès-France returned to the René Mayer attack. What was he complaining about? There were, after all, 175,000 French troops in North Africa now; this would have been impossible without the Indo-China settlement. And M. Mayer had thought fit to attack a great writer (Mauriac) who had done no more than denounce the atrocities committed by the French police—atrocities which should be stopped immediately.

Mendès then said that he had appointed Soustelle 'for the highest national motives' which had nothing to do with parliamentary trickery.

Speaking more particularly of Algeria, Mendès-France said he disagreed with the kind of 'priorities' that had been advocated: re-establish order first, then carry out social reforms, finally deal with political reforms. No; the re-establishment of order was inseparable from the rest: no military measure would suffice if, at the same time, political, economic, administrative and social measures were put aside; famine and unemployment were at the root of the problem. France had good reason to be proud of the dams, schools and hospitals in Algeria, which were more impressive than what could be seen in certain Moslem countries only too ready to criticise France; but the question of hunger and poverty had not been properly tackled yet. At the same time, mere budget grants from France for improving conditions in Algeria were not enough; a much broader programme must be considered.

After dealing with Tunisia where, he said, it would have been insane to try to 'negotiate' with mere French stooges who represented nothing, he concluded by referring to the low tricks to which the Opposition were resorting (such as refusing—which was unprece-dented—to grant the Government the *douzième provisoire* for

February[1]) in their endeavour to wear down the Government. And then, in a fine peroration, he said that the Government was pursuing in North Africa the only policy which, it believed, would not lead to disaster.

M. Fonlupt-Espéraber, one of the few members of the MRP who supported Mendès, stressed the soundness of Mendès's point of view: he believed that the reforms should be accompanied by a display of strength; but was against spectacular displays, against police tortures and the arbitrary arrests that were still going on.

M. Mitterrand, the Minister of the Interior, in a long speech, also stressed the panic and *'nervosité'* that were being constantly worked up among the French in Algeria by the French press there.

The debate dragged on into the early hours of the morning. Finally, about 3 o'clock in the morning, Mendès, exasperated more than ever by some of the remarks made by Alfred Coste-Floret, Maurice Schumann and some other MRP members, angrily remarked that it was all very well for the MRP to complain of prisons being crowded in Algeria and Morocco; they might have thought of this in the days when they ran the Government and when the prisons were packed.

In Tunisia in 1953 the prisons were packed; there were 5,000 people in prison then; now there are only a few hundred common criminals. Crowded prisons, my dear colleague—you should have complained about them not to me, but to the governments in which your Party was heavily represented! When the present Government was formed, it found that, in Morocco, too, prisons were packed to an inconceivable extent: mere 'suspects', without any charge against them, had been in prison for three or four years; and we found there some eight-year-old children who had been there for over a year! It was *your* governments that had filled these prisons; it was we who emptied them.

As for Algeria, I do not wish to dwell on certain particularly unpleasant facts already mentioned; but the Government has at least done something to reform the Algerian police, and has decided on the transfer of certain particularly undesirable police officials. And these transfers, let me say in passing, gave rise to some very curious interventions and attempts at wirepulling on the part of certain members of Parliament . . .

And then Mendès recalled that his policy had already saved numerous lives; in Tunisia during the four months before the Tunis visit, 145 people had been killed; in the next four months, 50 people; but between December 15, 1954, and January 31, 1955, the number of

[1] These 'votes on account' are normally passed every month when the year's budget has not yet been agreed upon.

victims of terrorism in the countryside had been : nil; and in the towns, also nil. 'Whatever the outcome of this debate, M. Coste-Floret, these figures will stand.'

He now spoke with much anger and bitterness. The North Africa debate, he said, was only an excuse for overthrowing the Government; but what was tragic was that the unholy coalition of colonialists, and lip-service Liberals and Communists which would overthrow the Government, would damage not only the Government, but France. There was no coalition which could replace the present Government coalition and pursue a salutary policy in North Africa . . .

Well, that was that. And now came the vote. At 4.50 in the morning, M. Schneiter, the President of the Assembly announced, in complete silence, the result of the vote : 273 for the Government, 319 against. There were 27 abstentions. With the silence still continuing, everybody expected M. Mendès-France, followed by his Ministers, to leave the hall, on his way to the Elysée. Much to everybody's surprise, Mendès-France went up the tribune, and started his famous 'farewell speech', unprecedented in the annals of the French Assembly. At first the Assembly listened with a kind of stunned surprise; but soon all hell broke loose. It was when Mendès proceeded to demonstrate that his Government had been different from other governments and that what it had been doing must continue to be done:

What was done in the last seven or eight months, all the things that have been put in motion, will not stop. Men come and go, but national necessities remain.

This 'arrogance' was more than the Assembly could stand. There was a chorus of booing and interruptions from the Communists, the Right and the MRP.

Trying to drown the din by shouting into the microphone, Mendès cried:

How can the nation forget the hopes we have aroused? . . . How can you doubt that the nation has acquired a taste for truth, now that it knows its bitter, but salutary flavour?

The uproar went from bad to worse. M. de Menthon (MRP) announced that this was wholly irregular. Others shouted that this was a violation of the Constitution, that this was Fascism; and that the tribune of the National Assembly was not intended for personal propaganda. The uproar went on for about twenty minutes, with Mendès still trying to read the end of his paper (which he had obviously prepared in advance) in the hope that at least the stenographers would hear him, and so record his final words in the *Journal Officiel*. But he had to give up. The President, more and more bewildered, went on asking Mendès to conclude, or at least to say something about the *douzième provisoire*, as was customary in the circumstances.

Mendès-France: Indeed, I was about to ask the Assembly to meet on Monday to deal with the *douzième provisoire* . . .
M. Bouxom (MRP): Full stop.
Mendès-France: You will excuse me, my dear colleague, it is I who will put the full stop, and not you.

The pandemonium was now indescribable. An infernal din was caused by the banging of desks so that only the stenographers below the tribune could hear more or less Mendès's final words:

I hope that tomorrow, in a better atmosphere, we shall give the country new reasons for hope, and that we may overcome those hatreds of which we have often given such a sorry spectacle to the world. *Vive la France!*

Looking livid with anger, and followed by his Ministers, he at last left the hall, amid loud booing from the Right, and MRP and the Communists, and cheers from the Socialists and a few others.

But even Mendès's best friends were not pleased with this final exit. What had been his motives—was it a bitter resentment against all those culprits of the mess in North Africa who were now daring to attack him and criticize him? Was it a desire to be *different* from anybody else, as he had tried to be throughout his 7½ months in office, so that he should always be remembered as the man who would not take the overthrow of his government as a bit of routine to which France had learned to react with ever-growing indifference?

Men like Lyautey—and in a slightly different way, Clemenceau— had treated the Chamber with such contempt. But Mendès-France? Did he also have an authoritarian streak, which, on that night of his defeat, came out as never before? He clearly wanted it to be remembered that *he* would still be there, if necessary, to save France from the disasters that were threatening her . . . But one thing was certain: he did not make it easy for himself to find political partners in future. For the National Assembly—this one and perhaps even the next—would still remember that fantastic spectacle—'that horrible scene', Mauriac called it—in the early hours of February 5 . . .

CHAPTER 16

AFTER THE FALL

THE reactions to the fall of the Mendès-France Government
were curious to watch. The *Figaro* and a few other Right-wing
papers shed some crocodile tears over Mendès who, as the *Figaro*
put it, 'deserved credit for his attempt to draw the country out of its
political inertia'; but others were more frank, notably in the French
press in Algeria and Morocco. 'Thank God, they've finished off the
brute', one Casablanca paper wrote. Much regret was expressed on the
Left, but, as *Combat* put it, the whole set-up had become 'artificial';
the Mendès Government had lasted three months longer than it would
have done only thanks to Mendès's complete surrender to the United
States over Germany. On the whole, everybody agreed that 'something would remain' of the Mendès 'style' of governing France; but
there were, on the whole, fewer lamentations than abroad. The Communists' first thought was that the Senate might still be induced, now
that Mendès had been overthrown, to reject the ratification of the
Paris Agreements.

The most ferocious attack on the men who brought down Mendès
came from the *Canard Enchaîné*, which spoke of the 'circus': 'How
jubilant they were as they watched the tamer being gobbled up—
gobbled up by René Mayer the python, now sitting there peacefully
digesting his prey'.

And it went on to draw a thumb-nail sketch of René Mayer, *le
tombeur:*

Descendant of the Rothschilds; a high official who, before
the war, held one well-paid job after another; Vice-President of
the *Compagnie des Chemins de Fer du Nord*, and of the *Compagnie
Internationale des Wagons-Lits;* then a director of the State
Railways, and co-founder of Air-France; and of a large number
of financial and industrial companies, both French and foreign
... And then, on June 18, 1940, he happened to be on a government mission in London; but because of the London fog, he did
not hear de Gaulle's appeal, and returned to Vichy France ...
Then, in 1943, he went to North Africa and joined Giraud, from
whom de Gaulle later inherited him ... And, after the war, with
the blessing of M. Borgeaud, the uncrowned kind of Algeria, he
became the *colons'* deputy for Constantine, in Algeria.

178

He belongs to that brilliant association of ex-premiers who have given France the EDC and Dien Bien Phu, and the Tunisian and Madagascar massacres . . . And now he is pining to become Minister of the Interior, so that, under the vigilant eye of M. Borgeaud, he can show Algeria where she gets off . . .

He is right; for since the end of the Indo-China war, France is bored. So let's have a new war in Algeria!

And the *Canard* also had a few digs at certain other Radicals. What, for instance, was M. Edgar Faure doing about it all—the 'faithful Edgar', Mendès's new Foreign Minister? Edgar did not want to take sides; he said he loved both Mendès and Mayer and hoped they would be friends. Which meant, in effect, that he was willing to serve in any new team. Also, he was on the best of terms with M. Coty, the President of the Republic, who had his own ideas about Mendès-France.

M. Coty's chief worry, in fact, is to prevent PMF from becoming a centre of attraction to the Left before the General Election of May 1956, and, meantime, the leader of the Opposition. And the very best way of stopping this is to make Edgar Faure the next Premier, so as to neutralize Mendès . . . For it doesn't really do to criticize too severely so dear a friend. These Normans are cunning old devils . . .

The *Canard* was perfectly right; and it foretold that, after futile attempts by Pinay (Right), by Pflimlin (MRP), and by Pineau (Soc.), to form a government, Edgar Faure would succeed and be the next Premier. Which would be the best way, as already said, of 'neutralizing' Mendès-France for a good long time. And that is precisely what happened.

A very curious document, published the week after the fall of Mendès-France, was an unsigned article in *L'Express* called 'The things he could not say.' If not written by him, the article was, at any rate, obviously inspired by Mendès-France.

Why, the article asked, had the net result of Mendès-France's $7\frac{1}{2}$ months in office been less fruitful than might have been expected? And the answer was that, in all fields, Mendès had met with ca' canny, obstruction and sabotage.

In the case of *Tunisia*, the negotiations had proceeded very slowly because the Radicals had tried to prevent Mendès, while the Gaullists had tried to prevent Fouchet, from having regular talks with Bourguiba, who was interned in France, but who was, in effect, the only man with whom negotiations could be rapidly conducted. The campaign against any talks with Bourguiba was conducted by Martinaud-Déplat, one of the Radical pillars of the North Africa lobby. Further obstruction came from the Gaullists who summoned Fouchet not to negotiate so long as the fellaghas has not surrendered. When these did, new objections were made by Martinaud-Déplat. However, the negotiations with the Tunisians went on, but had been badly delayed by all these manœuvres.

Secondly, there was continuous sabotage of M. Sainteny's mission in *North Vietnam*. Sainteny was negotiating with Vietminh, and the prospects of close economic co-operation between Vietnam and France seemed good. But the old MRP gang, together with the USA, were supporting Diem, and were doing their utmost to sabotage the general election in Vietnam, provided by the Geneva settlement.

Algeria: Rioting broke out on November 1, but within a few days order was restored, and the Government disbanded the MTLD, the principal Algerian nationalist party. The *colons* had really nothing to complain of. However, once order had been restored, Mitterrand embarked on a modest programme of reforms; result: terrific campaign against Mitterrand in the French press in Algeria. One of the great Algerian potentates, Senator Borgeaud, raised such a storm over it that most of the other *colons* joined in the uproar. This reached its climax when Mitterrand announced his intention of amalgamating the Algerian and French police; which meant that the Government could not only transfer police officials from Algiers to Oran, but also from Oran or Algiers to Clermond-Ferrand.

This simple project endangered the whole police organization in the hands of the feudal lords reigning over Algeria. At present, the Minister of the Interior is unable to carry out an enquiry into tortures and other police methods employed in Algeria—if only because certain police officials are in the service of the feudal lords of the North Africa lobby, much more than in the service of the French Government.

Nevertheless, the Government persisted in its plan; but now M. Borgeaud found a staunch ally in Paris, in the person of M. René Mayer, deputy for Constantine; René Mayer launched an ultimatum: 'No changes in Algeria, or I vote against you.' Which he did. In short, Algeria is a territory over which the French Government has no control. It belongs in reality to a group of people who control everything, above all the police. The slightest attempt by the Minister of the Interior to interfere in Algerian affairs comes up against the powerful feudal machine, and its allies in the Paris parliament.

And, finally, what went wrong with Mendès's economic programme?

Reconversion was the principal feature of Mendés's plan. Which meant the modernization or 'reconversion' of French enterprises that could not stand the strain of international competition. It was necessary that France should catch up with the industrial progress of the other industrial countries . . .
Everybody agrees with the idea; and yet nothing much happened. Why? Thanks to the economic euphoria enjoyed during that period by the USA, the feeling developed in France that there was no great hurry to resort to any drastic measures. The Ministry of Finance, under Edgar Faure, decided that it was no use, in the midst of this euphoria, taking long-term measures, however salutary in the long run, which might however cause some short-term 'upsets' . . . Mendès-France, who believes in 'sacrificing the present for the future', was too busy with other things . . . The decrees prepared by the Government were not spectacular, and when they were, the lobbies always came into action. Every lobby—for instance the *betterave* lobby—has its representatives in Parliament and its friends in the Administration . . . Thus, when a meeting was held at the Ministry of Agriculture with a view to reorganizing the sugar-beet 'system', men like M. Cayré (head of the beet growers) and M. Legendre, the 'beet lobby's deputy', were immediately informed and thus were able to prepare their counter-attack. After that, the only thing for the Government to do was to 'negotiate' with them; for these people are sufficiently powerful to command an important number of votes. Sometimes, the Government is reduced to playing off one lobby against a rival lobby—the beet growers against the petrol trade, etc. Although some seemingly revolutionary measures were taken by Mendès-France, especially in the matter of alcohol, it all amounted to very little in actual practice; and when it was learned that he was going to devote himself to economic affairs, the lobbies hastened to turn him out.

A good deal more was to be heard of the Lobbies in the following year. The *betteravier* lobby moved heaven and earth to have the Mendès decrees on alcohol revoked or at least watered down: the *bouilleurs de cru* decrees were toned down, and the North Africa Lobby became more active than ever under the Edgar Faure Government . . .

'*Le gang*' (Mendès remarked in the summer of 1955) '*le gang*' —it's not just this or that lobby; it's not only the *betteraviers*, or

the colonialists—it's an *ensemble,* the whole damned lot of them,
who have become, as it were, part of our system. It isn't only a
case of defending this or that private interest; it's also political;
one of the strongest men working with the lobbies is a man like
Tixier-Vignancour, a real Fascist. He works hand-in-hand with
the Legendres, the Quilicis, and the various other 'lobby deputies', not necessarily in order to help them, but in order to weaken
the whole fabric of our democratic institutions. This Vichyite is
an important person.

I often remembered these words early in 1956 when Tixier-
Vignancour, as Counsel of Baranès, the famous pseudo-Communist
in the *affaire des fuites* trial, made this trial an occasion for insinuating
that the whole Left—from Mendès all the way to the Communists—
had been engaged for years in treasonable activities . . .

PART V

1955:
THE CONQUEST
OF FRANCE THAT FAILED

CHAPTER 1

ENTER EDGAR FAURE

E ARLY in the morning of February 5, 1955, Mendès left the National Assembly a bitter, angry and frustrated man. The last meeting of the National Assembly, when he was howled down and insulted by what he later called 'the zoo' and the 'madhouse', left him with a bad taste in the mouth. He stayed on in Paris for a few days. There was the usual succession of prospective premiers who failed to 'make it'; first Pinay, on the Right, and then Pineau, the Socialist, and Pflimlin, the MRP. Pineau asked Mendès to enter his Government, but Mendès refused, knowing that, in any case, Pineau would fail to get a majority. And then, as all the best tipsters had foretold, it was Edgar Faure who formed the government—a government comprising Robert Schuman and P. H. Teitgen of the MRP (Mendès's most passionate enemy), and various members of the Right—in short, something remarkably like the old Laniel Government . . . with just this difference, that Edgar Faure was a man to be reckoned with. And M. Pinay, the 'small industrialist of St. Chamond'—of all people—was made Foreign Minister.

The best thing Mendès could have done—and he did it—was to go off to Megève for winter sports. For several weeks nothing more was heard of him. Mme. Mendès-France was reported to have said, 'Well, I am very glad, in a way, that he *was* overthrown; now at least I've got him to myself.'

The period between Mendès's overthrow on February 5 and the beginning of the election campaign in December, 1955, may be said to consist of the following main elements, as far as Mendès himself was concerned:

1. His attempt to 'conquer' the Radical Party, and the preparations he was making for conducting a resounding election campaign.

2. His attempt to enforce on Edgar Faure the acceptance of the *scrutin d'arrondissement* which he believed the indispensable weapon for strengthening and 'renovating' the Radical Party.

3. The nation-wide campaign he began to conduct in the summer of 1955, after he had been elected to the head of the Radical Party at the May Congress, where he had announced

that the Radical Party must have an election 'platform' in the British sense.

4. His furious clash with Edgar Faure at the November Congress, followed, a month later, by his final breach with Faure and the split in the Radical Party, from which, by hook or by crook, Mendès simply eliminated the 'old gang', and thereupon formed an election alliance with the Socialists.

5. The *mendésiste* campaign—with special emphasis on Algeria—which began to be conducted on a large scale by *L'Express*, after it had become a daily paper on October 13, 1955.

This enumeration of the main elements of which Mendès-France's activity in 1955 was composed, suggests perhaps that during this period Mendès-France was in a state of feverish activity. But in reality that was not the case; and that is the strangest and most frustrating aspect of this period in Mendès's life—particularly of the period between his overthrow in February, 1955, and the beginning of the *Express* campaign in October. The truth is that, during the greater part of this period, Mendès was *reduced to silence*—for the very simple reason that his Radical colleague, Edgar Faure, was Prime Minister. He was about the only possible Premier whom it was exceedingly difficult for Mendès to attack: and the cunning President Coty—who, long before Mendès had been overthrown, had already decided that Faure was to be the next Premier—knew it. The abortive Pinay, Pineau and Pflimlin 'premierships' were merely so much window-dressing . . . For it would have been awkward to call on Faure rightaway.

Aware of the popularity of the 'Mendès style', Faure tried to give the impression—even though he was head of a Right-Centre Government—that he was somehow following in Mendès's footsteps. On one occasion—over Morocco—he even adopted Mendès's famous 'deadline' technique—though wholly unsuccessfully.

But, apart from North Africa, Edgar Faure was remarkably lucky. Economic conditions were reasonably good, and he hastened, almost as soon as he had formed the Government, to make a number of concessions to small shopkeepers so as to cut the ground from under the feet of the Poujade movement which was showing signs of becoming dangerously popular among wide sections of the population—though, at that stage, still chiefly for fiscal, rather than for any major political reasons. Internationally, all seemed to be going well. Without much difficulty, Faure got the Senate to ratify the Paris Agreements, and the feeling grew in the country that the question of German rearmament no longer mattered very much, with H-bombs accumulating on both sides of the curtain. *La question est dépassée*, was a phrase with which many former enemies of German rearmament were consoling themselves. Moreover, the Russians had become almost unrecognizable.

The Summit Conference at Geneva was in the offing; the Russians, far from carrying out any of the dark threats they had uttered before the Paris Agreements were ratified, were now more forthcoming and friendly than before. They carried out, to Dulles's dismay, the neutralization of Austria; they apologized to Tito, and declared, in short, that they wanted to be friends with everybody. At heart, Mendès must have felt that fate was being unkind to him; why should life have been so hard for him in 1954 and the first few weeks of 1955, and why should it be so easy for Edgar Faure; and why should Edgar Faure and Pinay (who had been made Foreign Minister merely in virtue of some shabby parliamentary *dosage*) now be talking like equals to Eisenhower, and Eden, and Bulganin?

However, there was a big fly even in Edgar Faure's ointment; and that was North Africa. No doubt, there was still not much to worry about until June. But from June onwards, the situation in Morocco grew more and more critical every day . . .

This whole period cannot be dealt with without a close examination of what was happening in Tunisia, Algeria and Morocco—especially Morocco which created, at one stage, an altogether unprecedented situation for the Faure Government, when the French generals on the spot broke into open rebellion against the government of the French Republic.

All the discussions on North Africa during that period were, in one way or another, mixed up with Mendès-France, even though he took at first very little part in the discussions himself. But his Tunis Journey of July 31 the year before was considered the beginning of it all, both by those who saw in it the beginning of a constructive policy which might save North Africa for France, and by those to whom it was 'the beginning of the end'. Highly characteristic of the manner in which the 'policy of surrender' was invariably attributed to Mendès-France, was the haste with which the diehards denounced M. Gilbert Grandval, when Faure appointed him Resident-General to Morocco in July, 1955, as 'Mendès-France's nominee'.

I shall deal later with this truly astounding episode, in which the Resident-General of France was all but lynched by the French diehards of Morocco.

Edgar Faure tried throughout to reconcile the irreconcilables: to appear to be *mendésiste*, and to pursue a policy which would be acceptable to his Right-wing partners.

The field in which he 'continued' the work of Mendès was Tunisia. Here the negotiations on the Conventions, already prepared in the days of Mendès, took their course, and after several months these Conventions were signed, and then ratified by Parliament by a large majority. It was as if the Right had decided to surrender the smallest of the three North African countries to the *mendésiste* wolves—but be, as against this, more determined than ever to hang on to Morocco and Algeria.

But when it came to the crucial question of Morocco, Faure showed more clearly than ever before how 'compromise' between all kinds of irreconcilables was what he believed in; and it just didn't work.

I must recall here a conversation with Mendès-France in the summer of 1955. After recollecting his early days at the *Faculté de Droit*, where he first met Edgar Faure, and the journey they made together to Russia in 1932, and their wartime association, Mendès said:

'You see, the fundamental difference between me and Faure is this: I approach every problem with some theoretical basis to it; Faure's approach is purely and exclusively empirical.'

'You mean,' I said, 'that you believe in something, and that Faure really believes in nothing?'

Mendès smiled. 'Well, yes, that's one way of putting it. Faure does not like anything clear-cut; he does not like drastic action, prompted by some hard-and-fast principle. Take, for instance, this question of alcohol. I must say that I really put the fear of death into all these gangsters and racketeers. Not Faure; he is always willing to 'negotiate' with anybody, so that nobody is made unhappy. He believes in slowing things down, in going easy, in hurting nobody. Therefore, the moment my Government was overthrown, he began to tone down my anti-alcohol decrees, because so-and-so thought they were "excessive", and so on. The lobbies have their people planted pretty well anywhere; well, I happen to know that one of Faure's close associates went to see him and said it would be ever so much better, if only in the name of Right-wing support at the National Assembly, he (Faure) came to some kind of agreement with the *betteraviers*. "*Il faut faire un accord avec ces gens*", he would say. But the trouble is that if you compromise with all and sundry, and make little concessions and render little services here, there and everywhere, you really don't get anything serious done at all.'

There was a good deal of this technique of give-and-take, and 'little services' and 'little concessions' in Faure's management of his Government's affairs. As *France-Observateur* wrote on one occasion, in July, 1955, 'the peculiarity of Faure is that he is scarcely ever *personally* attacked by anybody. He asks people to nice lunches, and renders them all sorts of little services, and is personally liked.' It was quite true; he wasn't disliked even by the Communists. There would even be an occasional spot of *badinage* and good-natured leg-pulling in the Chamber lobbies between him and Duclos. All of which really amounts to saying that Edgar Faure had, to an extraordinary degree, managed to revive some of the old *République des Comarades* spirit of the better days of the Third Republic.

The truth is that while Mendès was acutely disliked and, indeed, hated by hundreds of his fellow-deputies, Edgar Faure was scarcely hated by anybody. Also, he was an 'intellectual', rather than a business-man or an economic theorist, and, unlike Mendès-France, he had his hobby—his *violon d'Ingres*—which was to write detective stories. He also had another hobby—reading and talking Russian. Altogether, he had an amiable human side which Mendès lacked . . . And, after all, even the extreme Left—the Communists and *progressistes*—liked to think that he couldn't, after all, be such a bad chap if he was so attached to his wife Lucie, who was editor of the NEF and whose *salon* was awfully 'fellow-travellerish' and very *Saint-Germain-des-Prés*, and one of her dearest friends was Roger Stéphane, who wrote lyrical books in praise of homosexuality, besides getting into hot water for publishing military 'secrets' on Indo-China in *France-Observateur*.

Faure, in short, appeared to be a genial cynic who took nothing desperately seriously; who was quite capable of presiding over a Left Government just as easily as over a Right one; who liked to consider himself—which, indeed, he was—a very able economic and financial technician, but one who preferred to do things without upsetting any apple-carts, and without treading on too many toes . . . He liked to say that he could do all this *mendésiste* stuff in a quiet and leisurely way, without having to strike revolutionary poses.

This attitude had, of course, its pros and cons; in the end, he got rather less done than Mendès; but his parliamentary position was always a much sounder one—which is not perhaps the best possible recommendation, when one considers that, of all the Governments of the 1951 Parliament, it was the disastrously inept Government of M. Laniel which lasted longest!

In short, as Mendès put it, Faure had an 'empirical' approach to things. And, during the first months of his 1955 Government, every-thing seemed to be going reasonably well in all fields; the Tunisian negotiations were progressing; Soustelle *seemed* to have struck a happy medium between liberalism and firmness in Algeria; Morocco had not yet blown up in a very big way; Russia was more peaceful than she

N

had been for years; economic conditions inside France were fairly good (it wasn't till August that Mendès came out with a statement to show that they weren't quite as good as Faure tried to imagine); and there was really very little that Mendès could do to prove to French opinion that he would be a much better man to have at the head of the Government than Edgar Faure. So for some time, he had to confine himself to a task which he considered essential in terms of the future: the reorganization of the Radical Party and preparing for the next General Election. To this he attached the utmost importance; for only after the General Election, he thought, would France have a chance of 'renewing herself'.

CHAPTER 2

CONQUERING THE RADICAL PARTY IS NOT ENOUGH

MENDÈS'S chances were not necessarily good. He liked to think of himself as a sort of Left-wing de Gaulle; but the analogy was an artificial one. It was, for one thing, difficult to imagine Mendès-France starting anything in the nature of a *rassemblement*, like the Gaullist RPF. De Gaulle, in 1947, appealed to what one observer has called 'a Boulangist mob', whereas Mendès could only appeal to a Republican electorate. That is to say, he was *nothing* without the Socialist Party and the traditional Socialist electorate; and the Socialist Party were certainly never in any mood to become dissolved in a sort of Left-wing RPF, with Mendès-France as its leader.

On the other hand, the Radicals—or most of them—were unwilling to drop the time-honoured routine of the Radical Party, with all their traditions, their committees and their *notables;* for the Radical Party is, first and foremost, a party of *notables*. And the joke of it was, of course, that, despite his aloofness and his apparent contempt for the old fogeys of the Radical Party, Mendès himself was a Radical who could, somehow, never really see himself acting independently of the Radical Party, a kind of life-belt to which he had clung all his life.

And when it came to talking of a true *politique de gauche*, the very awkward question arose of how this could be pursued *without* the 5 million Communist voters . . .

Another awkward question was this: what was the Radical Party without Edgar Faure, the head of the Government? Later Mendès tried to show that it could manage perfectly well without him; but even when Faure was called upon by President Coty to form his Government in February, 1955, Mendès had still hoped that he would refuse. 'You and I', he said, 'form a tandem—a very strong team. We can be powerful if we get the Socialist vote; since you can't get it, your alternative is to form a government with the MRP and all those monsters of Dien Bien Phu; better say no, and the future will be ours.' But Faure, feeling that on a Faure-Mendès 'tandem' he would always have the back seat, declined Mendès's offer. 'Sacrificing a long political and personal friendship, Edgar Faure chose the road that Paul Reynaud had mapped out for him.'[1]

[1] Claude Estier in *France-Observateur*, May 24, 1955.

Mendès was, in the circumstances, in an awkward spot, and he knew that it would not be easy for him to gain control of the Radical Party. With Edgar Faure having turned his back on him, the outlook was very different from what it had been only three months before. At the Radical Congress at the *cinéma Rex* at Marseilles in October, 1954, Edouard Herriot had cried: 'This is the Congress of Mendès-France. *Devant lui j'incline ma personne et mon passé. Je lui confie le Parti.*' 'My person and my past bow to him. I entrust him with the Party.' Quite a sublime moment, in the grand declamatory style of the heroic days of the Third Republic. And Emile Roche—that strange hybrid animal who combined a verbal *mendésisme* with the function of leader of the Moroccan Lobby (for he was one of the most influential men in the *Présence Française* in Morocco) said that Mendès's speech at the Marseilles Congress should be adopted as 'the traditional declaration of the Party, since nobody and nothing could improve on it!'

Yet three months later, on the morning of February 5, 24 Radicals —or one-third of the Radicals at the Assembly—voted against Mendès and so greatly contributed to his overthrow. And then, on February 23, only seven Radicals followed Mendès-France in abstaining in the vote investing the Edgar Faure Government. Such rapid changes are surprising, but not in the Radical Party, the most opportunist, the most weathercock party in France.

As Mendès looked back on his great apotheosis of the Marseilles Congress, he knew that the Radical unanimity behind him had been merely a façade. He was popular in the country then; and he could have twisted the Party round his finger. One word from him, and he could have got Martinaud-Déplat deprived of his post as Administrative President of the Party. But he had his moments of hesitation; Mendès had, indeed, an appalling weakness, which many have pointed out: he has always tried to make friends with his enemies.

It was even whispered that he was slightly scared: Martinaud-Déplat knew a few things about Mendès—and had raked up a few indiscreet odds and ends from the past which, if brought out, might harm him with the Americans. It was better, on the eve of the Washington visit, to let sleeping dogs lie; and not have Daladier elected in Martinaud-Déplat's place: for Daladier, though, by and large, a *mendésiste*, was against the ratification of the Paris Agreements, and if Mendès patronized him, it would make a bad impression in Washington... And so Martinaud-Déplat, member of the North Africa Lobby and a 'neo-Radical' of the McCarthyite variety, was left in charge of the administrative apparatus of the Radical Party. During the weeks that followed the Marseilles Congress, Martinaud-Déplat—though backed at the Congress by only 60 mandates out of the 1900—patiently and silently worked for Mendès's overthrow; for he had not forgiven him—and never would forgive him—that Tunis visit.

During March and April Mendès and his followers were asking that an Extraordinary Congress of the Party take place soon, at which the 'traitors'—who had stabbed Mendès in the back—would be punished. There were few wholeheartedly *mendésiste* federations. On the whole, in the spring of 1955, most of them were *fauriste* rather than *mendésiste*, displaying Faure posters rather then Mendès posters.

Although it did not look as though Mendès had any very wide support in the country, or, at any rate, among the Radical Federations, Martinaud-Déplat was not at all pleased at the clamour for a Radical Congress. And here was a typical example of the kind of hanky-panky of which a dyed-in-the-wool reactionary like Martinaud-Déplat was capable of. When as Administrative President, it fell to his lot to look for a place where the Congress could be held, he discovered that the Salle Wagram in Paris would be free all day on May 2 and 3; but that it would be free only till 6 p.m. on May 4—after which it was booked for a boxing match. So he promptly booked the place on May 4, so as to cut the discussion short. Which meant, as one paper put it, that 'Mendès-France will only have 2½ hours in which to carry out his *coup d'état*.'

M. Herriot was furious when he heard of this piece of trickery from the Administrative President of the Radical Party, and agreed to withdraw his resignation as President of the Party only if Martinaud-Déplat promised that 'all problems would be discussed that had arisen since the fall of the Mendès-France Government.' In the end, Martinaud-Déplat had to give way, and it was decided that time would not be limited and that, after clearing out of the Wagram at 6 o'clock, the Extraordinary Congress would continue its discussions at the Mutualité, a hall on the other side of the Seine.

This Extraordinary Congress was certainly one of the most violent the Radical Party had known. There was no doubt about it: it was a duel between Mendès and Martinaud-Déplat, between two policies, two temperaments, two traditions. Mendès, on this occasion, was so incensed by Martinaud-Déplat that, in the opinion of many impartial observers, he did not even shun a little trickery himself by having Martinaud-Déplat's post as Administrative President abolished on a show of hands, instead of going through the procedure of a regular vote by mandates. But then, it must be said, there had been so much trickery in the past with these mandates that they were no more reliable a yardstick than a show of hands at a Congress of this kind. The Congress, in the same way, decided on the 'reorganization' of the Party, and a directorate of Seven was appointed, with Mendès-France at its head. It *was* a little *coup d'état*—even though the powers of the directorate—called Action Committee—were rather smaller than what Mendès had hoped for.

The significance of this Radical Congress was considerable: it really meant a clash between two conceptions; that of a Party of *notables*, controlled by a small general staff in Paris, and that of a much more 'democratic' party, capable of being swayed by a strong personality towards the Right or the Left. The trouble with the Radical Party, of course, was (and this became particularly apparent when the Party split in December, 1955) that it was, by its very position in French political life, a Centre party; in some departments it found it profitable to be allied with the Socialists, in others it found it more advantageous to be allied with the MRP or the Right. Mendès was acutely aware of this; and one of the first things he did, at the Congress of May 4, was to obtain (by a narrow majority, it is true) that the 'reorganization of the Party' be included in the agenda.

M. Herriot, Life President, gave Mendès some support. He obviously liked Mendès, and hoped that he would put new life into the Party, which ought to be Left, rather than Right:

> It must remain a people's party. Even if certain coalitions are sometimes necessary, I do not think that it is our business to defend certain vested interests, which can do very well without us ... I am a man of the people, and my heart is with the least fortunate and most long-suffering part of our people. The Radical Party has a greater mission before it than ever it had.

However, having said that the Radical Party must be a party of the Left, he concluded, in the best fatherly manner, that he hoped all Radicals would be friends and brethren. Which was asking rather a lot from Mendès and Martinaud-Déplat.

It was certainly a stormy affair. There could be little doubt that the majority of the delegates at the Congress were Mendès men. An Algerian delegate, who started a speech by paying compliments to M. René Mayer, was howled down, and dozens of whistles were blown from all over the hall. On another occasion a bunch of young men in the gallery—they were not delegates, but 'public' (it was said that Martinaud-Déplat, just like Mendès, had his particular 'commandos' in the hall) greeted the appearance of Mendès on the platform with loud shouts of '*A bas les Juifs!*' Booing, cheering, the blowing of whistles took up a good part of the time at the Congress.

Mendès-France who rose to speak amidst a tempest of cheering and
booing, began by saying that the Party was dominated by a bunch of
bureaucrats and that this Congress—though 'the immense majority of
of the *militants* had been clamouring for it'—would never have taken
place at all, but for the insistent demands made by M. Herriot. Several
provincial delegates, he declared, had been prevented by Martinaud-
Déplat from entering the hall, and there was clearly a total lack of
harmony and understanding between the *militants* and the leaders. It
was essential, he said, that the Party's propaganda be developed, that
the inner organization of the Party be changed, and that it became
clearly a Party of the Left. This last remark was greeted with a storm
of applause.

> We must remake a party doctrine; what we need for the
> election is not a shop sign, but a proper election platform, with
> half-a-dozen basic ideas, definite commitments, and a time-
> table . . .

After saying that the young people of France would not follow the
Radicals if they continued to be a Party of '*vieilles barbes*', Mendès
concluded:

> Some have spoken of the Communist danger and of a new
> Popular Front. I want to avoid both. But we shall only play into
> the hands of Communism if we persist in our political errors and
> practise social conservatism. A will for renewal has been aroused
> among the young people of France; it *is for the Radical Party to
> become a centre of attraction to the young generation* . . .

There was loud cheering; and when Martinaud-Déplat rose to
speak, all hell broke loose. From all over the hall came cries of 'Resign!
Resign!' Finally he was able to speak—'looking like a toad', one reporter described him, 'and spitting venom'. The gist of his argument
was that it was much more advantageous for the Radical Party to be
a doublefaced Janus, and not a monolithic Party like the CP; because
the Radical Party represented all the variety of France. There could
be no common doctrine; for what were you to say to people if they
asked 'What do you think of German rearmament—do you agree
with Delbos, or with Daladier, with Herriot or with Queuille?' And
then he exclaimed, as tragically as he could: 'Are we to ally ourselves
with the Communists, and suffer the tragedy of Prague?' And he ended
with a nasty little dig at Mendès, whom he reminded of the fact that,
in the Eure there was not *one*, but there were *three* Radical deputies,
thanks to their *apparentements* with the Right!

In the evening the discussion was resumed at the Mutualité, where

the first thing Mendès did was to call upon Martinaud-Déplat to resign voluntarily, in the name of the Party's unity, his post as Administrative President. (Roars of delight from Mendès's followers, howls
of rage from the others.) Then roars of rage came from Mendès's
followers when Martinaud-Déplat, recalling the services he had rendered to the Party, concluded with a great display of pathos: 'For
seven years I have worked for you! And it is I whom you now want to
strike down!'

A conciliatory note was brought in by a brief statement from M.
Faure, who paid compliments to Mendès, and said that his action as
Premier had been the best 'propaganda' for the Radical Party; it was
also by belonging to *every* Government, whether Right or Left, that
the Radicals were serving the country.

The clash was between two conceptions of that Radical Party which,
in the past, had produced men so different as Clemenceau, Caillaux,
Herriot, Daladier and Bonnet: that of the 'hinge' party, for which
there was a place in almost *any* coalition; and that of an essentially
Left party.

In the end, in the midst of appalling confusion, there was a clash
over the method by which the Doubs motion (supporting the Mendès
line) could be voted. Herriot—possibly with his tongue in his cheek,
for all his 83 years—said that those favouring the vote by mandate had
the Party regulations to support them; but those favouring a vote by a
show of hands had speed and common sense on their side. At this
point Martinaud-Déplat, bursting with rage, picked up his papers and
left the hall. On a show of hands the Doubs motion was passed—and
Herriot declared that it was carried. Martinaud-Déplat later said the
whole thing was a swindle and a double-cross; and M. Lafargue said
it was a 'real political *coup d'état*'. But Herriot had, after all, given the
somewhat dubious procedure his blessing.

On the following day the *Dépêche du Midi* of Toulouse said it
didn't matter very much; if Martinaud-Déplat wasn't quite regularly
turned out of his job in Paris, he was, at least just as irregularly, maintained in his job at Marseilles six months before.[1]

---

[1] What had always given rise to much hanky-panky at Radical Congresses was
the strange machinery whereby the Radical headquarters in the Place Valois in
Paris sold membership cards at 300 francs each, at their demand, to the local
Federations. These then sold them to *bona fide* members. But the Place Valois had
to take the Federations' word for it that they *were*, indeed, *bona fide* members. The
trafficking in membership cards in cafés adjoining a Radical Congress when, for
the purpose of influencing some particular vote, membership cards were 'sold' to
all sorts of strange characters, has been a time-honoured custom in Radical
politics. M. Martinaud-Déplat is said to be by no means the only virtuoso at this
game.

The fact remains that it was during this Extraordinary Congress of May 4 that Mendès made his first major bid to conquer the Radical Party.

But did the Radical Party really lend itself to 'conquest'? Many careful observers had the impression, even after the little *coup d'état* of May 4 that Mendès-France was biting off more than he could chew. Thus, M. Jacques Fauvet, a leading authority on French party politics, wrote in the *Monde* soon after the Congress:

> M. Martinaud-Déplat was wrong about many things, but he was right about a few others. He was accused of having neglected the propaganda of the Party. But that, surely, overlooks two conditions underlying any effective propaganda campaign: namely, the existence of a doctrine at the top, and the existence of a great deal of genuine devotion at the base . . . In recent years there has never been anything even approaching a Radical 'doctrine' . . . For one thing, on foreign policy, the leaders were sharply divided.
>
> In the past, too, it is true, the Radical Party was never a united Party; neither in the days of Clemenceau and Caillaux; nor in the days of 'the two Edouards' [Herriot and Daladier]. M. Herriot, chiefly owing to his old age, had to leave the party, more and more, in the hands of its administrative president, Martinaud-Déplat. It was only a question of time before a sufficiently strong new personality emerged, who would inevitably clash with Martinaud-Déplat. Mendès-France is the man.
>
> M. Mendès-France errs on the side of wishful thinking, if he imagines that there can be a rapid Radical revival. Without a thorough renewal of all the *cadres*, he will have to cope with the inertia of the party machine, the absence of any real organization at the base, and the various 'vested interest' millstones—to which both Herriot and Daladier alluded.

Fauvet here touched on one of the most important aspects of the Radical Party—its dependence on 'subsidies'; and it was very significant that the Treasurer of the Party should have resigned at the same time as M. Martinaud-Déplat.

> But, despite his popularity among so many of the younger people, Mendès will have neither much time, nor much money (in view of what has happened) to remould the Party before the General Election.

This was a gloomy forecast, made all the gloomier when in retrospect one considers that the General Election was not held (as was thought at the time) in June, 1956, but in January, 1956.

Fauvet thought Martinaud-Déplat quite wrong to treat Mendès-France as the maker of a new Popular Front—a Popular Front which, he said, could only result in a 'Prague situation'; one only had to read the comments on Mendès in *Humanité* to see that nothing was further from the truth.

Naturally, what Mendès was trying to do was, above all, to come to an agreement with the Socialists; and (said Fauvet) the creation of such a 'dynamic Left-wing bloc' outside the CP was something that was bound to give the Communists bad dreams: hence their hostility to Mendès.

But, on the other hand, there would be, at least for a long time, a hankering among many Radicals to 'look both ways'; Edgar Faure represented that 'moderate' Right-wing tendency. His attitude, on the whole, should not be confused with that of Martinaud-Déplat and the like of him, who stood for the *status quo* in all fields; whether at the Radical headquarters in the Place Valois, in Indo-China or in North Africa. Since medicine had failed to cure the Radical Party (Fauvet argued) Mendès had resorted to surgery—with a technique reminiscent of his premiership.

That was all very well; but now came the time to build a new Radical Party; and that was where Mendès's troubles started.

For one thing, where was Mendès going to get the money? The truth, of course, was that the money—which every Party needs—came, in the case of the Radical Party, not from an unenthusiastic and almost non-existent army of *militants*, but from big business, and, above all, from the Radical Federations in North Africa, and Algeria in particular. Just as the French in Morocco were predominantly Vichyite, and those in Tunisia Gaullist, so the French Big Bosses in Algeria were 'Radicals'—but Radicals of the René Mayer and Martinaud-Déplat school of thought. One of the richest and most powerful men in Algeria, who virtually controlled the police and the administration, was Senator Borgeaud; and as *France-Observateur* wrote on May 12, 1955—

> The war-chest in the Place de Valois is filled from North Africa, and it is hard to see Borgeaud supplying money to Mendès-France. Anyway, what was this money used for? Unlike other Parties, the Radical Party does not subsidize any press in a big way, and most of the Radical papers, like the *Dépêche* of Toulouse, are prosperous, anyway. As for propaganda, Martinaud himself admitted that the Radical Party hardly went in for any. So the truth is that most of the Radical money goes into something else, namely the Lobbies . . . And it mightn't be such a bad thing, after all, if Mendès-France stopped this flow of money into the Lobbies, particularly the North Africa Lobby.

The relationship created between Mendès-France and Faure after Mendès's little *coup d'état* of May 4 was a curious one. It had an historical analogy in January, 1936, when, after the fall of the Laval Government a Right-Centre Government under the Radical Albert Sarraut was formed (with P. E. Flandin as his Foreign Minister); at the same time other Radicals—notably Daladier, Cot, Zay, etc.— were preparing to enter the Popular Front Government which was to emerge from the May, 1936, elections.

Except that Mendès was not going to be allied to the Communists, but only to the Socialists, the situation was similar: the Radical Party was, as it were, riding two horses all at once—not a very comfortable seat. And while Faure was reassuring his Right-wing colleagues that he was all in favour of retaining the *apparentements* system, which had benefited the Radicals, the MRP and the Right in 1951, so Mendès was agitating for an alliance with the Socialists and for the *scrutin d'arrondissement* which, in his view, would knock out the Communists almost completely.

Mendès, at that time, was hoping to draw up a precise election platform which would be more or less acceptable to the Socialists. For one thing, he was extremely North-Africa-conscious: he could always argue that his 'Tunisian trick' had worked admirably—for in Tunisia alone there was peace and quiet. In Morocco things were going from bad to worse, and there might soon be a major explosion there; while, in Algeria, the Aurès rebellion was continuing to smoulder.

The Socialists, for their part, while generally sympathetic to Mendès-France, did not feel like letting him play first fiddle in all circumstances. The leaders were, in fact, somewhat disturbed by the great popularity of Mendès among the Socialist rank-and-file, and particularly among the younger people—who were more numerous, for one thing, than the enthusiastic young 'Jacobins' who made a lot of pro-Mendès noises at Radical Congresses and other gatherings. Also, the Socialist rank-and-file, and, indeed, a large number of Socialist deputies greatly admired Mendès, and had followed him almost blindly during his premiership. The Socialist leadership thought that they should show a little more initiative themselves in future.

It was thus that in the early summer of 1955 M. Christian Pineau, noted for his strong support of EDC, the Atlantic Pact, and European-ism in the past, set up a predominantly Socialist 'brains trust', called *Comité d'Etudes pour la République*. This comprised several SFIO deputies—Gazier, Tanguy-Prigent, Lacoste, Savary, Jacquet, Defferre and Verdier (most of these were, indeed, to become Ministers in the Guy Mollet Government of January, 1956); a number of technicians, like M. Marjolin, formerly Secretary-General of OEEC; a number of Socialist (*Force Ouvrière*) trade union officials; a member of the 'Socialist Movement for the United States of Europe', a notable Radical, and a future member of the Mollet Government, M. Maurice Faure; and a few more-or-less Left-wing members of the MRP, such as M. Lecourt, M. Joseph Dumas, etc. Mendès-France was also invited; he accepted the invitation, but showed no hurry to attend the meetings of the Socialist brains trust.

CHAPTER 3

MENDÈS ASKS
'WHAT'S WRONG WITH FRANCE?'

DESPITE his February defeat, Mendès did not consider himself beaten; far from it. He was busy working on that election programme—or rather, platform—which he was going to submit to the Radical Congress in November. Meantime, he went on a tour around various towns in Eastern France, and he became pleasantly conscious of the fact that his name was a very big draw. At Strasbourg, at St. Dié, at Colmar—that is, even in cities with no strong Radical influence—his name was enough to produce overflow meetings. There hadn't been anything quite like it since the de Gaulle rallies some years before . . .

In the course of those meetings in Alsace and Lorraine, Mendès went over an enormous amount of ground. At Strasbourg, after recalling that he had spent many happy days in this city with his mother's family—a 'family which was cruelly decimated during the last war'— he spoke of the international situation.

He spoke of the *détente* that was characteristic of that summer of 1955—that summer of the Austrian settlement, of the Russian visit to Belgrade, of the Summit Conference at Geneva, etc. Needless to say, Mendès made the most of the part he had played in 1954 in creating the present *détente:* he had put an end to the Indo-China war. Mendès also congratulated himself on having brought about the ratification of the Paris Agreements—which was the only possible solution in view of the Russian attitude. It had made Russia's attitude not more hostile and uncompromising, but less. In short, if there was a better atmosphere in the world in 1955 than in 1954, it was thanks to the Geneva Agreement and the great organization of European defence.

Then came a typical Mendès reflection—in fact the kind of line of argument that Pineau, Mollet's Foreign Minister, was to adopt with so much effect in March, 1956:

The trouble now was that the *détente* had been created by the Russians, and that the Western Powers were silent, and were not

201

proposing anything. They should press for a constructive disarmament agreement, for one thing . . .

On the organization of 'Europe', Mendès was rather cautious and
already used many of the arguments he was to use against the Common
Market in his famous speech in January, 1957. He said he believed in
supra-national schemes, but it would be quixotic to open all frontiers
in Europe to labour and commodities; France would be the first to
be swamped. If 'Europe' was to be developed, it was essential for
France to become much stronger in the competitive field.

It is highly significant that already then, in the summer of 1955,
the audience—even at Strasbourg—should have been particularly conscious of the danger to France coming from North Africa. Most of the
questions put to Mendès at Strasbourg concerned North Africa. He
expressed strong views on the subject—views in the defence of which
he was to come into such sharp conflicts with his Socialist colleagues
in 1956:

> It is only too customary, when the North Africans make
> demands on us, to say: 'We shall not yield to force; we shall
> agree to reforms only once order has been re-established'. We
> have heard this kind of thing only too often. And so time has
> been allowed to pass, without anything having been done . . .
> In fact, we have never seen any policy, other than a policy of
> brute force, applied to these countries . . . No doubt there are
> cases when it cannot be helped. I have used force myself . . . But
> force never provides a real solution . . .
> We have brought up these people to believe in the principles
> of 1789, but we have constantly refused them the benefit of these
> noble traditions . . . We must have the courage to see that there
> can be no common future for us and the Moslems, except on a
> basis of voluntary understanding . . .
> Tunisia had been promised freedom, internal autonomy, even
> independence ever since 1950; but in practice, is was nothing but
> repression and more repression; in 1952 in a small country like
> Tunisia, there were 5,000 people in prison—often without any
> charge, and wholly arbitrarily.
> We lied to the Tunisians, we lied to the Algerians. And when
> we now propose to apply the *Statut d'Algérie*—a law passed in
> 1947—we are treated almost as revolutionaries! Yet the *Statut
> d'Algérie* is a law which must be applied fully, no matter what
> opposition may come from certain administrative groups and
> certain vested interests and lobbies. But Algeria is also an
> economic problem—and there are hundreds of thousands of
> hectares which could be irrigated for the benefit of millions of
> starving people . . .

He also talked at great length of a constructive economic policy in France, of productive investments, reconversion of industries, the development of French export markets, etc.

Production must be guided; it must not be at the mercy of old habits, of vested interests; it must be determined by real needs. In my little town of Louviers, the people have worked in the textile industry from time immemorial. It is a depressed industry: many work only 30 or 36 hours a week, and some are totally unemployed. If we take no precaution, if we don't warn them, they may well train their children to be textile workers ... Yet it would be a great mistake, since there are other industries with far better prospects of expansion ... Notably housing ...

He talked about housing, the modernization of agriculture, complete with lessons to be learned from Holland and Denmark, and a programme for training skilled labour. He quoted facts, figures, projects, plans, possibilities, with great knowledge and self-assurance. Everywhere he made a big impression: here was a man who thought in terms of turning France into a thoroughly up-to-date modern industrial country ... And yet, as against all these 'openings', 'possibilities', had to be put 'bad French habits', 'economic routine', 'vested interests', etc. And in Parliament, alas! there never seemed to be a constructive majority which could carry out 'a coherent, bold, and long-term economic policy'. In short, it was up to the electorate to return such a majority ...

Mendès tended to treat the Radical Congress of May 4 as a sort of turning-point in the history of France ... France was waking up; France was growing tired of political inefficiency, of all kinds of intolerable privileges, of triumphant—and well-protected—vested interests; she was tired of big blustering talk, followed by military disasters like Dien Bien Phu; and it was for the Radical Party—that old, despised Radical Party—to take a leading part in the *redressement* of France. There must be a live contact between the top of the Party and the rank-and-file; it was horrifying to think, said Mendès, that on the morning of May 4, a very large minority of the presidents and secretaries of Federations should still have been against any changes in the organization of the Party, and in favour of maintaining the *status quo*. It was a horribly rowdy Congress, Mendès said, but was it to be wondered at? The young people there were anxious, angry, furious at the thought that nothing might be changed.

And Mendès concluded by saying that 'the people of France' were telling the Radical Party what to do. The people of France had approved the decisions of the Congress of May 4. Thousands of new members had joined the Radical Party.

> Since May 4, not a single member of the Radical Party—not one—has resigned. But thousands of new members have joined. Every day, in the Place Valois, we receive new applications from all over the place . . . And the same happens in the offices of the local Federations. But this big mail that comes every day to the Place Valois—though a small thing in itself—is a reflection of the mood in the country. I made enquiries: in the past, applications did not come to the Place Valois by hundreds and by thousands. In the past it happened once, or perhaps twice a week for somebody to write a letter with some kind of enquiry, or a request for a brochure; what is happening now has never been seen before!

Here again, was something that was—at least slightly—reminiscent of de Gaulle. Mendès attached great importance to these applications for membership in the Radical Party. He felt that he had started some kind of mass movement. Was it only an optical illusion? What chance was there of a great *mendésiste* movement developing in France?

Although Mendès made great capital out of the flow of membership applications, these were not perhaps as spectacular as he had made out in his speech at Colmar; but they suggested, all the same that the Radical Party was, thanks to Mendès, at last beginning to gain some public support. There were about 100 applications a day: it wasn't much; but still, it was incomparably more than the total lack of such applications before Mendès had started 'reforming' the Party.

At last, after completing his various propaganda tours in the East and West of France, Mendès returned to his beloved Eure towards the end of July. His big speech at Evreux on July 23 was the most 'philosophical' he had yet made; it provided for a far-reaching reform of the State, and constituted a fundamental criticism of French Democracy as it was now working—or failing to work.

> True democracy, he said, is the intimate association, the fusion of the State and the citizen. But, in France, the citizen and the State have turned their backs on one another.

Voting Communist, he argued, was a form of 'abstention'. No doubt, there were some perfectly sincere Communists, who believed in the Communist doctrine. He regretted this, but he respected people who had a faith.

But there are an immense number of men and women in this country who are not Communists by either doctrine or conviction and who would be . . . most upset if the Communists came to power. They vote Communist because they are discontented or discouraged—and as a protest. They are wrong, because the Communists at the National Assembly vote against all Governments, and particularly against any progressive Government . . . The Communists do not believe any good can come of this régime in any circumstances; only a Communist revolution—in 20, 50, 100 years—can make life happier for the working class . . .

Mendès thereupon embarked on a eulogy of countries like Britain, Denmark, Switzerland and Sweden, where progressive, non-Communist Governments had achieved immense improvements in the welfare of the people.

He then quoted Malraux: 'Everywhere in France, the State is considered an impostor.' The State, he argued, was 'standoffish'; it had no live contact with the mass of the people; and that was why, Mendès said, so many politicians considered his Saturday talks on the radio such a scandal.

This was most regrettable, Mendès said, because it really meant that the State was hiding the truth from the people only too often. The State—i.e., Government after Government—had lied to the people— for instance about Indo-China, about EDC, about inflation. No Government, which had supported EDC, for instance, had taken the trouble to explain the pros and cons of EDC; it would have been more honest than to treat it as a cure for all ills.

And then he came to the Radical Party and the absolute need for parties—and particularly the Radical Party—to have a clear programme, and, secondly, to the need to practise democracy inside every party, instead of leaving everything to the 'professionals'. The *militants* were an essential part of every self-respecting Party, for it was they who maintained contact between the Party and the Nation.

Because the *militants* are inspired by a faith, by a disinterested conviction, they help the deputies to resist the pressure of demagogy and the pressure of vested interests . . .

Public life, he went on, must be made more moral. He denied that a great number of politicians in France were corrupt. That was not the case. But they had deplorably easy-going habits. He saw no reason why some system of checking and enquiring into the private means of a man before and after he had completed his term of office should not be tried out—as it was in certain cases in the USA. Also, official enquiries could be made into the money spent on election campaigns,

o

etc. Deputies should not be too easy-going; they should not, for instance, render improper services to their constituents—for instance, they should not intervene in favour of anybody who was in trouble with the tax authorities.

After discussing at some length the instability of French Governments, and the various classical remedies for this evil (right of dissolution, etc.), he dealt with the flaws of parliamentary routine in France. There had often been complaints in France about the 'absenteeism' of deputies, many of whom missed most of the parliamentary meetings, and voted by proxy.

> All through the year an enormous amount of parliamentary work goes on . . . For several weeks, especially during the budget period, deputies are supposed to attend the morning, afternoon, and sometimes evening meetings of the Assembly. Even apart from the Budget period, the Assembly usually meets six or eight times a week. Then, you have to add to this the meetings of the Committees; for a year I was President of the Finance Committee. Well, it used to meet every day, sometimes twice a day . . . Other Committees meet less often, but even so, seldom less than once or twice a week. That isn't everything. A deputy must go to his constituency. Even that isn't everything: for he also has his own personal work: he has to compile *dossiers* on this or that subject; or draft private Bills, take part in debates, make speeches, all of which means a great deal of preparatory work . . . And then there is all the mail to be attended to—letters from various professional organizations; not to mention the large mail from his constituents. He also has to pay visits to this or that Ministry about some business concerning his constituency—and which needs speeding up: few of you realize how much work has to be done if every constituency is to get its new schools, new houses, new water-mains, and so on . . .
>
> So you cannot expect a deputy, who has all these endless jobs to attend to, to be present at all the meetings of the National Assembly. If you are in favour—as I am—of every deputy attending every meeting, and voting personally in the divisions, then the number of meetings of the Assembly must be greatly reduced . . . There should not be, normally, more than two or three meetings a week, and more than two or three Committee meetings a week. That is, more or less, the system they have in England.

From there, Mendès went on to argue in favour of legislation by decree; the Assembly should have the right to overthrow the Government at any time; but until then, the Government should be in a position to carry out a vigorous policy by means of decree-laws.

It had often been argued, Mendès said, that during his 1954 Ministry, very little had been done in the economic field. This was not true. No doubt, foreign affairs required top priority during that period; all the same, a large number of decrees were issued concerning building, industrial reconversion, the reclassification of labour, the adaptation of agriculture to new requirements, the whole problem of sugarbeet, sugar, alcohol, anti-alcoholism, etc.

It was physically impossible to discuss at plenary sessions of the National Assembly all the legislation that was passed in the course of a year. French laws today had become infinitely complicated, simply because so many 'exceptional' cases and 'special' cases had to be provided for at the demand of this or that deputy, with some hard-luck story to tell, on the strength of which an amendment had to be incorporated in the Bill. The income tax laws, which were perfectly simple in 1917 and 1920, were now an almost inextricable jungle. The present legislation was so complicated that not only the taxpayer, but often the tax inspector found it hard to make out how much so-and-so was really expected to pay.

Although Mendès might have said that the same was equally true of England, he did not, in this case, dwell on the British parallel.

He did, however, when it came to discussing the budget: he thought the British procedure infinitely preferable to the French. In London the budget was passed in two or three days; in Paris the discussions dragged on for weeks and months.

Then came a discussion on citizenship, on the duties of the citizen, on the need to put the 'general interest' first; all of it ending with an appeal for a 'national awakening' of France—with the good old Radical Party showing the way, as it were.

The most interesting point in this part of Mendès's speech was his reference to the slander and libel, from which public men often had to suffer in France. The machinery for dealing with slander and libel was much too unwieldy—insofar as it existed at all.

Today anybody can say anything about any deputy or Minister. It's a sad fact: but the French love dirt about their public men. Journals specializing in blackmail and libel thrive in this country. And their victims have practically no means of defending themselves.

And then came this 'personal example':

Last year, a weekly paper published several articles in which it stated that I and members of my family had been selling arms to Vietminh and to the terrorists in North Africa. The paper insinuated that the Geneva Conference on Indo-China had succeeded because I was under an obligation to the Vietminh delegates who were, as it were, my associates. You see how serious these allegations are. I took action against the paper. It took months before the case came before the *tribunal correction-nel.* The people who had libelled me did not even try to make excuses, or produce the slightest shred of evidence, nothing! They were, of course, made to pay damages—rather mild ones, I must say. Because the judges, too, share in the general indifference. And then what happened next? They appealed. The case went before the *Cour d'Appel;* this lasted a very long time; in the end a slightly heavier penalty was imposed on them. They then went on to the *Cour de Cassation.* It's gone on for a year now; and meantime the readers of their journal go on believing what they were told, since no final verdict has yet been returned.

And then, another paper, last February, told a story of how the Egyptian Government had paid to members of my family several hundred millions as compensation, in order to influence my Tunisian policy. Of course, I again brought an action against these people, but the case is still pending; no doubt it'll travel all the way from the *correctionnelle* to the *Cour d'Appel* and on to the *Cour de Cassation* . . .

'No, honestly,' Mendès exclaimed (and he was obviously feeling very bitter and angry on the subject), 'how can any public figure in France enjoy sufficient authority, the necessary authority if he is not protected against this kind of thing?'

The Courts must hear cases of this kind without delay, he concluded.

It was curious how, at the end of this somewhat academic lecture on parliamentary reform and on 'citizenship', Mendès nevertheless found it necessary to say a few words on North Africa. Algeria—Algeria was, clearly, even in July, 1955, at the back of his mind.

I receive about ten letters a week from anxious fathers and mothers because their son has been called up to serve as a soldier in Algeria. How well I understand their anguish! I also have two sons. And, with all the love I bear them, I wish with all my heart they should be spared this danger.

All the same, he thought it would be wholly irregular for any Minister to intervene in a case like this; it would simply mean that X and Y would not be called up, but that A and B would be called up in their place. What was much more important, Mendès said, was that there should be no war in Algeria at all.

CHAPTER 4

NORTH AFRICAN SUMMER, 1955

BEFORE THE AUGUST EXPLOSION

THIS speech at Evreux was made on July 23. Already serious trouble was brewing in Morocco, where the Faure Government had just sent Gilbert Grandval to clean up the mess . . . if it still could be done. Algeria was restless, with Soustelle becoming increasingly discouraged, and his position becoming more and more ambiguous. In Tunisia alone, with the Franco-Tunisian Conventions having been ratified by the Assembly, all seemed reasonably peaceful.

These Conventions had, indeed, been ratified only a fortnight before, almost without opposition. Edgar Faure pleaded for ratification; he was supported by the Communists, the Socialists, and practically everybody else—since, in the phrase of one commentator, Tunisia 'had proved herself so reasonable that she was content with even less than what Libya had got'.

Faure tended to take all the credit for the Tunisian settlement— and hardly mentioned Mendès at all. One Right-wing deputy, it is true, was facetious about it, and said that Faure 'had given birth to Mendès-France's child'—a remark which rather scandalized a deaf old man in the public gallery, who commented on the strange morals under the Fourth Republic . . . Mendès delivered one of the very few speeches he made in Parliament since his fall in February, and, in the process, recalled some of the blunders made in Tunisia by the MRP— which made M. Bidault pretend that he had fallen fast asleep.

Among the few speakers who attacked the Tunisian settlement was the same old M. Legendre of the North African and beetroot lobbies, who spoke in a funereal tone; and M. Quilici who, in his infinite charity, suddenly decided that the French Government had been callous in not sufficiently protecting the rights of the Tunisian Jews. However, the ratification was voted by 538 votes to 44, and 24 abstentions. M. Martinaud-Déplat voted against.

But meantime, in Algeria, Governor-General Soustelle was between the devil and the deep sea. He knew that the opportunity of 'total assimilation' had been missed long ago; but, on the other hand, he was still refusing to admit that Algeria had a 'personality' of her own. Having by now abandoned his earlier 'federalist' view, he now advocated 'integration', by which he now meant the gradual—but not too slow—incorporation of Algeria in European France, but with the proviso that Algeria's 'religious, cultural and linguistic originality' would be respected.

All the evidence showed that this scheme was accepted by neither the Moslems nor the Europeans in Algeria. If logically applied, it would mean 120 Algerian deputies in the National Assembly—and Arab officials in France! All this, many now felt, might have been possible in 1870 when, instead of French citizenship being granted, under the famous *décret Crémieux*, to the Algerian Jews only, this had been granted to the Moslems as well. It might even have been possible in 1936—at the time of the Blum-Violette Plan—but not now, with the national consciousness of the Algerians having developed to a quite extraordinary degree.

Many authorities on Algeria now agreed that even generous economic and social reforms would settle nothing without proper political *réformes de structure;* that it was still not realized in France that Algeria was not (as Mendès-France tended to think) primarily an economic problem; it was, first and foremost, a national problem. The suppression of the mixed communes, the teaching of Arabic in all schools, the independence of the Moslem religion *vis-à-vis* the State were small stuff, part of that *Statut d'Algérie* which had been put in cold storage for nearly ten years.

So now Soustelle was, in effect, trying to square the circle by (*a*) admitting that the Algerian Assembly was 'unrepresentative', and (*b*) by doing nothing about dissolving it, and replacing it by a 'loyally elected' Assembly. Only genuinely free elections, supervised by all the Parties of the National Assembly could obviously produce those *interlocuteurs* with whom France could validly negotiate.

Yet Soustelle knew as well as anybody else that there was no getting away from the fact that there were over one million French in Algeria —which made the problem almost insoluble.

Soustelle who, in June, 1955, came to see Mendès-France, was so discouraged that he wanted to resign. It was, oddly enough, Mendès —who still had faith in a 'liberal' solution—who did all he could to persuade Soustelle to stay on, little realizing that he (Mendès) and Soustelle would soon find themselves at the two opposite extremes in respect of Algeria.

However, Algeria had not yet exploded in the early summer of 1955, and was only smouldering. The first major explosion was to occur there on August 20—which was marked by a series of mutual massacres, similar to those that occurred on that same day in Morocco.

GRANDVAL ALMOST LYNCHED IN MOROCCO

It was in Morocco that the major political crisis of 1955 broke out. Since the Sultan Ben Yussef had been deposed in August, 1953, and exiled, first to Corsica and then to Madagascar, the country had been in a state of constant agitation and ferment. The new Sultan was not recognized by the population; the French *administration directe* had been greatly reinforced, and there were frequent outbursts of Moroccan terrorism and French 'counter-terrorism', encouraged by the French He-men like Boniface, and other leaders of the *Présence Française*, the French Settlers' organization.

The ineffectual Resident-General, M. Francis Lacoste, was unable to cope with this counter-terrorism, and adopted a *laissez-faire* attitude, even though some of the members of his staff occasionally admitted that they had to 'fight two fronts'. Already early in 1955 there were a number of very strange happenings. There was the *affaire Forestier*, the case of a young and zealous police official who thought it his duty to help to stamp out the 'gangs'; after a very careful enquiry, he drew up a report on the assassination of moderate Moroccan nationalists by French gunmen, as well as the attempt made by them to kill M. Clostermann, the Gaullist deputy and famous French fighter-ace, who was a well-known supporter of the deposed Sultan. He also inquired into the circumstances in which the gangs were constantly threatening the life of Antoine Mazella, the Managing Editor of *Maroc-Presse*, the French liberal paper, controlled by Jacques Lemaigre-Dubreuil. Forestier, having drawn up a detailed report, in which he made grave charges against the various French terrorist gangs, handed it to M. Chevrier, the Director of Security at Casablanca. Ten days later, in highly mysterious circumstances, Forestier was killed in a motor smash on the Rabat-Casablanca road.

The 'thugs', who included big *trafiquants* and the editor of the extremist Casablanca paper, called *Paris*, Camille Aymard—already notorious in Paris in the days of the *affaire Stavisky* in 1934—had, of course, close contacts in Paris, among them some of the bigwigs of the Radical Party.

Acts of terrorism continued throughout the early part of 1955. But what brought it all to a head was the assassination by several gunmen of Jacques Lemaigre-Dubreuil at Casablanca on June 12. Lemaigre-Dubreuil was a major public figure. A big businessman, who controlled the largest French peanut-oil company, the Huiles Lesieur, he did not believe that the policy of repression in Morocco— or in North Africa generally—was in France's interests. Undeterred by constant threats, he ran a boldly-liberal policy in his paper, *Maroc-*

Presse. It was also he who, particularly in the *Monde*, conducted a strong press campaign against the policy that had led to the overthrow of Ben Yussef and the establishment of the French police régime in Morocco, with the puppet Sultan, the senile Arafa, at its head. Though a hardboiled businessman—but one who had also had his romantic past, as one of the leaders of the 'Weygandist' Resistance in North Africa, which had done so much to prepare the American landing in November, 1942—Lemaigre-Dubreuil came to be regarded as a kind of Moroccan François Mauriac.

In one of his rare moments of determination, Edgar Faure decided, when he heard of the murder of Lemaigre-Dubreuil, that he had had enough of it. At the National Assembly a few days later, on June 21, Faure bluntly announced that he could not accept the conclusions of M. Francis Lacoste, the French Resident-General in Morocco. Lacoste was just trying to shelve the problem of the Throne—which was Number One problem—and talked instead of 'decongesting' the whole situation by 'rejuvenating the Meghzen', which meant, among other things, replacing the Grand Vizir, now over 100, by his son. Faure thought this plan 'completely inane', and suddenly decided on a very bold step; he appointed M. Gilbert Grandval, former French High Commissioner in the Saar, Resident-General in Morocco.

How badly the He-men of Morocco took the Grandval appointment may be seen from this strange episode which showed that they were even thinking of extending their terrorist activities to Paris. I remember calling on Mendès-France at his Passy flat at the end of July; and after a long talk, he offered me a lift back into town. As we approached his car, a young man came up and asked: 'What time do you expect to return, *M. le Président?*' Plain-clothes man, obviously. I had also noticed two policemen in uniform outside Mendès's house that morning; and they were still there. As we drove off, Mendès remarked: 'I've had these chaps around for some days now; I have been getting quite a number of letters from the Moroccan gang threatening to murder me. They tell me that Grandval is my 'nominee'. What's happening just now in Morocco is very, very ugly. However, I don't suppose they'll extend their activities to Paris.' All the same, I had the impression that Mendès didn't mind having those cops around the place . . . One could never tell . . .

Rivarol, Aspects de la France, and other extremist and anti-semitic papers were, indeed, having the time of their lives over the Grandval appointment; and it was they who invariably associated 'Jew Grandval' and 'Jew Mendès-France'. A few samples of this type of journalism will give the reader an idea of the kind of propaganda these papers are capable of. Thus *Rivarol* wrote:

THE POPULARITY OF M. GRANDVAL

This is how the *Vigie Marocaine* of July 17 described the French demonstration against M. Grandval:

The Resident-General received blows and various missiles. He nevertheless managed to reach his car, but this was attacked by the crowd. They prevented the car from moving. The lights were smashed by some hard kicks. One demonstrator slapped M. Grandval's face through the lowered window of the car . . . Another demonstrator tried to tear off one of his epaulettes; but in the end the whole of the Resident's tunic was in shreds . . .

There followed a long article on this 'FFI General', whose real name was Hirsch-Ollendorf; the fact of having been a General in the Resistance army seemed even more ignominious to a Vichyite paper like *Rivarol* than being merely a Jew. Then there was this paragraph:

A GREAT FAMILY

M. Gilbert Grandval, who is making himself famous in Morocco just now, is not the only neo-Grandval whose name is recorded by the *Journal Officiel*. This M. Gilbert-Grandval was allowed to change his name from Hirsch-Ollendorf by a decree of 25.2.46. But the Grandval family is not limited to this eminent personage. There is also a M. Paul Léon Grandval, né Lévy Grunwald . . . as well as a Roger Lévy, metamorphosed into Grandval on 2.7.48.

From all this mud-slinging at Grandval, *Rivarol* went on to his 'crony' Mendès-France with this poisonous kind of story, illustrated by a drawing in the best *Stürmer* tradition:

THE SUPERMAN ON TV

So the Americans celebrated our 14th of July in a particularly picturesque way. Namely, by showing on their TV screens a film about our Superman. Or rather, the story of Superman's escape. For our Superman, as we all know, was locked up for desertion in a Vichy prison; nevertheless, he managed to get away and find his way to where he belonged—London. The Superman was impersonated by a professional actor, not by himself—which is rather a pity . . . But I hope the Americans won't be selfish, and also let us have this film—complete with its love-interest and a long close-up kiss. It's not so often these days that we, in France, have any real fun.[1]

[1] *Rivarol*, July 21, 1955.

The above little digression helps to understand the poisonous atmosphere which surrounded the whole Grandval episode in Morocco. If the *Rivarol* style of writing was still an exception in France, it was almost the general rule in the French press in Morocco.

On June 23, M. Faure held a press conference, at which he again said that the Throne was Morocco's Number One problem, adding that the time had come to put an end to the *administration directe* and to set up new institutions 'of the kind to which the people of Morocco aspire'.

It was known that, at that time, M. July, the Minister for Tunisia and Moroccan affairs was thinking of a 'transition stage', in the course of which some solution might be found. He thought, in particular, that it would be a good idea to get the puppet Sultan Arafa out of the way —for instance, by persuading him to take a cure at Vichy; and then to settle at Tangier, after handing his seals over to the Grand Vizir. This would create on the Moroccan throne a '*de facto*' vacancy. Meantime a Regency Council might be set up, representing the various Moroccan currents. However, the Government had not yet firmly made up its mind about what to do, and decided to see first what would come of the Grandval 'experiment'.

Grandval was ready for a showdown. Before leaving for Morocco, he said: 'I shall act, if necessary, without the consent of the Government; and may even act regardless of its advice'. For one thing, he seemed determined to take the French police in Morocco in hand. Even a month after the murder of Lemaigre-Dubreuil, not a single administrative chief, no *chef de région* (i.e., Prefect), no high official of any kind had been dismissed, transferred or suspended. The French 'counter-terrorists' in Casablanca were active. The Arabs were hitting back—in a variety of ways. Between June 1 and 24 alone there were 200 harvest fires, especially on big French estates round Meknès; there had been 43 bomb explosions and 39 people had been killed and 40 wounded. The 'general strike' of Moroccan shopkeepers, which had begun on May 16, had gone on for six weeks. This movement was showing a striking unanimity throughout Morocco.

M. Francis Lacoste, the Resident-General, was given a cordial send-off by the French community at the beginning of July; but this community was now going to make it hot for his successor, Grandval. The 'gang' was busier than ever. M. Boniface, the former *chef de région* of Casablanca, who had provoked the famous massacres of December, 1952, and now a financial power in the land, had ordered his followers to greet Grandval with the slogan: '*A bas les Juifs*'. The Glaoui and Marshal Juin had, in various ways, warned against any tampering with the Sultan Arafa's throne. Jo Renucci, Dr. Causse, president of the *Présence Française* and others were receiving every encouragement from the colonialists in Paris, like Martinaud-Déplat, Emile Roche, etc. These people even started the more than improbable story that Lemaigre-Dubreuil had not been murdered by any of the gangs, but by the regular French police, the DST. Apart from a few of the small fry, who had been made the scapegoats of this affair, all the killers, and their accomplices and bosses were going strong at both Rabat and Casablanca by the time M. Grandval arrived in Morocco in the second week of July.

On July 9, he drove through the Moroccan quarters of Casablanca. Everywhere large crowds were shouting *'Vive Ben Yussef!'*; he thus learned at first hand what the population wanted.

On the same day, he had his first meeting with the Sultan Arafa, and found the old man quite conciliatory and willing to give way. Grandval told him that, in his opinion, the *administration directe* should be replaced by that *autonomie interne* implied in the Protec-torate Treaty. He also said that he was in favour of setting up a repre-sentative Moroccan Government. Arafa admitted that he wasn't quite the man to have at the head of Moroccan affairs in the midst of such far-reaching changes.

On July 12, Grandval saw the Glaoui, and was pleasantly surprised to find that the wicked old man, who was more responsible than anyone else for the expulsion of Ben Yussef, was no longer 'absolutely determined' that Arafa be maintained on the throne.

The trouble began on the following day, July 13, when Grandval started his 'purge'. Nine *directeurs d'administrations* were suspended. A *communiqué* from the Residence said that a 'new spirit' was wanted in the Administration and that these men were 'unfit to carry out any reforms'. What is more, Grandval announced that he was going to purge the police. Moreover, he eliminated a number of officials, who had been highly influential in the days of Francis Lacoste: M. Guira-mand, *directeur des affaires chérifiennes*, roughly the Moroccan equiva-lent of Minister of the Interior, Colonel Pommerie, Director of In-dustrial Production and Mines, and M. Girard, Director of Public Works. An entirely new atmosphere was about to be created, with all these suspensions and dismissals, the release of 43 interned nationalist and trade union leaders, and the abolition of the Aghbalou N'Kedrous internment camp. Grandval even took the unprecedented course of holding a reception at the Residence in Rabat to which a great variety of French and Moroccan personaliites were invited, including some Nationalists. At this reception he had talks with two Istiqlal leaders, Lyazadi and Ben Barka.

Only a few hours later, a bomb exploded in a café in the Rond-Point Mers-Sultan, in the heart of the European city of Casablanca, killing six people and wounding 30. About the same time, in the new Medina, hand grenades were thrown at a police jeep; and although the five policemen in it were slightly injured, they fired back, killing four Moroccans, and wounding several others.

It was after the bomb in the European part of Casablanca that the European riots started. For hours a crowd of 4,000 Europeans went on burning down and looting Moroccan shops, lynching Moroccans, rioting outside the *chef de région's* residence, and distributing thousands of leaflets calling on the French of Morocco to 'oppose the liquidation of Morocco in the Mendès-France style'.

On the following day, when it was learned that Grandval was about to arrive in Casablanca, the rioting became even more violent and widespread. Thousands of demonstrators, singing the *Marseillaise* tore through the city, totally unhampered by the police, smashing cars and buses and beating up and lynching numerous Moroccans. An attempt was also made to lynch Maître Legrand, a liberal French lawyer, in his own home, but he shot one of his assailants, and the others fled. There was more rioting outside the *Région Civile*, and the premises of Lemaigre-Dubreuil's newspaper, *Maroc-Presse*, were smashed. In four hours, 150 fires were started. By 6 p.m. the entire European city was in a state of insurrection.

At 7 p.m. Grandval was still in conference at the *Région Civile;* a detachment of *gendarmes* alone, using tear-gas, prevented the building from being invaded. Otherwise, the police seemed completely on the side of the rioters.

But the rumour now began to spread that, after 24 hours' of looting of Moroccan shops and of numerous lynchings, thousands of Moroccans were preparing to 'descend' upon the European city. Grandval, in the midst of all this chaos, realized that the police were both helpless and wholly unreliable, and decided that the Army alone could restore order. He first called on General Duval, Supreme Commander of the French forces in Morocco, but merely met with the response that he had no troops to send to Casablanca. Grandval then appealed to General Franchi, military commander of the Fez Region, who agreed to send several battalions of the Foreign Legion. A 9 p.m. curfew was announced in Casablanca that night. On the following day, July 16, the Residence announced that the Civil Region of Casablanca had been transformed into a Military Region, under the command of General Franchi. The police having proved 'inadequate' in maintaining law and order, the Army now took over.

That was the day on which the funeral took place of the European victims of the bomb explosion in the Rond-Point Mers-Sultan two days before. The funeral service was held at the Catholic cathedral; and it was here that the riotous scenes took place in the course of which the Resident-General had his face slapped, was insulted and had his tunic torn off his back. It was these scenes which caused such delight to the *Vigie Marocaine* in Morocco and to *Rivarol* in France. And, indeed, not only to *Rivarol*.

Grandval did not, however, take it lying down. On the same day he had two of the chief organizers of the riots of July 16 expelled from Morocco—Cambiazo and Mattei, two secretaries of *Présence Française*, and suspended one of the heads of the French police at Casablanca, the *commissaire principal* Vergnolles, one of the chief instigators of the December 8, 1952, massacres. The Army and the *garde républicaine* were placed in charge of law and order in the native city, and the police were forbidden to enter it. Among members of the French Government it was the prevalent opinion that the bomb of July 14 was a quite deliberate provocation by the French extremists. The mass demonstration followed so closely upon the explosion that it seemed highly probable that the same people had had a hand in both . . .

This wasn't the end of Grandval's troubles. A few days later, as he entered Meknès on an official visit, the Arabs arranged a pro-Yussef demonstration. Clashes broke out between Arab rioters on the one hand and Europeans and French troops on the other. The 'Arafist' Pasha of Meknès was assaulted, and the Military Commander of the Region, General Miquel, noted for his violent manner, ordered the troops to fire. There were fifteen dead. After that Grandval, 'to avoid more bloodshed', cancelled his visit to Fez.

Rioting also broke out, about the same time, at Marrakesh, known until then for its alleged opposition to the deposed Sultan. During that one week, the official figures showed that 40 people had been killed at Casablanca, 6 at Marrakesh and 15 at Meknès. Unofficially, it was estimated that at least 230 people had been killed in Casablanca alone.

In spite of all this, Moroccan opinion was still favourable to Grandval; and one Moroccan nationalist is supposed even to have made this wisecrack—which can't have helped the Resident-General: 'Ben Arafa, Sultan of the French, and Grandval, Resident-General of the Moroccans'.

Grandval went on with his 'liberal' policy; despite protests from the Glaoui, he brought back from France one of Ben Yussef's chief supporters, Si Bekkai, the Pasha of Sefrou (who, after the return of Ben Yussef, was, indeed, to become the first Moroccan Prime Minister).

At the same time, Grandval submitted a plan of reforms to the French Government, a plan the principal features of which was the replacement of Arafa by a Regency Council. Even in France, among some of the Right-wing members of the Cabinet, the feeling was growing that Arafa was not worth backing much longer. It is true that Marshal Juin was still a believer in *administration directe* and in the strong hand; so also was M. Boussac, proprietor of *L'Aurore* and of numerous cotton mills in the North of France, to which Morocco was a privileged market. But even Right-wing leaders like M. Pinay and M. Duchet now felt that the outcry among the more extreme diehards, like M. Groussaud, that Gilbert Grandval should be recalled, somewhat excessive.

Grandval's idea was to set up a Regency Council, which would then nominate a *representative* Moroccan Government; this would then try to reach an agreement with the French on the problem of the Throne, on the future of Franco-Moroccan relations, on the new Moroccan institutions, etc. The exiled Sultan would be allowed to settle in the south of France before the end of 1955, pending these negotiations.

So, to begin with, a number of moderate Moroccan nationalists were brought back to Morocco—Si Bekkai, Ben Sliman (who, as pro-Yussef Pasha of Fez, was dismissed in 1953), and several others.

'Time is blood', Grandval had announced soon after arriving in Morocco. There was no time to lose if more bloodshed—like that of the two horrible days at Casablanca in July—were to be avoided. Speed was all the more essential as very serious trouble was likely to break out on August 20, the second anniversary of Ben Yussef's overthrow. On August 16, while Grandval was in Paris, he and Edgar Faure agreed on the main lines of what came to be known as the 'Faure Plan'. But certain members of the Government were pulling the other way. This became clear to Faure when, only a few days before the fatal 20th of August, he visited President Coty. It seems that Coty was in favour of avoiding over-dramatic action, and suggested that the Sultan Arafa be *asked* to form the 'representative' Moroccan Government, instead of this being done by the Regency Council, after Arafa's departure.

The news of these developments in Paris immediately started the rumour in Morocco that Arafa was staying, and Yussef not returning.

Grandval, though greatly worried by these new developments, and exasperated by Edgar Faure's shilly-shallying, decided that trouble in Morocco must be avoided at any price on August 20; and the Moroccan cities were all heavily occupied by troops and gendarmerie. In the circumstances, the Moroccan nationalists issued watchwords to the effect that it would be 'too stupid' in such conditions 'to get yourself massacred'; and they recommended the greatest calm among their followers.

What happened instead was unexpected—and horrible. There was no serious trouble in any of the large cities; but it was at the 'loyal' Berber end of Morocco that the trouble broke out. The most horrible massacres of Europeans—including children—occurred at Oued Zem, Khenifra and other places, where some of the Berber tribemen ran amok. There were hundreds of dead. On the same day, there was a rising of the Maquis in the Constantinois in Algeria: here too, hundreds of Europeans were reported to have been killed.

In Morocco, this explosion of rage among the most backward people—regarded until then as loyal supporters of the Glaoui by the French—was ominous indeed. It was largely from these tribes that the French used to recruit soldiers for their own army—soldiers, many of whom had only recently been fighting in Indo-China. Was Dien Bien Phu now suggesting to them that Frenchmen could be murdered with impunity?

Not unnaturally, the Europeans in both Morocco and Algeria were scared to death, and could see Moslem cut-throats (in the most literal sense) everywhere. Slogans like 'Kill off 100,000 and we'll have ten years of peace' came into vogue again. The *politique du massacre* was beginning to make headway. In the midst of these appalling dangers, Edgar Faure was now being attacked for conducting this whole Moroccan affair '*avec des petites ruses de maquignon*'.

This also seemed to be Grandval's view; for Grandval was, clearly, not pleased with Faure's plan to hold a 'Moroccan Conference' at Aix-les-Bains on August 21—as it happened, the very day after the Moroccan and Algerian massacres. Grandval—understandably—thought that Faure was playing for time; and, in his opinion, there was no time to lose. In a way, he was right; and it soon became apparent that the events of August 20 had cut the ground from under his feet. But Faure's idea of the Aix-les-Bains Conference was, potentially, a fruitful one—if only its results were not going to be sabotaged—as, indeed, they were to be.

At Aix-les-Bains a 'jury' of five French Ministers—M. Faure, the Premier, M. July, the Minister for Tunisia and Morocco, General Koenig, Minister of Defence, M. Schuman, Minister of Justice, and M. Pinay, the Foreign Minister, met to discuss the future of Morocco with a strange assortment of 'representative' Moroccans: among these were not only the old-time stooges, like the 100-year-old Grand Vizir, and a moderate nationalist like Si Bekkai, but also representatives of

the two main nationalist parties, the Parti Democratique de l'Independance (represented by Bendjelloun, etc.) and the Istiqlal (represented by Lyazidi, Bouabid, etc.). Even the Grand Vizir thought the
idea of asking Arafa to form the Moroccan Government incongruous.
The two nationalist parties, for their part, continued to express confidence in Grandval. On the other hand, Pinay and Koenig kept
pressing Faure to recall Grandval—but Faure would not yield.
(It was, indeed, the hostility of the Right-wing members of the
Cabinet that partly accounted for Grandval's refusal to go to Aix-
les-Bains.)

Very striking at Aix-les-Bains was the moderation—some called it
the 'reformism'—of the two nationalist parties, who now no longer
even insisted on the early return of Ben Yussef. What happened in the
end, after endless discussions, was the elaboration of the so-called
Aix Plan; which was rather more 'liberal' than what Edgar Faure had
even hoped for. But, to get it adopted by the Right-wing members of
his Government, he had to sacrifice Grandval, and not insist in maintaining him in Morocco, in face of the furious opposition he had aroused,
not only among the French extremists, but also among the Army
leaders . . .

The story of how Grandval resigned is a truly fantastic one.
It was little short of being a revolt of the Army against the Government.
What happened was this. General Duval, the commander of the French
forces in Morocco, discovered, not long before August 20, that there
was growing agitation in the formerly always reliable Berber country.
This agitation was also becoming very noticeable in the Khenifra
region, particularly among those very Tabors who had supplied so
many men for the French forces in Indo-China. They were becoming
increasingly affected by pro-Yussef propaganda, all the more so as
many of them had only recently been recruited to keep order in Casablanca.

There had already been signs of agitation in the *bled* during the
summer of 1954; this was a phenomenon which was worrying even
the leaders of the Istiqlal, one of whom was said to have remarked to
the French—'Once the *bled* starts moving, we won't be able to stop it.
Nor will you'.

Shortly before August 20, General Miquel, the French commander
at Meknès, warned the Residence at Rabat that trouble was brewing
in the Meknès area. At Rabat these reports from General Miquel were
taken rather too lightly, it seems; Grandval—after the experience of
his Meknès visit—thought Miquel a deliberate trouble-maker, who was
either inventing these stories, or else trying to provoke trouble. But

whatever Grandval really thought, he did his utmost to impress upon Paris the need of some spectacular gesture, which would prevent trouble on August 20.

The Resident-General had taken the greatest precautions in the cities, but had refrained from taking such precautions in the country-side, where he thought that a military display would only increase the *énervement* of the population, and possibly act as a provocation. When things turned sour in the countryside the Generals rebelled against Grandval and declared him responsible for the Khenifra and Oued-Zem massacres . . . General Leblanc, General Director of Internal Security, resigned in protest on August 22. Grandval asked him not to make his resignation public; but this was nevertheless announced in the diehard Casablanca paper, the *Petit Marocain*. Leblanc then declared that he had warned Grandval at 8 a.m. on August 20 that the situation was extremely dangerous at Oued Zem; but that Grandval did not okay the dispatch of reinforcements to that area until 4 p.m.—that is, after the massacres of the Europeans had already occurred.

It was during one of the punitive expeditions around Oued-Zem that followed the massacres of August 20, that General Duval's plane crashed and he was killed. On August 25, his funeral took place at Casablanca, and this was again marked by violent demonstrations against Grandval.

By this time Grandval was abandoned by practically everybody at the Residence. General Miquel, the Acting Supreme Commander, de-liberately ignored Grandval, and would not even send him any reports on the *ratissages* he was carrying out. On August 27, Grandval flew to Paris. The next two days were marked by a long succession of resigna-tions from the Generals in Morocco; these resignations were not with-drawn until the resignation of Grandval and his replacement by a new Resident-General. General Boyer de la Tour . . . Now the Generals were satisfied . . .

Grandval, 'Mendès-France's nominee', had started well in Mor-occo. But he was sabotaged throughout, first by the Settlers and the police, and then by the Army. At one stage, he had even won over the Glaoui; but the Glaoui had got tougher again, after receiving a number of visitors from Paris.

THE GLAOUI 'SAVES' FAURE

Having sacrificed Grandval, Edgar Faure nevertheless went on with the Aix-les-Bains programme. Five emissaries—General Catroux,

P

and M. Yrissou, M. Pinay's *chef de cabinet*, and three Moroccans—
travelled to Antsirabé in Madagascar, where they had talks with the
ex-Sultan, who, on September 15 agreed to the Aix Programme: a
Throne Council was to be set up; and this would then appoint a
representative government, which would thereupon negotiate with
the French on the basis of 'independence within interdependence'.

But on neither side were the extremists satisfied. The Right in
France grumbled against the very idea of the Antsirabé visit; and
Catroux was, in any case, a Mendès-Grandval-Mauriac type of 'liberal'
whom they had always distrusted. On the other hand, Si Alal el Fassi,
the extremist Istiqlal leader, who was in Switzerland at the time of the
Aix Conference, thought the Istiqlal representatives at Aix rather 'on
the feeble side'. The 100-year-old Grand Vizir, for his part, had been
offended by the Nationalists' objections to his becoming a member of
the Crown Council; and now appeared to be in no hurry to exercise on
the Sultan Arafa that 'discreet and respectful pressure' which he had
promised to do, so that Arafa could be said to have abdicated *almost*
voluntarily'. Worse still, once Grandval had gone, Arafa now declared
that he had no intention at all of going.

Edgar Faure was now at sixes and sevens. Striking a Mendès-
France pose, he declared at the end of August that there *must* be a
Moroccan settlement on September 12. He was setting a 'deadline',
just as Mendès had set a 'deadline' for his Indo-China settlement in
July, 1954. Only the trick didn't work this time; far from it.

In Morocco, after the departure of Grandval, *Présence Française*
felt that the time had come for a counter-offensive; many of the
officials purged in July were reappearing again, expecting to be reinstated at any moment. In Paris, at the same time, General Koenig
was creating more and more difficulties inside the Government, and
deputies of the extreme Right were becoming dangerously active. M.
de Bénouville rushed to Morocco; here he urged Arafa not to abdicate
on any account, and extracted from the Glaoui a declaration to the
effect that if Arafa was deposed, he (the Glaoui) would lead an armed
rising against the French! M. de Bénouville—who, though an *Action*
Française man before the war, had a distinguished record in the Resistance—belonged to the extreme Right of the Gaullist movement,
and then to the Gaullist parliamentary group; he was also associated
with the magazine, *Jours de France*, belonging to the Dassault group,
with large business interests in North Africa.

Another emissary of the extreme Right in France who went to
Morocco and assured Arafa that he would be defended, was M. Pierre
Montel, the Right-wing deputy who was chairman of the Defence

Committee of the Assembly, and a close associate of General Koenig, the Minister of Defence.

Marshal Juin, for his part, made a speech in which he said he feared that the French of North Africa might soon have reason 'to curse their ungrateful Motherland'.

The new Resident, General Boyer de la Tour, readily lent himself to all these machinations. On September 13—just after Faure's 'deadline' had expired—President Coty wrote a letter to the Sultan Arafa which Boyer de la Tour was to transmit to him. The Resident-General's instructions were that Arafa be sent to Tangier and that a Crown Council be set up.

No sooner had this letter been taken to Rabat than General Koenig protested, saying that the Cabinet had not been consulted on its contents; thereupon M. Pinay—though partly won over by Faure—phoned Boyer de la Tour instructing him to hold up the letter. Boyer was only too glad to oblige, all the more so as he was trying to live down, vis-à-vis the French in Morocco, the rôle he had played, by Mendès-France's side, in the famous Tunis visit of July, 1954—in the course of which he was appointed Resident-General in Tunis, where he more or less co-operated with the Tunisian authorities.

Despite the decisions taken at Aix-les-Bains, and the approval given them by Ben Yussef, nothing was settled about the Throne Council. The Faure Government was so divided on the issue that, in its bewilderment, it even went so far as to request General Nogués, Vichy's Governor-General in Morocco who had, for years, been living in exile in Lisbon, to come to Paris to help them out in their attempt to find the 'third man', in addition to the Grand Vizir and Si Bekkai, the moderate 'Yussefist'. Everything continued to be in a muddle. General Boyer de la Tour, after deciding not to give President Coty's letter to Arafa, returned to Paris a few days later (on September 16) and announced that the French in Morocco would 'rebel' if Arafa were deposed. The 'colonialist' counter-offensive was now in full swing against the Grandval policy and against the decisions of the Aix Conference. Boyer de la Tour himself, who had been a second lieutenant in Morocco in 1923 was, like so many other French officiers d'affaires indigènes, thinking back with nostalgia to the Lyautey and immediate post-Lyautey period, when France seemed to be playing so brilliant and constructive a rôle in Morocco. And then, despite his display of 'liberalism' in Tunisia the year before, Boyer de la Tour had, after all, been a close associate of Marshal Juin in Morocco in 1949-51; and he had then taken part in the severe repression of disorders in the Tadla country . . . Also, he had taken part in Juin's attempt to overthrow the Sultan in March, 1951.

The Moroccans' attitude to the Boyer de la Tour appointment was unmistakable: they had no illusions about him, and soon came to the conclusion that he intended to sabotage the Faure Plan. Unrest was growing both in the *medinas* and in the *bled*.

The line Boyer took was to ignore the Aix and Antsirabé decisions, and to start a new series of 'consultations' all over again. In any contacts he now had with Moroccan nationalists, his manner was sharp and studiously disagreeable. Among wide masses of the Istiqlal rank-and-file, the extremists were now distributing leaflets in favour of a general strike; the Istiqlal leadership were having the greatest trouble in restraining the growing revolt, and the tendency to agree with Allal el Fassi's uncompromising stand during the Aix Conference—when he thought the French were trying to double-cross the Moroccan representatives.

Some highly suspect 'delegations' of *caids* started, around the 20th of September, arriving at Rabat to assure Arafa of their loyalty. They also declared themselves hostile to any Crown Council, and particularly to Si Bekkai, whom they called 'an enemy of France'.

Faure at last realized that it couldn't go on like this; for the Moroccans, who had anxiously been waiting for the Aix decisions to be applied, were now in a state of growing exasperation. So on September 28 he gave Boyer de la Tour 36 hours in which 'to get rid of Arafa'.

At this point Boyer realized that if nothing was done, he would be recalled: and he started thinking up a 'compromise' solution with the help of the *Présence Française* leaders. Finally, it was decided to send Arafa to Tangier, and let him, before that, hand his seals to a cousin.

When, on the morning of October 1 it was learned that Arafa had actually flown off to Tangier, there was rejoicing in the *medinas*. But it did not last long; for soon it was learned that the cousin, called Moulay Abdallah, had been appointed to act as 'heir'. Rioting broke out in Casablanca and other cities. Worse still, a large-scale insurrection broke out in the Riff country, where Riff soldiers, armed with automatic weapons, started pouring in in large numbers from the Spanish Zone into the French Zone. Several towns were captured by them, and some were burned down. The rebellion showed signs of spreading to the Middle Atlas, where the Djebel Bou country was occupied by swarms of armed mountaineers. The Residence spoke of 'commandos of dozens of men' operating in various parts of the country. It declared that a large-scale 'fellagha movement' had begun in Morocco. In short, after 30 years of relative quiet, the Riff was on the move once again . . .

That was not the end of the trouble yet. True, the Riff rebellion was a strangely elusive one; and often it was hard to say whether the rebels had 'gone home' for good, or were preparing new attacks.

The National Assembly discussed Morocco during the first week of October, and—and this was one of M. Edgar Faure's *tours de force* —whereas the Right had voted for him on the Algerian issue, the Left now voted for him on the Moroccan issue: his line was that the two problems were different—in Algeria France must be tough; in Morocco she must stick to the Aix and Antsirabé agreements. However, not to antagonise the Right unduly, he declared (later he said it was a man-œuvre) that Ben Yussef's restoration was 'out of the question'. It was then that another Revolt of the Generals—even more serious than that of August 22—broke out. General Leblanc arrived in Paris and threat-ened that he and all the other high-ranking officers in Morocco, in-cluding Boyer de la Tour would resign if the Settlers were not given satisfaction. He demanded that the Throne Council be reduced to the rôle of a mere rubber stamp, with the elimination of Si Bekkai—the only Yussefist member on it—and his replacement by a stooge. 'In-stead of putting the General in jail for insubordination' (as Bourdet put it), 'Faure thought it more "expedient" to start negotiating with the rebellious Generals.'

All these further delays increased once again the great feeling of unrest in Morocco; and it was then, on October 25, that the great *coup de théâtre* occurred. The Glaoui (who, already a few days before, had reacted remarkably mildly to a Yussefist demonstration in Marrakesh) appeared before the Throne Council and solemnly declared that he favoured the return to the throne of Ben Yussef.

The French were completely stunned by this *volte-face*, and the Glaoui, for the first time in years, was given a tremendous ovation from the populace as he returned to Marrakesh the next day.

What were the reasons for this *volte-face*? There were several. One of his sons—whose influence with the old man was considerable—had become increasingly convinced that the Sultan's return was the only solution. For one thing, with the pro-Yussef agitation growing in the Riff and the Atlas, the Glaoui's own position was being endangered. Secondly, the nationalists might try to 'monopolize' Ben Yussef, and since, in any case, his return was probably only a matter of time, it was best to be the *first* among his enemies to back him. The 'alliance' of the two richest men of Morocco—the Sultan and the Glaoui—might prove a move in the right 'conservative' direction. Further, the Glaoui had been disappointed in the way French Big Business had treated him.[1] And lastly perhaps, the Americans—who, with their four enormous bases in Morocco, had a special interest in the country—were believed to have urged the Glaoui to come out in favour of a Restoration—which alone could bring law and order back to the country.

The rest of the story can be briefly told. The Sultan arrived in France soon afterwards; there was a jubilant rally of Moroccans to meet him on the Riviera; then he stayed for some days near Paris, where M. Pinay, the Foreign Minister, begged him to return to Rabat as quickly as possible. Arafa had abdicated in the interval, and there was nothing to stop the Sultan from returning. Less than a month after the Glaoui's dramatic move the Sultan was back on his throne. The scenes of jubilation that accompanied his return were marked by some savage lynching of former Arafa supporters outside his palace. Juin and Boniface, and the rest of the He-men now knew that their *coup* of August, 1953, had been in vain; and that it had proved a short cut to that Moroccan Independence which, in 1953, the Sultan was still willing to achieve by slow degrees, over a period of 25 years or more . . . Also, many hundreds of French, and many thousands of Moroccan lives had been lost in vain.

Anyway, the *dénouement* of the Moroccan tragedy was a great help to M. Edgar Faure who had, for months, been trying to solve the problem of the Throne, while being, at the same time, constantly bullied and blackmailed by the *colons* and the Generals. As far as it went, it was a 'happy ending' for Edgar Faure.

The curious thing is that although he played a tricky and awkward

---

[1] The Glaoui who, together with Marshal Juin, had played the leading part in the overthrow of the Sultan Ben Yussef in August 1953, had a vast range of business interests. One was prostitution. In 1955 the Movement for Colonial Freedom published in London a study from which it appears that the Glaoui was in the very centre of the gigantic white-slave traffic and of the network of brothels of North Africa. In particular, it was asserted that he levied a daily tax of 100 francs on each of the 6,000 prostitutes of Marrakesh—which made a daily total of about £600. This part of the Glaoui's business activities seemed, however, to be flourishing, as before. Where things started going wrong was in another field—that of mining concessions which, in virtue of a traditional *droit berbère* the Glaoui had been granting to various French companies, which were, for a time, willing to overlook the fact that all mineral wealth in Morocco belonged under the *loi chérifienne*, to the Moroccan state. With political conditions very uncertain in Morocco, it was doubtful whether backing the Glaoui 'against Rabat' was a sound way of carrying on business in Morocco; it was even more uncertain whether the *droit berbère*, in virtue of which the Glaoui was granting his mining concessions, was a sufficiently sound basis on which to develop big capitalist concerns in Morocco. The Glaoui was, in short, becoming a liability to the mining companies, as well as to the numerous 'politico-financial middlemen' between the mining companies and the French banks on the one hand, and the political forces in France (including the Radical Party), on the other.

delaying game (largely in order to keep his Cabinet and his Government majority from disintegrating)—a delaying game which produced tragic results like the August 20 massacres—he was, according to Grandval, convinced from the start that the restoration of the old Sultan was inevitable, anyway!

WAR IN ALGERIA

What, in the meantime, had been happening in Algeria?

Soustelle had landed in Algeria, intending to pursue a liberal policy. But he soon found that he would make a deadly enemy of the settlers and of Big Business if he embarked on far-reaching reforms. The *communes mixtes* he found run by narrow-minded French officials; and the *Gouvernement Général* itself was not run by the Governor-General, but by those high officials who had been born and bred in the *colon* society, or specially selected by the North Africa Lobby. Instead of proceeding with the election of a regular Algerian Assembly, Soustelle preferred to play for time.

Nevertheless, until June, he was still fairly optimistic, believing that minor concessions and the prospect of some economic improvements would keep the country quiet. This optimism was rudely shaken by the riots and massacres in the North-Constantinois, which revealed the existence of a genuine 'Algerian Liberation Army', a great deal more co-ordinated than before. The French reprisals were fierce; numerous villages were bombed and burned down, after women and children had ostensibly been evacuated. Many of the rebels' attacks were on French arms dumps. In the punitive expeditions that followed these raids and the massacre of Europeans, some five thousand Moslems were rumoured to have been killed in forty-eight hours . . .

During the weeks that followed, the French press began to take an ever-growing interest in Algeria, realizing, somewhat belatedly, that the trouble in Tunisia and Morocco during the last few years (mostly through the fault of the French diehards) was bound to have repercussions in Algeria. In Algeria the situation was, in several respects, potentially more dangerous than in the two protectorates. For one thing, the country was much poorer, and the over-population more acute than in the other two countries. There was also an important psychological difference : if, thanks to the fiction of a throne, in both the protectorates, Tunisians and Moroccans could still, up to a point, talk to the French as 'foreigners' and 'equals', in Algeria the feeling was much stronger that the French looked upon the natives as 'slaves' belonging to France, with no regular native institutions, or even a semblance of autonomy to fall back on. As distinct from Tunisia and

Morocco—which had all the trappings of Eastern monarchies—Algeria had nothing; not even that 'personality' of her own, the 'principle' of which Guy Mollet reluctantly granted it in 1956.

In September M. Robert Barrat, the ex-Secretary of the *Centre Catholique des Intellectuels Chrétiens*—a body closely connected with *Témoignage Chrétien* and other progressive Catholic circles, published in *France-Observateur* a reportage, after which he was arrested. This was an account of his visits to 'the Algerian outlaws'. While he was at Algiers, he was contacted by emissaries of the Algerian Resistance, who then took him into the Kabylian mountains some 60 miles from Algiers. Here he met Krim Belkacem, known as the 'Leader of the Kabylian Maquis'.

This is what these outlaws with whom he spent some hours told him:

> We are patriots who are fighting for an ideal. We face death, not because we like to kill, but because our confidence in France has been destroyed. The word 'France' which meant so much to so many of us before, now means police, tortures, and persecution . . . We do not believe that the French Government can put an end to the injustice and oppression that the Moslems of Algeria are suffering in their own country . . .

Some of these outlaws were students who had learned to believe in 'democratic France'. But most of these men whom Barrat was now seeing, had, at one time or another, been tortured by the French police. They were also saying:

> Our objectives are political. This is not simply a spontaneous rebellion. The CRUA is a para-military organization, which has little in common with the old MTLD, which, in any case, split in July 1954, after Messali had demanded dictatorial powers for life. Messali—who has been interned in France for years—has no authority in Algeria any more . . .
>
> When our movement first manifested itself in November 1954, the population of the whole of the Constantinois was already on our side. The people are solidly behind us: it is we who ordered a 15-days' boycott of the state tobacco shops, and the boycott was complete. We can also order the closing of shops at any time. The fact that we are never denounced shows that the people are with us. Even the Algerian representatives of the Second College are on our side now, and send us money. You French attribute our activities to 'the hand of Moscow', or 'the hand of Cairo', etc. But what you forget is the will of the Algerian people. Amongst us are NCOs of the French Army . . . Of course, we are

in contact with Algerian leaders in Cairo. You can threaten us as much as you like; but modern tanks are of no use in these mountains; if you want to fight us, you will have to fight us with the same weapons as we use . . . Repression will only strengthen us . . . We distinguish, of course, between good Frenchmen and bad Frenchmen; but even the good ones tend to think it is all a question of 'no schools', or hunger, or poverty; it has become, in reality, a national question . . . We shall create, before very long, a free zone in part of the Algerian territory, and shall proclaim Algerian independence and appeal to foreign countries, so that the problem of Algeria becomes internationalized.[1]

No doubt, there was an element of sentimentalization in this account of the Kabylian 'outlaws'. For Arabs in revolt do not usually conform to the romantic pattern of the European 19th century fighter for freedom; and a story like Barrat's inevitably struck a false note in trying to represent them as such. What had started in Algeria was a particularly ugly and cruel war—or rather, a Revolution which the French were now trying to smother. In such a struggle there was little room on either side for chivalry.

While, in Morocco, one *coup de théâtre* followed another, the Faure Government continued to be in a state of complete confusion about Algeria. The three-day debate in the middle of October was extraordinarily inconclusive; the watchword that had made headway for some time past, on the initiative of M. Soustelle, was 'integration' —but what this meant in practice, nobody could tell. It looked as though the French Government were willing to agree to some degree of 'economic integration'—which, as one Moslem speaker remarked, merely meant that the French winegrowers in Algeria could flood the French home market with Algerian wine without any barriers whatsoever. As for 'political integration', which would, if strictly applied, mean that 120 Algerian deputies would sit in the National Assembly, it was as far off as ever; and so was also the 'social integration', which should, logically, mean the same wages and the same family allowances in France as in Algeria.

Even the representatives of the Second College of the Algerian Assembly were now in open revolt against the Soustelle proposals; but the explanation offered by a Right-wing deputy in Paris that these *beni-oui-ouis* of the Second College were merely scared of the 'terrorists', did not provide the true explanation. Algeria was in the throes of a nationalist upsurge. It was, indeed, largely as a result of this revolt that the majority of the UN Assembly assumed an attitude which

[1] *France-Observateur*, September 22, 1955.

forced the French delegation to walk out of UN in a huff—not to return until two months later.

In fact, neither M. Bourgès-Maunoury, the Minister of the Interior, nor M. Faure himself gave the impression that they were doing anything other than playing for time. M. Faure's speech on October 14 was one of the worst strings of platitudes he had yet produced. Nevertheless, the debate, though totally inconclusive, was not without interest. The Communists, in particular, harped on the atrocities committed by the French in their reprisals for the August 20 massacres. Thus, one of their speakers quoted at length the gruesome account of the *Monde* correspondent, Georges Penchenier, who described his visit to the village of Carrières Romaines, near Philippeville, where he found that fifty Algerians—old men, women, children—had been murdered in the course of a 'punitive' raid.

Duclos directed his attack against the 'Hundred princes of Colonization', and particularly against Senator Borgeaud, the 'Wine King of Algeria', who, to save their privileges, were willing to see France start a major war in Algeria. He also protested against the prohibition of the Algerian Communist Party, which, he said, included both Algerians and Frenchmen, as well as against the closing-down of *Alger Républicain* which, though not a Communist paper, was the only daily paper in Algiers in opposition to the colonialist diehards.

Bourgès-Maunoury: You have been talking about the 'Hundred princes of Colonization'. Let me tell you that there are in Algeria 40,000 families of European stock; of these 20,000 are landowners, and among these 20,000, 18,000 own less than 200 hectares; 17,000 are the families of farm labourers, and 3,000 manage the estates. There is also the industrial and trading community, as well as a lot of small people; and all of them feel that their very lives depend on what happens in Paris these days.

Duclos pointedly remarked that the people who really mattered were the 2,000 families who owned *more* than 200 hectares, often *much* more; it was they who were preventing any land reform in Algeria.

The most moving speech was made by the 85-year-old Maurice Violette, who had been Governor-General of Algeria before the war and who had attempted, in 1936, together with Léon Blum, to introduce in Algeria a series of far-reaching liberal reforms. But every time he attempted anything, he met with opposition, and 'now, at the end of my career,' he said, 'I am carrying the intolerable burden of thirty years of deceived hopes and of broken promises.'

Yes, I know, the Algerians are using the roads and railways that we built. But what do these roads and railway mean to them?

What does property mean to them, except the rags they wear? I should like the Premier to give Algeria a bunch of fine reforms. For surely, the time for study is over. This is our last chance to avoid disaster. If the Government can break certain egoisms, there may still be a hope . . . As much as 30 years ago, I said that if the Moslems of Algeria were not given a square deal, they would take the law into their own hands . . . My long parliamentary career is coming to a close; and great is my sorrow in leaving this tribune, haunted, as I am, by the thought of what is to happen to both France and Algeria.

The debate went on for three days, but ended in an atmosphere of confusion, and M. Faure's final speech did nothing to dispel it. It was not clear whether he was in agreement with Soustelle or not. It was, indeed, only a few days later that M. Faure made it quite clear that he had no intention of taking any final decisions on Algeria, and preferred a General Election to take place in France without delay, so that the new Assembly could deal with this terrifying problem.

In the final vote there was a Socialist motion in favour of the 'strict application of the 1947 Statute of Algeria' and an honest election at the earliest possible time; but only three Radicals voted for this, among them M. Mendès-France. A few days later he spoke at Caen. It was a stormy meeting, at which an organized and rowdy opposition was conducted by M. Dorgères, who had been the leader of the Fascist movement among the peasants before the war. 'You've sold Indo-China! Better talk to us of alcohol,' (the main city of the Calvados *département* had, of course, strong views on the subject) were among the least unpleasant cries with which Mendès was greeted. The next meeting became so violent that the police had to intervene in the end.

'The unkept promises,' Mendès said, 'are at the root of our present troubles in Algeria. We shelved the 1947 Statute. Election returns have been constantly tampered with. The Algerian representatives were in fact appointed by the administration . . . The Statute must be promptly applied, and there must be real elections in Algeria. Even if the people elected are not our friends, we must negotiate with them; because they will be the real representatives of the Algerian people . . . Integration, to the Algerians, implies complete equality; but in Paris the word is often used merely as a meaningless slogan.'

As we have seen, the Moroccan problem was 'solved' in the most unexpected way by the end of October, after the Glaoui's spectacular *volte-face*. M. Faure, if anything, felt relieved at having what seemed a wholly insoluble problem solved for him in this way by an 87-year-old *deus ex machina* . . . As far as he was concerned, what was to happen in Morocco next was really the business of that new Assembly, the election of which he desired to be held as quickly as possible. That the whole Moroccan policy of France had been disastrous during the past three years was apparent from the simple fact that if, in 1953, and even at Antsirabé in 1955, the Sultan was still willing to agree to a 25-year 'time-table' before full independence was reached, the Glaoui's *volte-face* had now made independence an immediate reality!

CHAPTER 5

THE RADICAL CONGRESS OF NOVEMBER 1955

AS in the old days, the *Salle Wagram* was decorated with bunches of tricolour flags, and plaster busts of Marianne, and Phrygian bonnets painted above the slogans:

L'opinion publique est impatiente.—*Saint-Just.*
La République se construit sans cesse.—*Herriot.*
La République est toujours en péril.—*Alain.*
Organisons-nous, disciplinons-nous pour l'action.—
Camille Pelletan.
Le véritable danger, c'est la misère.—*Ledru-Rollin.*
Les républiques manquées rendent inevitable la dictature.—
Cudenet.
Il y a encore des féodaux à abattre.—*Herriot.*
Le Parti Radical est le Parti qui tient parole.—*Herriot.*

There was a musty smell of 19th century idealism about it all. And then, on the platform, or close to it, one suddenly caught sight of some ghosts—Third Republic politicians, some of whom one was startled to see, for one scarcely knew whether they hadn't died long ago. Even Georges Bonnet had turned up, as well as some others who had discredited themselves in the Vichy days and had been lying low for years. Some of them were very old men.

These ghosts had all come to hear Mendès-France explain his programme, and to watch his imminent duel with Edgar Faure.

The great majority of the delegates were pro-Mendès and anti-Faure. Mendès's programme speech—'the platform', as he preferred to call it—was an impressive document, and he took the greater part of the whole afternoon session of the first day, and part of the next morning session to read it. It was a brilliant job, and contrasted strangely with the well-meaning blah of the slogans around the hall . . .

What didn't he talk of—housing, wages, pensions, education, agriculture, the reconversion of industrial undertakings, revision of the Constitution, electoral reform, the 'purification' of public life, etc., etc., and, of course, North Africa and, in the first place, Algeria.

Just a few samples of this Mendès 'Platform':

. . . Our stock of housing has not been well used. We must develop hostels for unmarried persons, for old people, for North

233

Africans; every single person should have the opportunity of securing a single room to himself, without having to invest in a whole apartment . . . So long as there is full employment—and, indeed, a shortage of labour—in the building trade, the building of luxury flats must be prohibited . . . Insufficiently-occupied flats must be heavily taxed, and credit facilities should be given for the conversion of large flats into two or three small ones . . .

The racket of furnished rooms must be stopped. This is a racket from which the working class suffers most; the kind of robbery under which, openly or secretly, a worker is made to spend half his wages on 'rent'. It is intolerable that young married couples should be condemned to living in hotel rooms for which they have to pay exorbitant rents . . .

We cannot allow slums to survive 'until the housing shortage is settled'. Do you know that in such condemned property the incidence of T.B. is 600% higher than elsewhere? There must be a temporary rehousing plan for slum-dwellers; they can live in prefabricated houses until permanent new homes are built. In Paris alone 200,000 people live in houses officially classified as 'slums'. In four years all such slums in the Paris area must disappear.

He also spoke of agriculture, which was passing through a 'crisis of adaptation' to modern conditions.

In the Savoie, for instance, milk marketing is well organized, in the Eure it is still very bad and wasteful. French peasant economy should keep an eye—much more than it is doing now—on export markets; large quantities of fruit could be exported; but the organization is wholly lacking. With a sufficient degree of organization, stable prices could be made a general rule in the case of meat, eggs, fruit, vegetables, dairy produce; the export of all excess food production could be organized; it would cost the State something—but this is a more profitable form of expenditure than armaments. The peasant is not by nature a speculator, and the greater part of the peasantry would surely welcome the kind of stability which a *planned agricultural programme* could provide.

He then came to what he called *les classes moyennes*—by which he meant the small-producer and shopkeeper class, rather than the 'middle class' in the English sense.

The example of Scandinavia shows that the *classes moyennes* can flourish—provided they adapt themselves to new conditions . . .

And there followed a detailed exposé of his views on the reconversion of outmoded or uneconomical or redundant enterprises.

At present big enterprises have no difficulty in securing credits for buying new equipment; such credit should be extended to small businesses whose modernization can be said to be in the general interest. There should be an Equipment Fund for small industries, and a *Banque d'Artisanat* for artisan enterprises.

Plan, plan, plan . . . the word kept recurring over and over again in Mendès-France's 'platform' . . . Some of the 'old beards' in the audience muttered through their whiskers: 'Socialism'; but most of the younger people—who were the most numerous in the audience—were impressed.

And, in the case of Algeria, Mendès pleaded for democratic reforms and for an honest application of the 1947 Statute, complete with honest elections—a theme he was to develop in much greater detail during his election campaign a month later. His main theme then was that, unless a peaceful settlement was reached in Algeria, it was practically useless to talk about housing and the essential reorganization in France itself—for Algeria would absorb all financial resources which could otherwise be productively used . . .

But here, at the Radical Congress, Mendès's immediate worry was less Algeria than the *scrutin d'arrondissement*—a point on which he enjoyed overwhelming support from the *militants* in the audience. It was largely that which accounted for the extreme hostility with which the Premier, M. Edgar Faure, was received at the Radical Congress. For there was, clearly, a conflict between the Congress and the Party, on the one hand, and the Radical group of the Assembly on the other.

Faure's conflict with his own Party was, of course, nothing new in French political history. There had been similar conflicts in the past between the Party and some of its most prominent leaders—Daladier, Herriot, Sarraut, Doumergue, Caillaux, Clemenceau and others. It is true that, at the Senate, favourable to the *scrutin d'arrondissement*, Faure enjoyed less support than at the Assembly.

The General Policy Committee of the Congress had already passed a motion on November 3, i.e., before Edgar Faure had been given a chance to speak, in favour of Faure and the Radical Ministers committing themselves to the *scrutin d'arrondissement*, or else resigning. If they failed to do so, they should be expelled from the Party.

It was curious how Mendès-France had succeeded in giving this issue all the aura of a *mystique*—as if a return to the pre-war election system was the sole condition on which France could be 'reformed'.

The sceptics, indeed, recalled that the same election system did not necessarily produce the same results. It was under the *scrutin d'arrondissement*, for instance, that two such entirely different Chambers were elected as that of 1928 (Poincaré, Tardieu, Laval) and that of 1936 (Popular Front) which, in the end, endorsed Vichy!

On the afternoon of November 4, came the great clash between Faure and Mendès-France. All hell broke loose the moment Faure appeared in the hall. There was a chorus of booing and cries of 'Resign!' Faure gradually succeeded in making himself heard. His arguments were not altogether unimpressive.

> The Radical Party, he said, was essentially a government Party, not an opposition party. The choice, soon after the Liberation, lay between taking part in the Government and playing Cassandra, with her constant refrain: 'I told you so'. No: the Radical Party which, in 1945, had only 16 deputies, was proud to have been 'alone': it had been alone in criticising the Constitution, and certain nationalizations, and much else; but later the Radical Party had assumed its natural and traditional rôle, which was that of a Government Party. And it had proved that it was not a party of 'old fogeys'—it had produced two Prime Ministers under 50—[Faure and Mendès]. And then Faure proceeded to show (and now, in spite of itself, the Congress, did not fail to be impressed) how since 1953, when he became Finance Minister, economic conditions in France had vastly improved; thus, in 1953 only 119,000 new houses had been built; in 1955, 210,000 would be completed; and the minimum wage had, over the last three years, been increased by 26%. 'Unlike some others,' said Faure pointedly, 'we believe in social reform, but within the framework of personal freedom and private enterprise.'

He went on like this for a long time, without much interruption. Then he came to North Africa—'the most anguishing problem of all'. In Tunisia, he said, the Government had followed the policy inaugurated by Mendès-France; and despite much opposition from the Right, he (Faure) had established the most satisfactory relations with Bourguiba. In Tunisia the intellectual élite, of whom Bourguiba was so eminent a representative, had made agreement relatively easy. In Morocco it was infinitely more difficult; but here, too, he (Faure) had attempted, without waiting for the horrible explosion of August 20, to find a solution.

Faure then claimed great credit for having, even despite the massacres of August 20, pursued his plan of holding the Aix-les-Bains Conference, followed by the Catroux mission to Antsirabé . . . As for

Grandval, he had not been 'sacked'; but, after the massacres of August 20, he had cabled to Faure to say that he was not receiving sufficient co-operation from the Generals, and that a military man should be sent to replace him.

The most important point Faure made on Algeria (a problem, he said, over which he and his Minister of the Interior, Bourgès-Maunoury had worried more than any other) were these:

1. Soustelle considered that the re-establishment of order must have priority over reforms;

2. Nevertheless, a large number of reforms had been drafted, and were under consideration; but what was really needed was a more *general* solution to the Algerian problem.

That is why (Faure said) we have proposed that we be given a few weeks in which to hold very complete consultations, with both the Moslems and the Europeans of Algeria. In this way we might be able to draw up, possibly by January 1956, a Charter of Algeria. The matter is so important that it is in fact the chief reason why I am in favour of an early General Election.

It is no use having an eight-months' hiatus, with Algeria calling for urgent decisions. It is no use for an Assembly, with only a few months' existence before it, taking far-reaching decisions; Algeria might not know whether such decisions were binding on the next French Parliament.

As for electoral reform, Faure suggested that he personally preferred proportional representation on a departmental basis (not, of course, on a national basis—for this was a monstrosity); he was against the *apparentements;* he was not greatly in favour of the *scrutin d'arrondissement;* but if the National Assembly wanted it, it was free to vote for it. It had not done it so far. Anyway, a change in the election system would not necessarily bring governmental stability; other remedies were needed for that.

There was a curious incident, when a woman heckler exclaimed that Faure had made use of Communist votes on a number of occasions.

Edgar Faure: Madam, if there are Communists on the National Assembly, it is not because I invited them there. If, in certain cases, the Communists vote for me, I can draw whatever conclusions are to be drawn from it; but I am not going to be offensive about our parliamentary system because the electorate has returned so-and-so and so-and-so . . . The Communists voted for our policy in Tunisia, Morocco and Indo-China, and they were quite right to do so. It is no use saying that Communist votes are valid one day, and not valid another day.

Q

Here was a crack at Mendès-France, if ever there was one!

And then came this dramatic—and cunning—conclusion:

Faure recalled that, at the time of the Anschluss in 1938, France was without a Government. The situation in Algeria was, in its own way, just as dangerous. Now was not the time for France to be without a Government. However, since so many people at the Congress desired him (Faure) to resign, he wished to submit the matter to the arbitration of M. Herriot: if Herriot told him to go, he would.

Herriot, for all his 83 years, had lost none of his old cunning. No, he said, this was a matter for Edgar Faure's own conscience. He must decide for himself. Was it a veiled suggestion—as some of Mendès's followers thought—that it *was* Faure's moral duty to resign? But many, on the contrary, felt that Herriot—with his extraordinary instinct for guessing which way the wind was blowing—was, at heart, no longer as wholeheartedly *mendésiste* as he had been a year before.

There was a touch of comedy—almost buffoonery—in Mendès-France's reply to Faure.

'Shall I,' he said, 'call you Edgar Faure, or *président?*'

A delegate (ironically): Call him '*cher ami*' . . .

Mendès-France: (con dolore): Yes, I have a right to call him *cher ami*, and he knows what I think. I have the right to call him that, because our friendship is sufficiently old and sufficiently deep, so that no one can mistake this for a platform effect. He knows what I think, and how unhappy I am at this very moment.

And then Mendès embarked on a long discussion on the utter incoherence of the Faure Government; nothing could be settled about either Morocco or Algeria (except by outside factors, beyond the Government's control, as in the case of Morocco) because the members of the Faure Government were all at sixes and sevens—and not only on these two fundamental issues, but also on many others, and not least on electoral reform. And then he declared that a great new hope was sweeping the country; at last France—and especially the young generation—was regaining hope and confidence in the Republic; but, if Faure had it his own way, there would be another ungovernable, incoherent Assembly, and, in the end, the Republic would be muzzled and strangled.

There followed a grand ovation, with cries of '*Vive Mendès!*' and the singing of the *Marseillaise*.

In a sense, Faure and Mendès had been talking at cross-purposes. Faure had talked of the past and drawn up a fairly impressive balance-sheet of his own economic achievements; Mendès was talking of the future, and in terms of a programme. He was unwilling to look upon the Radical Party as the nucleus of a Centre Coalition, inevitably tied to the MRP; and thought in terms of an alliance with the Socialists; for that reason he (at least nominally) repudiated the *loi Barangé* of 1951, giving state grants to religious schools.

There was certainly a serious split, at that time, in the Radical Party. Mendès had created among the *militants* a kind of fanaticism over the *scrutin d'arrondissement;* so much so that even while Faure was discussing Morocco, he was interrupted by cries of '*scrutin d'arrondissement!*'

But for Mendès the whole thing was something of a gamble—and a gamble for high stakes, too; and Robert Barillon, the *Monde* commentator was shrewd enough to realize it when he wrote at the height of the Congress:

> Either the Radical Party will transform itself immediately, even at the risk of losing some of its members, or else Mendès-France will lose his bet within a relatively short time.[1]

Was it a personal triumph for Mendès? In a sense, yes. Herriot was unanimously re-elected President, and Mendès was elected First Vice-President by a large (but not overwhelmingly large) majority. His 'Platform' was adopted on a show of hands. Yet he was conscious of his supremacy not being the same as at the Marseilles Congress a year before, when Herriot had given him his solemn blessing. He therefore avoided a final showdown with Faure, and went back on the 'ultimatum' demanding the resignation of Faure and the other Radical Ministers from the Government. Many of the younger *militants* were bitterly disappointed by this climb-down. They attributed it partly to the pressure exercised on Mendès both by the Senators and by M. Herriot. They felt that these men were behind the times, and could not appreciate all the possibilities provided by the Mendès 'platform' . . .

---

[1] *Le Monde*, November 6–7, 1955.

CHAPTER 6

FAURE DISSOLVES THE ASSEMBLY

IT would be neither amusing, nor even very instructive, to recount in detail the highly tortuous parliamentary game that was played throughout November in connection with the date of the General Election and the voting system. But a few landmarks should be noted.

On November 7 the National Assembly once again rejected the *scrutin d'arrondissement* and Faure announced that he would make the maintenance of the electoral system (i.e., single-ballot departmental P.R.) of 1951, but without *apparentements*, a question of confidence. The Senate, largely favourable to the *scrutin d'arrondissement*, now resorted to delaying tactics, partly, it seems, under the influence of Mendès-France, who assured many Senators in private that if enough time was gained, the Assembly would adopt the *scrutin d'arrondissement* in the end. After a great deal of wire-pulling, the Senate introduced an amendment into the Faure Election Bill, this amendment amounting to a proposal that the *scrutin d'arrondissement* be adopted.

At this point the bulk of the Gaullists who were feeling increasingly uncharitable to Edgar Faure (chiefly because of his handling of Morocco) voted in favour of a motion whereby the Assembly 'took the *scrutin d'arrondissement* into consideration'. This motion was carried by 311 votes to 286, and Mendès rather rashly jumped to the conclusion that the idea of returning to the pre-war voting system was making rapid headway.

It was then that Faure—no doubt quite consciously—added to the confusion by embarking on a re-drawing of the electoral map, with a view to cutting up France into constituencies of almost equal size in terms of population. During the following week-end prefects and deputies spent their time examining the Government's *découpage* proposals, and two such *découpage* Bills were submitted to the Universal Suffrage Committee of the Assembly.

The confusion was now at its height, and finally Faure, in the face of these interminable discussions, and the Assembly's apparent unwillingness to make up its mind, announced that it must choose between elections in February and a Cabinet crisis.

The reason for this announcement was the motion in favour of a general discussion on the Government's policy—which implied the shelving of all further discussions on the date of the new election. M. Faure made the rejection of this motion a question of confidence.

The truth is that a part of the Right, and the Gaullists in particular were beginning to treat Edgar Faure as a 'liquidator of France's greatness', just as they had treated Mendès-France as such in the past. Just as Mendès was held responsible for the 'loss' of Indo-China and Tunisia, so Faure was now being blamed for the 'loss' of Morocco.

In the short debate which ended in the overthrow of the Faure Government, Faure was attacked by practically all parties other than the Radicals and the MRP. But M. Mitterrand (UDSR) spoke in reality on behalf of Mendès-France. He declared that Faure had merely paid lip-service to any changes in the electoral system, and that he was determined by hook or by crook to maintain the 1951 system, complete with *apparentements:*

> Every time, during the past month, when you thought you could bring off a snap election under the old system, you stepped on the accelerator; every time you saw the *scrutin d'arrondissement* making headway, you put on the brake.

Mitterrand then charged Faure with having done all within his power to discredit the National Assembly in the eyes of the electorate, and with wanting to bring about a snap election in these conditions: the electorate was expected to choose between M. Faure, a virtuous and patriotic statesman, and an irresponsible Assembly. By demanding a discussion on the general policy of the Faure Government, the Assembly wished to show the electorate how little M. Faure was worth.

What Mitterrand, Mendès-France and their friends were really hoping for was that, after the overthrow of the Faure Government, a caretaker Government under the aged M. Queuille would take over, and that the *scrutin d'arrondissement* would then be rapidly adopted.

They then made a catastrophic mistake. They did not realize that by working up all this agitation against Faure, they were playing into his hands: for it was not until the vote was announced—318 against the Government, 218 for it, and 83 abstentions—that they realized what had happened: the Government, under Article 51 of the Constitution, could now dissolve the Assembly; for it was the second Government to be overthrown, within 18 months, by an absolute majority of the Assembly. The decision could be taken, after the President of the Assembly had expressed his opinion (*avis*).

The ruling of M. Schneiter, the President of the Assembly, was that the Government was, constitutionally, within its rights to dissolve the Assembly; but, inside the Government a conflict broke out between the majority who were in favour of the dissolution, and those who were against it, on the ground that, whatever the letter of the law, it would be contrary to its spirit to dissolve the Assembly in the circumstances. In the end, five Radical members of the Government resigned, among them M. Bourgès-Maunoury, the Minister of the Interior; but Faure refused their resignations.

The whole situation was, indeed, highly paradoxical: in dissolving the Assembly, the Government was, in fact, precipitating precisely the kind of General Election which the Assembly had tried to prevent, and had, for that very reason, overthrown the Government. The *apparentements* system would, in the absence of a new electoral law, be now applied.

Technically and tactically Faure had outwitted Mendès and had achieved his purpose by denying him the time required for reforming the Radical Party and for shifting the whole political balance of France towards a reorganized and revived non-Communist Left grouping. But Faure himself was also to be denied the fruits of victory, and the winners of the contest (if there were any winners) were to be people with whom the contestants had hardly reckoned in their elaborate calculations and manœuvres.

The *mendésistes*, in particular, who felt that they had been badly outwitted by Edgar Faure, screamed about a *coup de force*, and compared 'little Edgar' to Marshal MacMahon, and even to Napoleon III —all the more so as the President's Dissolution Decree was dated December 2—the anniversary of the *coup d'état* of 1851.

Faure himself seemed undecided at first on what to do; but two factors played in favour of dissolution: the Right-wing and MRP members of his Cabinet—who thought they would benefit again from the *apparentements* system—urged Faure to use the dissolution weapon; secondly, Faure had reason to believe that, for all the screaming about MacMahon and Napoleon III, the country, on the whole, was not unfavourable to a new election. All the hanky-panky of the last six weeks over electoral reform and the date of the election had caused a great deal of irritation against the Assembly.

As for the Parties, they were not, in the main, violently hostile to a new election: the Communists and the MRP—and even part of the Right—were in favour of preserving the old electoral law[1]; the Socialists, though openly hostile, did not feel very strongly on the subject; and the only group that felt that a very dirty trick had been played on them were Mendès-France and his followers; to them, the *scrutin d'arrondissement* was the one great chance of winning a lot of seats.

[1] Although the CP had been its chief victim in 1951, it did not think the *apparentements* system would greatly harm it this time. Anything was better, from the CP point of view, than the *scrutin d'arrondissement*.

Not that, in the opinion of the *Monde*, there had ever been any likelihood of the Assembly adopting it.

Mendès-France was now on the war-path. Even before the Dissolution Decree had appeared in the *Journal Officiel* on December 2, he called a meeting of the bureau of the Radical Party—a body composed of 38 members, about two-thirds of whom were Mendès men. After a brief and acid interview with Edgar Faure, who was accused of having become 'the pensioner of the MRP', the majority of the bureau decided to expel Faure from the Radical Party. During this interview Faure had remarked with a touch of nonchalance: 'I did my best, after all, to get you your precious *scrutin d'arrondissement*.' 'Yes, you did, didn't you?' said Mendès with cold rage.

A few days later, Faure's expulsion was followed by a number of other expulsions—including that of several of the Radical diehards—Martinaud-Déplat, J. P. David, René Mayer, etc. All these, as well as Faure, while denying that they were no longer Radicals, decided to fight their election battle under the banner of the RGR (*Rassemblement des Gauches Républicaines*), a loose formation of various (mostly Right-wing) Radical and UDSR members. Shortly before, Faure had been elected President of this body.

To Mendès-France, Edgar Faure had now become Enemy Number One. His own personal resentment at having been foiled by the Dissolution Decree was best reflected in *L'Express* which conducted against the Premier a campaign of almost unprecedented ferocity.

CHAPTER 7

MENDÈS'S ELECTION BATTLE:
TOP PRIORITY FOR ALGERIA

THERE was a feeling of *malaise* in the country, at the time of the dissolution of the Assembly. Nothing seemed to be going quite right, and many things were going seriously wrong. In Europe, the second Geneva Conference had produced no results, and soon afterwards the Saar election was to prove another humiliation for France: it was as if, in a country like Germany, France could now be treated as of no consequence at all. This view had, of course, been greatly encouraged by what had happened during the past six months in North Africa, with the Sultan being triumphantly reinstated two years after he had been deposed by the French; with Tunisia showing great signs of intending to 'ask for more', barely a few months after the ratification of the Franco-Tunisian Conventions; while in Algeria, things were going from bad to worse as the weeks rolled by.

Mendès-France was in a difficult position. He had, on the face of it, 'purged' the Radical Party; he was ready to fight a spectacular election battle; but, at heart, he knew that the Dissolution had given him very little time either to organize his following in a big way or to make a major impact on the country. It was partly for that reason that he decided that, instead of trying to impress upon the electorate the far-reaching importance of his elaborate election 'platform'—in which every economic, social and financial problem had been worked out in great detail, it was perhaps best to concentrate on the one issue which, he felt, dominated all the others—and that was peace in Algeria.

In any parts of the country where Mendès was a familiar figure, he made a great impression. In his own constituency, the Eure *peparté-ment*, he had a large and enthusiastic following, and within the narrow limits of that constituency, the result amounted to almost a personal plebiscite in favour of Mendès. In the Paris area, too, he had a substantial following among many of the politically most mature and sophisticated voters, and some of his enthusiastic and devoted lieutenants, like M. Hernu, did very well indeed. But in the rest of France, especially in provincial France, the Mendès label did not cut as much ice as Mendès had hoped. If he was a great local figure in the Eure, and a great national figure in Paris, he was neither in the greater part of the country, and many of his lieutenants lacked both his dynamic vigour and his power of conviction.

Moreover, there was too much ambiguity about it all. The 'Radical' label was too old, and the 'Mendès' label too new; it was often not quite clear what the relations were to be between the *mendésistes* and the Socialists (let alone between Mendès and the rest of the Radicals), while the Communists often fought Mendès with much greater vigour than they fought Pinay or Teitgen, if only because he had flatly turned down the Popular Front.

It was Mendès, however, more than any other man during the election campaign who helped to make France 'Algeria-conscious'. But even this was not without its dangers, and a widespread impression, even among his followers, was that Mendès's (now) official propaganda organ *L'Express* was badly overplaying its hand. It soon came to be accused of being 'cosmopolitan' and 'un-French', and *apatride* (all of them, indeed, euphemisms for 'Jewish'), and one publication—the influential newsletter *Perspectives*—even proceeded to refer to it as 'the daily bulletin of the fellaghas'—the Algerian rebels.

The impression Mendès made on many, on closer examination, was that he did not really himself believe in a sweeping election success, but that he was determined, nevertheless, to make a tremendous effort, both mentally and physically, to achieve the absolute maximum that could be achieved in highly unfavourable circumstances. For at heart Mendès knew perfectly well that his personal triumph in the Eure and that of a few of his lieutenants in the Paris area were not enough.

With the General Election fixed for January 2, there was not much time to lose. Even so, the various preliminaries of the election campaign took up the first half of December, and there was little more than a fortnight left for the election campaign proper.

In the case of Mendès, First Vice-President and virtual head of the Radical Party, the first few days of December were taken up with purging the Party, and with organizing the electoral alliance with the Socialists, the UDSR, and certain Gaullists. These last two formations were, however, much less *mendésiste* than some had expected. Only one prominent member of the UDSR—M. Mitterrand—was an open ally of Mendès, while, among the Gaullists, only a small number of men, headed by Chaban-Delmas, fought under the banner of what came to be known as the Republican Front. This was officially formed on December 6, after the majority of the Socialists had rejected an alliance with the Communists.

To their right was a motley 'coalition' of Faure's RGR, the MRP, the 'classical' Right; and still further to the right, various groups of

'Fascist riff-raff'—under Poujade, Tixier-Vignancour, Dorgères and others—whom the Republican Front were not, however, taking seriously yet. 'These people,' wrote *L'Express* on December 7, 'can hope for no more than to snatch a few seats from Pinay and Duchet . . .'

On December 8, the Republican Front published an appeal to the Nation, signed by Mollet, Mendès-France, Mitterrand and Chaban-Delmas, and saying that, by holding their snap election, 'the Guilty Men of Dien-Bien-Phu, of the Morocco *coup*, of the 1,000 milliard deficit, of the chaos in North Africa, of France's numerous humiliations in the international field, and of the social *immobilisme* at home' were trying to evade responsibility for what they had done.

The electoral alliance was, of course, a reality—though not a very important reality, since the *apparentements* worked in only a few constituencies; as for a common programme, there wasn't any. The Socialists had their ideas, and Mendès stuck to the Radical 'platform'; it was not till after the election that the two could be co-ordinated, as far as possible . . .

Almost from the outset it was clear that Mendès was going to make Algeria his Number One Election Issue.

L'Express concentrated all its heavy guns on Algeria, and Mauriac —Mendès's most devoted and wholehearted supporter—regarded him as the one and only man in France capable of giving the Arabs a square, Christian deal.

'Whatever the outcome of this battle,' Mauriac wrote on December 5, 'everything will truly *begin* on January 2 . . . History, the bloody History, the criminal History that these people have been writing for the last ten years is on our side . . . I do not blame you people for hating Pierre Mendès-France. But to all those madmen who keep on screaming: "Anything, anything rather than Mendès-France!" I just want to put one question. Who is the man you have to put beside him, a man whose intelligence has passed as many tests as his has, and which is recognized by the whole world; who had the courage to stand up to the oligarchies, and to the gangs who are poisoning our race with their hard liquor; or who had no responsibility for all those disasters? Those disasters which, during the last ten years, Pierre Mendès-France foresaw and denounced relentlessly, until the day when his enemies had to call him to the rescue. Who, among your people, has been able to drag France out of her lethargy for even only a few days, as Mendès did during his term of office? Don't talk to us of Pinay or of Edgar Faure . . . that Faure who at last managed to achieve something the other day: a dirty trick. Our faith in Mendès-France is based on facts . . .

And what we can reproach you with is the thought which you would not even admit to yourselves: "May the nation perish, rather than be raised to its feet by this man!" '

Could anything be more strange or striking than this admiration, this adoration (one might almost say), certainly this hero-worship of Mendès-France by this great novelist, this old but passionate man, embodying as it were, the Catholic conscience of France? Just as in the past he had, contrary to all the traditions and reflexes of his own *milieu*, fought for Abyssinia against Mussolini, for Republican Spain against Franco and Hitler, for the Resistance against Vichy, for the Sultan of Morocco and the Moroccan people against Big Business and the He-men of Morocco, so today he was fighting another crusade for Mendès-France against the men of Dien Bien Phu, against *La Croix* (i.e., against the French Church Hierarchy), against the MRP, against the *Osservatore Romano* and the Vatican itself . . . He wanted the Catholics of France to stop voting for the MRP—'*démerpisons la France!*' he wrote; he wanted passionately that they vote for Mendès. Never, he swore, had Mendès done anything against the Church while in office, or against the Church Schools, and in January, 1955, the Holy Father had benevolently received him in Rome . . .

Mendès said No to war, he stopped bloodshed wherever he could (wrote Mauriac a few days before Christmas). But no; it is foreigners now—the Reverend Fathers of the *Osservatore Romano*—who have to interfere in our election affairs, and have to tell the faithful of France how they are to vote . . . Yet *La Croix*, like the *Osservatore Romano*, is against the men who have stood for justice, and it wants the victory of the gang of Dien Bien Phu . . . Oh, I know that the great mass of French Catholics will vote as they are told . . . But it will be enough for us if we have on our side some of the wide-awake youth of our country, a youth faithful to its mission. I watch them and I listen to them as they stand there, facing that boundless desert of conformism with its deadly resistance to the human spirit. The Little Child that will be born on Saturday night, will be born in a prison cell, jealously guarded by a class and a caste. All we can do is to attempt to liberate Him.

Such was Mauriac's crusading spirit. As an unkind critic remarked: 'Isn't he beginning to confuse Mendès-France with the Infant Jesus?' In a way, it made it all a little awkward for Mendès in his election campaign, when hecklers pestered him: 'Are you or aren't you for the *école laïque* . . .? You've always been vague; you've always tried to wriggle out . . . ' And the Socialists were a little uneasy about Mauric's *mendésiste* zeal . . .

Was it mistaken, misdirected zeal? Anyway, Mauriac had convinced himself, deeply, genuinely, that there was only one man in France with sufficient breadth and clarity of vision to save her from disaster—and that man was Mendès. One of the strangest human—and social—relationships in French history.

But it was all there—the spirit of the Dominicans, of the worker—priests, of the Vatican-banned *Cahiers de la Quinzaine*, of *Esprit* and *Témoignage Chrétien*, with its humanism, its lofty human values, its pity for the underdog—the Arab underdog. How different it all was from the bosses of the MRP who now, as Mendès himself noted in one of his articles in *L'Express*, had somehow 'forgotten' to include among their election candidates, M. Fonlupt-Espéraber, the Alsatian, who was the only MRP deputy to have gone to Tunisia in 1952 and to have publicly denounced the atrocities committed in the Cap Bon area by the Foreign Legion under the command of General Garbay, the 'killer of Madagascar . . .'

The *Express* pointed out that the Faure Government was deliberately hiding the real gravity of the situation in Algeria from the electorate. On December 5 it reported that the Moslem town councillors of Algeria and Oran had resigned to protest against

> the unprecedented repression and the war atmosphere; against the stamping out of any political life among the Moslems; against the inability of Moslem councillors to obtain a hearing from anybody; and against the French Government's determination to impose its policy of integration.

It also reported that the Algerian Assembly had decided to suspend its session on December 9 and to postpone its examination of the Soustelle Plan. It referred once again to concentration camps and police tortures.

On December 9, under the title 'Anarchy in Algeria' it reported that the two Colleges of the Algerian Assembly had by 67 votes to 10, adopted a motion asking the Government not to hold elections in Algeria on January 2. There was so much terrorism, the Moslem delegates declared, that it was useless for Moslems to vote in such conditions, and if the Government insisted on holding the elections in Algeria, the Moslems would boycott them.

The Government decided that no candidates, either Moslem or European, would stand in the circumstances. The *Comité de coordination des musulmans*, comprising 62 Algerian deputies, senators and members of the Algerian Assembly, most of them French stooges in the past, now nevertheless announced their 'solidarity with the other national movements, with a view to securing the triumph of the aspirations of the Algerian people'. They also demanded a 'Charter of Algeria'. It showed that even the 'stooges' were, willy-nilly, being driven into the arms of the Rebels.

On December 14 *L'Express* announced that General Billotte, Minister of Defence, has asked that reinforcements be urgently sent to Algeria; the Government decided to postpone the question until after the Election. Yet only a few days before, 22 French soldiers had been killed in an ambush at Gualma. In Algiers itself, two bombs had been thrown, wounding 22 persons. The paper recalled that in less than a year the number of troops in Algeria had risen from 75,000 to 180,000, and now many more were wanted.

On December 21, it reported that the Algerian Resistance had sent an ultimatum to all Algerian deputies, members of the Algerian Assembly, town councillors, etc., demanding that they all resign their functions before January 2. There was danger of growing anarchy in Algeria as a result. The paper also stated that the Government was *secretly* sending reinforcements to Algeria.

On December 23, *L'Express* revealed that the military were now demanding 60,000 new men in Algeria, which would raise the number of troops there to 240,000. It also showed that 'the scandalous *dossiers* of the French repression in Algeria fully explained the complicity of the population with the Rebels'.

On December 24 it reported that Soustelle had made an official statement showing that he had been clamouring for reinforcements 'for months'. The Faure Government, with an eye on the elections, had kept this dark, and had kept Soustelle waiting . . .

On December 28 the paper carried a detailed *reportage* from Algeria by Jean Daniel, which concluded that the divorce was now complete between the French and the Algerians, and that further repression would only end in a blood-bath. But the military were still talking of 'pacifying' the country; they were now already demanding 300,000 troops.

The next day the paper published a strip of four photographs, taken from a film, showing a French gendarme raising his rifle at a prisoner some twenty yards away, firing the shot, with the Algerian slowly collapsing and then lying dead on the ground. This sequence of stills, it was explained, came from a film on French atrocities which had been smuggled into America and shown to countless people, especially around UN.

At this point pandemonium broke out. What was the *Express* up to? The way it presented the story was this:

> The French gendarme you see in this picture had, together with some comrades, been entrusted with the task of guarding a number of suspects, who had been arrested in some villages in the Constantinois after the horrible massacre of several European families. To help the cameramen, who were shooting a newsreel on the war in Algeria, the gendarme put to death one of the prisoners in his charge.

This story constituted part of a great double-page spread on French atrocities in Algeria, including details of the Djorf concentration camp and of the bombing and burning of villages, whose inhabitants were then reduced to 'joining the Maquis'.

The Faure Government was, clearly, taken aback by the *Express* revelations. After a long conference at the Premier's office, a semi-official communiqué was issued, saying:

> It has been established that an auxiliary gendarme arbitrarily shot a Moslem who had taken part in the massacres of August 20. The matter is all the more serious as this was done at the instigation of the representative of a foreign film company. This person bribed the gendarme to help in the 'scenario', and the film shot as a result has indeed been shown in various cinemas of North and South America, and has certainly encouraged anti-French propaganda at the time of the UN session [in the course of which the vote on Algeria forced the French delegation to walk out, not to return until two months later].

The Government's communiqué stated that proceedings had been taken against the gendarme. But it then added that *L'Express*, in over-dramatizing an admittedly serious incident, was trying to discredit the whole of the French army, and to make political capital out of it on the eve of the Election.

Fox-Movietone then issued its own version:

> This film was taken at the end of August at Ain-Abid. Our cameraman is a Frenchman, born in Algeria; he was competing with the CBS TV-man and with several other cameramen. The scene in question was merely accompanied by this brief commentary: 'Film taken in the course of a battle while the forces of order break into a mechta [Algerian village].

That wasn't the end of it yet: the incriminated cameraman, Georges Chassagne gave a press conference on December 30, at which he denied having bribed any gendarme: the French authorities had asked him no question at all, until the *Express* story had appeared, and the 'bribery' story was a pure invention. The incident of the shooting had taken place during a 'clean-up' operation in the village of Ain-Abid. French gendarmes were searching the village for rebels who had committed some horrible atrocities only two days before.

Outside one house there was an old Algerian of about sixty; the gendarme asked him if a certain Algerian (whose name he gave) was hiding in the farm. The old man denied it. Nevertheless, in searching the stables, the gendarme found the man. He seemed unarmed. The gendarme then ordered him to walk down the road, and, when the man was a few yards away, the gendarme shot him. That was the picture we took. At no moment did we have any dealings with the gendarme. I must, however, say that the latter was closely related to a family, all of whom had been massacred only two days before. Like every other European in the area, this gendarme was sickened and furious by what the Moslems had done.

M. Chassagne thought, however, that the killing incident was an isolated case. He strongly protested, in conclusion, against the charge made against him, as well as against Fox-Movietone, by the Government. Soon afterwards, indeed, an apology was made to him.

The reaction to the *Express* 'scoop' was, in the main, unfavourable: it was charged with fouling its own nest; and it was this scoop, more than anything else, which started cracks like the *Express* being 'the fellaghas daily bulletin', the kind of thing that, in some measure, rebounded on Mendès-France himself and made him, more than ever, Enemy Number One of the French community in Algeria. The instinctive reaction of very many people was to sympathize with the gendarme.

The emphasis in *L'Express* had, indeed, throughout December, been on French, rather than on Arab atrocities; it was a bad psychological mistake to make during election time, even if, statistically, more Arabs than Frenchmen had been killed . . . No allowance at all had been made by *L'Express* for those my-country-right-or-wrong feelings which had been steadily growing in France for the past year . . . It was something fundamental which it had, somehow, overlooked.

It was widely felt that the *Express* had, on balance, done Mendès more harm than good.

Whatever the final outcome of the Election, Mendès-France was personally invariably a great draw during the election campaign. His first big meeting was at the *Mutualité* in Paris, and only half the 6,000 people who had come to listen to him could find room in the hall. There was some rowdyism outside, but not much. The audience, largely composed of women (for it was announced that he wished to address 'the women of Paris') was a friendly one, and a few cries of '*Mendès au poteau*', '*Mauriac aux chacals*' and '*Herriot au Panthéon*' were drowned in the much more numerous cries of '*Mendès au pouvoir!*'

He spoke of Indo-China, Algeria and—Drink. In the case of Indo-China he stressed the grave danger of 'internationalization' that the world had escaped and revealed that he had taken a much graver risk than people realized when he fixed his deadline on July 20.

I gave myself a month to make peace in Indo-China, and was accused by some of 'defeatism'. In reality, I can now reveal that the French Generals in Indo-China were desperate to have the cease-fire within a fortnight, i.e., on July 5; as they could not guarantee being able to hold out any longer.

On Algeria he said that reinforcements were being sent there, but that the Faure Government was making sure not to make this public until after the Election.

When at last (he exclaimed) are these people going to realize that these military measures do not constitute a policy? When will they realize that this method, which was practised for years in Indo-China, can only lead to disaster? We must make peace in North Africa. We cannot maintain ourselves there if we depend on nothing but the army, the police and repression. A deep understanding must be achieved between the two peoples of Algeria. But to want this is not enough: our will must be imposed on those monstrous feudal interests who see no solution other than a bloody and perpetual process of repression. So long as we go on ruining ourselves on military expenditure, there can be no question of building enough houses ...

That, in a nutshell, was the policy that Mendès-France was going to stick to in respect of Algeria—even during those melancholy months when, as Minister of State without portfolio in the Mollet Government, he tried to make his voice heard in the councils of Government ...

War in Algeria would mean economic and social stagnation—or decline—inside France: that was to be the principal theme of his whole election campaign.

But in December, 1955, there was still an occasional note of optimism in some of Mendès's speeches: he still spoke of a French 'awakening', of a new desire among ever-growing masses of Frenchmen and Frenchwomen to put their house in order. One of the trickiest subjects in this connection was alcoholism. Now, at that *Mutualité* meeting, he appealed to the women of France to help him in his anti-alcohol drive:

> Not a day passes (he said) without some evil brute ill-treating his children. The lives of innumerable women are in constant danger. Half the road accidents are due to drink. Alcoholism costs the State £250 million a year—enough to build 150,000 houses . . . Whatever your political views, please use your vote to safeguard the health of your family.

Mendès believed that, whatever the men felt about it, countless women in France considered alcoholism in France a major evil, affecting their personal lives, and the heredity and health of their children. Perhaps this anti-alcohol drive would have yielded rich returns, if alcoholism were the only—or the principal—election issue. But it wasn't.

Mendès spent the next ten days electioneering in his own constituency, the Eure, and held there four or five—sometimes six—election meetings a day; he met with some opposition from Communist hecklers and Poujadists; but his personal prestige in the Eure was so high that most of his meetings were orderly and, indeed, enthusiastic. He met with none of the systematic opposition, violence and deliberate sabotage which, at the end of a few days' electioneering, gave M. Mitterrand a heart attack and a nervous breakdown.

Just after Christmas, Mendès went to the south of France, where he held a number of mass meetings. The most important of these was at Marseilles, where he produced his 'Algeria Plan'.

> At any price (he said) we must find a solution to the Algerian conflict before March, as otherwise the war will take on tragic proportions. The Algerian Assembly no longer represents anything, and must be dissolved. After a number of stages—but within six months—an honest and controlled general election must be held in Algeria. We can then freely discuss the future Statute of Algeria with the legitimate representatives of Algeria, *so as to find a solution on Tunisian lines*. The premier of the post-election French Government must go to Algiers and stay there as long as may be necessary to break the resistance coming to any

R

such solution from the Administration and from the financial
and military feudal forces now holding Algeria in their grip . . .
Between the dissolution of the Algerian Assembly and the
Election six months later, a number of economic and social
reforms must be undertaken so as to absorb the unemployment
among 850,000 Algerians.

He also advocated the distribution of food in the neediest areas, the
redistribution of the large estates, the recuperation of abandoned
arable land, and measures which would 'compel the vested interests
in Algeria to work for the common good'.

> Let us not wait till Algeria rots away as Indo-China did, and
> as Tunisia nearly did. Remember that, between November 1,
> 1954 and February 5, 1955, when I was still at the head of the
> Government, not a single European was attacked in Algeria. I
> know that we are being attacked for our 'policy of surrender'.
> The phrase has always been applied in the past to statesmen who
> wanted to keep in step with the times.

This Mendès-France Plan aroused the greatest fury among the
French in Algeria; on the other hand, some Left-wing critics thought
it unrealistic. They said that if he really wanted peace in Algeria, the
first thing to aim at was a cease-fire with the Algerian Rebels . . .

All the same, *L'Express* claimed that, whatever the reactions of the
French in Algeria, the Moslems had been tremendously impressed by
the Plan, saw some hope for a peaceful settlement of their troubles,
and were less keen than before to follow counsels of despair . . .

Mendès's biggest Paris meeting was on December 27 at the Porte
de Versailles, a 'contradictory' meeting to which he had invited Pinay,
Bidault and Duclos, the Communist leader. Only Duclos accepted the
invitation. A Mendès-Duclos duel was, however, sufficiently interesting to draw a bigger crowd to this meeting than to any other throughout
the whole of the election campaign. 25,000 or 30,000 people came, but
only about half were able to get in to the hall; there was a dangerous
stampede; police barriers were broken through, doors were broken
down; the crush was such that a number of people had to be carried
away unconscious.

At least half the people present were Communists, but, despite
much singing, chanting and shouting of rival slogans—'*Mendès au
pouvoir!*' and '*Front Populaire!*'—both the principal speakers were
able in the end to get a hearing.

Mendès reiterated his 'Algeria Programme'; while Duclos chiefly
dwelt on the need for a Popular Front, and deplored Mendès's record

—he had rearmed Germany; he had done nothing in Algeria while in office; he had pursued an economic policy which was hostile to the working-class.

In replying, Mendès said that in January, 1955, he had prepared a programme for Algeria; if it was not applied, it was because his Government was overthrown soon afterwards—with Communist help; therefore, the Communists were as much responsible as anybody for the present war in Algeria.

> You treat us as traitors to the working-class; why then is it, Monsieur Duclos, that you should have been so persistent in offering us an election alliance? Had we accepted, you would have treated me very differently tonight, even though my programme would have been precisely the same one.

And Mendès advised the Communist leader to read the *Humanité:* he would find that the Communist paper reserved all its choice attacks for the Republican Front, and not for the reactionary Government of Edgar Faure.

CHAPTER 8

MENDÈS IN THE EURE

I SPENT the last two days of the election campaign in the Eure *département*, following Mendès from meeting to meeting. One thing was very striking: the man really felt at home here. He seemed to know personally half the people at his meetings; he referred to them by their names; and appeared to enjoy all the prestige of a 'local boy made good'. He was a famous man—one might say, a world-famous man, and the good people of the Eure seemed to take a distinct local pride in him—even those who were not going to vote for him. He, after all, was their deputy, the president of their *conseil général*—in short, Number One celebrity. No doubt, café proprietors tended to snarl and sneer at the mention of Mendès; he was the enemy of the café proprietors, and of the drink trade, and of the *bouilleurs de cru;* he wasn't easy to swallow. And among shopkeepers, there was a little whispering campaign saying that he had a big financial interest in Uniprix or Monoprix—the French variety of Woolworth—and that his wife was an Egyptian department store heiress. But all this did not outweigh his popularity.

Here, at Louviers, and Evreux, and Gaillon and in the little villages of the Eure he was at ease and self-confident, as though he were among people, most of whom were friends. Or, at any rate, people who admired and respected him. Those five or six daily meetings were exhausting—and yet Mendès seemed inexhaustible, always at the top of his form, dazzling in his replies, his repartee, his presence of mind... A familiar, friendly tone marked most of the meetings; even the Communist hecklers—most of whom he knew by name—he answered in a friendly, familiar tone. He did not seem on edge, as he so often was in Paris. These people—even the Communists, and the devout MRP ladies, and the Poujadists—were all Eure people, and few of them were poisonous creatures like Teitgen or Legendre back in the National Assembly in Paris... They addressed him with respect, as it had been customary to address a great *notable* of the Third Republic. And, at most of the meetings, there was a nice, old-fashioned, Third-Republic setting—for instance, the schoolroom at Aubevoye, with its plaster bust of Marianne, with a tricolour ribbon tied round her neck; and, below her, the poster:

VOTER MENDÈS
c'est voter pour la Paix
Le progrès économique et agricole
Le progrès social

Agricole . . . économique—a mixed area, partly rural, but also partly industrial, with a lot of new industries sprung up since the war so much so that the Eastern parts of the Eure were almost like an extension of the Paris *banlieue*.

It was interesting to watch Mendès-France's election tactics. Although he always spoke more or less extempore, with hardly any notes, it was clear that he had carefully prepared the general line of all his arguments, and had an answer ready for practically every conceivable —or inconceivable—question, with the possible exception of the question of the *école laïque*, in the case of which he tended to resort to evading tactics.

Like every parliamentary candidate seeking re-election, Mendès thought it necessary to justify his past record; here his main arguments were simple: it was he who had foreseen disaster in Indo-China long before others had done; it was he who had made peace *in extremis*, and had not allowed the senseless Indo-China war to degenerate into a major international war, which some of the MRP leaders were prepared to 'risk'. It was he, too, who had started the only possible policy in North Africa—a policy which, if pursued, could bring peace and friendly co-existence there. Germany and German rearmament he preferred not to mention—it was an unpopular subject. As for home affairs, he had done what he could, within the very short time allocated to him, but even so, a good deal was done, and even more was started, including the battle against alcoholism—a particularly tricky subject in the Eure, as we shall see.

But at all the meetings, whether they dealt with foreign affairs or (more often) with home affairs, Mendès stressed that, at the present juncture, there was really one thing that mattered, and which dominated all the rest—and that was peace in Algeria.

The discussion was, on the whole, on a fairly high level, and dealt chiefly with major national, and not local issues. I cannot describe all the meetings I attended, and shall confine myself to three—a small meeting in a village school in Aubevoye, which lasted only 15 or 20 minutes, with only some 25 people there; a medium-sized meeting at Gaillon, a town in a very 'mixed' area; and the great mass meeting at Evreux, the capital of the Eure. At Aubevoye, Mendès started with a few minutes of 'self-boosting'. He had made peace in Indo-China, he had re-established peace in Tunisia. Despite some extremist elements

in Tunisia, the attitude of the Tunisian Government towards Franco-
Tunisian co-existence was highly satisfactory. But Algeria was causing
him the gravest anxiety.

We must act very quickly to avoid a repetition of the appalling
Indo-China tragedy. The winter is not conducive to the development of civil war; but all the information we have shows that in
the spring more and more Algerians will leave their villages and
join the *fellaghas*. It is essential, at any price, to find a rapid
solution, which would give confidence to the Algerian people.
We promised them fair elections, and these elections were a
swindle. We must have controlled elections now—controlled by
all the French Parties without exception.
Sixty-thousand new men are being called up; but even if
600,000 were called up it still wouldn't make any difference;
because such problems are not settled by violence. The problem
of Algeria is today the most important problem of all; a peaceful
solution must be found: otherwise, if we have to spend many
hundreds of milliard francs every year on a war in Algeria, there
will be nothing left for anything else.

Except for an incoherent old drunk, who reminded Mendès that,
in 1932, he had been elected in the Eure with the help of Communist
votes, there were no hecklers at this meeting; and Mendès seemed,
indeed, in a hurry to get away to the much more important meeting at
Gaillon.

Here, in the tightly packed hall of the *mairie*—with the audience
consisting mostly of workers and farmers from the neighbourhood—
Mendès played very much on the 'local boy' string.

Ça fait 25 ans que nous nous connaissons (he began). At
Gaillon I have always met with comprehension and sympathy—
even from those of my friends who do not always agree with me
politically. And, by the way, this hall, as you see, is very cramped;
and I do hope that, in the next few years, you are going to have a
large and lovely spacious new *Salle de fêtes*.

After having got that one off his chest, Mendès turned to more
serious matters.

People always say: 'This is the turning point of history'. In
most cases it's an exaggeration. But this time I must tell you, with
all the earnestness and sincerity of which I am capable: This time
it *is* true. This *is* a turning point. In the next few years we shall
know whether the problem of North Africa is to be peacefully
settled, or whether we are to lose North Africa after a hopeless
war.

There followed a few minutes of self-boosting, and a sharp criticism of the *immobilistes*, who had allowed problems like Indo-China and EDC to drag on for years; also, in countries like Britain, Belgium and Germany, far greater economic progress had been made than in France in the last ten years.

He went over the usual ground about the Indo-China settlement, his methods of governing the country—methods which had proved distasteful to the National Assembly, but which had much to recommend them, all the same. He told the story of Indo-China and Tunisia not without a touch of pride and even arrogance.

'And the Paris Agreements?' somebody cried.

Mendès ignored the question, and went on:

In Tunisia the number of French troops has been reduced from 50,000 to 20,000. What better proof is there that my policy was the right one? But meantime, in Algeria the zones of rebellion are growing in number and are becoming a terrifying problem. Some say 'repression' is the solution. I say no, no and no.

There were questions—mostly from Communists—on a number of labour problems: what was Mendès's attitude to the abolition of the *zones d'abattement* (i.e., differential wages, according to zones); the protection of trade union freedom against victimization; the three, instead of two weeks' holiday with pay; the nationalization of the oil trade, etc. And why, he was asked, had he voted against the sliding scale in wages and against other labour measures favourable to the working-class? In replying, he insisted that wages could not be treated independently of production, and showed that the Communists, in a spirit of demagogy, had, in the last few years, asked for a huge increase in expenditure, without much to balance it on the revenue side.

The discussion grew much hotter as the drink problem was brought up. Mendès's chief heckler was an 'ambulant distiller'—who distilled the fruit of the *bouilleurs de cru;* a monstrous campaign, he said, had been conducted—and who had financed it?—against the small *bouilleurs de cru*. The man went on and on, complaining against Mendès's anti-alcohol decrees, some of which, unfortunately, he said, had not yet been repealed.

'I am a war veteran,' the man cried, 'I was in the Resistance, and it is shameful that old-time collaborators should worship on the tomb of the Unknown Soldier!'

It seemed rather irrelevant—but there it was.

And he continued:

'It is not the small fruit-grower who is responsible for the people in loonie-bins!'

Mendès now answered. First, the Communists, then the 'ambulating distiller'. He particularly addressed M. Fals, the Communist trade unionist, who had asked most of the questions.

You've asked me a lot of questions, Monsieur Fals. Don't tell me I am against the working-class. I was prepared to examine the whole question of wages in April 1955; it was not my fault if the Communists helped to overthrow me in February. But I *had* fixed the famous *rendez-vous d'avril*. Also, you asked me whether I favoured trade with China. Yes, I do. It was I who sent a business delegation to China, but the Communists overthrew me; Faure pursued the opposite policy towards China, and the Communists saved his Government on two occasions.

Now, Monsieur Fals, you are a Communist; I respect the sincerity of your opinions; you tell me I am against wage-earners, against old people, and in favour of the 'wages zones'. Surely, Monsieur Fals, if the cost of living varies from zone to zone, why shouldn't wages? But, as already said, I was willing to discuss the whole problem of wages in April this year; but your Communist friends overthrew me. But remember—when I was in office I was always willing, whenever possible, to talk to the representatives of the trade unions—of *all* the trade unions; I did not, as others did, discriminate against the Communist CGT. Monsieur Fals, you surprise me: if I were really the enemy of the working-class, why should Duclos have wanted an election alliance with me? I am a man of the Left, Monsieur Fals, and you know it. I supported practically all the reforms of 1936 under the Popular Front Government. Only, believe me, there is today something more important, far more important than whether you are going to have two or three weeks' holidays with pay—and that is peace in Algeria. And, another point—do you really think I could do everything in $7\frac{1}{2}$ months—the short time I was at the head of the Government?

Then he came to the drink problem. Here again he picked on one of the hecklers—the M. Chandelier who had declared himself to be an 'ambulating distiller'.

MENDÈS-FRANCE: Now, listen, Monsieur Chandelier; there is always a tendency to consider drink as a funny subject at any public meeting. Believe me, it is not a funny subject. We all know how many people died in the two wars—but how many people do you think have killed themselves with drink?

CHANDELIER (*plaintively*): Surely, Monsieur Mendès-France, every man has the right to choose his own way of dying!

MENDÈS-FRANCE (*sternly, and rather self-righteously*): Yes, he has that right; but he has no right to bring degenerate children into the world! Alcoholism costs the State 250 milliards a year—enough to build 150,000 houses . . . You have talked about the genuine *bouilleurs de cru*, that is, the people actually working on the land and—about the others, who are also enjoying the *bouilleurs de cru* privilege.

CHANDELIER (*triumphantly*): But, Monsieur Mendès-France, you are a *bouilleur de cru* yourself!

MENDÈS-FRANCE: Just a minute, I'll deal with that one presently. But please remember this: the *bouilleurs de cru* institution has given rise to one of the most scandalous abuses in our whole economy. There were, in the first place, at the beginning of this century, 800,000 *bouilleurs de cru* in France, allowed to distil 10 litres[1] of pure alcohol a year, free of tax. Now there are $3\frac{1}{2}$ million . . . or at least there were till I stopped this racket. I personally have lost my privilege as *bouilleur de cru:* and I am glad I have: it's perfectly normal I should *not* be one. Just like the 10,000 *bouilleurs de cru* in Paris—a notorious agricultural area, as you all know!

Now let me say something else. If a farmer distils 10 litres, it is not a serious matter. But there are some who distil 700 litres. And this illicit alcohol is sent to *apéritif* manufacturers; I happen to know that there are various booze factories which buy three-quarters of their pure alcohol from the *bouilleurs de cru*.

CHANDELIER (*furiously*): It's a lie! It's not true!

MENDÈS-FRANCE: Yes, it *is* true, Monsieur Chandelier. And will you keep quiet for a moment. There is a black market in alcohol, which causes the State a yearly deficit of 40 milliard francs; if it weren't for that, taxes could be cut by that amount. When a grower makes 10 litres, it doesn't matter, but there are certain areas where growers distil hundreds and hundreds of litres.

CHANDELIER (*hysterically*): But what with, what with?

MENDÈS-FRANCE: With *your* stills, *cher Monsieur!*

The 'ambulating distiller' was neatly demolished, and said no more. Mendès then said that there should be a very strict control, limiting the tax-free distilling to ten litres in the case of *bona fide* agriculturists; similarly, the whole system of 'ambulant distillation' should be thoroughly revised, as it had already partly been done under the Mendès Government. Alcoholism, he said, was a major tragedy in France; there were parts of France where eight per cent of the population were alcoholic, and where one person in 300 was interned in a mental home; in some places this infernal proportion was even higher.

[1] About 2 gallons.

Never have I opposed the moderate use of wine and alcohol; but if there were no alcoholism in France, there would be enough money to increase the standard of living of the French working-class by 10 per cent.

Naturally, in a country like the Eure, he had to pull his punches; to condemn the whole *bouilleurs de cru* institution would have been suicidal in electoral terms; that was why he had to dwell only on the abuses of the system.

There was one curious incident. It was when a heckler (quite irrelevantly) exclaimed *'Prix unique!'*

Mendès stopped, and turning to him, said: 'You said "Prix unique"? What did you mean by that?' It seemed an obvious allusion to Cicurel—and to the whispering campaign among shopkeepers that Mendès had financial interests in Uniprix or Monoprix shops (the French 'Woolworths').

The man was taken aback by Mendès's sudden sharpness.

'People say . . .' he mumbled.

MENDÈS: Say what?

THE HECKLER: Monsieur Mendès, you are a more educated man than I am, and you have more practice in talking in public, so it's hard to argue with you; but people say you have shares in *prix unique* shops.

MENDÈS: All this has nothing to do with your education or my education. But let me tell you just this: if you ever hear people say it, you can tell them that Mendès-France firmly told you that he hasn't, and never had, any money invested in any sort of *prix unique* shop . . . Is that clear?

THE HECKLER: Yes, Monsieur Mendès-France. But what can you do if people talk?

However, Mendès ended his meeting by warning his audience that the greatest problem of all was peace in North Africa, and it was up to the Electorate to decide on January 2, whether it was to be war or peace.

In the crowded café outside the *mairie* of Gaillon, the café proprietor was sneering at Mendès-France. He thought Poujade was his man. *C'est un bon Français, celui-là.* And he was *not* against the café proprietors, and the small shopkeepers. 'Don't you believe him; he *has* got financial interests in Monoprix and Uniprix; and, what's more, he's also a big shareholder in Esso-Standard Oil. *Un homme de gauche* —don't you believe it!—he's up to his neck in Big Business.'

The meeting at the Lido at Evreux was a great mass meeting, the biggest in the whole election campaign in the Eure. December 30 was only three days before polling day, and the opposition was there in strength. But even here Mendès had many more friends than opponents, and everything went off in a fairly orderly way. Mendès did not make an opening speech, and merely asked that the questions be asked first, and then he would answer.

First came several Communist speakers who insisted on knowing what Mendès's position was in respect of the *école laïque*. Was he, or wasn't he in favour of revoking the *loi Barangé*? He has formed his Republican Front with some of the worst enemies of the *école laïque*, such as Chaban-Delmas, the Gaullist, who had publicly announced that there was no question of revoking the *loi Barangé*.

Another speaker, obviously wishing to embarrass Mendès, asked that he say something about the Paris Agreements and EDC.

The next speaker was a tight-lipped MRP school-mistress, clearly from an *école libre* (a Catholic school):

We are against you, M. Mendés-France (she began). With your speeches you have created a fog of illusions. But your Republican Front is full of contradictions. You have created a gulf between two halves of the French nation. And yet you claim to be a leader of the youth of France. We happen to know what you replied to the *Action Laïque*. And yet, don't you realise that your Socialist friends would be the first to be extremely upset if the *loi Barangé* were revoked?

And then, turning to Algeria, she said:

In your paper yesterday, you printed some abominable photographs [a reference to the unfortunate film strip]. Don't you realize what you are doing? Don't you realize that you are attacking the very soul of France?

She was followed on the platform by a lanky young man:

I am a Communist (he said). May I ask why, throughout your speeches, you have avoided like the plague any mention of the Paris Agreements? Secondly, you have promised us a settlement in North Africa. And yet you are the first head of the Government to have sent *contingent* troops to North Africa. And it was you who sent Soustelle there—the Soustelle of the *ratissages* in countless Algerian villages. Do you, or don't you, approve of Soustelle? . . . Economically, you say you hadn't time to achieve much. All the same, you were in office for eight months. You found time to make a few nice little presents to the capitalists, with your 180 milliards of fresh capital investments . . .

The next speaker was a polished, well-groomed young barrister, a M. de Broglie, who was one of the Right-wing candidates in the Eure.

> You say you wish to negotiate in Algeria, just as you negotiated in Tunisia. But with whom are you going to negotiate? There is no Algerian *nation*. What, in fact, your proposals amount to is that you would like to negotiate with the terrorists. But beware! Already in Tunisia there are men more extreme than Bourguiba—I mean Ben Yussef. Just as in Algeria, so in Tunisia, the extremists are gaining ground, and what you want to do is to encourage them. Instead, you should negotiate with Algerian war veterans, with Moslem technicians, with people who would help us to isolate the terrorists. I would not say that your policy was a policy of surrender; but you are pushing the Algerian people into the arms of the terrorists; and if you try to apply the Tunisian solution to Algeria, then it'll be the end to French rule in North Africa.
>
> You say you've got a programme. But where's your majority? You say you will be supported by a lot of men of goodwill. But, for one thing, your Socialist friends have not accepted your programme, and, secondly, do you really believe that the Radicals you have expelled from your Party will forgive and forget so easily? M. Mendès-France, you have been a disruptive force; you have divided the country, and those who will vote for you will vote for a policy of reckless adventure in North Africa.

Another speaker asked what Mendès-France's attitude was to Europe. Mendès now replied.

> When I was still a student, I believed that the frontiers of Europe did not answer the economic needs of our Continent. I then wrote a book on Briandism. The weakness of EDC was that it made armaments the corner-stone of Europe . . . I have always encouraged Franco-German collaboration. But France was twice invaded by Germany within a generation; and I know that France's distrust of Germany is more than understandable. That is why I have never much believed in 'Europe', unless Great Britain took part in it . . . We tried to keep Germany unarmed, but I must say, with all due respect to our Communist friends here, that the violent Soviet Note of September 9, 1954, while I was in office, rendered this rearmament inevitable. We then saw that Germany might be rearmed without our consent, and we had no choice other than limiting the damage through the Paris Agreements. It was only after the Paris Agreements were ratified that the Russians became reasonable.
>
> I am glad we have some MRP speakers here (Mendès then

remarked); I gather they came here because they found that nobody had gone to the MRP meeting!

An MRP lady told us that that film—which was shown abroad—should not have been mentioned. I don't agree with that. We are entitled to know the truth. Even the ugly truth—for instance that the French police in North Africa use Gestapo methods. It was bad enough to have had the UN vote against France on the issue of Algeria; it hurt us all, I can assure you; it hurts even more when we hear that so many things happen in Algeria that are unworthy of France.

Answering M. de Broglie, he said that it was no use negotiating with *beni-oui-oui's* who represented nothing; that mistake had already been made with Bao Dai in Indo-China.

M. de Broglie mentioned Algerian war veterans. But these people do not want to dissociate themselves from their own people any longer. They do not want to be considered French *collabos*. What we must avoid is an Algerian Dien Bien Phu. No solution by armed force is possible.

He answered various other questions, but was extremely vague on the *école laïque*, saying merely that he was surprised to see the Communists being so interested in it, since the *Action Laïque* had already objected to the Communists trying to make political capital out of it.

The MRP, fearing defeat, he concluded, were now trying to come to terms with the Republican Front at the last moment; no; there would be no sordid negotiations with the MRP—either now, or after the Election. There must be no artificial majority.

But if the majority of the Assembly invest us, we shall form a coherent Government. That is what France needs. By voting for us, you will help us to save the country.

The large audience, favourable in the main to Mendès, burst into loud cheering. There were cries of '*Vive Mendès!*' '*Mendès au pouvoir!*' and it all ended with the singing of the *Marseillaise*.

A similar, and even more enthusiastic meeting took place the next day in Mendès's own stronghold, Louviers. It was December 31, the last day of the campaign. His face had a tired and yellow look, and he seemed worn-out. But he still spoke with vigour, and appeared confident that the polling would prove a triumph for Mendès-France—at any rate in the Eure. Which it did. But it did not in the rest of France ...

For one thing, many of the Radical candidates, who had conveniently adopted the 'Mendès' label, were easy-going old-time Radicals, and not Mendès men at all.

PART VI

THE ERA OF
NATIONAL—MOLLETISM

ENTER POUJADE

IT was one of the strangest elections in the whole history of France. Its result was baffling and bewildering. Something had been going on in France below the surface which all the election experts and tipsters had overlooked or greatly minimized. It was not only that the Poujade movement, which the tipsters had been generously giving half-a-dozen or ten seats, was given $2\frac{1}{2}$ million votes out of the 24 million votes cast, and 52 seats, but notorious pre-war and war-time Fascists like Dorgères, the 'peasant leader', and, worse still, Tixier-Vignancour, a notorious pre-war Fascist and rabid Vichyite had now made a spectacular come-back. Also, Georges Bonnet, a discredited Third-Republic politician, who was best remembered for his hob-nobbing with Ribbentrop in 1938, found 40,000 people voting for him in the Dordogne.

It was as if the war, the Occupation, the Resistance had receded far into the background of many people's minds, and as if the young generation (and there were close on three million new voters, compared with 1951) knew little or nothing about the war-time years, and had different criteria from the older generation in judging men and events. The home-bred Fascism of a Poujade was in no way associated in the minds of younger people with Hitler or Mussolini; they had hardly heard of them, and Poujade did not necessarily stand for anything discreditable.

Not that Poujadism was a Youth Movement—far from it. Its peculiarity was that it was, in reality, a middle-aged movement; nearly all the Poujade deputies elected were over 30; most of them were over forty, many over fifty, and a few over sixty. In reality there were two Poujade movements: a movement of discontent, especially among shopkeepers, who were 'defending themselves' against heavy and 'inquisitorial' taxation; and a much more consciously anti-democratic and Fascist movement into which this discontent was being canalized by the demagogues and the 'intellectuals' of the movement. These 'intellectuals', many of whom were running the Poujade paper, *Fraternité Française* were former *Action Française* men, Doriotists, and plain *collabos*—who had worked for the Germans during the Occupation of Paris. The record of Pierre Poujade himself, 'the little stationer of Saint-Céré', was not too good either. In his propaganda, he made much of the fact that he had joined the Free French late in the war; while nothing was said of the fact that, as a young man, he had been one of the Doriot boys. There was, in reality, nothing 'Gaullist' about this '*bon Français moyen*'. If he represented any French political tradition at all, it was the tradition of Right-wing thuggery, with Doriot as his most immediate predecessor.

With his slogan '*sortez les sortants*', so reminiscent of the Action Française's 1934 slogan, *A bas les voleurs*, he conducted an effective anti-parliamentary campaign during the election. He was young, vigorous, athletic, loud and foul-mouthed; he was 'one of us'; a *bon père de famille;* but crude and gargantuan, a heavy eater and good drinker, and with an implication of great sexual virility, as he resorted to his favourite platform trick of doing a sort of strip-tease in throwing off his jacket, his pullover and his shirt and showing off his pair of muscular arms. He tried, from the start, to build up his wife—the very type of the 'satisfied female'—as a sort of Evita Perón.

One of the favourite pictures to appear in the press after Poujade's election victory was that of Mme. Poujade, with a self-satisfied *Herrenvolk* smirk, dressed up in oriental garb reclining on an Algerian couch. For Mme. Poujade was a *Française d'Algérie*, whom he had married during the war; and if Madame hero-worshipped 'Pierrot', Pierrot had learned quite a few simple ideas about Algeria from his wife's peculiar 'settler's' mentality. It is a point which, in the context of 1956, was of considerable importance. Poujade, for one thing, had a very large following in Algeria (just as Doriot had had in the past); and his 'solution' for Algeria was a simple one: and that was simply to 'be tough with them'. One of the paradoxes of Poujadism was this curious combination: the outcry against taxation, and the willingness to embark on a very costly military campaign in Algeria which might prove even more ruinous than the war in Indo-China.

To complete the family picture of Poujade, there was also the inevitable *vieille maman*, whom he carried in his athletic arms as he waltzed round the room on hearing of the election results; and the two children who took part in the election campaign by chalking on walls '*Vive Papa!*' And on the well-laden dining-room table stood a pig-shaped water-jug, and, with a loud guffaw, Poujade would say: 'Pass me the Mendès!'

To a man like Poujade, Mendès-France was Enemy Number One. Not that he treated him with hatred; he treated him with a tremendous display of contempt—the chap who 'wasn't French'—who drank water and milk, instead of wine; who was an enemy of the hundreds of thousands of French café proprietors, a kill-joy and a spoil-sport, the chap with 'no roots in the soil of France', who had 'deserted during the war', who favoured the Monoprix and Uniprix and other Woolworth and department stores at the expense of the small shopkeeper (Cicurel wasn't forgotten either); who feebly sold out in Indo-China and started the rot in North Africa by throwing the French in Tunisia to the Moslem wolves, and who, if only he were given a chance, would throw away Algeria, too.

Poujade had, in short, come to 'replace' de Gaulle—the de Gaulle of the RPF of 1947 and 1951. The RPF had, in its later stages, not been entirely devoid of thuggery; but de Gaulle was a noble and respected figure, though with little political understanding; now he had come to be replaced by a table-thumping, soap-box demagogue who, better than de Gaulle, had learned all kinds of low tricks from Doriot and Goebbels. Anti-parliamentarianism, anti-semitism, racialism, Herrenvolk stuff, and the whole box of tricks.

Poujade's 2½ million votes were not all ex-Gaullist votes: some Socialists, Radicals, Right-wingers, MRP's and even Communists now voted Poujade. I know from my experience of South-West France that there even existed a curious form of 'bigamy'; Communist party members (who remained Party members) voting for Poujade, because he was going to (a) defend the 'small man' against taxation, and (b) save Algeria by killing off a million or two of Arabs—which the Communists were either unwilling to do, or were incapable of doing.

Poujade's success went to his head; for a few weeks after the election he threw his weight around mercilessly; talked of the *Etats Généraux* which would tell Parliament what was wanted, and claimed that 'his' 52 deputies were the '52 bristles of my broom which will sweep France clean'. And, finally, it was Poujadism which claimed the greater part of the credit for the Algiers riots of February 6, 1956, which forced the Mollet Government to abandon its peace programme in Algeria and made it submit to the will of the European community there. But this surrender was, in fact, what Poujade had least expected; and it was that which took the wind out of his sails. His decline was even swifter than his rise: National-Molletism, as we shall see, left no room for Poujadism.

During the election campaign, one of the most picturesque figures —'affiliated' with the Poujade movement—was the ex-police *commissaire* Dides—hero of the *affaire des fuites*. His constituency was the Sixth Sector of the Seine, comprising Vincennes and a large section of the industrial *banlieue* south-east of the capital.

Dides, contesting a constituency with many habitual Communist voters, pulled his punches where the Communists were concerned.

'To be apolitical is a policy,' he would say. 'Russia, America, China; I don't give a damn. What matters is *le biftek*. The real revolutionary is Poujade!' And then, with his expressive voice, and his good presence, *le commissaire* Dides (who, in the days of Mendès-France had been sacked by Mitterrand, the Minister of the Interior), would say:

> I have proof, positive proof, that military secrets were handed over to the enemy, handed over to the enemy by the Mendèsistes, progressistes and neutralists . . . And even if I do not accuse them formally of treason, I maintain that they were swimming in treasonable water!

There would follow a defence of Pétain: he had been sentenced to death; but what had the politicians of the Fourth Republic done but ruin all that Pétain had managed to save—the French Union above all? Innuendoes, innuendoes, still more innuendoes—all about a 'treason plot'; and in the centre of it, according to Dides, were people like Mitterrand and 'that great Frenchman' Monsieur Mendès-France . . .

CHAPTER 2

MENDÈS'S ELECTION FAILURE

ALTOGETHER, the election dumbfounded the prophets and tipsters. The Right-wing parties and the MRP who had persuaded Edgar Faure to dissolve the Assembly and hold a snap election were most disappointed of all. They thought that a lot of the Gaullist votes of 1951 would go to them; they went to Poujade instead. The *apparentements* had worked only in about fifteen *départements*, and usually only between the Mendès Radicals and the Socialists and, in some cases, between Faure's RGR, the 'classical' Right and the MRP. The fundamental feature of the 1951 election— the Socialist-MRP alliance, which was calculated to reduce the representation of the two extremes (Communists and Gaullists) was absent this time. Only in ten *départements* out of ninety did the *apparentements* achieve their object at all. In 1951 they had 'worked' in 39 *départements*. In the rest of the country a *départemental* PR was the system that had now worked in practice.

The results published on January 4, though not quite complete, showed sufficiently clearly what had happened. The Communists and *progressistes* had now nearly 150 seats between them as against 95 in the previous Assembly; the Socialists 90 as against 100; the Radicals having contested the election under at least three different labels, had, indeed, become three splinter parties who, instead of holding the 82 Radical seats of the old Assembly, now shared some 70 seats, of which only 34 were shown (somewhat arbitrarily) by the semi-official returns to be 'Mendès' seats, and 15, 'Faure' seats. The MRP were down from 85 to 70 seats, and the 'Classical' Right from 125 to 95.

These two groupings, which had pressed for the Dissolution more than any other, had badly miscalculated their chances.

On the extreme Right, there were now a group of 52 Poujadists, besides a handful of pre-war Fascists (Dorgères, Tixier-Vignancour, etc.).

The most spectacular failure was that of the Gaullists (16 instead of 57). Even such 'stars' of Gaullism as M. Gaston Palewsky, M. Philippe Barrès and General de Monsabert were eliminated. Much of the Gaullist vote went to the Poujadists. These also gained a number of Right-wing votes, as may be seen from the loss of 30 seats by the Right. The MRP lost heavily chiefly because the *apparentements* did not work in 1956 as they had worked in 1951.

French election statistics are always a little tricky, and, except for the Gaullists, practically everybody declared himself satisfied with the results. Even the 'classical' Right and the MRP claimed to have done 'rather well'. Although the proportion of the Communist vote had not increased, the Communist seats had increased by some 50 per cent, and the Communists were conscious of their strong strategic position in the new Assembly. The Socialists, like the MRP, had suffered from the absence of *apparentements*, but had, compared with 1951, substantially increased their vote. There is no doubt that the dynamic figure of Mendès—an election ally of the Socialists—had, in many constituencies, contributed to the Socialists' success. (Mollet hastened to forget this once the election was over.) On the other hand, neither the Faure, nor the Mendès Radicals had very much to be satisfied with, and Mendès-France was undoubtedly disappointed by the result. Not that this prevented *L'Express* from claiming a great Mendès victory, and from announcing in a huge headline on January 3:

LE FRONT REPUBLICAIN EN TETE

The fact remained that, at a pinch, the Republican Front could claim about 150 seats; but much more than half of these were Socialist seats. *L'Express* protested against the figure of '34 Mendès Radicals' in the semi-official statistics, and claimed 50 or more; but even 50 was not exactly a landslide. The sad truth was that *mendésisme* as such had made no impact on the country, and had produced only a few—very few—striking personal election victories, notably that of Mendès-France himself; the results in the Eure (where none of the *apparentements* had obtained an absolute majority, and so hadn't worked) were:

Registered voters	198,000		
Votes cast	161,000		
Radicals (Mendès-France and Gilbert Martin)	59,787	votes	2 seats
Socialist	7,807	„	nil
MRP	23,916	„	1 seat
Right	13,981	„	nil
Communist	31,401	„	1 seat
'Faure' Radical	8,653	„	nil
Poujadist	10,816	„	nil
Gaullist	2,522	„	nil

In Paris, Charles Hernu, head of the 'Jacobin' movement[1] (a small group of *mendésiste* intellectuals, with some following especially amongst students and officials) and a close associate of Mendès's, and a few others did reasonably well. But if in Paris the Mendès label that certain Radical candidates had attached to their election propaganda carried some weight, it made no great impact in the rest of France, except here and there, notably in the East. But, as already said, it helped the Socialists. At the same time, as was soon to become apparent, most of the Radicals who had presented themselves under the Mendès label were not *mendésiste* at all. Mendès must have foreseen this, but the election had been decided upon so suddenly that there wasn't much time to pick and choose the candidates.

Faure, for his part, also achieved a major personal success in his Jura constituency, but 15 was all the following he could reasonably claim.

---

[1] Its weekly paper, *Le Jacobin*, claimed a circulation of 12,000.

CHAPTER 3

ENTER GUY MOLLET

AT heart, nobody, except Poujade and the Communists, was satisfied with the election results. The immediate question that arose was what kind of government majority there was in the new Assembly. One thing was clear: there could be no Government without the Socialists. It is true that, in the second week of January, the Right-wing press, including the *Figaro* began to build up the uncouth Poujade boys as hard as it could, rather with the suggestion that their heart was perhaps in the right place, after all; and if, in the past, the 'classical' Right managed to win over a large proportion of Gaullists, why shouldn't it win over some of the Poujadists—all the more so as there were now a few signs of the 'shopkeepers' beginning to protest against certain unmistakably 'Fascist' tendencies displayed by some of Poujade's followers, and especially by Poujade himself. On the other hand, Poujade himself claimed that if only the electorate had known that his movement represented a major national force, there would have been not 50, but 150 Poujadists elected.

However, the overtures made to the Poujadists met with no response at the time, and no sooner had the Assembly met on January 20 than the other parties decided that it would be in their interests to write off the Poujadists as potential allies; and often against any rhyme or reason, the other parties, including the Socialists and the MRP, embarked on a highly dubious game of 'invalidating' some of the Poujadist seats, and taking them over themselves. In this way more than half-a-dozen Poujadist seats were 'distributed' among the other parties. It was thus that M. Alfred Coste-Floret (MRP) and a couple of Socialists were re-admitted to the National Assembly. The technical reasons for invalidating these Poujadists were usually extremely feeble, and the invalidations were accompanied by ugly rows and even fights.

Only a few days after the election results were known, Guy Mollet and Mendès-France, as the two principal leaders of Republican Front, claimed that it was for them to form the new Government. But on whose support would they depend, since they had barely 150 seats between them? The Communists started agitating in favour of a Popular Front—which would have something very close to a clear majority in the new Assembly; the 'classical' Right and the MRP started talking in terms of a 'national' Government including themselves, the Mendès Radicals and the Socialists. Finally, on January 17, at the Socialist Congress, Mollet rejected both the Popular Front and a National Government. Which meant, in reality, forming a minority Government, depending either on Centre support, or on Communist support—or, in a few cases, on both. Mendès-France took the same line.

It was then that a lot of hanky-panky started. The hanky-panky was chiefly over two problems: one was Algeria, the other was the place Mendès-France was to hold in the Government.

Who was the prospective new Premier, Guy Mollet? Born at Flers in the Orne *département* in 1905, the son of a textile worker, who was to be killed in the 1914 war, Mollet was brought up as a war orphan (*pupille de la nation*) at the expense of the State. In due course he took his *licence* and became a teacher of English. He taught in various *lycées* before the war and was, at the same time, active as a Socialist *militant* and strongly advocated the organization of the teaching profession on trade union lines.

Wounded and taken prisoner by the Germans in 1940, he was released in 1942, and joined the Resistance as a member of the (relatively Right-wing) OCM organization, which he headed in the Nord and Pas-de-Calais region, an area with which he was familiar, since, just before the war, he had been teacher of English at the *lycée* at Arras. He became a captain in the FFI and took part in the fighting at the time of the Normandy landing. The same year he became Secretary of the Arras Liberation Committee; was elected mayor of that city and, in 1945, he became *conseiller général* and Socialist deputy for the Pas-de-Calais. As leader of the 'anti-Blum' Left wing of the Socialist Party, he replaced Daniel Mayer as Secretary-General of the Party in September 1946, and his victory was hailed as one of 'Marxism' and of the 'revolutionary tradition' of the French Socialist Party over the purely 'reformist' outlook of Léon Blum.

Not that he was, in reality, any more Left-wing than Blum or Daniel Mayer, and the 'palace revolution' of September 1946 amounted to very little in practice, despite the ostensibly much more *dirigiste* tendencies of Mollet, compared with the more 'compromising' attitude of Daniel Mayer. Mollet took an active part in drafting the Constitution in 1946, and held his first Government post as Minister of State in Blum's stop-gap cabinet of December 1946.

After the breakdown of *tripartisme* in May 1947, Mollet became outspokenly anti-Communist and very much a Third-Force man, and one of the few *bons mots* attributed to him is: 'The Communists are not on the Left, they are in the East.'

Though looking, as somebody remarked, like ten thousand other *lycée* teachers, Guy Mollet is a man of character, and a very sharp disciplinarian inside his own Party—as some of his colleagues were to learn on more than one occasion. 'As big a bully as Herbert Morrison', one French paper described him at the time when he devoted most of his energies into disciplining the Socialist Party into accepting 'Europe', EDC and, after the breakdown of the latter, the Paris Agreements.

He and his Party supported Mendès-France throughout the latter's tenure of office; but there was undoubtedly a lack of personal sympathy between the two men; and Mollet was no doubt envious of the position Mendès had created for himself as the outstanding, and internationally-acknowledged personality of the French non-Communist Left. For one thing, Mollet was very jealous of his own position in the Socialist Party, and did not like the glowing admiration that so many of the younger Socialists were professing *vis-à-vis* Mendès—who had, indeed, far more admirers among the Socialists than among the Radicals.

The election alliance between Mollet and Mendès was a marriage of convenience, and when Mollet discovered that the Socialists had done very much better than Mendès in the election, despite the publicity that had surrounded Mendès's election campaign, he felt relieved.

And there was one important thing that played at that time into Mollet's hands. Unlike himself, Mendès was not a wholehearted 'European'—even despite his belated spell of 'Europeanism' in January 1955, when he went to see the Pope and Adenauer. Mollet knew that, to the MRP in particular, he (Mollet) was a much lesser evil than Mendès; and one suspects that it was not without some satisfaction that he learned of the MRP veto of Mendès as Foreign Minister. Guy Mollet, who, on the question of Europe, had always seen eye to eye with the MRP, and who, like the MRP, had shed tears over the death of EDC, still bore Mendès a grudge for having allowed EDC to be killed in August 1954.

This was all the stranger as EDC was dead and buried, and nothing seemed less urgent in January 1956 than the precious *relance européenne* the MRP were now talking about. Algeria was surely the first worry, and as for Europe, it presented itself in a different light from 1954 . . . Nevertheless the MRP persisted in its veto of Mendès-France.

*   *   *

IT was on January 11, even before the new Government had been
formed, that Governor-General Soustelle—who had been marking
time during the election campaign—came out with his Report,
which was examined by the Faure Government, during one of its last
cabinet meetings.

Soustelle was now much more precise in his policy than he
had been during the previous year. He rejected 'federalism'
absolutely, since this could only encourage separatism sooner
or later. He avoided the use of the word 'integration', but
replaced this by the phrase 'equality of rights and duties' among
both the French-born and the Moslem citizens in Algeria.

Absolute equality between French and Moslem citizens? Not
really. What Soustelle meant was this:

The public services of Algeria and metropolitan France would
be unified (transport, electric power, credit, etc.) and the status
of labour (wages, social security) would be the same in both
countries. All this would imply great financial sacrifices for
France; but these, in his view, were preferable to the even more
expensive alternative of the loss of 'French Algeria'.

The most original features of the Soustelle Plan concerned the
political and administrative side:

The abolition of the Governor-General of Algeria and of
the Algerian Assembly, and the establishment in Paris of a
Ministry of Algeria;

The creation of three groups of *départements*, each under the
authority of an Inspector-General or a *Super-Préfet*, as in
Metropolitan France;

The abolition of the *communes mixtes* and the establishment
of a 50-50 representation of Moslems and Europeans in localities
where the Europeans exceed a certain percentage;

The creation of a Single College in Algeria and of an election
system which would provide a much larger representation of
Algerians in the French National Assembly than hitherto.

Soustelle did not state how many Algerians should sit in the National
Assembly in Paris; his original proposal had been 30 or 35, but he was
willing to increase the number, if necessary, to 100—which would
almost correspond to the population of Algeria. Compulsory
European-Moslem parity on many town councils would, in Soustelle's
view, counterbalance the predominance of Moslems in the Single
College, for this College would compulsorily have to elect local
councillors on a 50-50 basis.

The reactions that the Soustelle Plan aroused in Algeria were just what was to be expected. The Europeans thought it might be accepted as a basis of discussion; the Moslems, on the other hand, were hostile, suspecting it of having all kinds of snags and catches, and of (naturally) perpetuating French predominance in Algeria.

At the Socialist Congress a few days later, apart from some not very far-reaching economic reforms which the Socialist Party was proposing to carry out when in office, Guy Mollet spoke chiefly of the government coalition and of Algeria. It was agreed that there would be a Republican Front Government, and neither a National Government nor a Popular Front Government. The latter was 'an unthinkable hypothesis', he said.

As for an alliance with the MRP, this also was out of the question because the MRP were insistent on maintaining the *loi Barangé* with its State subsidies to religious schools. As a working class Party, Mollet said, the MRP had betrayed their mission, and had given top priority to the religious question. (Not that, in practice, the Socialists were ready to scrap the *loi Barangé*.)

In spite of the Unity of Action pact in 1936, Guy Mollet said, there was nothing but demagogy on the part of the Communist Party. The Communists were now preparing to sabotage the Republican Front, and therefore there could be no question of a Popular Front Government. As for whether the Communists would vote for this Government or not, it was certainly not for the MRP to be self-righteous about it; they and Faure gladly accepted the Communist votes in November to bring about a snap election.

On Algeria, Mollet was in a distinctly liberal mood, though, significantly, he already said less than he did during the Election campaign about the urgent need of putting an end to 'this cruel, senseless war'.

There is no ready-made solution (he declared). We must therefore solemnly announce that *the fate of Algeria will not be settled unilaterally, but as a result of free discussions between the Algerians and ourselves*. We must take account of their aspirations, but they must, for their part, take account of the French living in Algeria and of France's legitimate rights in that country.

It is not true that the Republican Front Government intends to bring back rightaway the young soldiers sent to Algeria. But appeasement measures are possible; and these the head of the French Government must announce on the spot, at the same time as the dissolution of the Algerian Assembly, and the organization of free elections to a Single College—elections in which the same

thing as has gone into the ballot boxes also comes out of them.
On all these points I am in full agreement with M. Mendès-
France.

Up to a point (though how far exactly was not clear) he appeared to
be following Soustelle's lead. It is curious to observe that, inside the
Socialist Party, even at that stage, when Mollet seemed very liberal,
there were some who thought him unrealistic. The 'opposition'
speech that aroused the greatest attention at the Socialist Congress
was that of M. Oreste Rosenfeld, member of the Assembly of the
French Union, and a close associate of Léon Blum's in the past.

The Government will be judged on the strength of its Algerian
record (he said). We have no right to fail, for if we do, it will be
the end of democratic Socialism.

The Soustelle Plan is unrealistic, for it ignores the Algerian
National Movement; this is a hard reality, while 'Algeria is
France' is just à myth.

The policy of the Republican Front must be based on the
principle of Algerian self-determination. There must, *inter
alia*, be an amnesty, the dissolution of the Algerian Assembly,
the re-establishment of democratic freedoms, and early free
election. I hope it may still be possible to establish federal relations between Algeria and France, as well as between France and
her Black African colonies; the Assembly of the French Union
has, indeed, undertaken to study the possibility of such a Federal
French Union.

All this was rather more than, even at this stage, Mollet was
willing to subscribe to. All the same, the appointment of General
Catroux as Resident-Minister to Algeria a few days later was
intended to show that the Republican Front Government intended
to find a 'liberal' solution to the Algerian problem, through
negotiations with the Algerians themselves.

Seldom had a Government so badly misjudged the state of French
opinion in Algeria; nor had it fully realized the strength of opposition
in France itself to a 'soft' Algerian policy.

*   *   *

When in France did the idea first mature and spread that it was
'now or never'; that Algeria was the last trench, and that
too much had already been surrendered since 1945—Syria and
Indo-China for instance, and, what was much worse: Tunisia

and Morocco? These, it is true, had only been 'half lost'; but if
Algeria were lost, the loss of Tunisia and Morocco would also become
final and complete. And, after that, Black Africa would not take long
to go, too . . .

No doubt, appalling mistakes had been made in the past. Morocco
would have remained a loyal partner of France's if, in 1952-53, the
French had agreed to a minimum of concessions, instead of overthrowing the Sultan; in Tunisia, too, an agreement with Chenik in
1951 would have assured a peaceful co-existence for years to come.
Instead, the tough Hauteclocque policy was applied, just as the
Boniface policy was applied in Morocco.

Algeria, in the meantime, had been allowed to 'rot'. In 1954
Mendès-France had tried to save what could still be saved in Tunisia.
Order was restored and the French and Tunisian communities seemed
prepared to settle down to long years of peaceful co-operation.

But the trouble, which was bound to start in Algeria sooner or
later, started there in November 1954, and in Morocco, meantime,
nothing was done to ease the situation, so that in the end, the French
found themselves in the extraordinary position of having to be grateful
to the Sultan for being at all willing to co-operate with them—two
years after he had been deposed by them.

Both in Morocco and Tunisia the French were faced with strong
nationalist movements—but movements not headed by Arab League
fanatics, and at least that was something on which they could congratulate themselves. By treating with proper respect the *national*
states of Tunisia and Morocco, they could still hope to maintain
themselves in North Africa. But everything ultimately depended on
Algeria. Here, as distinct from its two neighbours, was a country
which had none of the trappings of a 'state', and which was not even,
legally speaking, a 'nationality'. On the one hand, it was important to
come to some agreement with the Algerians (whether one considered
them a 'nation' or not), if the country was not to be swallowed up in
a general massacre; on the other hand, what distinguished Algeria
from the other two countries was the presence there of a large and
extremely belligerent French minority, over one million strong, out of
a population of over nine millions.

The uneasy relationship between France on the one hand, and
Tunisia and Morocco on the other, which had come into being at the
end of 1955, could be protected against further deterioration only if
Algeria were 'kept in order' (as some said), or if an agreement with
Algeria on the lines of the Franco-Tunisian agreement were reached
(as others said). But it was not easy to negotiate with Algeria; it would
take time to produce 'valid spokesmen'; and both the Right in France

and the French in Algeria were alarmed at the prospect of Algeria being 'surrendered'.

Very widespread in France were the sentimental arguments (one million Frenchmen who cannot be deserted) and the international argument ('if we quit, the USA or Russia will take over'), and the prestige argument ('we've been in Algeria for 125 years; Algeria is part of France; without it we'll become a small continental power whom nobody will respect'); and it was these arguments which carried more and more weight as the days went by. As for the moral argument about France's duties to the Arabs—who cared about that? Did the USA care about the will of the South Koreans? Or Britain about the will of the Cypriots? Or Russia about the will of the Estonians?

One of the strangest phenomena in the whole post-war history of France was the nationalist revival of 1956, which soon came to be identified, not with the name of Poujade, but with the names of two Socialists, Mollet and Lacoste.

But the now familiar my-country-right-or-wrong movement, which soon came to be known as National-Molletism, had not yet quite crystallized in January 1956. At that time Mollet still hesitated. Who was to be sent to Algeria as Resident-Minister—the pro-Arab, liberal-minded 79-year old disciple of Lyautey, General Georges Catroux, or the blunt, Ernest Bevin-like Robert Lacoste? Which of the two was more suitable at Algiers in 1956?

Mollet dithered, and finally decided to try out Catroux. The ex-Gaullist General impersonated better than the Socialist Lacoste the lofty principles of the Socialist Party and the Mendès-Mauriac line of argument. But he *had* hesitated, for even as late as January 27 he still thought it might perhaps be safer to send Lacoste to Algiers.

*　　　*　　　*

The Assembly met on January 19 in a somewhat morose atmosphere; and it was not certain at first how the 'butchers and grocers' of the Poujade movement would behave. But nothing sensational happened; the Poujadists merely seemed even more surprised than anybody else to find that they were deputies now . . . Besides, the 'butchers and grocers' preferred to let themselves be led by M. Le Pen, a young Paris intellectual with strong *Action Française* leanings. Also, the Poujadistes had some allies with greater political experience than they: the famous *commissaire* Dides and the dazzlingly-venomous Tixier-Vignancour.

On January 24, M. Le Troquer (Socialist) was elected President of the new Assembly; and, a few days later, President Coty called on M. Mollet to form the new Government.

Meantime, the new Assembly had split itself up into *groupes* with the following result:

Communists	144
Progressistes	6
Socialists	95
Radicals (nominally Mendès's followers)	58
UDSR and African *Rassemblement*	19
RGR (Faure's followers)	14
MRP	73
Overseas Independents (affiliated with MRP)	10
'Classical' Right (Independents, peasants, etc.)	95
Gaullists	21
Poujadists (Union de Fraternité Française)	52
Others (including extreme Right)	6

Mollet was, as already said, greatly divided on the question as to whom to send to Algeria; and the problem of what to do with Mendès-France gave him an even worse headache. There had been, at the time of the election, a 'gentlemen's agreement' between them to the effect that if one was offered the Premiership, the other would automatically become Foreign Minister. So, at any rate, Mendès-France afterwards claimed, and was not contradicted by Mollet. But already the campaign against Mendès-France had gained in momentum. Partly because he was not sufficiently 'European'—always a sensitive spot with Mollet—but, above all, because of his alleged 'capitulationist' tendencies in North Africa.

A first Cabinet list was published on January 30, from which it appeared that Mendès-France figured in it merely as 'Minister of State without portfolio'.

The principal appointments were—

Premier	Mollet (Soc.)
Minister of State (without portfolio)	Mendès-France (Rad.)
Minister of State (Justice) ..	Mitterrand (UDSR)
Minister of State (War veterans) ..	Chaban-Delmas (Gaullist)
Foreign Affairs	Pineau (Soc.)
Defence	Bourgès-Maunoury (Rad.)
Interior	Gilbert Jules (Rad.)
Resident Minister in Algeria ..	General Catroux
Economic Affairs	Lacoste (Soc.)
Social Affairs	Gazier (Soc.)
Overseas France	Defferre (Soc.)

There were several Secretaries of State, of whom the most important were: Tunisia and Morocco (Alain Savary, Soc.); Algerian

Administration (Champeix, Soc.), War operations in Algeria (Max Lejeune, Soc.).

Why was Mendès not made Foreign Minister? Because the MRP had warned Mollet that if he were appointed to the Quai d'Orsay they would not vote for the Government. Mollet, unwilling to depend entirely on Communist support, gave way. The reasons given by the MRP for their veto related, on the face of it, entirely to 'Europe'; they could not forgive Mendès his 'murder' of EDC—even though in private many MRP members were now ready to admit that they should have supported Mendès's compromise proposals at Brussels—the adoption of which was, in fact, EDC's only chance of being passed by the National Assembly at all. Now they claimed to be worried lest Mendès-France, as Foreign Minister, 'sabotaged' Euratom, as he had 'sabotaged' EDC in the past. But, in reality, Mendès's lukewarm 'Europeanism' was not the real reason for the MRP's hatred of him; it was his whole attitude, his whole personality, his way of handling things, his Indo-China record, as well as his views on North Africa that aroused their undying resentment. They felt he had played his hand badly during the Election; that his great campaign had failed and that he had become fair game at last.

They knew that Mollet would be easier to handle than he; and it was important to impress upon Mollet that Mendès was a 'foreign body' in his Government; they also knew that something was on the point of blowing up in Algeria. A scapegoat was needed for all those future emergencies which a ruthless policy in North Africa might well engender; and Mendès had to be built up as a scapegoat. He was as suitable as anybody—indeed, more suitable for the part than anybody else. The legend of the 'liquidator of France's greatness' was making rapid strides.

That week which preceded the famous Algeria riots of February 6 (how providentially the date had been chosen!) was marked by an almost inextricable tangle of personal conflicts and political intrigues. Mendès-France and Catroux stood for one policy, the MRP and Soustelle and the RPF stood for another; Mollet was still full of indecision, anxious to try out first one, and, if this failed, then another policy. As for the Algerians themselves, they were taking an extremely gloomy view of it all.

Thus, Ferhat Abbas, leader of the relatively moderate nationalist Algerian Party, the UDMA, showed how gravely the whole situation in Algeria had deteriorated in the last few weeks; and how he had no excessive illusions about the Republican Front Government. 'We've been lied to often enough before,' he said. More important still, when

T

Ferhat Abbas was asked by *Action*, a Tunis paper, whether he considered himself as a possible Algerian negotiator (*interlocuteur*) he declared (and this was something new and ominous):

> I have no qualifications at all for negotiating with France. Only those who are leading the action [meaning the revolt] are qualified. My party and I have clearly stated that we fully support the cause defended by the National Liberation Front. A man like myself must today give way to the leaders of the armed resistance. The methods I have defended during the last 15 years —co-operation, discussion, persuasion—have proved ineffective; though I still believe that my notion of an 'autonomous Algerian Republic' remains valid. But I shall advocate neither this nor any any other solution unless I am commissioned by the National Liberation Front to do so. The first thing that should be done is to settle the military problem by negotiation.

A similar line was taken by other leading Algerians—even those who, like Ferhat Abbas, had only recently sat in the Algerian Assembly; it all pointed to a very marked hardening of Moslem opinion.[1]

*   *   *

Strange things were meantime happening in Algiers itself. Governor-General Soustelle, whose plan had not been adopted by the Mollet Government, and whose appointment had not been renewed in view of the decision to replace him by Catroux as Resident-Minister, left Algiers in the midst of a tremendous demonstration in his favour by many thousand of Europeans. Received a year before as a 'Mendès-France nominee' with great hostility, he had gradually come to be regarded by the European community as their best defender against *mendésisme* (as interpreted by them). On the face of it, his 'integration' plan of January 11 had not greatly pleased the Europeans, but they knew that it was little more than so much window-dressing and that the heart of de Gaulle's former right-hand man was in the right place. Not only had he been won over by the Algerian administration during the course of a year, but he had convinced himself, especially during the last few weeks, that France was now faced with the Revolt of Islam, with its vast international ramifications, and must meet the challenge.

On January 30, on his return from Algiers (where the pro-Soustelle demonstration had rapidly developed into a demonstration against the new French Government) Soustelle attended the meeting of the

[1] Cf. *Le Monde*, January 27, 1956.

National Council of the Social Republicans (Gaullists) and here he launched his first major attack on Mendès-France and Catroux.

Though reticent during most of the meeting, he nevertheless protested vigorously against the campaign that had been conducted against him, 'not by the Socialist Party, but by a certain paper to which I used to contribute in the past'. He meant, of course, *L'Express,* and thereupon wondered whether this paper reflected the views of M. Mendès-France, rather with the implication that it largely did.

On the military situation in Algeria, Soustelle was, if anything, rather optimistic.

This situation has not deteriorated in the last few weeks; we are now getting dividends from the policy we have latterly pursued; we are in a position now to liquidate the bands in the Southern Aurès. On the other hand, the civilian situation has badly deteriorated since November. There is a real 'confidence crisis' in Algeria, and if there are any signs of our wanting to negotiate with the Rebels, all those afraid of reprisals will go over to the rebels.

It was on the following day that Mollet presented his Government (from which the two Gaullists had—provisionally—dropped out) to the National Assembly.

The investiture of the Mollet Government was an extraordinarily morose affair; observers likened it to the investiture of M. Laniel in 1953—whom the Assembly accepted in a dreary mood of resignation, after a Cabinet crisis which had lasted for more than a month. Mollet, too, was the 'inevitable' new Premier—at least until further notice, and he aroused no enthusiasm anywhere, not even among the Socialists, who were about the only people to cheer politely his investiture speech. Mendès-France sat on the Government bench, looking glum, and flabbily clapping only once or twice.

Mollet spoke about economic and social reforms—or rather, read out his piece about them; and nobody was either interested or impressed. The only striking remark he made was that the French Government recognized an 'Algerian Personality', which seemed to mean something new—though nobody quite knew what. Presumably it meant that Algeria could not be treated simply as 'part of France', but that it had the specific character of a country where two distinct races were living side-by-side. The phrase meant the rejection of Soustelle's 'integration' formula, as well as of the federalist solution, complete with its 'Algerian National State'. The French in Algeria would be expected to consider themselves as being part of a 'Franco-Moslem community', which would, however, be 'indissolubly linked with metropolitan France'; but, at the same time, said Mollet, the future status of Algeria would on no account be 'granted'; it would be 'negotiated'. (This precisely is what was *not* done when it came to the point.)

Mollet made it clear that what he had in mind was the early election of a Single College—the very suggestion of which had already produced a violent uproar in the French press in Algeria. It was not easy; but Mollet still seemed to hope that it might be possible to ignore the nationalist movement in Algeria, and its Egyptian accomplices, and to convince the Algerian population that it was not in their interests to throw in their lot with the rebels. He also promised to release all Algerian political suspects, as distinct from the 'terrorists', who had been caught red-handed.

The discussion that followed Mollet's let's-hope-for-the-best speech also lacked distinction. A Poujadist made some very offensive remarks about General Catroux, whom he treated as a defeatist and capitulationist (a description of 'that highly honoured soldier, who is moreover, Chancellor of the Legion of Honour' against which Mollet strongly protested), but otherwise nobody could work up much interest in either Mollet's speech or in the new Government; and although this was given a large vote of confidence from all except the extreme Right and the Poujadists, it was known that nothing had yet been settled: the next few days would be decisive.

Mollet had, indeed, been ill at ease throughout. It was rumoured that he was very nervous about the Catroux appointment, and was going to go to Algiers himself, to see how things were, before 'installing' Catroux there. Catroux was Governor-General in Indo-China in 1940, when, after the formation of the Vichy Government, he was replaced by Admiral Decoux. He then joined de Gaulle; commanded the Free French on the side of the British in Syria in 1941, and ranked as de Gaulle's principal expert on North Africa, having, for many years in the past been associated with Lyautey in Morocco. Later, in 1946, he was appointed French Ambassador to Moscow. On his return to France he was given the honorific post of Chancellor of the Legion of Honour.

His ideas on North Africa were liberal, and, in 1953, he distinguished himself by writing a series of articles in the *Figaro* in which, taking a line not unlike that of Mauriac, he protested against the departure by the ultra-colonialists in Morocco from 'the Lyautey principles', and, in particular, against the attempts by the He-men to undermine the position of the Sultan. He annoyed the extremists so much that when it was announced in April 1953 that he would give a lecture at Casablanca on — Lyautey (of all subjects!), the He-men declared that they would make it so hot for him that General Guillaume, the Resident-General hastened to cable to Catroux asking him to cancel his visit. Later, in 1955, it was Catroux whom Edgar Faure sent to Madagascar to consult the exiled Sultan on the future of Morocco.

His critics often said that, being nearly 80, he was 'gaga'. In reality, his ideas on North Africa were lucid and clear, but they were rank poison to the colonialists. In the first days of February he was fully aware of the hostility his appointment had aroused amongst the French in Algeria, and had even offered to resign in favour of somebody more acceptable to the French community. But Mollet decided to give the Catroux appointment a chance. In a cautiously-worded statement, Catroux told the *Monde* that he did not believe in Soustelle's 'integration' proposals; since the Moslems would not hear of them. He dwelt instead on the 'particularism' of the French in Algeria, and endorsed the Mollet formula of a Franco-Moslem 'Algerian personality'.

> This, of course, means that we cannot accept a purely Moslem 'personality' of Algeria. We cannot, for one thing, ignore all that France has contributed to the progress of Algeria. Moreover, there is no historical basis for an Algerian National State; Algeria never was a unified state, and even the authority of the Dey before the French conquest was a very limited one.
> The administrative machinery of the Government-General will not be scrapped, but merely modified. There will be an Algerian Assembly, which might even in future be endowed with an embryo of executive power. This empirical structure might be useful if, in time, we adopt for the French Union a federalist Constitution.

All this, on the face of it, seemed meek and mild; but even the 'embryo' of executive authority for a Single College Assembly in Algeria, and the very possibility of a 'federalist' Constitution were dynamite to the French community in Algeria.

Moreover, Catroux said he intended to have talks with any Algerian representatives (*interlocuteurs*) whom he (Catroux) might consider valid, though he excluded—in a vaguely worded phrase—'those who had risen against France'. But he added as a dangerous afterthought: 'However, I shall be able to judge more clearly once I am on the spot'.

He also said that he, of course, realized that the rebels were enjoying support for three reasons: intimidation, military successes in certain areas, and the appeal they were making to 'Algerian nationality'. If a successful guerrilla war could be conducted against the rebels, Moslem opinion might switch over to the French side.

He concluded with some generalities about the 'indissoluble bonds' between France and Algeria, which could not be allowed to become a national Moslem State.

> Nor can there be any question of the French becoming a mere minority. The two communities must reach an equality in rights and duties. But an end must be put to injustice, and the human condition of the natives must be raised by social and economic measures.

What made Catroux even more suspect in the eyes of the Europeans was the announcement made by the Group of 61 (Moslem members of the Algerian Assembly, National Assembly and Senate) on February 2, saying that

> they had confidence in General Catroux, the Resident Minister, who had already greatly contributed to a happy solution of the Moroccan problem and who, they were sure, would find a solution in Algeria inspired by the Moslems' national aspirations.

In Algiers meantime the French press was up in arms against Catroux, and unsigned leaflets were being distributed calling on the French to demonstrate against him on the day of his arrival.

> Pedestrians shall boo him wherever he goes; motorists shall block the streets and blow their horns; shopkeepers shall close all their shops as a protest.

Various war veterans' organizations, Poujadist organizations and others were preparing for a showdown.

That was the atmosphere in which Guy Mollet landed at Algiers in the early afternoon of February 6.

CHAPTER 4

THE 6TH OF FEBRUARY AT ALGIERS

TO appreciate the full flavour and significance of that '6th of February' of Algiers, it is best to quote not those who were indignant at what had happened, but those who gloried in the 'operation' itself and in its after-effects. The account published in *Fraternité Française*, Poujade's paper is, in effect, not very different from all other accounts of that historic day, which truly became a turning-point in the history of French North Africa, but it gloats more shamelessly than any other over the vigour of the 'French awakening', the ruthlessness of the methods employed, and the true significance of it as a victory of the North-African He-men over the mealy-mouthed Socialists and the well-meaning intellectuals in Paris.

VIVE L'ALGÉRIE FRANÇAISE!

the banner-headline screamed across the front page of *Fraternité Française* of February 11 ; and, on page 3 there were these headlines—which were even more significant :

HOW THE HEAD OF THE GOVERNMENT BECAME AWARE OF THE REALITIES OF ALGERIA

And here came the story :

The people of Algiers won a great victory on February 6. So wonderful were their unanimity and their instinct of self-preservation that they not only forced the Resident Minister—whose very name was a symbol of defeatism and surrender—to resign but also made the Premier go back on his past prejudices and become aware of the realities of the Algerian situation.

And yet, no demonstration had been organized in advance. The Ex-Servicemen's Organizations and the [Poujadist] UDCA, who are, in Algeria, the true leaders of public opinion, had recommended calm and 'abstention'. Guy Mollet was to enter a city in a state of mourning. On that Monday, all shops were closed, as well as all cinemas, cafés and restaurants. Factories, too had closed down. The bakeries had baked no bread, and milk for children was distributed only until 8 a.m. . . . Several houses were displaying wide ribbons of black crepe. All public services had been slowed down to an absolute minimum . . .

291

Extraordinary precautions had been taken by the authorities. Apart from the city's regular police forces, 2,000 CRS troops had been brought from France, and whole regiments had been brought by air-lift from Oran and Constantine . . .

Between the airfield and Algiers there were thousands of armed and helmeted soldiers . . . A ridiculous and provocative display of armed strength. Were these soldiers there to protect the Premier against a fellagha attack? No; merely against the booing of honest Frenchmen who were unwilling to see the destiny of Algeria handed over to a professional liquidator and a real Jonah . . .

The real whistling and booing, however, did not start until Guy Mollet had reached the centre of Algiers:

Ten thousand people had gathered in the Boulevard Laferrière. They had no aggressive intentions. They intended to demonstrate their disapproval by a contemptuous silence . . . But the presence of the helmeted CRS guards rubbed them the wrong way. 'Are we being taken for so many rioters?' people were saying.

It was at this point that the convoy of official cars appeared.

Then, from 10,000 throats came a tremendous outburst of booing expressing all the suppressed indignation of many months past. It was spontaneous and irresistible . . .

Outside the heavily-guarded war memorial, Guy Mollet emerged from his car. The band played the *Marseillaise*. But the booing was now so deafening, that not a single note of the National Anthem could be heard. It was then that the first shower of missiles began to hit the group of flabbergasted official personages: oranges, and rotten tomatoes, and lumps of lawn torn out of the public garden. I saw an officer catch one of these missiles just as it was about to hit M. Mollet between the eyes. As the crowd was about to break through all the barriers, the guards threw their first tear-gas bombs. Meantime, to complete his programme, Guy Mollet still had to climb the steps of the war memorial and lay a wreath at the foot of it. All the time the whistling and booing continued. M. Mollet, after laying the wreath, was in an obvious hurry to get away from this unexpectedly hostile crowd.

And then came the story of Mollet's 'conversion'.

At that moment he had not yet understood anything about Algeria. He was still a prisoner of his absurd Socialist prejudices: for months he had been conditioned by all the Party chatter. He had expected to be received in Algiers, with half the people booing and half the people cheering, as if he were at some local election meeting at home. Now he was faced with the unanimous anger of the whole population. In the eyes of those very ex-servicemen, whom he thought to be his comrades, he could read nothing but indignation. As an honest man, he was visibly upset by it all. It began to dawn on him that he was in the presence of a people refusing to die ...

The conversion seemed complete:

Very pale, and with his eyes filled with tears—caused by emotion and perhaps also by the tear-gas, he entered his car, and drove off to the Summer Palace.

No sooner had he left than the crowd broke through all the barriers, snatched up M. Mollet's wreath, and threw its flowers to all the winds. This was not the end; it was only the beginning. Nothing could now stop the tremendous drive of that crowd which was determined that Algeria would remain French. Shouting in chorus: 'Hang Catroux!' and 'French Algeria! French Algeria!' they formed themselves into columns ready to march to the Summer Palace ... Fifty thousand people were now crowding the Boulevard Laferrière outside the main post-office. The uproar was terrifying. The CRS guards retreated, and formed a new barrage in the rue Michelet. But the most violent clashes occurred outside the Summer Palace, and it was here that the truly revolutionary nature of the movement became apparent. A number of students penetrated into the Bardo Gardens and even into the precincts of the Summer Palace ... Just outside the Palace, Senegalese troops, with their machine guns in place were awaiting orders. Fortunately these orders did not come; but it was touch-and-go. The whole town was seized with a fever of rebellion. Everywhere there were now merry-go-rounds of cars blowing their horns and sirens. The tension was terrific, and if anyone had fired a shot, heaven only knows what would have happened.

It was then that it was learned that General Catroux had resigned. From the balcony of the *Journal d'Alger* a blackboard was lowered with these two words written on it:

CATROUX RESIGNS

A roar of triumph rose from the crowd, an immense explosion of joy which almost made the shop-windows crack ... Receiving the War Veterans' delegation next morning, M. Mollet, his eyes miraculously unsealed, said the words which one wishes he had uttered the day he formed the Government: 'I came, I saw, I understood'.

But his hardest task is still ahead: he must convince the Socialist Party and all those deputies on whose votes his Government depends that there is only one solution for Algeria —and that is the solution advocated for months by the French in Algeria.

A fierce attack was made on Mollet a few days later by Mauriac in *L'Express*. After ridiculing his Algiers performance (Why did he have to go there? He could have learned all his lessons in Paris from Senator Borgeaud and the other diehards.'), Mauriac declared that he no longer felt any respect for a man who, to please these people, had started his career by throwing Mendès-France and General Catroux overboard.

Edgar Faure, though entangled in his own cobwebs, was still capable of a sudden stroke of invention, of an outburst of cunning intelligence. But from this motionless schoolmaster, sitting there in his chair, and allowing himself to be pelted by an unruly class with inky balls of paper, there is just nothing to expect . . . And outside, there are eight million Algerians, watching and waiting.

The Mauriac article caused an uproar inside the Government; Mollet accused Mendès of having inspired, if not dictated it. Both Mendès and Mauriac denied it.

All the same, it is quite clear that what Mauriac was saying was not very different from what an angry and embittered Mendès-France was thinking about the same time . . .

So that was that. The 6th of February, 1956, marked the great turning-point in the story of the young *Front Républicain;* indeed in the whole history of the Franco-Algerian problem, and of France's relations with North Africa. A few days after the 6th of February, Mollet returned to Paris, and Robert Lacoste, the Minister of Economic Affairs and Finance, was appointed Minister Resident in Algeria, in place of General Catroux. Lacoste was a Socialist, but of an intensely national, and indeed nationalist variety. During the months that followed, Lacoste became the 'Strong Man' of France as well as the 'Strong Man' of Algeria.

He took the wind out of the sails of the Poujadists and the Right. It was a Socialist who was now defending the 'heritage of France in North Africa'. He did it with drive, conviction and ruthlessness. The above-quoted article from *Fraternité Française*, the Poujadist weekly, already showed that, though it related with some relish how a rotten tomato had nearly hit Mollet between the eyes, it was willing to give

Mollet a chance; Mollet was a true Frenchman, merely slightly cor-
rupted by his Socialism, but sound at heart. The same was even truer
of Lacoste. In the last analysis, what Lacoste came to represent was
not substantially different from what Soustelle had represented during
the previous year.

Inside the Government there still continued an opposition to the
Lacoste policy in Algeria; it came from Mendès-France, Savary and
Defferre. But 'Strong Man' Lacoste dominated them all, and in May,
after another violent clash with Lacoste, Mendès-France was to resign.

There started after February 6, months of petty persecution of all
those who were now said to be 'sabotaging' the French war effort in
Algeria, who were preaching defeatism, who were following a Mendès-
France-Mauriac line.

Needless to say, there was no enthusiasm for the war in Algeria;
there were even a few cases of rioting among the conscripts who were
being called up. But, by and large, the country was impressed by
Lacoste—was accepting Lacoste. It became clear that the resentment
over the Arabs—the Tunisians and Moroccans who had defied France
and thrown their weight about in past years—was now expressing
itself in France in a thousand ways, small ways, but also big ways.
Mendès-France was built up as the bogey man: the 'defeatist' Trojan
Horse inside the Government; the rootless, *apatride* creature who
lacked all the earthy native virtues, and all the tough fighting spirit of
Robert Lacoste.

At the War Leakages trial, the famous *procès des fuites*, which
went on throughout March, April and a part of May, Mendès was
often alluded to as Number One Defeatist, as the Liquidator of France's
Colonial Empire and of France's Greatness. Lacoste had the majority
of the Cabinet with him, and one of his staunchest allies was the
Radical, M. Bourgès-Maunoury, the Minister of Defence.

The situation in Algeria was, indeed, alarming when Lacoste took
over. Things began to happen which had not happened before. Apart
from an increase in the number of acts of terrorism on the part of the
Rebels—including the massacre of whole French families living on
out-of-the-way farms—the French colonial troops were becoming unreliable. On February 21, fifty Algerian *tirailleurs* deserted, and went
over to the Rebels. A few days later, there was a similar case of
desertion. On March 8, seven Europeans were massacred only a few
miles outside Algiers. It was about that time that the *Monde* published
a map of Algeria showing that practically the whole of the country was
in a state of 'insecurity', and that there were large areas, especially in

Eastern Algeria, which were now fully under the control of the Algerian nationalists. Some people—M. Edgar Faure among them—were beginning to talk of a possible 'partition' of Algeria, under which a coastal strip, comprizing Algiers and Oran, might be turned into a sort of 'French Israel', while the rest of Algeria became an 'Algerian Republic'.

But the nationalist wave, the movement in favour of Lacoste, was beginning to sweep the country.

A Bill for Special Powers in Algeria was being prepared by the Government. On March 8 the Bill came before the National Assembly. The debate on the 'exceptional powers' in Algeria opened before a crowded House. After the various *rapporteurs* had spoken, the same old *grands tenors* of the extreme Right were let loose; M. Dronne, for instance, said that certain papers like *L'Express* 'had done France greater harm than ten fellagha divisions would have done'.

> France (he said) is already on the point of being evicted from North Africa. After the capitulation of the last French Government to the Sultan of Morocco, that country has now become independent, despite all the vague jargon about 'interdependence'; and Tunisia naturally wants as much independence as Morocco; if these two countries are lost, Algeria cannot possibly be kept.

M. Legendre also spoke, and protested against any suggestion of negotiations 'with the murderers'. Among these Right-wing speakers there was a newcomer, M. Le Pen, the leader of the parliamentary Poujadist group, who said that 'since you've got to make war in Algeria anyway, it's better to start it now than to wait.' He also fumed against the 'defeatist press' run 'by traitors and the enemies of France'.

The great speech of that first day was by M. Lacoste, the Resident-Minister in Algeria.

> On balance, he said, Algeria had benefited from France's presence in that country, and it was not for feudal states like Egypt, with their appalling social conditions, to criticize France. The morale among the Moslems was not good, and the Rebels had more and more accomplices amongst the population. The rebellion had now spread to one-third of the whole of North Algeria.
>
> Military action alone could not solve the Algerian problem, but since the Rebels were being supplied with arms from abroad, it was the duty of France to intensify her war effort, if necessary.
>
> There was no question of subordinating either the restoration of order to the introduction of reforms, or *vice versa*.

After enumerating a number of reforms (more jobs for Moslems in the administration, elections to a Single College even before the country had been 'completely' pacified; expropriation of the large estates and the reclamation of arid territories by means of an irrigation programme, etc.), Lacoste concluded however, in the best tricolour style:

> The time for promises is over; the time for action has come. France's presence in Algeria will be maintained. The conception of 'Algerian personality' [the phrase used in Mollet's Ministerial Declaration] will have to be moulded so as to fit into the indissoluble union between France and Algeria; No French Government will ever abandon Algeria.

Lacoste, heavy, massive, *bon Français* Lacoste, Lacoste the trade unionist, the native of Perigord, was not yet quite so full of self-assurance as he was to become some weeks later. His first impression of Algeria, when he had arrived there three days after the Algiers riots, was deplorable; 'A *l'époque*,' he said to a friend some months later, '*tout semblait foutre le camp.*' He was not yet fully reassured in March, but began to feel that there was still a good chance of saving Algeria 'for France'—*if the will was there.*

'France Awake! France awake with a start! Let your national consciousness awake!'—this was the theme of the most important of all the speeches in that Algerian debate which preceded the granting of 'exceptional powers in Algeria' to the Government.

Soustelle was determined to become a driving force in the country in this 'awakening' campaign over Algeria. A writer, an intellectual, a scholar, a former right-hand-man of de Gaulle's, and former Governor-General of Algeria (and, moreover, one who had gone there with the reputation of a great liberal), Soustelle was a man with considerable prestige in the country.

He certainly started his speech at the National Assembly that day with an effective clarion call:

> Algeria lost! Just imagine what this would mean if it came true! It would be a national disaster equal in depth and in its calamitous effects to the most terrible defeats in our history. Only Sedan, or June 1940 are comparable to what the loss of Algeria would mean . . .

If, he said, Algeria was lost, the whole of the French possessions in Africa would go. Moreover, the anger and despair in France would be such that democratic freedoms in the country could not survive, and France would inevitably embark on some perilous adventure.

After discussing a variety of social, economic and administrative improvements which should be introduced into Algeria (he particularly dwelt on the creation of 'social centres' in every town and village, which would—as in Mexico some twenty years ago—lay the foundations for universal education), Soustelle proceeded to defend the French of Algeria:

> These Algerians of European origin are being constantly dragged through the mud in France, as so many colonialists and blood-suckers. Ladies and gentlemen, may I just ask you for one moment to put yourselves in the place of such a 'colonialist', who lives on an isolated farm with his wife and his three children and who expects at any moment (and such things have happened) to see his farm invaded by a band of Algerians, who then, in his presence, cut his children's throats, and rape his wife and daughters before killing them. And then he himself is murdered, and his farm burned down. And so another point of *présence française* disappears . . .
> Whatever the faults of the Europeans in Algeria (and who hasn't faults?) are they so serious as to deserve the death penalty?

And then he spoke of the Moslems—humble officials and others —who, in areas dominated by the Rebels, lived in a constant state of terror, until (unless they were murdered) 'their nerve was broken, and they were reduced to a state of slavery by the powers of darkness.'

As for the time-schedule for pacification and reforms, Soustelle said that this was not an easy matter. While he was Governor-General, it happened that a new school or factory was in process of being built; but one day everything was destroyed, and the workers—Moslems, of course—were all found massacred. All the same, Soustelle thought that pacification and political and economic reforms should be carried out simultaneously. But it was a fact that everything had been rendered much more difficult in Algeria by the vast anti-French conspiracy that had been hatched abroad.

> Egypt is in the centre of this spider's web. For a long time now Cairo radio had been inciting the North Africans to murder and violence, and has encouraged all attacks on France. The *cadres* of the rebel forces in the Aurès, Nementcha and Kabylian mountains consist of men sent from Egypt via Libya and Tunisia . . . There is in Cairo, with the blessing of the Egyptian Government, a three-member committee composed of Ben Bella, Boudiaf and Mahsas, which is in charge of all the military operations against

France in Algeria. This committee is 'manipulated' by officers of a special Egyptian service, chief of whom is Major Ezzat Soleiman.

After giving some further details on this organization, Soustelle then dealt with the arms deliveries to the Algerian rebels—some of these being British or American, while others were bought in the black market, especially in Tunisia—and he quoted documents to show that the real chief of this arms traffic was none other than 'a certain Colonel Gamal Abdel Nasser'. Further, Soustelle quoted documents showing that Libya was a place from which much of the armament came to the Algerian rebels; and members of the Libyan Government were directly implicated. And then Soustelle dealt with other terrorists who had their base in Spanish Morocco—with the blessing of the Spanish authorities.

No doubt, Soustelle concluded (and this also was typical of the change of temper in France) *the Algerian nationalists could not seriously expect to defeat France militarily in Algeria; so what were they hoping for? They were hoping for several things: but, above all, they were hoping for a breakdown of the home front in France.*

To carry out pacification (and pacification meant, above all, the protection of the civilian populations) a lot of soldiers were needed. Two men with a mortar could destroy a village; but twenty men were needed to defend it. Secondly, apart from this defensive action, it was necessary to organize offensive action—which meant pursuing the bands into their mountain hide-outs: this meant a good deal of re-adaptation in the French Army, so that its soldiers could practise a sort of 'counter-guerrilla'.

What was essential (said Soustelle) was a quick French awakening—*un sursaut national:*

> For today we must sink all past differences, forget all past quarrels; for nothing, absolutely nothing matters today except our national salvation—and this national salvation today means the salvation of Algeria. (*Cheers on right, centre and some left benches.*) Let us all tell France that this is neither a vague police operation, nor a far-away colonial war . . . Algeria is not far. It is a French land, which is as close and as dear to us as if it were part of European France . . . Now is the moment for France to choose between salvation and irretrievable decadence. I am sure that the country will reject decadence. (*Loud cheers on centre, right, extreme right and certain left benches.*)

It was *the* speech of that debate; and few took much interest in the colourless speech of M. Mollet that followed, with its little sprinkling of liberalist and socialist ideas, and its nostalgic references to the 'great ancestors'—men like Blum and Violette—whose humanitarian plans for the benefit of the Moslems in bygone days had, alas! fallen on deaf ears. He spoke of the Government's 'triple action'—military, social and economic, and diplomatic. He would not negotiate with criminals; military action would be continued; more troops would be sent; meantime reforms would be carried out whenever possible; and, as soon as violence had ceased, there would be loyal elections in Algeria, and with the lawful representatives of the Algerian people a new Algerian Statute would be negotiated.

The end of the debate was marked by a statement by Raymond Guyot on behalf of the Communists saying, in effect, that they were prepared to give the Mollet Government a chance to pursue a democratic policy which, they hoped, would soon bring peace to Algeria; and by a very ugly row into which Tixier-Vignancour, the newly-elected Fascist trouble-maker (and the central figure in the *procès des fuites*) deliberately dragged the Left half of the Assembly. He started by saying that three Communist agents—whom he named—were supplying the Algerian rebels with funds received from Czechoslovakia. His whole manner was so provocative that not only the Communists, but also the Socialists burst into a chorus of angry abuse, calling him *Vichyste, hitlérien,* Gestapo agent, or simply *salaud* and *ordure.*

In the end, the plenary powers for Algeria were passed, on a motion of confidence, by 455 votes to 76, only the Poujadists and the extreme Right (Tixier-Vignancour, Dorgères, etc.) voting against the Government.

Throughout the debate, Mendès-France had not said a word.

The debate had, in fact, been a victory for Lacoste and Soustelle, and Guy Mollet's well-meaning generalities did not mean much.

CHAPTER 5

SEVERE SETBACK FOR THE INTELLECTUAL LEFT

THE Left-wing intellectuals and anti-colonialists were in a difficult spot. For years and years they had been right. For years they had campaigned against the war in Indo-China; for years they had warned the successive French Governments against the follies of their policy in North Africa. They had pleaded and pleaded in favour of constructive talks with Tunisia at a time when the Tunisians were willing to accept a bare minimum of internal autonomy; their pleading had fallen on deaf ears. Afterwards they denounced the crimes and follies of French policy in Tunisia at the time of the ruthless Haute-clocque régime of 1952-53, and argued that all this brutality would merely envenom Franco-Tunisian relations. Similarly, they campaigned against similar (and worse) follies in Morocco, showing up the crimes of the He-men (such as the Casablanca massacre of Moroccan trade unionists in December, 1952), and warning them against their plans for overthrowing the Sultan in the absurd belief that, in doing so, they could perpetuate in Morocco the French *administration directe*. When the behaviour of the French diehards in both Tunisia and Morocco led to a perpetual state of insecurity in both countries, complete with waves of terrorism and counter-terrorism, the intellectuals campaigned for new talks, new negotiations, and a peaceful settlement.

In Tunisia, in virtue of this 'intellectual' policy, an end was put to bloodshed by Mendès-France's famous visit to Tunis on August 31, 1954. In Morocco, after a half-hearted and confused attempt by Edgar Faure to achieve a similar result, a more precarious settlement was finally reached in much less favourable conditions, and through the Moroccans themselves forcing the hand of the French, and without the latter ever having seized the opportunity of showing any spontaneous generosity.

In their diagnosis of the trouble in Indo-China, Tunisia, and Morocco, the Left-wing intellectuals (represented by papers like *Le Monde, Combat, Franc-Tireur, Temps Modernes, Esprit, Témoignage Chrétien, L' Observateur* and, since 1953, *l' Express* (in which the articles of Mauriac were of particular importance) had been consistently, one might almost say, infallibly right. Events had more than justified all their criticisms of the perpetuation of the war in Vietnam, and of the senseless and shortsighted policies conducted in North Africa. The attempts by the Right to win the war in Indo-China, or to scare Tunisia into submission with the help of *ratissages*, police tortures, internment camps in the Sahara and the like had failed miserably.

Being sure of their own judgment, in view of the great wisdom they had shown in relation to Indo-China, Tunisia and Morocco, these people confidently proceeded to apply the same judgments and the same criteria to Algeria.

But here Mendès-France, Mauriac, Bourdet and so many others came up against an obstacle they had not encountered in their other three campaigns. In all these, they had (by and large) public opinion in France behind them. And if (as during the earlier stages of the Indo-China war) public opinion was sometimes more or less indifferent, it was never acutely hostile to the intellectuals, who, on the contrary, exercised an ever-growing influence on public opinion. By 1953 there was a nation-wide outcry against the war in Indo-China being continued; and there was also a widespread desire for a reasonable settlement in both Tunisia and Morocco, as conditions were becoming increasingly chaotic in these two countries. But the reactions to Algeria were different.

Algeria was, as already said, 'the last trench'. Algeria was 'part of France'. There were 300,000 or 400,000 Algerians in metropolitan France, and there was for them a widespread racial hatred—a hatred which was even shared by a large part of the French working-class, Communist or not.

The feeling had grown in 1955 that France had suffered humiliations, and had been outwitted, if not in Tunisia, at any rate in Morocco. Moods of irrational resentment had grown in the country and had crystallized in a thing like the Poujade movement. And then there were other factors: the most was made in the press of the unspeakably horrible Arab atrocities committed in Morocco and Algeria in August, 1955 (children with slit throats, piles of European corpses with their lips, and ears, and noses and genitals cut off by the fellagha killers, and so on). That atrocities were committed by the French also was true enough; but '*that* was different'.

And then, there was also a strong feeling—which was not nearly so strong in the case of Tunisia and Morocco—that, in Algeria, there were over a million of 'our own people' to defend. Maybe many of them were thugs, and Fascists and colonialists (some of whom were only getting what—in the abstract—they deserved) but—they were *French*. Strong nationalist, indeed racialist instincts had gradually been aroused in France—especially during 1955 and the early months of 1956.

The line of argument followed by a number of Left-wing intellectual papers during the early months of 1956 was something like this:

In Algeria, the Government was making *precisely* the same mistakes as those that had already been made in Indo-China, where the successive French Governments had missed every opportunity of reaching a peace settlement with Ho Chi Minh while conditions for it were still favourable to the French. In Algeria, as in Indo-China, the war would lead, in the end, to 'another Dien Bien Phu'. It was essential, therefore, to start right-away by negotiating a cease-fire with the Algerian Resistance; to call up more and more men would only lead to ever-growing chaos in Algeria, and this chaos would 'inevitably' spread to Tunisia and Morocco, where forces hostile to the French would, in the name of Moslem solidarity, gain the upper hand; and this general 'revolt of Islam' would rapidly eliminate the French from every part of North Africa. To try to subdue Algeria by sheer military weight was hopeless. Also, a long and hopeless war in North Africa could only create the greatest financial difficulties in France itself, followed by social and political unrest.

Especially after Mollet's surrender to the Algiers rioters on February 6, a paper like *France-Observateur* began to denounce the Government in no uncertain terms for launching France upon a hopeless adventure, simply because her Socialist Prime Minister hadn't had the guts to stand up to the Algiers mob on that fateful 6th of February. It went, indeed, out of its way to show that the Algiers riots were by no means a purely spontaneous demonstration; it gave a long list of names of the influential persons in Algiers who had set up a regular commando organization, with ramifications throughout Algeria.

After the Assembly had voted the Government's plenary powers for Algeria, Claude Bourdet in *France-Observateur* deplored the fact that the Government had now been given the means of choosing war, instead of peace; and this war, he said, could only end in disaster. A week later, the same writer published an article which was interpreted by M. Bourgès-Maunoury, the Minister of Defence, as a call to disobedience among the men called up for service in Algeria; and on March 31, the police raided the offices of *France-Observateur* and the homes of 12 of its contributors, and Bourdet himself was arrested on a charge of 'demoralizing the Army'. He was, it is true, let out the same day (without, however, the charge being dropped); but the publicity that was given to his arrest was precisely what Bourgès-Maunoury had hoped for: he wanted it to be understood that the Government—as he himself put it—wasn't going to stand for any defeatist nonsense any more. What was significant, however, was the comparatively mild reaction in the Paris evening press to the news of Bourdet's arrest. Even the *Monde*, while deploring this drastic application of a particularly controversial article in the criminal code, nevertheless suggested that Bourdet had latterly tended to 'overstate' his case. Other papers thought Bourdet had been unwise to write in such terms at a time when 70,000 reservists were on the point of being sent to Algeria. He, surely, could have no illusions that he would make the Government change its mind—Lacoste was, by now, obviously dominating the Government.

The Government was, clearly, succeeding in its attempt to create a sort of 'national discipline' over Algeria. Professor Henri Marrou, of of the Sorbonne, wrote on April 5, an article in the *Monde* in which he declared that 'a curious torpor had come over the nation during the last two or three weeks'.

> The Government's threat to exercise 'a certain control' over the press and radio has already resulted in their practising a severe 'self-discipline' . . . It is rather ominous that, as in wartime, we should now start listening to the Swiss radio to get any news about Algeria . . .
> Everywhere, strange voices are now whispering words of realism: 'Now that we've lost Indo-China and have thoughtlessly abandoned Tunisia and Morocco, Algeria is our last trench; if we lose it, it'll be the end of France as a great power . . .' Even among the clergy I find men now digging out of the archives some old and musty ideas of a Crusade against Islam's Holy War . . .

On balance, Marrou said, he was not proud of France's record in Algeria. And he did not see how there could ever be a peaceful settlement, following upon the loudly-promised Algerian elections, if, in the meantime, France used as her three principal weapons in Algeria: concentration camps, tortures and collective reprisals. What would be the good of these Algerian elections if the voters were mere survivors of concentration camps and burned-down villages? All this was unworthy of France; it all savoured too much of the methods used by Vichy, with its abominable concentration camp of Gurs.

> I cannot think without a shudder of the day when I was called upon to represent France at a Unesco exhibition in honour of Human Rights—an exhibition at which there was a whole section showing how police tortures had (oh, what a piece of hypocrisy!) been abolished.

To most members of the Government this was a lot of harmful sentimental tosh—and, just to show how strongly it disapproved of this kind of thing—somebody in the Government sent the police to search the professor's house. It is not at all clear what it hoped to find there. But it had become necessary to keep these 'liberals' in order. A few days later, M. Bourgès-Maunoury, the Minister of Defence, went so far as to state in the *Dépêche* of Toulouse that any words 'uttered either consciously or unconsciously' which were liable to demoralize the army were criminal!

Throughout April reinforcements continued to be sent to Algeria.

And the most significant fact is this: except for a few isolated 'railway station incidents', the hundreds of thousands of conscripts went off to 'defend Algeria' almost without a murmur. The stories which appeared in some English papers about mass desertions from the French Army were just untrue.

CHAPTER 6

MENDÈS-FRANCE'S 7-POINT PROGRAMME OF IMMEDIATE REFORMS

MENDÈS-FRANCE, whose position in the Government was becoming more and more intolerable, was not protesting against these reinforcements; but he repeatedly tried to argue that drastic reforms should be introduced simultaneously with the pacification process; after pacification had been achieved (even if this were possible), it would be too late to introduce the reforms. The pacification would be much easier to achieve if the Moslems were shown that France really intended to improve their lot.

But his clashes with Lacoste (who had no intention of 'fighting on two fronts'—i.e., against the Rebels and against the Colonialists) were becoming more and more frequent and bitter; and on April 10 Mendès-France offered to resign from the Government if no notice was taken of his proposals.

These proposals were the following:

(1) The release of political prisoners other than those with a precise charge against them. Despite assurances given by Mollet, these preventive arrests were becoming more and more numerous.

(2) A free press for the Moslems; in this they could express any ideas, other than incitement to hatred, crime and violence. Similar restrictions should be placed on the French colonialist and racialist press.

(3) The elimination of officials who continued to represent in the Algerian administration the contempt for the natives, as well as a contempt for law and justice.

(4) The dissolution of all municipal authorities guilty of victimising the native population. The enactment of a new municipal law. 'It must be constantly borne in mind that it is on the local level that the Moslem population is made particularly conscious of any humiliations it is made to suffer.'

(5) The effective expropriation of the large landed estates with a view to their transformation into small family properties which would be used for growing food. The abolition of the various safety clauses and the excessive delays in the recent decrees concerning this matter.

(6) A fundamental reorganization of the *Crédit Agricole* which has, so far, been merely a tool in the hands of a handful of large landowners, and has been of no help to small producers.

(7) A substantial increase in wages; the direct control of the social laws by officials animated by a new spirit, i.e., by persons determined to see the workers' interests loyally respected; active and loyal support, on the part of the authorities, to Moslem trade union organizations.

This seven-point programme of 'immediate action' in Algeria—an action which was to run parallel with Lacoste's 'pacification'—figured, indeed, as a conclusion to a *Note sur l'Algérie* published at the beginning of May in the first issue of a new publication, *Les Cahiers de la République*. This was published at the Radical headquarters in the Place de Valois, and the chairman of its editorial board was none other than Mendès-France.

The article, though presented as a 'collective' work by 'a group of Radicals' had, however, all the marks of Mendès-France's own style. Some of it was reminiscent of his 'Cassandra' speeches at the time of the Indo-China war.

Here are some of the main points of the article:

There were already close on half-a-million French soldiers in North Africa, and the question had arisen of sending 100,000 more. The 'military effort' in Algeria already represented an increased expenditure for France of 200 milliards a year; but this figure would be far greater before long. The country was faced with new taxes or inflation, and the shelving of economic and social reforms. The Algerian rebels were no great military force; there were believed to be not more than 25,000 men; but they enjoyed the full moral support of the mass of the Moslem population, and any losses inflicted on the rebels would be easily replaced.

Only bold political action by the French could restore any confidence in France among the Moslems. Otherwise there could be no lasting and real solution.

It was wrong of the Government to believe that it could pacify first, and hold free elections after that. At that stage the colonialists—the 'men of the 6th of February'—would feel sufficiently powerful to oppose any genuine election, let alone any far-reaching reforms. Before long, terrorism would flare up again.

In the past, the Moslems had had the impression that, sooner or later, France would treat them generously and fairly. All these hopes had been disappointed far too often.

Even so, just after the January 2 election, a bold move by the new French Government was possible; and conditions were favourable: the Moslems were favourably disposed to the Republican Front, and were genuinely hoping for a new deal. The election promises of the Republican Front parties had impressed them. Mollet's Ministerial Declaration had, on the whole, been well received, including his reference to the 'Algerian Personality', and his promise to have persons under preventive arrest released.

But after the 6th of February and the dismissal of Catroux, Mollet's speeches had become vaguer and vaguer. And the most serious result of the 6th of February was to unify the Algerian Resistance. Until then, it had been dispersed and unorganized. It was after February 6 that the fanaticism, the hatred and the despair of the Moslem population had grown.

The whole significance of this article became apparent very soon after its publication. The 'Seven Conditions' were, in fact, the conditions Mendès-France had made to Mollet for staying on in the Government. He did not resign in April, as he intended to do, for two reasons: the call-up of reservists for service in Algeria was in full swing (by the end of May there were to be about 500,000 French Troops in Algeria alone); and Mollet and Pineau were about to leave for Moscow. So he marked time, hoping against hope that Mollet might still accept his terms.

When Mollet returned from Moscow, he made it clear that he was not accepting them.

Should Mendès have gone long before? For instance, after the Government's capitulation to the Algiers mob, and the dropping of Catroux? At that time, Mendès thought it would be 'disloyal to Mollet' to do so; and too many people who had believed in, and voted for, the Republican Front would be too disappointed. He obviously also thought that he—and a few of the Socialists like Defferre and Savary—could exercise a moderating influence on the Government's policy.

Mollet, impressed, on the one hand, by Lacoste's self-assurance, and, on the other hand, by the smear campaign that was going on in the country against Mendès-France, did not try very hard to retain him in the Government.

'Don't throw stones at him; he is a sincere and tortured man'. There had been many things to torture him, and thwarted ambition was perhaps the least of them. He had been tortured by Mollet's 'disloyalty' and by the obsession that the Republican Front Government had embarked on a policy which could, he thought, only fail in the end. He was not prepared to surrender to the growing jingoism of French public opinion, to the country-right-or-wrong moods, to the signs of anti-Arab racialism.

And he felt acute bitterness at the thought that Mollet had done nothing to protest against, or even to show his displeasure over, the smear campaign to which he (Mendès) was being subjected at the War Leakages trial, a scandalously-conducted trial at which the lawyer of Baranès, Tixier-Vignancour and a variety of witnesses were constantly insinuating that Mendès-France was somehow mixed up with the leakages, and that in any case, he represented the Defeatist Gang in France.

All these insinuations were made with impunity, and with the obvious approval of the presiding judge. And even when, on two occasions, Mendès insisted on appearing in Court, to challenge his enemies, he could obtain no great satisfaction. On such occasions Tixier-Vignancour would merely remark venomously that 'the time was not yet ripe' for Mendès's defence, but that he regarded him as Culprit Number One in the disintegration of France's colonial empire! The legend was being vigorously built up that France would not have lost the war in Indo-China but for treason at home: the treason of papers like *Express* and *France-Observateur* with which (or with whose contributors) Mendès was 'somehow' mixed up. The Guilty Men—Bidault, and Letourneau, and Teitgen, and Frédéric-Dupont—who had persisted with the insane Indo-China war, were now making scapegoats of the 'defeatists', and, in the first place, of Mendès-France.

As the *Monde* wrote at the end of the trial:

> There is not the remotest piece of evidence that Mitterrand had anything to do with the leakage. But then, any man who embarks on a political career is bound to run grave risks. But neither M. Baylot [the Prefect of Police whom Mitterrand dismissed in 1954] nor M. Tixier-Vignancour was really interested in Mitterrand. The forgeries by which he got dragged into the Leakages Case had quite a different purpose: and that was to strike at quite another man—Mendès-France—and at the republican regime itself. No doubt, the enemies of Mendès-France had the right . . . to suspect him of betraying the interests of France. Martinaud-Deplat accused him of this as early as 1953, over the North African affair . . . Consciously or unconsciously, Mendès-France's enemies proceeded to manufacture the 'evidence' of his treason, so much so that the Mitterrand-Mendès case is becoming extraordinarily like the Dreyfus Case. But although certain professional patriots had the right to suspect Mendès, they had no business to fake the evidence.
>
> But it goes deeper than that. They identify Communism with treason, *progressisme* with Communism, and non-conformism with *progressisme*—with the odd result that, in the end, Mendès-France becomes more dangerous in their eyes than Thorez. If

only because Communism in France is isolated in its opposition, while cabinet rank still confers a special authority on a man . . .

As a result the Communists suffered less injury from this trial than anybody else . . . No doubt, it was difficult to treat Mendès and his friends as simple traitors . . . In one sense, they are innocent. But, on the other hand, their enemies argue, their actions, their speeches and articles betray the country's interests. Such is the intellectual perversion which makes people accuse others of treason, and do so in seemingly perfectly good faith . . . No doubt, there is something highly suspect about a missing police slip, or a forged document; but what's that compared with the alleged salvation of the country?[1]

In this respect, the *Monde* argued, the Mendès-Mitterrand case was extraordinarily like the Dreyfus case; but it went even further in some ways: the *affaire des fuites* gave the French public a general and nauseating feeling that 'everything was rotten' in the State of France; that there was no real authority left anywhere. That the rival police services were discrediting each other; that the whole legal machinery was rusty beyond repair if the presiding judge, M. Niveau de Villedary, could so openly identify himself with the Fascist lawyer, Tixier-Vignancour. Judges like him had served Vichy, just as they were—on the face of it—now serving the Fourth Republic. But they had lost the serenity which should be part of their function; they were willing, as on this occasion, to join in the Vichy vendetta; they were thereby discrediting the legal institutions of the Republic, while, at the same time, doing their best to undermine the authority of the Republic's Government personnel.

The lack of a republican *mystique* among so many French officials was something Mendès-France had often deplored; in the case of the *affaire des fuites* the trouble was even more blatant; here servants of the State were taking part in a vendetta against the Republic.

Simultaneously, at the MRP Congress, only a few days before Mendès's resignation, he was being constantly alluded to as a traitor, though no one had the courage to mention him by name.

To all these vicious charges Mollet did not react. His antipathy for Mendès was great, and he did not feel like compromising himself by standing up for Mendès and—indirectly—for the 'defeatists'— whom his own Minister of Defence, M. Bourgès-Maunoury, was trying so hard to frighten into submission.

A subsidiary reason for Mollet's dislike of Mendès was the latter's insufficient 'Europeanism'. Shortly Euratom would come up for discussion before the National Assembly, and Mollet knew that Mendès

[1] Jacques Fauvet in *Le Monde*, May 22, 1956.

was unfavourable to the scheme. Moreover, Mendès was highly critical of the financial policy of Ramadier, the Finance Minister—a policy which was a hand-to-mouth mixture of demagogy and inflation, and which was already beginning to show unmistakable signs of producing a sharp rise in the cost-of-living—for the first time since 1952.

Mendès felt that the flag-waving over Algeria could only be of short duration; even if it was not necessary to call up any more men than had already been called up, the country would soon become restive over the effects of inflation, a direct result of the new war expenditure. And, above all, there was his 7-point programme on Algeria which Mollet had rejected.

And so Mendès went—just as he had gone in 1945 when de Gaulle rejected his Financial Plan.

But in reality he had misjudged the real mood of the country. It was increasingly determined to 'keep' Algeria at any price.

A large part of France continued to be in a flag-waving mood. Lacoste, when he spoke in June at the Senate and, later, at the National Assembly, came very close to being treated as France's national hero— the man who had 'saved Algeria' in the nick of time. Everybody, from the Socialists to the Poujadists, cheered their heads off at the end of Lacoste's speech. Only the Communists and a handful of Radicals round Mendès-France, were silent.

Yet the Socialists, at heart, were not unanimously behind Lacoste. At the Socialist Congress at Lille at the end of June, grave doubts were voiced over the ultimate wisdom of the Lacoste policy.

CHAPTER 7

THE SOCIALIST MOTION FOR A CEASE-FIRE

IN June, Mendès-France was no longer in the Government. But he had not abandoned the fight. He knew that he had allies and sympathizers in the Socialist Party, and it was with an eye on the Socialist Congress, which was to meet at Lille soon afterwards, that he made a great programme speech on Algeria before the Executive Committee of the Radical Party on June 8. 1,100 delegates of the Radical federations from all over the country and numerous deputies and senators came to the meeting at the Salle Wagram. Again, there was something paradoxical about it all; the motion approving Mendès-France's policy was voted unanimously, except for a few delegates of the Radical Federations on Algeria; but, at the same time, the Radical Ministers in the Mollet Government, such as Bourgès-Maunoury continued their die-hard policy.

'For the past six months, French policy towards Algeria has been moving in the wrong direction,' was the main theme of Mendès's speech and he repeated the substance of his seven-point proposal which Mollet had rejected.

The Socialist Congress which met at Lille at the end of June was a stormy affair. The opposition, which largely thought along the lines of the Mendès-France proposals, and was led by Daniel Mayer, André Philip and Edouard Depreux voiced the great uneasiness caused by Lacoste's 'pacification first' attitude. They declared themselves wholly dissatisfied with the innocuous motion presented by M. Commin, and insisted on the insertion of some very 'anti-colonialist' paragraphs, to which, finally, Mollet agreed—though not exactly with good grace.

These 'inserts' were of the following order:

There was a reference to 'the monstrous errors of the past, inspired by the selfish colonialist spirit'.

There was another reference to 'the sabotage of the Blum-Violette plan of 1936 and the sabotage of the Statut d'Algérie of 1947';

There was a veiled criticism of Lacoste in the phrase which said that 'in present conditions, the French Government must wage war on two fronts: against the rebels and against the colonialist diehards, who are opposed to a Franco-Moslem reconciliation and to the creation of a new Algeria'.

There was a passage calling on the Government to put an end to the intolerable influence of certain colonialist monopolies, which were weighing so heavily on the press and on France's whole policy in Algeria; to take drastic measures against the press which was interfering with a Franco-Moslem *rapprochement;* and, finally, to eliminate from Algeria those who stood at the head of this press.

Another passage called for a purge in the administration, and the rapid training of new cadres, without distinction of race and creed, to promote a better understanding between the two races in Algeria. Municipalities which were weapons of colonialist oppression must be dissolved without delay.

And after agreeing to the Commin text concerning the future status of Algeria, the minority, nevertheless, insisted on the cease-fire clause being more categorical than it was in the Commin version. Instead of 'relying on the Government to do everything to bring about a cease-fire', etc., the final text of the motion said:

The Congress demands that the Government do everything to bring about a cease-fire with those against whom we are fighting, since such a cease-fire is the preliminary stage and the primary condition of any general settlement.

Although this final motion did not include the even more precise recommendations (or rather 'demands') concerning the cease-fire procedure proposed by M. André Philip, including talks with the Algerian nationalists 'on the highest possible level', as well as the 'pre-negotiations' which he recommended for preparing the elections to the Single College, it went as far as it could go, in view of the strong opposition coming especially from M. Lacoste, the Minister-Resident.

The importance of this Lille Motion cannot be overrated. It showed that, despite strong chauvinist currents which could be observed in France ever since the beginning of the year, there was still an articulate Left—which was manifesting itself inside the Socialist Party—and which was determined to take a long-term view of Algeria, and of the dangers of perpetuating the war there . . . This Socialist minority had, clearly, been strongly influenced by Mendès-France's seven-point programme, to which, however, it had added an insistent demand for a cease-fire—a point on which Mendès had (in public, at any rate) hesitated to commit himself.

But would Lacoste take any notice of this motion voted by his own Party? That was No. 1 question after the Congress.

CHAPTER 8

MENDÈS-FRANCE AT LOUVIERS

'This school, you say, wants to buy a typewriter with a wide carriage? It seems to me a totally unwarranted expense—about 20,000 francs more than an ordinary-size typewriter. If they were to use it five or six days a week, I could see some justification; but simply to have it there, so that they can use it a few times a year makes no sense. I think you had better make further inquiries before we agree to this grant.'

This was *M. le Maire* speaking at the meeting of the Town Council of Louviers on July 7, 1956. The crystal chandeliers were lighting up the room with its long table, at the head of which sat M. Mendès-France. There were 22 other town councillors present; a little man with a white *barbiche*, who was *l'adjoint;* and the rest of them, mostly large, sturdy Normans—shopkeepers, businessmen, one or two doctors and lawyers of the city of Louviers . . . And two Communists, who were as well-behaved as the rest. They had a large agenda that night. It started with some small items—a widow who had left furniture worth 60,000 francs to the local museum; and a Mme Gaillon who was asking the town council for an 'exceptional bursary' of 30,000 francs for her student son; and the case of M. Ebert, who had 12 children, of whom two were fighting in Algeria, and who had some hard-luck story to tell in his letter to the town council, and whose case raised the question whether a bursary of 8,000 francs should be granted to one of his children out of the council's 'unforeseen expenses'. And so on, and so on. Further, a decision was taken not to have any fireworks at Louviers on July 14, and so to save 50,000 francs which would be paid to the fund in charge of parcels for the French troops in Algeria.

M. le Maire: We must ask the Prefecture to whom exactly this money must be paid.

There were discussions on the way the Barangé funds were to be allocated to the various *laïque* schools (it was at this point that the question of the typewriter with the wide or ordinary carriage arose), and on the price of the musical instruments that were to be bought for a local school orchestra and music school, and a variety of other items, each one of which ended with *M. le Maire's 'adopté'*, or else with his decision that there must be a further inquiry. And then there followed a discussion on the longest of all the items—the water rates at

314

Louviers, the differential rates of 'small consumers' and 'large consumers' and *économiquement faibles*, and market gardeners, who were using a lot of water, and the slaughter-house, which was being unnecessarily wasteful with its water, and so on; and the comparative water rates at Louviers and Vernon; and the various reasons, such as the extension of the network, why Louviers had had to put up its rates—which were, however, even now still lower than in most other towns of the Eure.

It was curious to watch 'Mr. France', 'France's leading statesman', the idol of the international press back in 1954 talk with such expert knowledge of the water rates of Louviers, and of what to do about the 60,000 francs' legacy of furniture, and about the comparative cost of large and small typewriters, and on whether a school couldn't do with a small one instead of a big one.

M. le Maire presided over the town council with consummate authority and clearly knew what he was talking about. Local government was a fine art he had learned over a large number of years—ever since he had first landed at Louviers as a 21-year-old lawyer back in 1928.

He sat there, at the head of the table, a strange impassive figure, with jet-black hair, a tired look on his heavy eyelids, and a pale, almost yellow face, that seemed even more yellow than usual in the midst of the plump, ruddy-cheeked Normans around him.

Certainly they respected him; many of them admired him, and were proud of him. He was, after all, a very famous man. And they seemed a little afraid of him. 'He's very powerful,' a ruddy-faced jovial town councillor afterwards told me. '*Il a le bras long*. He's as thick as thieves with the Prefect, who just eats out of his hand. I am a friend of his. But he's got enemies here, too. Only they are afraid of him, and they want to keep in with him. They know that, when necessary, he can render them all kinds of services; and he is rather inclined to render services to his enemies—*de petits rubans, de petites promotions*. You know what French provincial life is like,' he added with a shrug.

I am not sure whether this man was really a friend of Mendès's or not. He agreed that Mendès had done extraordinarily well in the General Election: 'Ah yes, the people were very largely for him; no doubt about it. But, you know, his influence isn't quite what it used to be. He had the industrialists behind him, you know. And the Church, too—*mais oui, parfaitement*. At one time, he also had the Communists behind him; but they don't like him any more; and I am not sure who is really there to support him these days. All the same, *il a le bras long*. He's not merely mayor of Louviers; he's president of the *Conseil Général* of the Eure—a very, very powerful and influential man, and he's a very good *maire*. He has here at Louviers seven secretaries, and no letter ever remains unanswered.'

Mendès was proud of the Eure, and of all that he, both as mayor of Louviers and as head of the *Conseil Général* had done for the *département*. 'Yes,' he said that evening, as we were driving to a *manifestation artistique* organized by a *laïque* school some miles outside Louviers, 'it's very satisfying to be able to work on this local level. Here you see the results rightaway. Look at all we've done in Louviers by way of housing—and in the Eure generally. We have built, proportionately, more houses in the Eure than any other *département* in France, with one exception.'

And he talked at great length of the reconversion of industries that was going on in the Eure, and the inevitable decline of the textile mills, and the problem of re-training textile workers for other industries, and the persuasion that had to be used not to encourage textile workers to make their children follow in their footsteps.

And he talked about the *école laïque*, and the encouragement that he—together with the *Amis de l'Ecole Laïque*—had been giving to it, and the constant efforts that had to be made to counteract the propaganda of the *curés*, especially among the children. At Louviers the *école laïque* was dominant; there were only two small *écoles libres* in the town, and they did not amount to much.

We went to the *manifestation artistique* at the school of a small working class centre in the Eure. The children were doing a sort of *Cinderella* ballet, followed by three scenes from *Le Médecin Malgré Lui*—an awfully amateurish little show. But the children were gay and pretty with their fancy dress and their make up. In the interval between the two shows, the local president of the *Amis de l'Ecole Laïque*, a stout gentleman with a rosette of the Legion of Honour, announced that *le Président* Mendès-France had arrived, and there were loud cheers from the children. Mendès, sitting in the front row, watched the *Cinderella* ballet and the *Médecin Malgré Lui*, but his thoughts seemed elsewhere . . .

'Ah, the week-end, the week-end' he later remarked, 'it's the busiest time in the life of a deputy! That's the time when we keep in touch with our local people . . .' He commented on the devotion of the *instituteurs* who had organized this show. It was important to compete with the *curés* always hot on 'cultural' activity of this kind.

But his thoughts were elsewhere . . . Algeria was like an obsession with him. As we drove back to Louviers, he spoke with some bitterness of Mollet. This was the second time he had been forced to leave a Government, because he knew that it was doing the wrong thing . . . He thought an all-out war in Algeria absolutely hopeless. 'All right, we'll kill off a thousand rebels, ten thousand rebels. We'll go on advancing; they'll go on retreating. *So what?*' he added in English. 'We'll go on advancing. On to the Sahara, right on to the Belgian Congo—is *that* a solution?' There were nine million Arabs in Algeria to draw from; so, short of genocide, the rebels' manpower was inexhaustible. He thought the Socialist motion at Lille a very good thing, but would Lacoste stick to it?

He had known Lacoste for a long time. A man who had been anti-Munich and who had a fine record in the Resistance, who was a man of courage . . . And yet, he was a man with a terrible weakness. When, after the Liberation, he was Minister of Industrial Production, he was incapable of any serious planning effort, and was wholly under the thumb of the big industrialists . . . And it was much the same again: he couldn't get tough with the *gros colons* in Algeria and with their stooges in the administration, and he seemed incapable of fighting 'on two fronts' as the Socialist Motion had asked him to do.

But what could be done? Lacoste was working hand-in-hand with all that was reactionary in Algeria. The liberals among the French were terrorized. Even some of the most reasonable people among the Algerian leaders had had to escape abroad, or were in camps . . . If there was no solution to the Algerian problem, it was no use expecting any agreement with either Morocco or Tunisia. Bourguiba might sign anything in the world, but, even with the best will in the world, he couldn't stick to it; he would be carried away by Arab nationalism. He would think it his patriotic duty to follow that course, if France persisted with the war in Algeria . . .

Lacoste was very pessimistic in February when he got to Algeria; but now a few local military successes had gone to his head. He thought he could force the Algerians to surrender. And then, unilaterally, there would be a few minor concessions to the Algerians, and the old colonialist gang would take over again . . .

As I watched him talking that night, in the 'rustic' pantry of his house, up on the hill above Louviers, I could not help pondering on this remarkable man's strange destiny. Here he was, obviously dejected, frustrated, unhappy. He was terribly conscious of all the Parties being against him. There had been other men in the same position in the past. They also were rebels; they also had found it hard to stick to the rules of the political game—the rules of the System, as de Gaulle had called it . . . That evening one had the feeling that Mendès felt that there was perhaps only one French leader with whom he really saw eye-to-eye—and that was de Gaulle. Would de Gaulle ever return? Would he ever be called upon to find a solution to the infernal problem of North Africa—he, the man of an anachronistic

V

grandeur française? And if so, would Mendès be the real executive
power behind de Gaulle? It all depended . . . It depended, first and
foremost, on what de Gaulle was prepared to do. If his Government
was the usual 'national union' assortment of all and sundry—complete
with Bidault and Pinay and Mollet and what-have-you—it wouldn't
be any good. It would have to be a Government with a precise programme. Perhaps the trick could then work . . . Never again, I felt,
would Mendès go into a Government that did not know what it
wanted. He had had two 'accidents'—one in 1945 and another in
1956. Never again . . . But for the present, at any rate, few in France
wanted him, anyway. Or de Gaulle, for that matter.

Throughout the summer of 1956 Mendès-France remained grimly
silent. He was watching Algeria with ever-growing dismay. He did not
speak again until October.

PART VII
NORTH AFRICAN CLOSE-UP: JOURNEY TO ALGERIA, TUNISIA AND MOROCCO

CHAPTER 1

NATIONAL REVOLUTION IN ALGERIA

I T was on the Algerian issue that the Mendès-France Government
had been overthrown in February 1955. Throughout 1955 Algeria
continued to be Mendès-France's chief worry, and, in his election
campaign at the end of that year he kept on repeating that if the war
in Algeria—for it had become a minor war by now—was not
liquidated, the whole future development of France would be
jeopardized. He made Algeria the election issue on which everything
else depended.

The unity of the Republican Front Government, formed after the
January 1956 election, was disrupted on the Algerian issue. After
Mollet's surrender to the European rioters at Algiers on February 6,
1956, and his adoption of a diehard policy in Algeria, the conflict
between the liberal and diehard policy inside the Government was
personified, for several months, by the clash between Mendès-France
and Lacoste. In the end, after a hopeless four months' struggle,
Mendès-France resigned. Ever since 1954 there had been a campaign of
varying intensity against Mendès-France as the 'liquidator of the
French Empire'.

In the summer of 1956 I decided to see for myself what this North-
African Empire looked like in reality. In the foregoing narrative the
quarrel inside France over North Africa—with Mendès-France as one
of the central figures in this quarrel—is described in some detail; but
it was not always clear to me what it all looked like from the other side
of the Mediterranean, and also how relevant all the plans, mutual
criticisms and mutual accusations were to the real state of affairs in
North Africa.

So, on a hot day, on August 1, at Bordeaux, I boarded the *Provence*,
a double-decker Bréguet plane, bound for Algiers . . .

There were three women and three children among the 100 passengers of the *Provence;* nearly all the rest were soldiers or—policemen
in uniform. The plane had come to Bordeaux from Nantes, and the
25 or 30 policemen had boarded the plane there. Why all these French
policemen? Their presence on the plane gave me a first hint of the state
of great insecurity reigning in Algeria . . .

We flew, at 9,000 feet, over the high, black peaks of the Pyrénées,
still with a few patches of snow; then over brown desolate-looking

stretches of Northern Catalonia; and we crossed the coast of the
Mediterranean just south of Barcelona. After the usual euphoria-
creating Air-France supper with its cold chicken and other dainties
and its quarter-bottle of superior claret, we caught the first glimpse of
the coast of Africa in a lilac twilight. Some distance away, to the right,
we could see the thousands of lights of Algiers. We landed at Maison
Blanche, and were conducted into the sumptuous brand-new *aérogare*.
It had not yet been built at the time of my last visit in 1953 ...

Passengers, crews, officials, police, soldiers, gendarmes, milling
round the vast hall of the *aérogare*—they were all French without
exception. For the first few minutes on the soil of Algeria you would
not have guessed you were in Africa ... The first Arabs to be seen
were porters, and the man selling coach tickets, and the coachdriver.
Wholly uneventful eight-mile drive along a dark wide road towards
the twelve-storey Air-France terminal. Not much traffic at 9.30 p.m.,
but some, all the same. Everything looked singularly normal. I commented on this to a French officer sitting next to me. 'That's Algiers,'
he said, 'but if you flew to Constantine, you'd find the coach from the
airfield driving into town under a heavy escort of armed motor-
cyclists ... Things are still fairly all-right in Algiers,' he added with a
doubtful shrug ...

At the air terminal there was the usual bustle of 'authorized'
porters with armlets and 'unauthorized' ones—without armlets. These
were the usual ragamuffins of Algiers, who were being chased away
by the 'authorized' porters; no racial or national solidarity among
them ... My 'unauthorized' porter—a shabby pimply youngster of
14 or 15—carrying my case along the dark and almost deserted street,
said ingratiatingly: 'American?' When I said '*Anglais*', his deference
vanished. But, in broken French he started his little bit of propaganda
—a sob story of how 'you couldn't safely say anything these days', and
how he had spent a week at the Centrale (the prison), and if he hadn't
several young brothers and sisters to help out, he would long ago have
joined the fellaghas ... And here he was, he said, having to carry the
luggage of Europeans, instead of going to school ... Clearly somebody had filled him up with the right ideas ... All along the deserted
streets, we came across helmeted patrols of usually four men ... After
ten minutes' walk, we emerged into the Boulevard Laferrière, with its
Hotel Albert I-er, alongside the long strip of garden running right up
the hill as far as the *Gouvernement Général*, and with the very war
memorial where, on February 6, a frantic crowd of Europeans had
pelted M. Guy Mollet with rotten tomatoes ...

That night, I sat on the balcony of my room on the sixth floor of the
Hotel Albert. Sumptuous blocks of flats on the other side of the

Boulevard Laferrière, and all the way up the hill, as far as the eye could see. But very few lights in the windows. Had most of the inhabitants of French Algiers gone to Vittel and Vichy? At this late hour, this might be Cannes or Nice; nothing to show this was Africa. Down on the left, I could see a few lights on the ships in the harbour. The Arab Algiers might have been a 100 miles away. All was quiet in Algiers— too quiet. There was hardly a soul in the streets below, except the patrols. An occasional car raced past at breakneck speed. Were they scared of being attacked, or what? I wondered . . . At midnight came the curfew; the last of the pedestrians vanished; but a few patrol cars still raced about . . .

I spent ten days at Algiers, and found it more and more depressing every day. On the face of it, life was normal, almost absurdly normal in European Algiers. Everywhere there were, of course, patrols and sentries, but shops in the rue d'Isly and in the rue Michelet were doing a booming trade; restaurants were crowded with soldiers and civilians, and *à l'heure de l'apéritif*—which meant almost any time between 10 a.m. and 7 p.m.—you could hardly find a seat at the Coq Hardi and the other fashionable cafés. On the café terraces on the pavement, smartly-dressed civilians and officers and ravishingly handsome women were imbibing their coffees and pastis and *jus de fruits* . . . It might be Nice; except—except that, all the time, they were being guarded by armed patrols, and the shoeshine boys—about the only Arabs in this part of Algiers—were pestering everybody with their *'cirer? cirer?'*

In the morning and late afternoon, the traffic in the streets of European Algiers was about as thick as in Paris . . . The tramcars— these alone were crowded mostly with Arabs—jingled down the rue d'Isly.

'The new Algeria will emerge the moment the European and Moslem communities have regained confidence in each other, and both have regained confidence in France,' M. Lacoste had declared some months before. Alas, that was the one thing of which there was no evidence at all.

Perhaps the Europeans had, after the 6th of February, 'regained confidence in France'; but every day the gulf was widening between Europeans and Moslems. Even the old paternalism of some of the Europeans had given way to acute distrust, and there could be no illusions about the Moslems' attitude to the Europeans. They were filled with fear and hatred. Seldom did Europeans venture into the Kasbah. A French friend to whom I suggested one night having supper at a famous fish restaurant near the Mosque, said: 'Not on your life! The least we risk is having all four tyres punctured . . .' Although this same Frenchman had Moslems working in his small factory, he said they were 'a bad lot'; he couldn't trust them half an inch; relations with them were stiff and formal. '*Communauté franco-musulmane*', he said rather grimly one day, 'Believe me, there's no such thing; and I doubt whether there ever will be . . .'

This gulf between French and Moslems was one of the characteristics of Algeria. Another was the appalling insecurity in which the whole country was living. The 500,000 troops were creating relative security in some places, but no complete security anywhere. Economically, the country was in a mess . . . And, politically, there was an almost complete vacuum, with no Moslems representing anything on *any* level. Precariously, the country seemed to hang together more or less thanks to the presence of these 500,000 troops; they were there to save European lives and to enable the economic wheels to turn slowly— very slowly. Algeria was, in fact, run by a dictatorship of the Army and the French Administration, itself closely allied to Big Business.

* * *

Algeria has been, and continues to be, the playground of Big Business. Many French writers have dealt with the question of 'Who are the real masters of Algeria?' Without attempting here to give an exhaustive account of Algeria's economic structure, it is sufficient to quote a few important facts, which will give the reader an insight into this essential characteristic of Algerian economy:

> The group called *Banque de l'Union Parisienne-Mirabaud* controls the *Compagnie Algérienne* which, in turn, controls the *Compagnie Algérienne de Crédit et de Banque;* the *Société Financière de l'Afrique du Nord;* the *Société Finemaroc;* the *Fermes du Chelif;* the *Ouenza Mines* (78% of all Algeria's iron ore); the *Société des Lièges des Hamendes et de la Petite Kabylie* (the most important cork-tree plantation); the *Crédit Foncier d'Algérie et de Tunisie* (the principal European Settlers' bank) and the *Banque Industrielle de l'Afrique du Nord;* all these wield a powerful influence on the whole economy of Algeria, and, needless to say, in a manner favourable to European and not to Moslem enterprises.
>
> *Les Fermes Françaises de Tunisie* own seven very large estates in Algeria, and General Aumeran, who was Deputy of Algiers till 1956, is on its Board of Directors; *La Société de Keroulis* owns numerous estates and a great amount of house property in the cities.

The biggest *colons*, wielding immense political power are Borgeaud, Blanchette and Schiaffino.

Henri Borgeaud, of Swiss origin, is a Senator for Algiers and owns the largest vineyards in Algeria, the *Domaine de la Trappe* alone producing 40,000 hectolitres of wine a year, and the *Chapeau du Gendarme*, with 45,000 hectolitres. He fully or partly controls a vast number of Algerian companies: agricultural concerns like the *Compagnie Générale Nord-Africaine*, the *Union Foncière Nord-Africaine*, the *Domaine Beni Slimene*, mills, distilleries, cork-processing plants, timber concerns, shipping and textile companies, cement works, the biggest cigarette and tobacco factories (*Tabacs Bastos*), banking, phosphates (*Compagnie des Phosphates de Constantine*), etc.

Georges Blanchette, the richest man in Parliament, and, until 1956, deputy for Algiers, is estimated to have a net income of £21,500,000 a year. He enjoys a virtual monopoly in esparto grass (*alfa*), a vast crop stretching over thousands of square miles of central and southern Algeria, and notorious for the sweated labour used in harvesting it. Blanchette owns or partly controls numerous concerns (esparto, water, textiles, market-gardening, sundry agricultural concerns, stone quarries, etc.).

Laurent Schiaffino, senator for Algiers, is Algeria's shipping magnate, but is also closely associated with mining interests, banking, etc.

Nearly all the best lands are in the hands of Europeans. 25,000 Europeans own 2,720,000 hectares (average 108 hectares, 62 of them productive), as against 7,672,000 hectares owned by 532,000 Moslems (average 14 hectares, of which only five are productive). But these 'average figures' are misleading, because both among the European and Moslem landowners, one-quarter of the land is owned by three-quarters of them, and three-quarters of the land by one-quarter. Even so, the small French landowner has an average of 28 hectares, and the small fellah, five; moreover, the European lands are better and more suitable for irrigation.

Of the biggest estates should be mentioned the *Compagnie Algérienne* owning 70,000 hectares of the best lands; the *Compagnie Genévoise*, with 20,000 hectares, the *Société des Lièges de Hamendas et de la Petite Kabylie*, with 50,000 hectares of cork-tree forests; M. Dussaix, with 18,000 hectares, M. de Calen with 6,000 hectares, etc. The big settlers have, moreover, concentrated on the cultivation of crops for export—wine, citrus fruit, vegetables—with no proper market inside Algeria, and with only a doubtful or—in the case of wine—indirectly state-subsidized market in France.

The 400,000 hectares of Algerian vineyards are one of the worst economic anomalies of Algeria, but are nevertheless a source of huge profits to the growers, especially the large growers. At the same time, the quantity of wheat produced in Algeria is the same as that in 1911— sufficient for little more than half the present population.

With their desire to keep labour cheap, the colons have, for dozens of years, put the brake on the development of Algerian industry; and the customs union with France has discouraged the creation of major Algerian industries, all the more so as electric power is 70% dearer than in France. The output of the mining industry (3.3 m. tons of iron ore), is almost wholly exported in its raw state. The same is true of Algeria's oil (85,000 t.), phosphates (603,000 t.), lead ore (11,800 t.) and zinc ore (28,000 t.). Most of the coal alone (200,000 out of 295,000 tons) is used locally. There are four companies prospecting Algeria for oil reserves, but, so far, these projects have not made much difference to Algeria's economy.

On balance, it may be said that, whereas France has in recent years been lending Algeria substantial sums for equipment (from which, however, the Europeans have, proportionately, derived a far greater benefit than the Moslems), Algeria has, as an 'under-developed' country with a strikingly lopsided economy, been a liability, rather than an asset to France as a whole—though not to certain financial interests, both in France and in Algeria.

What has, naturally, immensely complicated matters has been the rapid increase in the Algerian population; the Moslem population, which was just over two million in 1872 and 5.5 million in 1930, was 8.3 million in 1954. The European population is 1,230,000, of whom only 11 per cent[1] are of French origin, the rest being of Spanish, Maltese, Italian or Jewish origin. It has been observed that the most extreme French nationalists in Algeria are usually not of French descent! There are over 300,000 Algerians working in France, but this has not absorbed the unemployment in Algeria by any means; a large part of the population (one million male adults, roughly) are partly or wholly unemployed, and, in the agricultural areas, the annual *per capita* income has been estimated at about £20. Many parts of Algeria are fairly near the starvation level. The schools are wholly inadequate: only 19 per cent of Moslem children of school age go to school.[2]

[1] According to Jeanson, op. cit. *Le Monde* (September 13, 1956), spoke of 'about one-third' being of French origin.

[2] Most of these facts and figures are derived from C. A. Julien's *L'Afrique du Nord en marche:* (Paris, 1952); G. and F. Jeanson's *L'Algerie hors la loi:* (Paris, 1956); and C. Bourdet's *Les Maîtres de l'Afrique du Nord* (Paris, *Temps Modernes*, 1952).

The capitalist and colonialist order pretended to be still going strong in Algiers in August 1956; the sumptuous blocks of flats, the vast office buildings of the *Compagnie Algérienne*, the *Société Financière* this and the *Crédit Foncier* that, the great Algiers branch offices of the main Paris banks seemed to suggest that the *héritage du père Bugeaud* was still in safe hands . . . And, among the Europeans, sipping their *apéritifs* at the Coq Hardi there was still much loose talk of *les bicots* and *les ratons* . . . How reminiscent of the talk about 'Wogs' among the British in Egypt only a few years ago . . . Only now *les ratons* were no longer merely creatures to be despised. *Les ratons* had become dangerous; the Little Rats had shown their sharp teeth just as Nasser, the King of the Wogs, had shown that they weren't going to be Wogs forever . . .

Nasser, Nasser, Nasser . . . What a blessing Nasser was to the French diehards in Algiers during that whole period! 'If Britain and France crack Nasser over the head, it'll be the end of the war in Algeria', a French-Algerian journalist was exclaiming frantically at a press conference up at the *Gouvernement-Général*. And a young man from the *Echo d'Alger* was drawing romantic fantasies of British and French troops landing at Port Said and occupying Cairo, and hanging Nasser, after which all the *ratons* would lose heart, and become once again the well-behaved subject race they had always been. Nasser was the straw at which the believers in Lacoste's policy of Pacification were now clutching. *Entente cordiale* . . . and *Vive l'Angleterre!*

Had England, which had betrayed the common cause in the Arab world by abandoning Suez in 1954—had England seen the light at last? Was England, whose agents in Libya—that artificial British-made monstrosity—had for years been feeding anti-French sedition in Tunisia and Algeria—as American agents had been doing the same in Morocco—was England having a change of heart? Would England and France, the twin spearhead of the Free World, now reassert themselves at last, and make the pan-Arab tide recede? Would the errors of Churchill in Egypt and Libya, the crimes of Mendès-France in Tunisia, and the blunders of Edgar Faure in Morocco be repaired and avenged? For months during the autumn of 1956, thousands of Frenchmen in Algeria day-dreamed about the restoration of past greatness, about a sudden revival of colonialism . . .

It was all a little pathetic. And it was, in itself, an admission that but for Nasser and that war against Nasser which would change everything, the policy of Pacification had failed. Up on the hill, in the sumptuous palace of the *Gouvernement-Général*, they were readily admitting that pacification had not produced the results it had been expected to produce. Far from it . . . They were admitting it ten yards away from Lacoste's own office.

What was the position in August 1956? For several months 'pacification' had been in progress. The *quadrillage*—the division of the country into small military units, in which the show of French military strength was supposed to 'persuade' the local populations of the towns and *douars* into loyalty and submission—had not succeeded. The French were up against something new—a kind of national unanimity among the Algerian masses they had not known before. Every Arab, almost without exception, had a soft spot for the Rebels, the National Liberation Front or at least for the remnants of the Messali movement.[1] Every Arab had mental reservations, and saw an enemy in the Frenchman; and, to the French, every Arab was a potential assassin and *égorgeur*.

Land reform? The papers had, during the previous month, talked a lot about sixteen 'indigent' Algerian families being settled on expropriated patches of land, somewhere near Oran; there was to be a great ceremony to celebrate the birth of this great land reform; yet the ceremony was called off; for the beneficiaries of the land reform were too scared to occupy the land allocated to them, since they might be looked upon as 'collaborators' by their fellow-Algerians.

'There *are* loyal Algerians,' I was told by a high official of the *Gouvernement-Général.* 'But what can you do? The people to whom we are willing to give land are too scared to occupy it. When we appoint Algerian officials to high posts in the Administration, they either refuse (for they are scared), or they accept, but ask that no publicity be given to the appointments. In the last few weeks, we have made 600 such appointments; but practically nobody's heard about them, and the whole business has got to be treated as a sort of guilty secret. It's hard to find these days able and reasonable men in Algeria who want to co-operate with us, and who *are*, at the same time, independent-minded Algerians; I don't mean *beni-oui-oui's* at all—good heavens,

---

[1] It was not easy to draw the line between the followers of the FLN and of the former MTLD, dissolved in 1954. Both were engaged in guerrilla warfare, but the degree of opposition between the two elements seemed to vary from place to place. The FLN claimed that Messali himself, interned in France, was 'completely out of touch' with Algerian affairs, that he had 'phoney' information planted on him by the French and that his opposition to a 'single party' (expressed in various press statements, notably in *Demain*) was unrealistic. He was no longer considered as uncompromising as before when, for the benefit of the *colons*, he had invented the slogan '*la valise ou le cercueil*', and the extremists of the FLN looked askance at Messali's proposal for a round-table conference on the lines of the Aix-les-Bains Conference on Morocco of August, 1955.

no! I mean people like Farès, the former President of the Algerian Assembly. But what's the good? He's scared. If we proclaim him an *interlocuteur valable*, he'll be bumped off the next day . . .'

It was revealing. Around Lacoste, they *were* thinking in terms of *beni-oui-oui's* as the most likely *interlocuteurs;* tame Algerians, Algerians believing in the 'indissoluble links between France and Algeria' (Mollet *dixit*). Yet even a man like Farès was to declare himself a 'rebel' only a few months later! Anyway, before there could be any negotiations with *any* Algerians (so the argument ran), pacification was essential. But what about pacification? There were 500,000 French troops in Algeria, yet the insecurity in the country was almost complete.

The railways were running, they were saying at the *Gouvernement-Général*. But how? It took 36 or 48 hours to travel from Algiers to Tunis. Repair squads had to travel on every train to mend the damaged line. Sometimes the trains, though travelling slowly, were derailed. Often, very often they were fired at, especially the *michelines* travelling from Biskra to Batna and thence to Bône.

A French friend, a small Algiers businessman, Henri L., was saying: 'My business takes me all over Algeria in my car. Now I never quite know whether I won't be the victim of some *sale coup* . . . A month or two ago it was still possible to travel safely from Algiers to Oran, but no longer. Did you see the story in the paper the other day of how a bus was stopped on the Algiers-Oran road; how all the European men were taken off by the fellaghas and shot there and then? Only one of them escaped; because he was born here, looked like a *raton*, and spoke perfect Arabic, and they thought he was one of their people . . . Already since March, I've given up going by car to Constantine and all those mountainous parts.'

'If there are any buses still running,' Henri said, 'it's only because the bus company in question pays ransom to the fellaghas. The owner of the bus that was attacked must have failed to pay ransom; or else it was attacked by some independent gang who hadn't been informed . . . Ransom, ransom—that's the only reason why anything is still working in Algeria. If not more French farmers have been murdered, together with their children, it's not because they are all that well protected by the French Army (the Army can't protect everybody at every moment of the day and night), but because they've paid ransom to the fellaghas . . .

'No doubt, the Army is of help; also the settlers are armed; but ransom is practically indispensable. The Army, it is true, has been of great help in one respect; but for the Army, the settlers would never have brought their harvest in this summer; they've managed it, all the same. But then, I ask you, how long is the Army to be employed at this kind of thing?'

How curious the mentality of the small or rather, medium, French-Algerian businessmen can be! What an odd mixture of prejudice and common sense! Henri drove me one Sunday afternoon to Alger-Plage and La Perouse—about the only places in the neighbourhood of Algiers where you could safely go without something unpleasant likely to happen. The whole of European Algiers seemed to be on its way to this 'Brighton' of Algiers. Along the 20 miles of the road, it was just one continuous stream of thousands and thousands of cars. There were armed patrols at almost every 200 or 300 yards. Sometimes there was a hold-up—why? Just because in the midst of all the European cars going to or from Alger-Plage there was a car with Arabs (or somebody looking like Arabs) inside it. It was immediately searched for bombs and firearms. Only through one small Arab village did we drive; and Henri commented on the miserable group of huts outside one of which stood a shabby old Citroen. '*Ils peuvent s'acheter des Citroen, mais ils préfèrent vivre dans la merde* . . .'

Bikinis, gramophones, loud-speakers, yachts with red sails, *pastis, jus de fruits*, coca-cola—such was Alger-Plage, with villas around, expensive villas which 'even now' you could still let for 150,000 or 200,000 francs for the summer . . .

As we drove back, as part of the same stream of cars, Henri became gloomy. 'I hate and despise the *ratons*,' he said. 'Often I feel that I'd like to get out of this damned place and settle in France. *On se fait du mauvais sang tous les jours* . . . The truth is, we've made an unholy mess of Algeria. It's probably too late now to do anything about it. I don't even know that having a crack at Nasser would make much difference. But it's not our fault, not the fault of the *petit blanc* . . . It's the fault of the *gros colons*. I pay my Algerian employees decently; there was one chap—*un vrai salopard*—who was getting 30,000 francs a month. He demanded 40,000. He wasn't much good anyway, so I sacked him. Now he's no doubt joined the fellaghas . . . But the *gros colons—c'est eux qui ont fait suer le bournous*. They've got a lot to answer for. It's they—and not small people like us—who paid the farm labourers 200 or 250 francs for a 12-hours' day. And it's also the big business interests in France who have always interfered with the development of Algeria. Why should Borgeaud grow all this wine which nobody wants? Why can't we grow sugar-beet and produce on the spot all the sugar Algeria needs? Oh, because the *betteraviers*, the *Raffineries Say* and the *Sucre Beghin* and other sugar refineries in France don't want to lose the Algerian market; so Algeria, if you please, has got to import sugar from France, at prices the *raton* can hardly pay . . .

'There's another thing,' said Henri. 'There are tremendous irrigation schemes which could be carried out, and could turn Algeria into a much more prosperous country. There's the Chott Chergui scheme in the Sud-Oranais under which thousands and thousands of hectares of land could be irrigated. They've talked and talked about it for years, but let's face it—France can't afford to invest all these milliards in Algeria. The whole of North Africa—if there's to be any *mise en valeur* on a big scale—will have to be done by some international body. There will *have* to be a North African Federation, with planning on a really grandiose scale. There's the Sahara. I am an old airman, and by plane, by car, and even by camel, I've seen most of the Sahara. There are possibilities there, I can tell you. 600 kilometres south of Gabès they've struck oil. I am told it may prove one of the richest oilfields in the world . . . Of course, we are slow and unorganized, and rotten with routine. It would be nice if France could get closely tied up with a new North African Federation, but I'm afraid it will be the Yanks . . . They've been buying up land—large pieces of property—round Mostaganem. All being done through a Swiss bank. Lacoste was right—damned right when he said at Colomb Bechar last month that there were two brands of Arab nationalism: the kind that wanted to follow blindly in the footsteps of Cairo; the other brand—a sort of "Western Islam"—that was willing to sell its bases and abandon its mining wealth and its natural resources for all time to the Americans. And there's not only oil in the Sahara, but also uranium and thorium, and all the Big Powers have an eye on it.'

'What do you think of Lacoste?' I asked.

'A good man, a very good man,' said Henri emphatically. But then he added doubtfully: 'He saved the situation here last spring; but I don't quite see where he's getting. The results of this pacification are nil, truly nil . . .'

'Did you take part in the 6th of February demonstration?' I said.

'You bet I did. Everybody in Algiers did. *We* weren't going to have Catroux here, *espèce de gâteux*. We had had enough of him in the lovely days of General de Gaulle—no more, thank you. Catroux and his *Collège Unique*—the man must have been crazy!'

'Yes, I know. But look, Henri—Soustelle, for whom you organized an ovation the week before, also proposed the *Collège unique*.'

'Ah well,' said Henri, 'you know as well as I do that he didn't mean it. But Catroux, that was different. He was quite willing to throw us to the wolves. He and his friends Mauriac and Mendès-France. *That* one had better not set foot in Algeria. My God, if *he'd* come to Algiers on that 6th of February, that would have been the end of him. We didn't even have to do anything about him ourselves. We only had to hand him over to the Jews of Algiers; they were saying: 'he belongs to us. We'll deal with him!'

'I daresay the Jews are even more scared than the Europeans at the thought of being "abandoned" to the Moslems. All the same, it all sounds rather absurd to me,' I said.

'Oh, don't you kid yourself about Mendès-France! We know why he sold out Tunisia. It was he who started all the rot in North Africa. He's in the pay of the Egyptian Government, don't you know?' I said I didn't know. And Henri burst into a harangue about Monoprix and Uniprix and Cairo department stores . . .

'Yes,' said Henri, 'everything was in a complete mess last February. Lacoste just arrived in time, and brought troops here, and order was restored.'

'But you have been saying that order had *not* been restored, and that things were going from bad to worse.'

'That's the tragedy of it,' said Henri. 'Lacoste was absolutely indispensable in February, but now I just don't know where his pacification policy is getting him.'

Henri had some wild stories to tell with some pretty wild figures. He thought 50,000 Algerians were in jails and camps, and that 'probably' half a million or so had been killed off since the beginning of the Rebellion in November 1954 . . . 'Some pretty grim stuff has gone on round Nemours and various other places—fierce *ratissage* stuff— women and children and all . . . But it's really not much good. The *ratons* are tough, and they've got money. Why should any of these loafers get himself a job if he can become a fellagha? They give him a rifle and 30,000 francs down—and *there's* another terrorist. There's no end to it . . .'

We dined that night in an open-air restaurant high up on the hill, at the far end of the Boulevard Télemly. The restaurant was crowded with young soldiers, who seemed to be happy and interested to be here . . . Below us was the city of Algiers with its thousands of lights, and the harbour with its ships, and beyond it, in the distance, a dim coastline. 'That's Cap Matifou over there,' said Henri. 'That's already where the danger zone starts. It's no longer safe to go there by car. That's where Kabylia begins . . .' And he started on another series of stories of fellagha hold-ups and murders and massacres . . .

Curious chap Henri, I thought to myself. As typical a French-Algerian as you could make them. Henri was nearly sixty, an airman of the first and second world war, and as hard as nails. And yet hard as he was, I could feel as he spoke, that here was something of a split personality. He was full of the old colonialist prejudices; and yet, and yet—he knew that the colonial problem no longer presented itself as it did before; that 'under-developed territories' were something different from colonies, even though the places were the same; that *something* had gone seriously wrong; that it was hard for France alone to cope with 'her' North-African territories with their surplus population; or that if she did, it would have to be on the basis of a free association between France and a more or less sovereign 'North-African Federation' . . . The development of the Sahara, for instance, could not be undertaken over the head of an Algeria at war. Above all, perhaps, a man like Henri had seen the light; he had realized that the '6th of February' policy was only a temporary solution . . .

And here a curious question arose in my mind: had not Mollet and Lacoste—perhaps without knowing it—done the one thing which it was psychologically and tactically possible to do in February?—which was to give way to the clamour of the French Algerians. By adopting *their* policy, instead of a liberal policy (which, at that time, was called treason) were they not going to prove to them in the most tangible manner the impossibility of the die-hard policy at the present stage of North-African development? In other words, only after a long try-out of the Lacoste policy, and after the demonstration of its failure, could the French-Algerians convince themselves that there was no practical alternative to a liberal policy?

I am very far from crediting Mollet and Lacoste with such foresight. Lacoste, at any rate, seemed genuinely convinced that his policy of Pacification could work the trick. A large part of France was carried away in this belief in the spring of 1956.

However, in August, while I was in Algiers, it was beginning to dawn on people—including the officials at the *Gouvernement-Général*—that Pacification had failed. There was still a crazy hope, however, that war against Egypt might make this Pacification a success!

Meantime, the political vacuum on the Algerian side seemed complete. The French had no Algerian partners on any level; these were either in prison or in the maquis. Even the Algerian Assembly had not been replaced by anything since the revolt of the Second College members and the Assembly's subsequent dissolution. As an official at the *Gouvernement Général* remarked, with a display of liberalism (and it was curious how his anti-*gros colon* line coincided with that of my friend Henri):

That Algerian Assembly wasn't any good anyway. You've heard a lot about the faking of the election returns for the Second

W

College; but, believe me, not only the Second College, but the First College, too, was wholly unrepresentative! The First (European) College was composed almost entirely of nominees of the *gros colons*, and your French *fonctionnaire*, and small businessmen, or *petit colon*, or bus-driver or trade unionist wasn't represented by anybody.

It was the same on other levels. Nothing had been done to demo-cratize the régime of the *communes mixtes;* the diehard Federation of Mayors was still going strong; Lacoste vaguely hoped that there might be, before long, municipal elections in some parts of Algeria, but all this was still in the dim future . . .

Opposition press—none. Or nothing to speak of. And also, no trade unionism to speak of. In the same street as my hotel were the offices of *Alger Républicain*, an opposition (near-Communist) paper; the windows had been smashed some time before, even though the paper had been out of action for a long time; but the shattered windows were left as they were, like a trophy of the 6th of February Spirit . . .

Only at Oran were a few Liberals still timidly speaking up. One small—almost clandestine—fortnightly, advocated cease-fire talks, and claimed that there were reasonable Algerians among the FLN; while *Oran Républicain*, a liberal paper which had been silent and non-committal for a long time, came out, in the middle of August with an article, which caused something of a sensation: by following in the footsteps of the die-hards, it said in effect, Lacoste had driven reason-able men like Ferhat Abbas into the arms of the extremists.

Also, at Algiers, I picked up on a bookstall a copy of a small weekly called *L'Espoir*, with an editorial by Brahim Bouakkoz, pleading in favour of a cease-fire, which could not, however, be achieved without the Rebels being given some preliminary assurances. The café waiter, seeing me reading it, said: '*Tiens!* I thought it was prohibited!'

The trade union situation in Algeria was peculiar. As distinct from Tunisia and Morocco, with their powerful 'native' trade union federations, the French authorities in Algeria would not allow the Moslems to have trade unions of their own. There was a branch section of the *Force Ouvrière* in Algeria, and another of the CFTC, the French Catholic trade unions; but the membership of both was small and almost exclusively European. The membership of the *Force Ouvrière* was so small that one of its officials, after fumbling and mumbling, told me 'he couldn't remember the figures', adding, however, that it included '400 Moslem miners'. The Communist-dominated CGT had gone underground, or rather, had lost its

membership to the new Algerian trade union federation, the UGTA
(*Union Générale des Travailleurs Algériens*). The story of this one is one
of the strangest and most sinister stories in the whole of French North
Africa, as shall be seen presently.

I could not help being startled by the curious mentality of
M. M——, an official of the *Force Ouvrière* at Algiers. He claimed to
be a Lacoste man, but was, in fact, much more representative of the
crusty colonialism of the *petits blancs* at their worst. He was convinced
that Pan-Arabism was a 'terrible force' which France would have to
fight for years. Arabs—the whole damned lot of them—were rotten.
Bourguiba, for whom the French liberals seemed to have a soft spot,
was as bad as any of them: *'un fou, un illuminé'*. Tunisia was hard-up,
and Bourguiba was sure to try to sell Bizerta as a base either to the
Americans or the Russians. The real trouble in North Africa, he said,
had been started at the Anfa Conference, when Roosevelt had
promised the Sultan of Morocco the moon. And then there were de
Gaulle's 'disastrous' speeches at Brazzaville and Constantine, which
gave the Algerians the idea that they could do as they pleased. Hence
the famous rebellion in the Constantinois in May 1945—it was that
which started the rot in a big way.

'France doesn't understand Algeria,' said M. M——. 'Three-
quarters of the people in France have been poisoned by Communist
propaganda. They don't know what they want. But the idea that
Algeria is entitled to some sort of self-determination has made great
headway, though people in France have no idea what Algeria is like ...
Personally, I believe in a *communauté franco-musulmane;* but the
French of Algeria are funny people; they do not *really* feel at home
here. Just you look at the hundreds of small ads. in the *Echo d'Alger*,
tempting the Algerian French to sell their properties here, to give up
their jobs, and to buy themselves a "profitable garage at Narbonne"
or some other quiet little funk-hole in the Lot-et-Garonne or the
Gers ...'

'Yes, I know,' I said. 'At the military press conference at the
Gouvernement-Général the other day, the Colonel was very indignant
about these small ads.; he said they were demoralizing the people of
Algeria, and he thought the Algiers papers should refuse to publish
them ...'

'I am glad to hear it,' said M. M——. 'But the mentality of the
French in Algeria is not good. If these people considered that they
belonged to this place, why should they go on receiving their colonial
bonuses—that *tiers colonial*, the one-third over and above their official
salaries?

'They do not invest their money in Algeria; they do not even *spend* it in Algeria; at the least excuse they dash off to France for their holidays. We haven't, mind you, any watering-places or health resorts in Algeria to speak of; they all rush off every summer to Vittel and Vichy to treat their livers, or even to Juan les Pins or Biarritz—as if we hadn't a perfectly good sea right in front of our noses. Yes, I believe in the *communauté franco-musulmane*; but what can you do? The Europeans—or most of them—don't give a hang what the Moslems think of them; they don't realize how it shocks Moslems to see French women walking about the streets of Algiers in shorts and bikinis!

'So the Europeans are really a lot to blame. There is no proper understanding between Europeans and Moslems. But then the Moslems live a life of their own, with their *lois coraniques*, their hostility to assimilation in any sense. Very unlike the Algerian Jews in that respect. And yet the Arabs now somehow imagine that they are grown up. They are *not*.'

Clearly the man was blaming the Moslems for not being more cordial to the Europeans, as if in Algeria, of all places, they had received much encouragement! All the same, like an official at the *Gouvernement-Général*, the *Force Ouvrière* man took a somewhat paternalist attitude, saying that the Algerians were wrong to be so distrustful; the French of Algiers knew they had to live with them, and they did not hate them. In Morocco, on a number of occasions, European civilians ran wild, and started lynching Moroccans; this sort of thing did not happen in Algiers . . . It wasn't much to boast of, but wasn't it significant of Algeria all the same?

'Maybe,' I said. 'But the fact that Europeans don't make a habit of lynching Arabs in Algiers still seems to me a rather flimsy basis for a *communauté franco-musulmane*'.

'All the same,' he said, 'I believe in it. What I do not believe in is the recognition of the *fait national algérien*. *Personnalité algérienne*, as Mollet called it in his ministerial declaration—well yes, at a pinch (since we don't know what it really means); but a *fait national algérien* —which is what the fellaghas want—no, no, no!'

And here M. M—— came to a matter that had been worrying him greatly: indignantly, he told me how the CGT had practically gone out of existence, but had been replaced by an autonomous and native trade union federation, the UGTA (*Union Générale des Travailleurs Algériens*), the Algerian counterpart of the Tunisian Trade Union Federation, the UGTT, and the Moroccan Federation, the UMT, the *Union Marocaine des Travailleurs*. Most monstrous of all, this UGTA had been admitted quite recently into the ICFTU (International Confederation of Free Trade Unions). This recognition by the

ICFTU of the UGTA amounted to a recognition of the *fait national algérien;* it was shocking to find both the British and American representatives of the ICFTU voting for its admittance. It was most indelicate both *vis-à-vis* France and *vis-à-vis Force Ouvrière*, which was itself a member of the ICFTU. It was really monstrous—a clear case of Moscow-Washington collusion.

'Oh, how's that possible?'

'Quite possible, don't you make any mistake about it! Most of the Communist CGT members—all the Moslems, anyway, joined the UGTA; while the ICFTU is, as you know, dominated by the American Federation of Labour, which, with its Mr. Irving Brown, has never ceased to play dirty tricks on France, in the name of its"anti-colonialism". They've encouraged the UGTT in Tunisia, and the Moroccan trade unions, much to the delight of the Communists!'

And M. M—— hinted at the same collusion of Moscow and Washington which could be observed in Egypt.

'There's only one way: France and Britain *must* stop the rot in Egypt. Nasser must be liquidated. If he isn't, all the Arab extremists will come to the top. The fellaghas in Algeria will think themselves the rulers of the country; and in Morocco Allal El Fassi will seize power; it'll be the end of everything . . .'

M. M—— praised the wisdom and patriotism of Lacoste, 'a great Socialist and Trade Unionist who has understood what ought to be done about the Arabs'. 'Of course,' he added, 'he is willing to open doors to Arab officials; but he knows it musn't be done too quickly. They are *not* mature. There are 200,000 French officials in Algeria, and I assure you, they know their job . . . Also, Lacoste has a healthy distrust for Communists, Egyptians and Americans.'

And again came a reference to the Colomb Béchar speech: 'He was quite right to say that there were two brands of Arab nationalism— there were those following in the footsteps of Cairo—that is, Nasser; and those representing a sort of "Western Islamism", as he put it, willing to surrender bases and the wealth of their countries to the United States. He said "certain great powers"—but we know whom he meant! And of course, Lacoste was a thousand times right not to have allowed Irving Brown of the AF of L and of the ICFTU to set foot in Algeria, when, he meant to pay an official visit to the new Algerian Trade Union Federation!'

'What's happened to it?' I said.

'Oh, I don't know,' said M. M—— evasively. 'We wanted one or two of their people to come and discuss something with us the other day; we just couldn't locate them. They seem to have gone underground, just like the remnants of the Communist CGT.'

Clearly, the UGTA had been driven underground; and I was determined to find out what had happened to it. I found their headquarters in the Place de Chartres locked; but managed to meet one of the officials of the Algerian trade union federation. And this was what this Arab told me: The Algerian UGTA, following the pattern of the Tunisian UGTT and the Moroccan UMT, had been formed last February. Almost from the start, it had 100,000 members; but Lacoste had refused to recognize it, he considered it a branch office of the fellaghas.

'In fact, we are not a political body, and are only concerned with trade union matters,' my Arab friend said, 'but I need hardly tell you that we are completely in sympathy with the Liberation movement of the Algerian people.'

The entire leadership of the UGTA was arrested on May 24. However, another team took over. This team was holding a meeting on July 3, when a bomb exploded in the premises of the UGTA, and 17 of the leaders were wounded; one of them so badly that he had to have both legs amputated. The police merely had to walk in and pick up the wounded. Nevertheless, the general strike the UGTA had called for July 5—i.e., two days later—was strictly observed throughout Algiers. (July 5 was the anniversary of the French occupation of Algiers in 1830.) It showed that among the working-class of Algiers, the orders of the UGTA were strictly followed. Despite this act of terrorism—this 'second decapitation' of the UGTA, a third team took over; but now, of course, its work had become pretty well impossible: it could only continue a clandestine existence. But my Arab trade union official (an intelligent little man, who spoke perfect French) thought the UGTA was destined to play 'as great and honourable a part in the Liberation of Algeria as the UGTT and the UMT had played in the liberation of Tunisia and Morocco'.

It was obvious to me that, to the diehards, 'native' trade unionism was an enemy to be fought by every means. My Arab's story reminded me of how, in the days of M. de Hauteclocque in Tunisia, Ferhat Hashed was considered the most dangerous man in Tunisia, next to Bourguiba, and of how, in December 1952, the French gunmen of the Red Hand, murdered him. In Morocco, too, the French He-men struck in December 1952 at the trade unions, a blow to be followed by other blows—one at the Nationalist Istiqlal, and another at the Sultan himself. Both in Tunisia and Morocco the trade union organizations were invaluable auxiliaries to the nationalist parties, and sources of political and social consciousness and enlightenment among the most down-trodden parts of the population. As in Tunisia and Morocco, so in Algeria, an organization like the UGTA was bound to arouse the greatest disquiet among the French ... The UGTA was driven underground in July 1956, just as the UGTT was practically disbanded in Tunisia in December 1952, after the murder of Ferhat Hashed, while in Morocco, after the lynchings of December 1952, trade unionism was altogether stamped out for a while ... They were allies of the Neo-Destour and the Istiqlal, just as the UGTA was, in a sense, an ally of the Algerian fellaghas ...

The UGTA man spoke as follows, as we sat there, at the far end of a small café near the Kasbah:

'In France today they've managed to focus all attention on Suez. It's merely a trick to gain time—and get nothing done in Algeria. And even if they do produce a new *statut* before the meeting of the UN Assembly—a *statut* not to be negotiated but granted—it will only be another piece of delaying tactics.

'True, the Socialist Motion of Lille was a step in the right direction, and I know that many Socialists in France believe that we—the UGTA—could act as a link between the French and men like Ferhat Abbas. But Lacoste will not hear of it. He is in the hands of the *ultras*. We have men in Algeria—like myself—who've been brought up in French schools; but the number of Algerians appointed to responsible posts has been negligible. Out of 800 *administrateurs civils*, only 12 are Algerians.

'Now such little concessions no longer arise. The whole of Algeria today is a *maquis;* practically the entire Algerian population now stands solidly for the liberation of Algeria. They can think up all the *chocs psychologiques* they want; it's too late. What we want now is a satisfaction of our national aspirations: in the first place the recognition of the Algerian Nation.

'They've been talking about "*personnalité algérienne*" since 1865. What's it all mean? It's all mixed up with the old notion of the *statut personnel*, complete with Moslem divorce laws and the acceptance of the *caid*, as though he were a real *juge de paix*. In Tunisia, Bourguiba has had the sense to realize that all this religious jurisdiction over family life must end. Or else, what can one make of all this quibbling over the *fait national algérien?* There is one thing, and one thing only that must be recognized: Algerian nationality. Oh, I know all the objections—the French will be outnumbered, and all that. No; the interests of the French will be respected; we need teachers and technicians. Of course, the French authorities like talking about "French interests" as though every Frenchman in Algeria had the same interests—the worker, the *petit fonctionnaire* and the *colon* with 20,000 hectares!'

He again talked about the UGTA, his clandestine Trade Union Federation. After the *coup* of July 3, its paper, *L'Ouvrier Algérien* was prohibited, and throughout July, there were mass arrests. In the Algérois alone—in the camps of Aflou, St. Leu, Berroughia and M'sila there were 5,000 to 6,000 internees. There were many more in other areas—in the camps of Lambèse, Bossuet, etc. These people were trade unionists and other 'suspects'.

'There is no trade union life in Algeria at present, and the authorities prefer it that way. They know that the UGTA has by far the largest following among the workers. Each of our members belongs to one of our 83 unions. I'll give you an example of how the authorities want to suppress the fact that we have this large following. Recently the election of trade union delegates was organized in two places—in the tobacco factory at Blida, and among the tramway workers of Algiers. By 5.30 p.m. when 90 per cent of the votes cast was for the UGTA— i.e., just as the election returns were about to be announced, the police arrived and declared that "in view of the military situation", no such elections could be held! I am really not far wrong in saying that, fundamentally, the authorities consider the UGTA even more dangerous than the fellaghas. The colonialists were always scared of "native" trade unions: whether in Tunisia, Morocco or—now— Algeria . . .

'They know that our aims—social security, decent wages, etc.— are incompatible with the regime they are trying to perpetuate. As you know, the social legislation of France is not applied to Algeria. There are about two million unemployed in the country; in agriculture, the present "minimum wage" is 360 francs a day—but few work more than half the year—with luck. The French say these people are lazy; it's not true; there just isn't enough work for them. There are practically no family allowances, no social security, no accidents insurance . . . And when they do get work, they have to work damned hard for their 360 francs a day—12 or even 14 hours. It's not enough to keep themselves and their families alive. So masses of farm labourers ask the *colons* for advances; at the end of the year these have to be repaid—but how? simply by going on working for the same boss. This indebtedness is something chronic and terrifying. There are entire families who have worked for the same landowner for generations. Oh, not *colons* only; a few rich Arab proprietors, too. It's truly medieval . . .

'Since the UGTA was founded, we have set ourselves the task of drawing up detailed programmes for practically every branch of our national life. In the matter of civil and public servants (*la fonction publique*), we are in favour of complete racial equality—and the whole of it based on the particular candidate's qualifications. There must be no *numerus clausus* against Moslems or anybody else.

'As regards education, we are in favour of a bilingual system, with Arabic as the basic language, but French holding an important—and compulsory place. We have drawn up programmes for the widest possible extension of social security legislation—including its extension to the rural areas. We have drawn up proposals for the more rational development of Algeria's national wealth; for industrialization; for the replacement of thousands of hectares of vineyards by wheat and other useful crops. Under proper industrialization, 400,000 Algerians now in France could find employment in their own country. For in France, too, the Algerian is a slave; he has to feed and lodge himself; and pay his fare to and from Algeria, and send money to his family at home; and most of the Algerians in France live in appalling housing conditions, and the T.B. rate is higher than if they had stayed at home.'

And again—it seemed like an obsession with him—he started on the discrimination against Arabs: why, at the university of Algiers in 1954, he said, were there 4,500 European students and only 557 Moslem students? 'In fact, you claim,' I said, 'that the French practise a sort of *apartheid* policy, like the white South Africans towards their own natives?'

'Precisely,' he said; but then added, with superb pride and a touch of arrogance: 'Only it isn't the same thing really., The South African blacks are a *very backward* people. But the Arabs of Algeria have a thousand-year-old civilization behind them. It was *we* who built Granada!'

And he concluded with some general reflection about the French attempt to convince the world that this was a war against the Arab League. 'It's a pathetic piece of eyewash! They want to dodge their responsibilities in Algeria and perpetuate the colonialist system. Only they can't get away with it! Not even if they invade Egypt. If they do that, they will create a pan-Arab *mystique* which is really a myth for the present! "War against the Arab League"—it's just a slogan calculated to deceive the halfwits.'

'But what's happening to the various UGTA programmes you've been telling me about?' I said.

'Nothing. They refuse to discuss them with us. But they'll *have* to discuss them sooner or later . . . '

I tried to see M. Jacques Chevalier, the Mayor of Algiers, but he was not keen on seeing anybody. He had been a Minister in the Mendès-France Government of 1954-55, and ranked as a 'neo-colonialist' who had many Big Business contacts himself. As Mayor, he had certainly done a great deal to make Algiers beautiful, and, in the process, even a proportion of the inhabitants of the *bidonvilles* had been rehoused. Like Mendès-France and Mitterrand, he liked the idea of 'turning North Africa into another California'—if only there were enough funds. It was rumoured at Algiers that Chevalier was in disagreement with Lacoste, did not believe in the effectiveness of his 'token concessions' and 'reformlets', and believed that Pacification had already proved a wash-out. He was feeling it more and more as the 'zone of insecurity' was spreading into the very heart of Algiers. However, at that time it was emphatically denied at the *Gouvernement-Général* that M. Chevalier was in disagreement with M. Lacoste. All the same, M. Chevalier preferred not to discuss the matter with foreign visitors, and I was brushed off with something closely resembling the Soviet 'formula': 'He's gone out for five minutes; will you phone again next week?' Clearly M. Chevalier was not ready yet in August to make the statement he was to make a month later to *France-Soir*:

> I am sorry not to be able to share in the official optimism, but judging from what is happening in this city of 500,000 people, which I have to administer daily, the situation, far from improving, is growing worse every day. Why this determination to treat the Algerian problem as a war? This is a revolution, taking place in the midst of complete political confusion. This revolution must be treated politically. Yet all the innumerable statements—many of them contradictory, have not made it possible to advance half-an-inch in this field. A great variety of projects are put forward, but none is discussed. What is more, no Algerian of either College is being consulted about them. People behave as if the fate of 10 million people could be settled without them . . .

There was only one way of re-establishing confidence, M. Chevalier said, and that was to start talking to the Algerians themselves:

> We shall get nowhere by trying to *impose* our solutions. We must re-establish contacts with the very people with whom we are no longer on speaking terms. You don't get anywhere by having discussions with people with whom you are in agreement. The immediate problem for Algeria is a question of procedure: we've got to decide first and foremost how we are to start the discussions, and not decide in advance what is going to be discussed. It's only in the course of the discussions that we shall see where we stand.[1]

[1] *France-Soir*, September 7, 1956.

Needless to say, there was immediately afterwards an angry editorial in *l'Echo d'Alger* by its editor, that spokesman of the diehards, M. Alain de Sérigny, saying it was monstrous that M. Chevalier should want to start talks with Ferhat Abbas and Ben Bella—a lot of Nasser stooges. And he hinted at a Chevalier-Mendès–France plot.

In reality M. Chevalier said in September what had been at the back of the minds of an ever-growing number of Europeans in Algiers during the previous weeks . . .

'This is a Revolution, not a War,' Chevalier said on September 6. At the back of his mind, every soldier in Algeria had known it for months. Pacification meant that the Algerians—or at least a substantial proportion of them—were willing to submit to French rule, and try to make the best of it. Every French soldier knew that, inwardly, at any rate, every Algerian was hostile.

But it would be rash to generalize about the state of mind of the French troops in Algeria. There were, for one thing, hard professional troops, like the *paras*—the paratroopers—and the Foreign Legion, to whom this war was like any other war. They were not squeamish. Shootings and massacres and *ratissages* did not make their stomachs turn. They—or many of them—had seen and done the same kind of thing in Vietnam. I met some paratroopers at Algiers and at Bône who, with the wild look in their eyes, gave me the feeling that here were desperadoes. One, to whom I talked, made no secret of it; but he also claimed that this kind of warfare was the only possible one; that the *paras* were the real backbone of the war in Algeria, and that they alone were fully conscious of their duty to France. Of the *rappelés*, the reservists, he spoke with condescension, if not contempt . . .

The attitude of the *rappelés* varied greatly—and usually varied according to where they happened to be. They did not much care for patrolling up and down the rue Michelet to see to it that no harm came to the Europeans having their *apéritif*, and were not enchanted by the attitude towards them of the greater part of the Algerian French, who took the 'protection' France was giving them as rather too much for granted. For one thing, the Algerian French, many soldiers thought, were not really doing as much as they might be doing to protect their 'own' country. It is true that most of them were doing what might be called 'home guard' duty—that is, patrolling at night, and so, relieving the army and police patrols. (In Algiers alone, there were some 400 patrols, representing about 2,000 men.) But there was no *levée en masse* of the Algerian French; and the explanation given me for this strange phenomenon at the *Gouvernement-Général* was something like this:

1. Since the official view is still that Algeria is as much a province of France as Normandy or the Limousin, it is no use applying—or even encouraging—much greater enrolment than elsewhere;

2. It's no use expecting too many able-bodied Europeans in Algeria to go into the army; it is very important that the economic life of Algeria should run as smoothly as possible;

3. No Government of the Republic would care to have any specifically French-Algerian army units; it doesn't trust them; it thinks there are too many Fascists among them . . .

Apart from a certain lack of sympathy between the *rappelés* and many of the Algerian French, many of the soldiers still felt that this was 'part of France', and that Lacoste had managed to 'save' Algeria 'just in time'. But such thoughts were more prevalent in the early months of the Lacoste rule than later. So long as they were in relatively quiet places like Algiers, many of the young metropolitan soldiers didn't much mind being here. When not on duty, they crowded the cafés and restaurants as they would have done anywhere else.

It was different in the *bled*. At the *Gouvernement-Général* an official spoke with great satisfaction of the 'magnificent morale' of some of the *rappelés*. 'They can be much tougher than our regular African troops. At Palestro, where there was a horrible massacre of several French soldiers, the other *rappelés* ran wild, and did a counter-massacre which the Foreign Legion might have envied them! They are not used to this kind of war, and when any of them gets killed, they see red.'

A well-known phenomenon was also this: it often happened for a young *rappelé* to be armed with a tommy-gun; having paraded 'French might' throughout the Arab countryside, the day came when he could no longer resist the temptation of using his tommy-gun—sometimes on some wholly unsuitable occasion.

My more general impression, however, was that most of the *rappelés* were 'browned-off'. Those who were helping the *colons* to bring in their harvest, were not, as a rule, impressed by the *colons;* but there were also those who were solely employed to 'impress' the Arab population by marching in great strength through the countryside, ostensibly in search of fellaghas. To many, these long and exhausting marches at the height of the African summer seemed wholly pointless. They were convinced of the hostility of the Algerian population. And when it came to *ratissages*, and the rounding up of villages, and the interrogation of suspects, at least some of the *rappelés* thought it nauseating. What kind of cause was France supposed to be defending?

Many of the French *rappelés*—perhaps the great majority of them —were deadly bored. I remember, for instance, talking to a young sub-lieutenant who was stationed with a dozen men on the border of Algeria and Tunisia. They were miles from anywhere, practically in the desert. They were supposed to look out for fellaghas smuggling arms from Tunisia and Libya into Algeria. 'For weeks,' he said, 'it's been 120° in the shade (that is, if there *were* any shade) . . . There's almost no water in the God-forsaken place. We have seen no fellaghas, but I and my men have to wage a war, day and night, against scorpions. The place is teeming with black and brown scorpions. The black ones are the most dangerous. Two of my men were stung, and had to be taken to hospital.' He was a young man of about 26, who had done his *licence*, and was preparing his *doctorat* in Paris, when he was called up; he didn't like it at all.

'And don't you imagine that, in these conditions, morale among the troops is good. It is not. And, above all, they keep asking me: "I wish you would tell us what we are here for?" Honestly, I don't know what to say to them . . . '

But one thing was certain to me: *few of the French soldiers serving in Algeria had come to like the Algerians*. And, in spite of much grumbling, there was still a fundamental feeling of solidarity towards the "Algerian French" on the part of the soldiers who had come from France. And to most the "defence of Algeria" was a necessary duty.

In itself, the war was not a major war. In July and August, the French Army's losses were about 150 or 200 a month. But insecurity and terrorism were spreading all over the place. One night I was at Algiers, a bomb went off in the rue Auber, only a couple of hundred yards from the *Gouvernement-Général*. Shortly before that, a 'Moslem fanatic' had shot several European pedestrians, for no apparent reason, at Bab el Oued, on the northern outskirts of Algiers. Terrorists were killing off a few policemen or soldiers in the centre of Algiers from time to time. Then one night—only a few minutes before curfew— Algiers was shaken by a terrific explosion, which wrecked five houses in the Kasbah. The official story was that a bomb, belonging to a secret arms dump, had blown up by mistake, and that 15 people had been killed. The streets leading to the scene of the explosion were roped off the next morning, and no independent enquiry was possible. But an Arab I met that day told me, with tears in his eyes, that 190 or 200 people had been killed in the blowing-up of the five overcrowded houses, and the arms and legs of small children could be seen protruding from the wreckage. He was certain (and this seemed highly probable) that it was a deliberate piece of counter-terrorism . . . a warning against any bomb-throwing at Europeans.

But the bomb throwing and the shooting continued, and went from bad to worse. It *was* a revolution, rather than a war.

Before leaving for Algiers, I had somehow imagined that, at some stage, I could become a 'war correspondent'. This was a complete fallacy, and added point to Chevalier's remark that this was not a war, but a revolution. One evening, at the *Gouvernement-Général*, I had a talk with the Colonel who, night after night, read out the 'war *communiqués*'. These were nothing but an enumeration of 'incidents'— This, for instance, was the substance of the *communiqué* (called *'bulletin de presse'*) of August 2 :

> *Algérois:* A military convoy was ambushed yesterday at 6 km south of Tizi Ouzou. Three French soldiers were wounded.
> Near Haussonvillers several outlaws were killed; numerous suspects were rounded-up; two shotguns, two revolvers, ammunition, and a quantity of clothing were captured. Some losses among our troops.
> Near Maréchal Foch one outlaw was killed and his shotgun captured.
> Several suspects were captured North-West of Lodi.
> In numerous local operations in Kabylia some losses were inflicted on the Rebels, and 16 shotguns were captured.

There were further sections on the *Constantinois* and the *Oranais*— much on the same lines.

There was no 'front' to speak of. There were ambushes and skirmishes here and there. A number of regions were pratically rebel-controlled; to these, punitive expeditions were occasionally sent. Correspondents were, obviously, not encouraged to accompany the punitive expeditions (*'chez nous,'* said the Colonel, *'on ne fait pas de Tours Cook'*); but otherwise, there was nothing to report in the way of regular warfare. Where the rebel forces (estimated at only 20,000) took the initiative, you could never get there in time; and if the French took the initiative, correspondents in Algiers weren't usually warned about it in advance. I was told I could have a *carte rouge* for 'travelling in the zone of operations'; but (with his tongue in his cheek, I rather suspect) the Colonel said: 'You can always take a plane to Batna; there you can take a taxi. If you're lucky (and provided the taxi takes you anywhere outside Batna), you'll be turned back by a French patrol; if you're not so lucky you'll be ambushed, captured and perhaps massacred by the fellaghas . . . *Enfin, débrouillez-vous.'*

The local French correspondents were 'browned off'. For a day or two they pretended to me that they were doing a lot of war *reportage;*

but, over a drink, one of them confided: '*C'est plutôt du bluff.* Very occasionally we get outside Algiers. Then if the local commanding general is in a good mood, he might take you on a 20 minutes' run in a helicopter; but I've never seen anything much that way . . . Then you are taken back to the command-post, where, with the help of a map, they explain some local operation to you—but usually, in terms of the war in general, it doesn't mean a damned thing . . .'

Sometimes, he said, correspondents were taken along to witness the 'submission' of some particular region to the local French commander. Most striking of all, in all such 'ceremonies', was the total lack of sincerity and conviction on both sides. . . .

I did not stay at Algiers to wait for my *carte rouge*. What was the good, anyway? As a *Monde* correspondent wrote sometime later: 'Some Arab atrocities; some French atrocities—same thing, over and over again. That's not the real problem of Algeria.'

One day, with 112 in the shade, and a high sirocco blowing from the Sahara furnace, I took the Tunis-Air plane to Bône, and thence to Tunis. Bône was not very different from Algiers, except that the tension was even greater. A few days before, 20 Europeans had been murdered by Arab gunmen in broad daylight . . .

Flying over the brown mountains of Kabylia, with its numerous, miserable-looking mountain villages, I remembered that it was from here chiefly that the hungry *bicots* migrated by the thousand to the industrial belt of Paris. No wonder! Perhaps to avoid any possible anti-aircraft fire (it was rumoured that the fellaghas had now a few ack-ack guns, too), the plane flew a large part of the way over the bright-blue sea, with a rocky brown coast to the right. Only shortly before reaching Bône, did it fly inland again. It was the same brown, desolate-looking country of Kabylia. In one or two places there were large forest fires, forming large clouds of black smoke. Had the fellaghas set fire to them, as only a few days before they had set fire to 1,000 acres of forest outside Algiers?

Suddenly the scenery changed: it was green again, and the roads were regular, and in the small towns and villages there were churches. 'The Europeans have the best land . . .'

On the following day, from Bône we crossed the Tunisian border near Tabarka (it was here that Bourguiba was first interned, back in 1952); and after flying over more mountains, looking like the mountains of Kabylia, we landed at El Alouina airport. French passport and customs officials, as usual, and the usual stink from the Lake of Tunis, the lake into which all the sewers run, but alongside which passes the great motor road to Carthage and Sidi Bou Said, and

Gamarth and La Marsa, the playground of the Diplomats and the Rich . . . I remembered 1952, and M. de Boisesson, and the dinner party at his villa at La Marsa, attended by pompous puppet ministers in dazzlingly white jackets—puppet ministers of the puppet government of M. Baccouche. M. de Boisesson was the second-in-command of M. Jean de Hauteclocque, the Resident-General; '*Jean le Terrible*', the Tunisians used to call him . . .

CHAPTER 2

A REASONABLE ARAB LAND:
BOURGUIBA'S TUNISIA

TUNIS had greatly changed since I was here last in June and July 1952. Tunisia was independent! Back in 1952, M. Baccouche, the 'Tunisian King of Coca Cola' and an amiable cynic, was the puppet Prime Minister; the centre of all political and military power was the Residence; French troops—though fewer than in Algiers just now—were patrolling the streets; the Bey was being tolerated—and no more—by the French; M. Chenik, and other Ministers who had had the insolence to ask for a few minor concessions only a few months before, and had then been dismissed and exiled to the Far South, had only recently been allowed to return to Tunis, and were lying low. Bourguiba, after his arrest in January, 1952, had since been transferred to the Island of La Galite, and M. de Hauteclocque was confidently declaring that the Tunisian people had forgotten him. The Neo-Destour had, more or less, been driven underground, and some 5,000 people were in jails and camps, though a few of the leaders were still about—for instance, Dr. Moqqadem, now Tunisian Ambassador in Cairo. The worst thorn in the side of the French authorities was Ferhat Hashed, the Secretary-General of the UGTT (*Union Générale des Travailleurs Tunisiens*), the trade union federation which, like the UGTA today, was being encouraged by the ICFTU. Ferhat Hashed was said to be in constant contact with the American Consul-General.

A few months later—in December, 1952—Ferhat Hashed was murdered by the gunmen of the Red Hand; and although there was a lull during part of 1953 (the storm centre had shifted to Morocco), terrorism and counter-terrorism flared up again, and reached its height in the summer of 1954. It was then that Mendès-France came on his famous flying visit to Tunisia to grant her 'internal autonomy'. But in Morocco events took a new turn with the Sultan's return in November, 1955, and since, soon afterwards, Morocco proclaimed her independence, it was natural for Tunisia to do the same, and no longer to be content with Internal Autonomy and with the Franco-Tunisian Conventions negotiated and ratified in 1955.

And now a 'semi-stooge' and great landed proprietor like Tahar Ben Ammar, who became Premier in the days of 'internal autonomy',

x   349

after the Mendès visit, had been replaced at the head of the Government by Bourguiba—Bourguiba, the fire-eater, the arch-enemy of the French Right, the bogey-man of the Martinaud-Déplats and the Quilicis . . . In the days of Internal Autonomy, Bourguiba suddenly became a moderate in the eyes of the French; the bogey-man was now Salah Ben Yussef; and not until Tunisian independence was proclaimed did the Yussefist tide recede, while Ben Yussef himself became the man of Cairo. He was in Cairo now, criticizing Bourguiba and calling him a French agent and a traitor.

How things had changed in four years! More than Morocco (as I was to observe soon afterwards), Tunisia was concentrating on 'external signs' to show that things had changed. Everything had become bilingual—street signs, shop signs, and the number-plates on cars. Motorists were given up to the First of September to change their French plates to plates with both French and Arab figures; most drivers had already changed them, because it was not thought safe to have merely a French plate; tyres were apt to be punctured . . . True, the avenue de France (with the same written above it in Arabic) was still the avenue de France; and there was still a rue Charles de Gaulle; but the avenue Jules Ferry had become the avenue Habib Bourguiba, and, at the far end of the avenue de France, outside the British Consulate-General (now Embassy) the statue of Cardinal de Lavigerie had disappeared—moved to some back garden at Carthage. The place de la Résidence—the centre of Tunis—was now called the place de l'Indépendance, with a specially rich display of Tunisian flags—red crescent on white background—in the middle of the square between the Catholic Cathedral and what was now merely the French Embassy. Tunisians were grumbling because there were still French sentries outside the French Embassy—this wasn't 'regular'.

Now Ferhat Hashed was the National Martyr of Tunisia; his mausoleum had been erected just outside the Kasbah, and the long avenue leading up to the Kasbah, the Seat of the Government, was now named after him . . . And there were postage stamps with pictures of Ferhat Hashed—the very Ferhat Hashed whom, four years before, I had seen in the humble tumble-down building in the Medina, with its creaking wooden stair, when he told me about the *ratissages* of the Cap Bon a few months before, and the police tortures, and had shown me a letter of threats he had received from the 'Red Hand' . . .

The central police station, where the tortures and the *passages à tabac* had taken place, had now been transformed into the headquarters of the UGTT, and a big bank building in the centre of Tunis had been taken over by the Neo-Destour party headquarters . . . And even the words 'Théâtre Municipal de Tunis', on the façade of the theatre had been replaced by an Arab inscription. *Afrique Française* had a melancholy article about it, saying how sad it was to think that 50 years of *rayonnement français* were now at an end. The Tunisians weren't very appreciative . . .

All this was perhaps a little childish; but, paradoxically enough, despite these little demonstrations of defiance, the whole attitude in Tunisia towards the French was less bitter than in Morocco. Since March, 1956, Tunisia had been independent—this was a fact which took the wind out of the sails of Salah Ben Yussef's propaganda. But in the autumn of 1955, in the days of Internal Autonomy, the conflict had been sharp between Bourguibists and Yussefists, and the two factions had even begun to murder each other. Not that Tunisia's independence was complete by any means, despite her embryonic army and the few Ambassadors she had sent to a number of foreign capitals.

Just as last time, in 1952, I lived at the Hotel de France, an old and slightly grubby hotel in a narrow side-street a few yards away from the Medina. Although, in Tunis, there is what might be called a 'purely European' part, a great deal of Tunis is *mixte*. The neighbourhood of the Hotel de France was such a 'mixed' area, full of spicy and rancid oriental smells and guttural voices and thumping sounds. There was a Moslem café next door to the hotel, and, just round the corner, a 'snack bar' with nickel-tubed furniture and Italian waiters, but patronised by Moslems as well as Europeans. Not only now, but even in the days of M. de Hauteclocque, Europeans and 'natives' mixed in Tunis far more than they did in Algiers. Now there were lots of Tunisian customers even in what used to be almost purely European cafés in the old days . . . For one thing, the Tunisians never suffered from the same inferiority complex as the Algerians. Moreover, within a short time, a new class of Tunisian Government officials had sprung up—and many of them were reasonably well-paid.

Most of the customers of the Hotel de France were French soldiers on leave. 'It's they,' said the French *patronne*, 'who keep the place going. Otherwise there's not much in the way of tourism . . . People in France seem to be afraid to come here, though, heaven knows, things are a good deal more quiet than they were two years ago'. Business was bad, she complained. And there was awful unemployment in Tunisia. 'All the same,' she said, 'things might be much worse. We hear dreadful stories about Algeria every day. And my impression is,' she added, 'that Bourguiba is a very reasonable man, who doesn't want to break with France altogether, don't you think so?' I said I didn't know, but hoped to find out . . .

That first night—it was hot, but not quite as bad as in Algiers the day before—I was joined by my old Tunisian friend Ahmed, whom I had warned of my arrival. Ahmed is a very progressive Neo-Destour *militant*, aged about 33, and a junior official in a government office connected with the Ministry of Finance. Since our last meeting, he had got married to a lovely Tunisian girl, but one belonging to an extremely conservative Moslem family. They had a tiny little black-eyed daughter, now aged 2½, who babbled in Arabic, and they lived in a small modern house about five miles outside Tunis, together with the young wife's widowed mother—a very traditional Moslem, who had abandoned the veil only very recently. She wore Moslem robes and spoke no French. She was a handsome, though white-haired lady of about 50, gracious in her manner, but reserved, and a little bewildered, it seemed, by her son-in-law's modern ways. However, she liked being taken for drives in the second-hand 4-*chevaux* Renault which was Ahmed's proudest possession... A promising sign of the evolution of Tunisia was the fact that Ahmed's wife, despite her traditional back-ground, was working in a sort of 'maternity guidance' clinic in Tunis —one supported from private funds. For there were some wealthy Tunisians—notably M. Chenik, the former Premier—who were sup-porting such social institutions... Between them, Ahmed and his wife were earning about 60,000 francs a month, and were living frugally but decently.

From my numerous conversations with Ahmed—and many others —it was clear to me how powerful the national consciousness of Tunisia was; it had already been powerful enough in the days of M. de Hauteclocque; now it was combined with a strong social conscious-ness—with a keen desire to turn Tunisia into a 'model Arab State'—a shining example to the rest of the Arab World... No doubt, there were dangers and pitfalls. Was not a well-paid, self-contented Government class growing up too rapidly? Were there not rather too many educated Tunisians to whom Independence was providing opportunities which might go to their heads, and lay the foundations for a new kind of moneyed bourgeoisie and privileged bureaucracy? Rather too many young people had the ambition of becoming Cabinet Ministers, draw-ing salaries of 400,000 francs a month—or Ambassadors... It did not take long to discover that there were signs of friction between the Government personnel and the Trade Unions, with their particularly acute social consciousness...

That first night, Ahmed talked about these frictions; he also said that, in the days of Internal Autonomy, the conflict between Bourguiba and Salah Ben Yussef was very sharp, and that a large part of the

Neo-Destour intellectuals tended to become Yussefists. But now Ben Yussef no longer mattered; he had become a Cairo stooge; there was no great admiration in Tunisia for Nasser. He was spending practically the whole Egyptian budget on the Army, and social conditions in Egypt were as bad as ever . . . Tunisia was not impressed by the social and economic record of the Arab states. Tunisia intended to become a Modern State. and Bourguiba today was universally accepted in Tunisia. 'There's one thing I can tell you,' said Ahmed, with a threatening little note in his voice, 'if Bourguiba were assassinated today, there wouldn't be a European left alive in Tunis. Wouldn't matter who he was, nationally or politically. The whole lot would be murdered . . .'

Relations between France and Tunisia were rather complicated. On the one hand, Tunisia was making the most of her Independence; but on the other hand, economic conditions were difficult, and she was badly in need of French help. But, at the same time, she was protesting against this independence not being sufficiently respected by France. And the war in Algeria was a disturbing factor of the first magnitude. There were many thousands of Algerian refugees in Tunisia. The negotiation for a Treaty of Alliance and Friendship between France and Tunisia had come up against grave difficulties, and had broken down in July, but were being resumed in a somewhat piecemeal manner. At the same time, there were negotiations with other countries, notably with the United States, which had promised to send wheat in September, to relieve the famine in central and Southern Tunisia.

Things were difficult. Shopkeepers in Tunis were complaining that business was at a complete standstill. *C'est le marasme* . . . The export of European capital—'a milliard francs every month'—seemed like an obsession with them. '*Les Européens foutent le camp*', said an Italian shopkeeper. 'Even the Italians are packing up; there are 100,000 of them in Tunisia. But then, there's no work for them in either France or Italy. But here, there's no money, no capital, and no building is going on. They change the street-signs; but that's not enough to keep the place going . . .'

I called the next day at the new headquarters of the UGTT to see Ahmed Ben Salah, the Secretary-General, and successor of Ferhat Hashed. At the large headquarters of the UGTT—the former French Central Police Station of Tunis—in the rue de Constantine (now re-named rue Mohammed Ali)—there were dozens of offices, and in each was a portrait of Ferhat Hashed; in the yard, crowded with Tunisian workers, most of them wearing *chechias*, there was a statue of Ferhat Hashed. Ahmed Ben Salah was out of town, but I saw his assistant, Mahmoud Ben Ezzedine. With him, as with so many other Tunisians, Algeria was an obsession.

Nothing is going to get properly done in either Tunisia or Morocco (he said) so long as the war in Algeria goes on. It's a fire that is sure to spread. The gulf shouldn't be allowed to widen any further between the French and the Algerians. If the French persist in their obscurantist policy, they will play straight into the hands of the Americans, keenly interested in the North-African market . . .

It's extraordinary how blind the French are (he said). What is Lacoste? He's just the Hauteclocque of Algeria. It was Hauteclocque who said in 1952: 'Bourguiba is just a myth, a legend. The Tunisians have already forgotten him'.

He then talked about the UGTT. In 1952 it had 100,000 members; now it had 200,000; the Communist USTT had dissolved itself; there were small branches of the *Force Ouvrière* and of the CFTC in Tunis, but they only had 2,000 or 3,000 European members between them . . . There were quite a number of Europeans belonging to the UGTT.

'We have got past the purely nationalist stage of our activity,' Ben Ezzadine said, 'the stage when national liberation was our chief concern, and when we were a powerful auxiliary of the Neo-Destour Party . . . Today our people are learning to think in social terms.

'Have you ever had any strikes?' I asked.

'Yes, indeed. The trouble is that the Tunisian employers are learning new ideas and new habits very slowly; they are apt to ignore the minimum wage fixed by the Government. The agricultural employees of Tahar Ben Ammar—at the time he was Prime Minister!—went on strike. Tahar Ben Ammar, as you know, is the president of the Chamber of Agriculture; and there's a sharp conflict between the Chamber of Agriculture and the Government. The former is strongly opposed to any nationalizations and land reform, and the fixing of agricultural wages. We, on the other hand, hold that these big landowners needn't complain of the low output of agricultural labour, if they don't treat it properly . . . These employers won't pay the workers the legal wage of 350 francs a day (it's not much, is it?); and although we have agricultural inspectors, they are not numerous enough to enforce the payment of the legal wage. That's how strikes break out in the agricultural areas . . .

'We are in favour of building up professional cadres. We have set up a popular university with six-weeks' courses for forming economic and cultural cadres for about 100 students at a time. Once a year we have also a fortnight's course for about 60 people to discuss general trade union matters; we have had here comrades from Tripolitania and Morocco; the whole of it was done under the auspices of the ICFTU . . .

'We are in close contact with the Ministry of Education; and we advocate a kind of programme which would enable most young Tunisians to get some degree of education. Of course, it's a desperately hard task. The French boasted a lot about all they had done for Tunisian education. True enough, proportionately far more Tunisians than Algerians or Moroccans received a secondary or higher education, either here or in France; but the fact remains that 80 per cent of children of school age in Tunisia are not at school. We are determined that the Government introduces compulsory elementary education and free secondary education . . . I know the French are now complaining about our wanting to introduce Arabic as a compulsory subject in all schools; but then isn't Arabic the language of our country! They talk about "discrimination" against the European minority; this, surely, is unreasonable . . . But of course, it's a terribly hard uphill fight. There aren't enough school buildings, thousands of teachers remain to be trained; and above all, there's no money. It's the lack of money that's the most heart-breaking thing in Tunisia. And I must say that we, at the UGTT, are not entirely in agreement with the latest economy cuts—chiefly in officials' salaries—decreed by the Government. What's needed is a major fiscal reform; there are far too many businessmen—both Tunisian and European and, above all, the Jews—who don't pay anything like the taxes they ought to pay . . .

'There's a lot to be done in other fields. The UGTT is trying to deal with the Nomad problem in the south. We are trying to create agricultural villages there, with a co-operative system . . . There are two million hectares of fallow land that could be recuperated. Of the 400,000 unemployed in Tunisia, many have patches of land, but it's of very small value. All this land was badly neglected under the *ancien régime* . . . We are always told about the dams and the irrigation in various places. "*Voyez ce que la France a construit* . . ." But who benefited from these dams? Not the poor people of Tunisia! To make all these places habitable, we need money. Will France lend it to us? Or why not other countries? Why not UN? Last year, UN set up a special fund for the development of Libya. Why not one for Tunisia? Frankly, we prefer not to be too dependent on the French. We'd rather have an international loan . . .'

'And what do you think of Egypt?' I ventured to ask.

'Oh,' he said, 'of course we have a sentimental attachment to Egypt. But after all, here in Tunisia, our whole upbringing has been Western. At the UGTT we have' (and here he said what I had already heard from Ahmed) 'no respect at all for the economic system of the other Arab countries. These have not made the most of their independence . . . They have perpetuated a sort of feudal system. Here in Tunisia we are determined to get rid of all feudalism. We've already sacked all the caids. Tunis is teeming with sacked caids—good luck to them! To us Tunisians Independence is not an end but a means. Political reforms are inseparable from social and economic reforms.

'The most important reform introduced just the other day by the Government has been the prohibition of polygamy. This was absolutely essential. So long as there was polygamy, it was no use expecting women to develop a social consciousness. After developing their social consciousness, we shall develop their political consciousness. It scandalized a lot of the older people, but, believe me, we are taking the creation of a Modern Tunisia very seriously, and we don't want to muddle along like some of the other Arab countries, with their veiled women and their polygamy and their caids and their feudal system . . .'

The man was impressive. He seemed full of faith himself, and was certain to inspire faith in others . . .

'We have the solid foundations,' he said, 'for building a modern state of nearly four million people. We are not scared away by the word "nationalization". If necessary, we shall nationalize the big estates; and we shall carry out a land reform. It's true that, for the present, we don't intend to nationalize them: because we must try to avoid difficulties like those Nasser brought upon himself with his nationalization of Suez. There are other lands, other than the big *colons'* estates, or the estates of the big Tunisian landowners, which can be developed. There is all the *habou* property which can be put back into production. The institutional *habous* have been taken over by the State; private *habous* can now be sold by one family to another; none of this land will remain "immobilized" and so, in most cases, neglected; this is one of the big achievements of the Bourguiba Government: I've mentioned some of the others: the dissolution of the *caidal* corps; the "westernization" of the divorce laws (so that a man can no longer simply "repudiate" his wife), and the transfer of the jurisdiction concerning family relations from the religious to the state courts; the prohibition of polygamy; and last, but not least—the fact that the Bey's civil list has been cut down from £35,000 to £8,000 a month. This made a tremendous impression, I can tell you! The record of the Bey hasn't been all that hot; he's not like his predecessor, Moncef Bey, who was popular. Most of our people wouldn't mind if Tunisia became a republic . . .

'But our No. 1 problem today is unemployment. A large part of our people are on the brink of famine. In the South and Centre many thousands of families should be settled on the land; and we ought to create new industries, which would absorb at least 60,000 workers. Our present commercial conventions with France aren't making this easy . . . And there's also the problem of housing which is causing grave concern to the UGTT. We've started a housing co-operative among our members; we hope, in this way, to build 6,000 small houses ("villas") near Tunis by next year, so as to decongest the *bidonvilles*. Already, we have helped our dockers to build "villas"—complete with bathrooms. It's a case of their paying 6,000 frs. a month for the "villas". Similar schemes are now also in operation in the mining concerns —with the help of the mining companies.

'We intend to have a Modern State; we must have full employment; we must have old-age pensions. We've already managed to obtain pensions for the dockers and miners . . . But to get all this, to get unemployment relief, and all that, it'll take a long time . . .'

Tunisia—a Welfare State: that seemed the UGTT's ideal. Tunisia, with a network of schools and hospitals for everybody. The most advanced and modern Arab State in the world . . . But, of course, he said, everything was being held up by the war in Algeria. Algeria must become a sovereign State. Only then could the three North African countries play the rôle they deserved to play in the Mediterranean . . . And it was not true that the French had no *interlocuteurs valables*. What was wrong with Ferhat Abbas? Four years ago, they were saying the same thing about Bourguiba. 'We represent nothing' or 'The Istiqlal in Morocco represents nothing.'

'What about Salah Ben Yussef?' I asked. 'Has he no following in the UGTT?' 'No,' said Ben Ezzedine. 'He's dead. Dead politically. Completely dead.'

One Sunday Ahmed packed his whole family—wife, mother-in-law and the black-eyed Arabic-babbling baby—and me into his 4-*chevaux*, and we drove to Nabeul, through the lovely rich country of the Cap Bon, east of Tunis, with its vineyards and orange-groves and olive trees. Here were some large estates, many, but not all, owned by French *colons*. A few miles outside Tunis Ahmed pointed to a spot where Ferhat Hashed's car was held up, on December 4, 1952, by French gunmen of the *Main Rouge*, who then murdered him, and battered his face to pulp, so that it should be unrecognizable, and then abandoned his body by the roadside.

'His murderers still hold posts in the French police' said Ahmed, 'though most of them were recently placed at the disposal of the French Embassy and so are no longer in Tunisia. But one of the people implicated in the murder still holds an administrative post at Sfax. We Tunisians are pretty tolerant people, you'll agree! But of course, everybody knows that these gunmen were just carrying out the instructions—and written instructions, too—of a high official at the Residence. I can tell you that a photostat copy of these instructions is in existence.'

And Ahmed talked of how, after Internal Autonomy was granted to Tunisia, there was the solemn re-burial of Ferhat Hashed at the Kasbah at Tunis, and of how 300,000 people came to this immense state funeral. And since then, he said, there was a continuous pilgrimage to the Ferhat Hashed mausoleum, and during the year after his murder nearly all the children born in Tunisia were called Ferhat . . .

'Didn't Mendès-France become the lawyer of Ferhat's widow?' I asked.

'No; it was Maître Izard; but Mendès came to Tunis and took a great interest in the case, and it was certainly an eye-opener for him on the gangs who were reigning supreme at the Residence . . . He got a pretty good idea of the kind of activities certain big shots encouraged . . .'

Ahmed seemed to have friends all over Tunisia; and at Nabeul, a small market-town on the Gulf of Hammemet, we called on his friend Mahmoud, an orange-grower in the district, who promptly instructed his women-folk to prepare a big dinner for us. Mahmoud, wearing not a *chechia*, but a fez (a sign of belonging to a superior layer of the bourgeoisie) and a long white robe, was a man in his late fifties, with a large family of children and grandchildren. I reckoned that he must have an income of about a million a year, for he complained of having to spend 'nearly half his income' on keeping his son at the Polytechnique in Paris . . . This was a very traditional Moslem family, in which it was still not customary for the women to eat at the same table as the men; and yet, they were all very proud of the young man studying at one of the most select *grandes écoles* in France. The inside of the house was a curious mixture of some beautiful oriental objects (particularly some exquisite pieces of Nabeul pottery) and extremely shoddy bits of European furniture, crystal chandeliers and a gigantic patriarchal bed with a vast canopy. The Louis XV bed might well have come from Lévitan or the Galeries Barbès.

And what a meal it was! Various kinds of roast meat, accompanied by corrosive vegetable salads, then the traditional *kuskus*, with its mixture of semolina, potatoes, mutton, and an intriguing bright-green and highly-spiced sauce, and then fried aubergines and courgettes, followed by enormous chunks of exquisite iced melon and water-melon . . . No alcohol, of course, but water and, later, very sweet and strong mint-flavoured tea. And after the meal, you washed your hands —with a vulgar piece of soap—-over the traditional copper basin.

What a curious mixture Tunisia is! At Nabeul it was as apparent as anywhere else. The chief local industry is pottery; and there are—which is quite a symbol!—two kinds of pottery they make here: the heavy and very oriental pottery with its bright reds, blues and greens and the lighter pottery—Tunisian, too, but covered with black-and-white designs of deer and horses—which are in the purest Graeco-Roman tradition, when you come to think of it.

Indeed, as you look to the north from the beach of Nabeul, you see the dim outline of an island. That's Pantellaria—Italy! On the beach of Nabeul, hundreds of children and young people splashed about in the bright-blue waters of the Bay of Hammamet, and Euro-peans and Jews and emancipated Tunisians danced in a blue-and-white café to the tune of jazz records. Yet a few hundred yards down the road from the beach, you are right in the centre of Nabeul again, and here the Arabs in their long robes sit about the Moorish cafés, as they have done in the last hundred years, reading the Arab paper, and discussing the price of olives and oranges . . . But there are now Tunisian flags on many houses, and in the cafés there are large pictures of Bourguiba—and sometimes of Ferhat Hashed. But never of the Bey. He might not exist . . . Everybody was saying that Tunisia would soon be a republic, and that the Bey and his family (they had all, more or less, 'collaborated' with the French) were costing too much to keep.

Late in the afternoon we drove with Mahmoud to visit his orange plantation. About 30 hectares of it, most of it reclaimed from the sand-dunes. We drove through Tazerka and Beni Khiar and one or two other villages which had been scenes of much savagery during the *ratissage* of this area by the Foreign Legion, back in 1952. About 200 people were killed round here . . . But now life seemed to have returned to normal again. We came across several camels, some of them—surprisingly—making a meal of prickly cactuses lining the road. Mah-moud had seven labourers working on the reasonably well-kept orange plantation, and most of them living there. They were receiving the legal wage of 350 francs a day. Mahmoud was particularly proud of the rich new well from which they pumped the water and irrigated the former sand-dunes. There were still some giant oranges of a pound or more on some of the trees. But it was a hard life, Mahmoud said. He sold his oranges at 11 francs a kilo, and they were sold in Tunis at 70 or 80 francs. He paid a tribute, however, to the co-operative system which was making things easier for him, and to the STP (the *Société Tunisienne de Prévoyance*) a Government organization, which had already existed in the French days, and which had helped him to acquire his pumps and irrigation equipment . . . Mahmoud thought that, in spite of everything, the French had done quite a few things for Tunisia . . . And already Mahmoud had ideas on how the new régime might improve things still further: since the oranges were hard to sell, couldn't a canning-plant for orange juice be set up in this area? . . . There was no conflict between the fez and industrial progress.

At Nabeul there was still a French gendarmerie, but now—provisionally, and pending their withdrawal—the gendarmes were under Tunisian authority. In this small Tunisian town, there seemed no hostility between the French and the Arabs, or between the Arab shopkeepers and the numerous Jewish shopkeepers.

In one of the towns we passed on our way back, I noticed a French Consulate. 'That,' said Ahmed, 'is a trick. They left in Tunisia a lot of the old *contrôleurs civils*, and these now call themselves consuls . . . The biggest joke are the *caids*. They have all been sacked. They were so dependent on the *contrôleurs civils* that they now keep pestering the French consuls for jobs and instructions! Of course, we've still got 20 out of the 75 French *commissaires de police* in Tunisia. They're a pretty scruffy lot—nearly all of them mixed up with *les affaires les plus louches*—drug traffic, white-slave traffic, *bordels*, and all the rest of it . . .'

BOURGUIBA WOULD LIKE TO MEDIATE IN ALGERIA

Habib Bourguiba has been called 'the world's most intelligent Arab statesman'. And latterly some have called him 'France's only statesman'!

With lucid enthusiasm and faith he has struggled for the last 25 years for the emancipation—and, eventually, for the independence—of Tunisia. He has what's called 'a magnetic personality', and can, on occasion, be a noisy demagogue, capable of arousing tremendous mass enthusiasm. But he has always been careful not to overdo it. Because Bourguiba is a man who is never carried away by irresponsible slogans and wild enthusiasms, and has always carefully calculated every step. Not that that is the popular French view of Bourguiba. '*Un illuminé*', a French lady I know in Tunis described him; it was meant to be both a criticism of his 'fanaticism' and a tribute to his sex appeal. For at 53, Bourguiba is still a handsome man, and one of great personal charm—more than charm: magnetism. And he has deep-blue eyes which many of the French find disconcerting, like the sign of something unusually superior in an Arab!

The curious thing about Bourguiba is that he has, throughout his life, been pro-French . . . in a certain sense. Though belonging to a family which had been half ruined by the confiscation of his grandfather's property, following the Sahel insurrection in which this grandfather had taken part, Bourguiba received his education in Paris, and, being brought up in the cult of Michelet and Victor Hugo, he liked to think that the French left were the allies of the colonial peoples.

As a student, he married a Frenchwoman—a sign in those days of highly progressive ways of thinking. Full of ideas on *liberté*, *égalité* and *fraternité*, he asserted himself as a leader of the Neo-Destour movement around 1930. It was, indeed, in 1930 that a Eucharistic Congress, which met at Carthage with the approval of the French Government, had the bad taste to hold a procession through Tunis, with a statue of St. Louis at its head. The whole thing was intended to celebrate and commemorate the Crusade of the Christian French against the Moslem Infidels. With speeches and articles in *L'Action Tunisienne*, the organ of the Old Destour, and later of the Neo-Destour, Bourguiba started a nation-wide campaign against colonialism, of which the Eucharistic Congress had been a particularly shameless example. He soon became Secretary-General of the newly-founded Neo-Destour Party, and was arrested soon afterwards. During the next 25 years, Bourguiba spent eleven years in French prisons or as an internee.

Not till 1936, under the *Front Populaire* Government of Léon Blum, was he released; and, for a time, he genuinely believed in the establishment of lasting bonds between France and Tunisia. He was, throughout his career, a 'possibilist'; and he tried to believe that there were enough men in France who could exercise their influence in favour of Tunisia. In 1936 he was particularly impressed by a man like Pierre Viénot, Blum's Under-Secretary at the Quai d'Orsay, and believed that a new era had dawned. But, only a few years later, he was again in prison—from which, in 1943, he was to be released by—the Italians! His faith in France had, by now, been severely shaken. Admiral Esteva, Vichy's Resident-General in Tunis, was collaborating with the Germans and Italians and, at the same time, pursuing, *vis-à-vis* the Tunisians, an ultra-colonialist policy. Bourguiba's flirtation with Italy was not, however, 'collaboration' in the Vichy sense; he merely declared on Bari radio that he was prepared to negotiate with Italy, 'provided Italy recognized Tunisia's complete and entire independence.'

After the war, charges were brought by the French against Bourguiba, on the ground that he had 'collaborated' with the Axis Powers. These contacts with Italy as late as 1943 were no doubt a mistake; but it was perhaps too much to expect an Arab leader, who had spent years in French prisons, to be over-squeamish—least of all at a time when the French Resident-General in Tunis was, in his own way, also collaborating with the Germans!

Nevertheless, these planned negotiations with Italy, made his position very difficult after the war; and, in 1946, we find Bourguiba in Cairo. His line now was that little was to be hoped from France (especially after the Constantinois massacres in Algeria during the previous year); and he wrote that, although he would prefer Tunisia to be associated with France, there was no denying that the British and especially the Americans had an eye on North Africa, and that, if French colonialism did not mend its ways, it might be necessary to establish contact with the USA. But whether it was France, or the USA, Bourguiba always preferred to look West. He was not impressed by Cairo or the Arab League; and he consistently hoped that France would not drive Tunisia into the arms of Egypt. Throughout his career, he had always taken a keen interest in Algeria, and was aware of the grave dangers of Algeria becoming fanaticized and being driven into 'pan-Arabism' by the misdeeds of the French colonialists . . .

Some years after the war, Bourguiba returned to Tunis, and then, in 1951, went to France, England and the USA, where he pleaded the cause of Tunisian liberation—a case incorporated in his famous 7-point programme. Although M. Schuman, the Foreign Minister, seemed, for a time, reasonably well-disposed, the 'Bourguiba programme' appeared excessive to the French Government, and M. Chenik, the Tunisian Premier in 1951 asked for much less. But when even Chenik's very mild proposals were turned down on December 15, 1951, Bourguiba flew into a rage, and returning to Tunis soon after the new year, proceeded to harangue his fellow-countrymen, calling on them to prepare for a bloody struggle. He called a Congress of the Neo-Destour, but this was prohibited by the new Resident-General, M. de Hauteclocque; Bourguiba was arrested, and there were thousands of other arrests throughout Tunisia. For a long time Bourguiba remained a prisoner of the French on the island of La Galite, off the North coast of Tunisia.

Bourguiba, who had meantime been transferred to France, did not come into his own again until 1954 when, to put an end to the ever-growing chaos in Tunisia, Mendès-France went there on his famous visit. Bourguiba got on well with Mendès-France, who soon saw that

Bourguiba was not, as was asserted by Martinaud-Déplat and other diehards, France's Enemy Number One. He became indeed, the Man of Internal Autonomy and resisted the outcry of Salah Ben Yussef and others in favour of immediate independence. It was not until Morocco had received her independence that Bourguiba's position in Tunisia became almost untenable—unless he obtained for her the same degree of independence immediately. He travelled to Paris, and persuaded the French that, without this independence, Tunisia would become more and more attracted to Egypt . . .

Though perhaps wondering, in his heart of hearts, whether events had not moved a little *too* fast, and whether economic difficulties would not increase as a result, Bourguiba was now nevertheless acclaimed as the man who had secured Tunisia's independence, and as Tunisia's great national hero.

Scene: the Dar el Bey Palace at the Kasbah in Tunis. He was sitting at his desk, wearing a fez. He took this off when I entered and we sat in two armchairs beside a side-table. It was curious to be in the same office again—the office where, four years before, I had been received by M. Baccouche, the puppet premier whom M. de Hauteclocque had invented . . .

So here was Bourguiba, at the same desk. I was struck by the man's extraordinary personal charm, the great clarity of his mind—but also by the fact that he was worried.

Not that he was particularly worried about Nasser. The Suez Crisis had now been going on for nearly a month; and the line Bourguiba took was this: the principle of nationalization had been accepted; the Canal ran through Egyptian territory; Nasser had had the sense to guarantee the freedom of navigation on the Canal; he had agreed to negotiate a new treaty to replace the Convention of 1888; the United States was very reluctant to get involved; so a compromise would no doubt be worked out in the end.

'But what if Britain and France attack Egypt all the same?' I said.

'I think it highly improbable,' said Bourguiba, 'but if they do, then Nasser will have the whole Moslem world and the whole of French North Africa on his side.'

I said that at Algiers they were, on the contrary, hoping that war against Egypt would put an end to the war in Algeria.

'*Ils sont fous*—they're crazy,' Bourguiba briefly replied.

I could see what he meant; the reasonableness, the *bourguibisme* he was trying to apply in Tunisia would be thrown to the winds; in Algeria, pan-Arab nationalism—and with it, the war—would grow in intensity; while the precarious peace in Morocco would be blown sky-high.

But what was worrying Bourguiba far more at that time was Algeria.

'What we are trying to do in Tunisia,' he said, 'has not really been done in other Arab countries. We want to create a state which would set an example for them: a state where there would be respect for the human person, and respect for social justice. We have undertaken some very bold and far-reaching reforms. Our reform of the divorce law (no more repudiation of a wife by her husband without her consent), our prohibition of polygamy, are reforms of profound significance; and they have naturally met with some opposition among the more obscurantist of our people. It implies the interpretation of the Koran in the light of the requirements of a progressive modern state. But the vast majority of our people are favourable to these changes; they had been expecting them for a long time, but my predecessors were afraid of clashing with certain religious traditions in our country. These reforms are absolutely essential; without them, Moslem countries will never be taken seriously as fully grown-up partners by the rest of the world. There can be no emancipation of women without such reforms . . .'

But the building of the Modern Tunisia was faced with two sets of terrible difficulties. Economic difficulties and those arising from the war in Algeria.

'I am expecting the United States to send some important wheat shipments to Tunisia in the course of next month,' Bourguiba said. 'For four years the harvest has been bad in the south and centre of Tunisia. So there is practically a famine in some parts of Tunisia. France is helping us, too, but chiefly with equipment—for this purpose we are getting a loan of £17 m. this year. But, in the long run, we must chiefly depend on our own plans: we must increase production; we must make the most of the *habou* lands that have now been freed from their *main-morte* stranglehold. We must, at any price, increase production—food production, as well as industrial production.'

'Are you proposing to have a land reform, complete with the nationalization of large estates?'

'No; there is no hurry about them. Most of these are fairly efficiently run; and we have masses of other lands to develop.'

I recalled what somebody else had told me: that Tunisia was avoiding any measures which might bring upon her the wrath of the Great Powers—and was therefore careful about nationalization, especially of European property.

Bourguiba smiled. 'Well, yes—there's something in that argument.'

'And France, *Monsieur le President?*'

'France helps us with some credits, and she supports our applications to international organizations. But, apart from that, France has not helped to create in Tunisia an atmosphere of confidence. We are having the most appalling difficulties to get the French authorities to accept the logical conclusions of our political independence. They do nothing with good grace. We have to haggle about every little thing. And about the big things, too. The French security police, the DST, is still active in Tunisia. We have to haggle about it, about the *controleurs civils*, who are still hanging about in some capacity (usually as Consuls); we even have to squabble about the evacuation of this or that barracks, or this or that public works department. And, worst of all, there are still 40,000 French troops in Tunisia. It embarrasses us enormously, both economically and, above all, psychologically to have them here. And the DST police go about the country, arresting people—especially Algerians. After all, we aren't at war with Algeria!' Bourguiba added angrily.

'Seydoux, the French Ambassador is doing his best, I must say, to reduce friction wherever possible; all the same, there are constant rows which don't make it easy for the Government to carry out its reforms.'

'What about foreign investments,' I said, 'and all the talk about the "flight of capital" from Tunisia?'

'Foreign investments—yes, by all means. We welcome investments—from Germany, Czechoslovakia, America, or anywhere else. As for the capital that came here during the colonial regime, and which is no longer satisfied with the present conditions, let it go! We are not keeping it back. What we want are *bona fide* investments, which would do some good not only to their owners, but also to the Tunisian people. The colonial era is over; and more intelligent capitalists realize it.'

'And Algeria?'

'That's our biggest worry of all,' said Bourguiba. 'As long as the war goes on there, our own instability is complete. Surely, the Algerians are entitled to self-determination. It'll happen quite

Y

inevitably—sooner or later, but the sooner the better. The colonial regime is bound to disappear. But so long as there is all this hatred and anarchy, all peace and co-operation between us and the French remains difficult.'

'Don't you think France should have a privileged position in North Africa, all the same?'

'Of course, she'll have her privileged position,' said Bourguiba, a little impatiently, 'but not until she has understood the aspirations of the Arab people. If this atrocious war of extermination, with its horrible repression, continues much longer, there cannot be any reconciliation between France and Algeria, and, indeed, her relations with both Tunisia and Morocco will become increasingly difficult and strained. What France ought to realize is that there *can* be close and fruitful co-operation between her and the three sovereign Arab states of North Africa. The French talk a lot about the "marvellous possibilities" of the Sahara. Quite true; there are great possibilities there. The Sahara will be a valuable outlet for the unemployment in North Africa. But you can't start developing the Sahara over the head of an Algeria that's at war!'

'There has been some talk, *Monsieur le Président*, about your acting as a possible mediator in an Algerian settlement.'

'Of course, nothing would please me more than if we could mediate in this tragic conflict, and put an end to it. Mind you, there are extremists on both sides; and we already do all we can to bring the two viewpoints closer together. We are telling the French that the era of colonialism is closed, and that they must recognize this fact. We are telling the Algerians that they cannot get everything overnight, and that they've got to proceed by *stages*. I believe there are some reasonable people among the FLN who fully agree with us . . .'

I recalled to Bourguiba the strong line taken by Ahmed Ben Salah, head of the Tunisian trade unions, who had said shortly before that Tunisia must help her Algerian brethren by every means—not only give them moral support, but arms and men as well. Bourguiba made a face; he was obviously not in agreement with this, and thought it, indeed, an embarrassing point.

'Frankly,' he said, 'I don't consider the military side as the most important one. What is important is that France should realize that there must be a form of free co-operation between her and the North-African countries which alone can solve her problems. I believe that this idea is making headway in France. The idea of a compromise in Algeria is gaining ground, now that the 'pacification' policy has failed. For our own part,' Bourguiba added, 'we are doing all we can to show both parties the living example of Tunisia—a Moslem country in which the French can feel at home, and in which the strength and prestige of France is based on this Moslem country's national sovereignty. The French are not in danger in Tunisia. There were Frenchmen who imagined that the moment we became independent, all the French would be chucked into the sea. Well, nobody has been chucked into the sea. Only, the present situation will not be made any easier if the war in Algeria continues, and if we remain a semi-occupied country . . .'

Tunisia was, clearly, a poor country, a badly under-developed one, and it was difficult for Bourguiba, as a 'possibilist', not to take account of it. Tunisia needed capital from abroad; and there was no eagerness on the part of foreign capital to invest in Tunisia, so long as the war in Algeria was continuing. It was this war in Algeria, more than the 'semi-occupation' of Tunisia by French troops that worried Bourguiba. The troops were merely an accompaniment of the Algerian war, and, so long as this continued, Bouguiba knew that there was little prospect of the French moving out. Perhaps he felt it necessary to stress the need for their evacuation so as not to appear 'soft' to the more impatient people in Tunisia, and in order not to lag behind the Moroccans, who were very vociferous on this question of French troops.

Except that they tended to extend their operations against the fellaghas in Algeria into Tunisian territory, the French troops in Tunisia were not very troublesome. What struck me in Tunis, in particular, was the extreme mildness of their manner; many of them, indeed, expressed the feeling that Tunisia was a 'much nicer' country than either Algeria or Morocco, and that the Tunisians were, somehow, 'different' from ordinary Arabs. And one had the curious feeling in looking at these French soldiers in the cafés and restaurants of Tunis that they wanted to leave a good impression and were being almost apologetic to the Tunisians for being here at all . . . Not that many of them had yet made up their minds *ever* to hand over the naval base of Bizerta to the Tunisians; a kind of 'Gibraltar' *mystique* surrounded this question, even though the Tunisians all glibly argued that it was 'part of Tunisia—and that was all there was to it'. The French, on the other hand, strongly suspected the Tunisian Government of planning to lease Bizerta—for a very substantial consideration—to the Americans, the British—or perhaps even to the Russians!

The corridors of the Dar el Bey Palace looked very different from what they were in the days of M. Baccouche. Then one saw nobody there, except some local fez-wearing worthies, or an occasional haughty

French official bringing instructions from the Residence. Now the corridors were crowded with important-looking diplomatic personages —including top-ranking members of the French Embassy waiting for an 'audience'—and with various Tunisians, some in oriental, others in European clothes. Business-like Tunisian officials—all in European dress—were darting from office to office. This was a genuine Seat of Government, and no longer the comic opera Arabian Nights palace of the Baccouche days . . .

I paid several more visits to the Dar el Bey, and met many of Bourguiba's closest associates. Some were more outspoken than himself—above all on the question of the commercial conventions with France. These were still a hangover from the Internal Autonomy days. They tended to paralyse Tunisia's freedom of movement in foreign trade; and the Conventions also interfered with the development of certain Tunisian home industries. Germany, Switzerland and even countries of the Soviet bloc were interested in trade with Tunisia which had phosphates and olive oil to export; but the trade conventions with France were interfering with the development of Tunisian trade with countries other than France. Also, the conventions were hampering the development of certain local industries: for instance, when the question arose of beginning to manufacture ordinary tea glasses in Tunisia, it caused an uproar in France—a real storm in the National Assembly, *une flambée parlementaire*—with 100 deputies specially intervening to protect the French export of tea glasses to Tunisia!

Only since Tunisia had become independent had it been possible to start growing sugar beet here—the experimental first 10 hectares had proved a success: in a few years it would be possible for Tunisia to grow most of her sugar, instead of buying 60,000 tons of sugar a year in France; the dearest sugar in the world . . . The 17 milliard francs France had lent Tunisia this year wasn't enough to make any major changes in the economy of the country; and too many conditions were attached to this loan . . . All the same, the end of the Protectorate offered some new economic possibilities to Tunisia in the field of international trade. America, Germany, Czechoslovakia, Switzerland —these names recurred over and over again in any talks about future economic developments in the country.

Most of the plans were, however, vague, terribly vague so long as the Algerian war continued; and Nasser hadn't made things any easier . . . The opinions expressed on Nasser at the Dar el Bey were not all too favourable. '*C'est un gaffeur*', an official was saying. 'It was stupid of him to say that Pineau's threats would be answered by the Algerian fellaghas. Suez isn't the capital of Algeria, after all! But, on the other hand, your Sir Anthony is a bit of a *gaffeur*, too! Really, these Palmerstonian shock tactics are a bit out of date . . .'

There was much talk of the contacts existing between the Tunisian Government and the FLN leaders, the rebel command.

'We keep telling them: "for heaven's sake accept a compromise—something that would contain all the germs of future independence. *We've* done it: why the devil can't *you* do it?" '

'Of course, so long as the Mollet-Lacoste team are running the show, there's not much hope. And yet there are some very reasonable Algerians who would accept a minimum arrangement: Ferhad Abbas, for instance. And there are some others who are *not* the maniacs they are pictured by the French to be. The real Ben Bella is not at all the monster that the French *images d'Epinal* make him out to be.'[1]

Curious were the reactions to French politicians. What was the attitude to Mendès France? I wondered.

Two opinions. *One:* 'He's the only man in France in whom Tunisia has any faith at all. His visit to Tunis on July 31, 1954, was the greatest date in the post-war history of France.' *Two:* (by a Tunisian official of equal importance): 'All I would say about Mendès is that he's an enlightened colonialist. He knew that he had to give us Internal Autonomy; it was the only way of saving Tunisia for France, and he knew it. He's concerned about the interests of France first and foremost, and he's more intelligent than the diehards, but we would have remained a French Protectorate a damned sight longer if he were Prime Minister than we actually did . . . He's a sly one . . .'

And again, there was talk of the North African Federation of three sovereign Arab States, which, in close co-operation with France, could make a great thing of the Sahara. '*L'avenir de la France, c'est le Sahara*'—this ambiguous jest was being spoken of now as a genuine economic reality in all the three North-African countries. But again and again they were saying that everything depended on the war in Algeria ending quickly. If—an idle hypothesis—pacification produced results, it would be the end of an independent Tunisia and Morocco; but 'pacification' could produce results only if it took on the form of large-scale extermination. In some parts of Algeria this was precisely the policy that was being adopted; Algerian refugees were telling of whole villages being 'smoked out' . . . There seemed to two schools of thought among the military in Algeria: for instance General Ollié, the French commander in Kabylia, no longer believed in pacification; whereas General Lorillot, the supreme commander in Algeria believed that results could still be achieved provided 'much more brutal methods were used'.

[1] See below the serious effect of the kidnapping of Ben Bella.

The UGTT was preparing for its next Congress. The last Congress took place in July 1954; now, for the first time, Ahmed Ben Salah would put forward his programme.

Ben Salah, like the late Ferhat Hashed, his predecessor, like the Algerian UGTA leader I had seen, like the Moroccan trade union Leaders, belonged to that type of North African with whom it is easier for a European to talk than with any other. Trade unionism in all three countries represents certain values which are easy for the European to understand. Arab nationalism often abounds in obscure implications and contradictions; Arab trade unionism—even though it functions less effectively than European trade unionism—largely represents the same kind of emancipatory movement as earlier trade union movements in Europe. The UGTT is a powerful force in Tunisia, and several of its leaders are in the Bourguiba Government; but Ahmed Ben Salah refused a government post, and took the line that his function was to act as a *corrective* to government action. The trade unions in Tunisia, while apparently loyal to Bourguiba, tend to play the part of a constructive Opposition. One of the functions of the UGTT was, as it were, to present a maximum programme—which it was then for the Government to apply as far as possible.

'There are a number of essential points in our programme about the application of which we feel very strongly,' Ahmed Ben Salah said. 'There must be a complete change in our tax system, so that the rich pay their due share. Secondly, we intend to set up an *Office de mise en valeur du Sud et du Centre;* further, we propose the creation of a variety of training centres, to be called Centres Bourguiba; it's a case of creating skilled labour in sufficient quantities, of creating the right kind of *cadres* . . . The *mise en valeur*—the development—of the South and Centre of Tunisia should be financed by the Ministries of Agriculture, National Education and Public Works; and there should be a great loan, to be called *emprunt Bourguiba.*'

'Are you,' I said, 'in agreement with Bourguiba or not?'

'Fundamentally—yes. But on various details we disagree. We were against the uniform wage cuts which were recently enacted; they affected the low-grade government servants very severely, and the high-grade officials only slightly; it should have been the other way round. We are great believers in social security, complete with adequate health services, maternity guidance centres, etc. Already the UGTT has set up a number of such services—a medical centre outside the central market in Tunis, and other medical centres at Sfax and Sousse. Ben Ezzedine told

you the other day about our educational efforts—our popular
education courses. Although about 40 per cent of our members
are still illiterate, it is not really our job to teach them to read and
write; that must also be done; but not by us. What we are trying
to teach them is some elementary economics, and to give them
some ideas on social security, on the history of trade unionism in
the world in general, and in North Africa in particular. The fact
that a man cannot read or write does not necessarily mean that he
is stupid; our members, whether literate or not, are all anxious to
learn. And there is a genuine eagerness among all these people
to create a modern state in Tunisia—a state in which illiteracy
would disappear within a short time.'

I found this rather new and not without charm: even before they
had learned to read or write, many people in that under-developed
country of Tunisia attended lectures on economics. Absurd on the
face of it? Not at all. It seemed to me on the contrary, a very significant 'under-developed country' phenomenon. Get a smattering of
economics and politics and social sciences first—and then learn to
read and write . . . Was not this, after all true of many revolutions in
the past—not least the Russian Revolution?

There was no 'fundamental' disagreement between Ahmed Ben
Salah, the trade union leader, and Bourguiba, the head of the Government. And yet . . . Ben Salah was less of a 'possibilist' than Bourguiba;
he was less pro-French; he was even, I suspected, less hostile to Salah
Ben Yussef—now in Cairo—than Bourguiba himself.

'Salah Ben Yussef,' said Ahmed Ben Salah, 'was opposed to the
Franco-Tunisian conventions, and to the armed forces and diplomacy
remaining in the hands of the French. Well, since we got our independence, he hasn't much of a leg to stand on. But he still argues in
favour of our breaking with France and of joining the neutral bloc—
that is, in the first place, Egypt. Another string on which he has been
playing good and hard is Algeria. He says we must be more openly
pro-Algerian.'

'But then you said so, too: There can be no independent Tunisia or
Morocco so long as the war in Algeria goes on; we must help our
Algerian brethren by every means—moral support, financial support,
arms and men. That's not quite the Bourguiba position is it?'

'No; but the Government *nearly* agrees with me. There are, mark
you, a lot of Algerians in the UGTT; and we cannot ignore them. The
Government cannot, on the other hand, ignore a mass movement led
by the UGTT. And we cannot stand by while the Algerians are being
massacred. What would you say if one of these days there was an
attack on the Maison de France, the former Residence?'

'Pretty serious, I should say.'

'Well, it hasn't come to that yet,' said Ben Salah, 'and I hope it never does. But a lot of things are seriously wrong, and we must go on prodding the Government. It's true, there are four UGTT men in the Government—the Ministers of Education, Posts, Public Works and Agriculture. And we expect them to get tough. For the UGTT demands, among other things, a revision of our customs union with France, and of the commercial and financial conventions. Income tax must be higher; we can't allow Tunisian businessmen to pay income on only 5 or 10 per cent of their real income . . . It's scandalous to watch all the plutocrats feeding their faces at La Marsa and the other luxury places on our coast. Don't you realize that this is the doped part of Tunisia; the real Tunisia is in the south—it's a land of poverty and starvation. And once the situation becomes catastrophic, we shall all go out and fight for the Algerians. But it's not true that foreign capital is afraid of the UGTT, as some people say; it's afraid of the instability and insecurity in North Africa.'

And here was another curious difference between Bourguiba and the UGTT: the UGTT was more 'internationally-minded'; it did not believe much in Tunisia becoming a 'model state' while the rest of North Africa was in flames.

'Mind you,' said Ben Salah, 'the Government and the UGTT are both mobilized for the defence of Algeria—mobilized in different ways, but mobilized all the same. We do what we can; and of course, it's no use broadcasting everything we do . . . But we cannot consider that Tunisia is living in a vacuum. The three countries of North Africa are inseparable. Tunisia and Morocco must enter into negotiations with France; even before dwelling on the greater independence or the complete independence of Tunisia, it is essential that we persuade France to discuss Algeria with us. Both in France and in the outside world there is more support for us than for Algeria. And so long as France refuses to negotiate on the *ensemble*, on the whole of North Africa with all three countries, there'll never be a satisfactory solution . . . All this, as well as our economic development are being sabotaged by both the French and our own big bourgeoisie. And the French are hiding behind the backs of these big shots . . .'

And Ahmed Ben Salah angrily exclaimed:

'Tunisia is *not* independent. And Suez is being used as a piece of psychological warfare to maintain the whole of North Africa in a state of servitude or economic impotence.'

Was the man slightly muddled-headed? I wondered. And also was he representing all the tendencies in the UGTT? Apparently not. On the other hand, Bourguiba's mind was clearer; Ben Salah was hinting

at great things that were being done for the Algerians by Tunisia—
which just wasn't true. It made him feel better. But behind all this
demagogy, I felt, there was an eagerness for a quicker and more
violent movement, and a certain impatience with Bourguiba's
'possibilism'. Algeria and Suez had, below the surface, aroused
political passions which suggested that the influence of Salah Ben
Yussef was not as 'stone-dead' as Ben Salah's own deputy had
assured me it was . . . I could see the UGTT driving Bourguiba, before
very long perhaps, into an extremist course if the war in Algeria
continued; if economic conditions in Tunisia went from bad to worse;
if, above all, Egypt was attacked.

I talked about it to my friend Ahmed that night; what did he
think, as a member of the Tunisian Government personnel?

'Ahmed Ben Salah is a brilliant chap,' he said, 'but he's a bit of a
hothead. He'll go on pushing Bourguiba as far as he can; but I don't
much believe in any Tunisian large-scale intervention in favour of the
Algerian nationalists; people are apt to be selfish, and they won't
stick their necks out, unless they are driven to it by hunger . . . Only
heaven alone knows what'll happen here if the British and French do
invade Egypt. I think I can tell you this: most of our people here don't
like Nasser. But if Nasser is attacked, every Arab in the world will be
Nasser's ally: Ben Salah, and Ben Yussef and Bourguiba and everybody in Tunisia. Except perhaps your old friend Baccouche, our
Coca Cola King . . .'

Later, I often remembered these words, and wondered what *would*
really have happened in Tunisia and Morocco if the Suez Operation
had been allowed to develop into a major war?

Fortunately it hadn't. On the other hand, it was not long before Ben Salah was eliminated from the leadership of the UGTT:
the man was becoming too embarrassing with his interventionist zeal.

I spent my last evening in Tunisia at the enchanting country
house of a Tunisian friend—a French-trained doctor. We had a
traditional Tunisian supper in the garden among the jasmin bushes.
The doctor's wife—a very 'progressive' lady—had recently returned
from a trip to Russia and China, and said she was greatly impressed
by the 'optimism' of these people—despite the still very low living-
standard of the Chinese. But she felt that both countries had 'something' which the old world lacked, and which the newly-emancipated
colonial peoples, with their terrible living conditions, were bound to
find interesting, to say the least. . . . And, after speaking of Russia
and China, she talked, a little jocularly, about her grandfather and

the complications he had with his four wives. Both she and her husband agreed that Bourguiba was absolutely right to have prohibited polygamy. While there was polygamy, there could never be democracy or social progress.

At the end of the table sat a very ancient old Arab, the doctor's father; he wore a *chechia* and had a small wrinkled face with tiny watering eyes and a white *barbiche*. He was eighty-five, spoke no French, and was treated with great reverence by both his son and his daughter-in-law; and although the son was over fifty, he did not dare light a cigarette until the old man had retired to bed. . . .

The air was filled with the scent of jasmin, and there was perfect peace, except for the song of the crickets and the rumble of an occasional car along the near-by Tunis-Bizerta motor road. It was cool after the stifling heat of Tunis that day, and a bright moon in the African sky was shining through the orange trees.

Here was a prosperous, hard-working Tunisian family, with their roots still deep in the Moslem past. But they had also been nourished on French culture; and now, with a puzzled look, they were throwing side-glances at still another world. Where, they themselves wondered, would the future for them lie? Would Tunisia—their Tunisia—become some day an amalgam of all these three worlds?

For even in an office adjoining Bourguiba's, an official had said to me only a few days before: 'Sooner or later, we can't avoid it. There will have to be a land reform in Tunisia—on Socialist lines or on Communist lines, doesn't matter what you call it. But it'll have to come.' And he added: 'Not to scare the West, Bourguiba's got to pull his punches. So Tunisia remains, for the present, a bourgeois state, with all its good—and bad—points. For, let's face it: we have not yet seriously tackled, let alone solved, our No. 1 problem—which is the hunger, the hideous poverty and unemployment among our people, especially in the central and southern parts of Tunisia. We can't become a truly modern, model Arab state until we've done that. And if we don't do something quickly, some of our intellectuals and trade union boys will be tempted by Communism. It may be discredited in the West, but to many hungry Arabs it is something new and strange. . . .'

CHAPTER 3

SOCIAL REVOLUTION IN MOROCCO?

AIR journeys are the same the world over. Whether in Tunis, or Algiers, Bangkok or Amsterdam, the glass panelling of the airport buildings, the nickel tubing and the comfortable arm-chairs in the waiting-rooms, the spotless cleanliness of the bars and restaurants and *lavabos*, and the anonymous smiling benevolence of the air-line employees are always the same. Everywhere air-hostesses are well-groomed, discreetly lip-sticked, motherly and with a not-for-you sexiness written all over them.

To fly in one day from Tunis to Algiers, and from Algiers to Casablanca is to escape for 12 or 14 hours from the realities of Tunisia, Algeria and Morocco. In Bône alone, where we landed for half-an-hour, the new airport building had not yet been completed, and passengers were escorted into a corrugated-iron army hut, a survival of the Allied Occupation of 1943. In the small bar, where they drank Alsatian beer, were a couple of *paras* in their green camouflage overalls. There was something tragic about these two young men's faces. What all hadn't they done in the course of their punitive expeditions? One of them I remember particularly well. His face was scarred, there was a mad look in his eyes, and one side of his face twitched all the time. He looked like a madman, or at least like someone who was near the end of his tether; he seemed to hate not only the Arabs, but to hate and despise everybody. He seemed to be bearing the brunt of this whole senseless war, just as he had borne the brunt of the equally senseless war in Indo-China. He would go on with it—even if everybody else gave up. I had seen such faces among S.S. prisoners in the final stages of World War II . . . He drank his beer silently, grimly, without saying anything.

Again we flew over the sea and over the brown mountains of Kabylia and were then 'offered' a free lunch at Algiers airport by Air-France. Then on to Oran, where we waited another hour. Oran airport presented the picture of a huge holiday exodus. Every few minutes the loud-speaker would announce: '*Messieurs les passagers à destination de Marseille*', '*Messieurs les passagers à destination de Nice*', '*Messieurs les passagers à destination de Toulouse et Paris . . .*' Like journeys to the Moon. From talks with various people I learned that at Oran—where the proportion of Europeans is higher than anywhere in Algeria, there was practically no trouble at all. But it was hell at Tlemcen, it was hell at Nemours, both of them not far away. '*L'Afrique du Nord, c'est moche*', was the simple summing up given by one middle-aged French businessman . . .

And then the last 2½-hour hop, over the desolate Riff Mountains, and then, just as we caught sight of the Atlantic, over the white twin cities of Rabat and Salé, and then over New York . . . well, not quite New York, but something extraordinarily reminiscent of it—an immense city, with vast buildings and a 'Central Park' and the sky-scrapers threatening to hit the plane's underbelly: Casablanca! Here, as in Tunis, the passport and customs officials were French, and the coach-driver was a jovial back-slapping Frenchman, a *vieux Marocain*, who had come here 30 years ago.

The streets of Casablanca were as crowded as when I was last here in 1953, and there was the same bustle of cars—mostly driven by Arabs—and buses and trucks in the place de France, that great square with its vast European luxury buildings on one side and, hidden behind a high wooden hoarding, the labyrinth of the Old Medina on the other. And down the avenue des Quatre Zouaves, leading to the Port, were the same hundreds of small shops selling leather goods, and blankets and rugs and souvenirs. Some of the traffic police were still French, but were being progressively replaced by Moroccans.

That first night I took a bus—packed with Moroccans, including some spick-and-span soldiers of the new Royal Moroccan Army—to the outskirts of Casablanca to see a French friend, the owner of a fairly large tannery. The place stank of hides and chemicals and the heaps of hides in the yard were infested with clouds of flies. We had supper in a small house adjoining the tannery. The French owner was being optimistic. 'I've no intention of clearing out of Morocco,' he said. 'Of course, the good old days when we could kick our Moroccan workers about are over. But we've got to adapt ourselves to new con-ditions. It's all the fault of these idiots—Boniface and General Guil-laume, egged on by that old scoundrel the Glaoui—who turned out the Sultan in '53. That's what really started all the trouble. I daresay if we'd hanged twenty Moroccans in the place de France every day, it might have worked the trick; but these things aren't done any more . . . It's not easy, of course. My Moroccan workmen are tricky people. They're full of new-fangled ideas. They get 45 per cent more pay than before—'trade-union rates', if you please!—and they work 30 per cent less and often, when they're in a bad mood, they laugh in your face when you give them orders . . .'

And my friend's wife complained of the servant problem. A few

years ago, you could get all the Fatimas—the charladies—you needed ;
today they don't want to come and work for a few hours two or three
times a week; it's got to be a full-time job, or nothing . . .

'However, you still make ends meet,' I said.

'Yes, indeed, and our exports of leather have gone up in the last
year. The Moroccans need foreigners here; it's a lot of irresponsible
hooey if they say they don't. No doubt, some Frenchmen have got
cold feet in Morocco, and are hastening to clear out. But we know that
if we go, others will take our place. The Americans have got an eye on
Morocco, and the Czechs are setting up three new factories—an
automobile plant, a sugar refinery and a Bata shoe factory . . . Some
Frenchmen may tell you that the Moroccans wouldn't mind who came
here—Americans, Russians, Germans—provided it wasn't the
French; but that's an exaggeration . . . All the same, the Bonifaces
have a lot to answer for . . .'

I went back to the tannery a few days later when work was in full
swing. In the stinking inferno the Moroccan workers—mostly young
men—were working hard and conscientiously. Some of the foremen
were French, others were Arabs . . . The men were now clamouring
for higher wages; higher prices had swallowed up their increases, and,
on the following day, they were not going to work: they were having
a 'Solidarity with Nasser' strike . . .

Curious, all the same, how normal and unchanged everything
looked in Casablanca. Outside the spectacular Town Hall—an
architectural symbol of the Lyautey days—the equestrian statue of
Lyautey was still there; in the luxury shops and luxury hotels of
European Casablanca, it is true, business had badly slowed down, but
the Café des Arcades near the central Post Office (with its mostly
European clerks, now selling stamps with the Sultan's effigy) and in the
big café at the Rond-Point Mers-Sultan, where several people were
killed by a bomb at the beginning of the brief Grandval régime, there
were the usual crowds of Europeans—and looking less nervous than
back in 1953 . . . The *Vigie Marocaine*—the most ferocious 'colonialist'
paper—was still appearing, but merely a shadow of its former self,
and full of reverence for *Sa Majesté le Sultan* . . . This was the evening
paper; the morning paper, the *Petit Marocain*—was also remarkably
mild in tone. *Maroc-Presse*, the liberal paper, owned by Lemaigre-
Dubreuil, who was assassinated by French gunmen in June 1955, had
closed down . . .

The French in Casablanca were less nervous than in 1953; but, on
the other hand, they were much less self-assured, much less *Herrenvolk*.
Some were preparing to pack up; others, with more or less good grace,
were hoping to adapt themselves to new conditions, hoping at heart

that the 'more reasonable' Moroccans (with the Sultan at their head) would make it possible for the French to stay on. Most were scared of an Istiqlal dictatorship—which would make things extremely difficult for the French. And yet, some big-business people were in contact with the Istiqlal, and were prepared to play ball with them; even the Istiqlal (was the argument) needed French capital and French technicians and French brains, and even if there were some fanatical pan-Arabs among the Istiqlal (like Allal Al Fassi), there were also some good liberals, who had a healthy respect for French culture, and were *sure* to be at least slightly grateful to the French for having laid the foundations for a modern Morocco . .. It was the French, after all, who had built this superb city of Casablanca, with its public buildings and its magnificent gardens . . . There were, of course, the filthy old medinas, and the *bidonvilles*, but all that would sort itself out in time.

It did not take long to discover that, unlike Tunisia—which was, more or less, united round Bourguiba—Morocco was sharply divided into two main factions, which might conveniently be called the Right and the Left. No doubt, the Sultan was generally accepted as the Symbol of Unity; but each faction, while expressing its undying devotion to the Sultan, was trying to win him over to its own side, hoping that he would help to crush the other faction.

The struggle, broadly speaking, was between what they themselves called 'the live forces of the nation'—i.e., the Istiqlal, the UMT (*Union Marocaine des Travailleurs*), the great trade union federation, and a number of Resistance organizations on the one hand, and the wealthier, more conservative and more traditionalist elements on the other. To say this, however, is to oversimplify matters: for the Independents and the PDI, the *Parti Démocratique de l'Indépendance*, forming part of the coalition Government under Si Bekkai, represented not only (as the Istiqlal claimed) the 'feudal order', but also the relatively well-to-do bourgeoisie and a variety of other people who regarded the Istiqlal's and the trade unions' clamour for a 'homogeneous government' as an attempt to set up a one-party dictatorship.

The truth, of course, was that while the 'Right' was reasonably satisfied with having achieved Morocco's *political* independence, the 'Left' considered this political independance 'all-right as far as it went', but thought that this must be followed up without delay by a major *social* revolution.

Clearly, in both Tunisia and Morocco, ideas of Social Reform had made tremendous headway in the last few years; but while the Tunisians were conscious of their economic limitations and were 'possibilists' by temperament, and had no desire to quarrel violently with

France (after all, Tunisia had been treated rough for only a relatively short period by the French), the Moroccans were impulsive, more violent and arrogant in temperament, and were conscious of having a larger and potentially much richer country than Tunisia. Independence had gone to the Moroccans' heads, much more than to the Tunisians' heads. The progressive unification of the French, Spanish and Tangier zones (already it was no longer necessary to have a permit to cross the old demarcation lines) was now being accompanied by much flag-waving and by much talk of an even 'Greater Morocco', including the vast French and Spanish territories to the south (Mauretania, Rio de Oro, Ifni, etc.), almost all the way down to the Niger and Senegal.

Although the Moroccans were worrying less than the Tunisians about the more childish manifestations of independence (new street names, road-signs and number-plates in Arabic, etc.), anti-French feeling was much stronger than in Tunisia; much stronger, too, were the pan-Arab influences. Inside the Istiqlal (by no means a homo-geneous party) there was a powerful pro-Egyptian faction led by Allal Al Fassi; the Istiqlal Minister of Education was favouring all-out Arabization; and in *Al Alam*, the Istiqlal's paper, one came across items almost inconceivable in Tunisia: for instance the Arab League's proposal for creating a 'pool' of Moslem technicians, who would replace European technicians throughout the Arab-speaking world . . . Altogether, there was more violence, more passion, more irresponsi-bility and amateurishness in much of the talk to be heard among 'progressive' Arabs in Morocco than in Tunisia. I was often reminded of a Tunisian's boast that there were 1500 *licenciés en droit* in Tunisia, and only 120 in Morocco! Tunisia, I somehow felt, could be a Euro-pean intellectual's paradise; Morocco never . . .

No doubt, Morocco, which only a few years ago was still a capital-ist Eldorado, a land of feudal lords, of an uncouth new urban pro-letariat, and of medieval pageantry, had still preserved many of its features. Outside the Sultan's palace at Rabat I still witnessed scenes of almost unbelievable 'picturesqueness'—tribal chiefs and their retainers in fantastically coloured costumes waiting around for hours in the August sun to present a petition to the Sultan, or simply to assure him of their allegiance; or other 'delegations' arriving on horse-back; or Superior Persons, Arab or European, arriving in their Cadillacs and being escorted into the Palace by the bayonet-carrying Negro Guards in their red-and-gold uniforms.

Yet now both the capitalists and the feudal lords were in retreat or, at any rate, on the defensive. The rebellious proletariat of the Casa-blanca *bidonvilles* now had their recognized spokesmen,while many of the capitalists, subdued and no longer arrogant with their Moroccan workers, were thanking their stars for being here at all . . .

No man in Morocco impressed me more then Mahjoub Ben Saddik, the Secretary-General of the Moroccan trade unions. Small, wiry and sparkling with intelligence and an acid kind of humour, Mahjoub seemed to personify the social revolution that was on the way in Morocco. He received me in his large office on the eighth floor of the vast building in the avenue de la République, now the Labour Exchange and the Trade Union headquarters at Casablanca. His office looked on to a vast panorama of Casablanca harbour and the Atlantic beyond . . . 'This building wasn't originally meant for us', he said with a grin. A native of Meknes, he had been a railwayman for many years, and was head of the railwayman's federation in 1952 at the time of the 'massacre of the trade unions' on December 8 by the He-men of Casablanca. 400 or 500 Moroccans, mostly trade unionists, were then murdered or lynched by Europeans . . . Mahjoub was arrested that day, was beaten and tortured and was then kept in jail for nearly three years. One of his hands was deformed as a result of the torture he had undergone . . .

'Hah, that's ancient history', he said with a shrug. 'There are more important things to talk about. The most outstanding fact about Morocco is the extraordinary evolution and adaptabilty of our work-ing class. They have acquired a social consciousness and a mental maturity you wouldn't have believed possible a few years ago.'

I said I thought I had heard a good deal of irresponsible talk since arriving in Morocco.

'That's different,' said Mahjoub. 'Of course, Government offices and some of our politicians are full of wild talk. I mean the change in the mentality of the Moroccan working man. *He's lost his slave mentality*. He is very rapidly becoming a *citizen* in the true sense. Our masses are not frantically interested in flags, or even in a Moroccan army; they are, however, acutely conscious of the social problems of our country. And the trade unions, with their 600,000 members, are a force with which *everybody* must reckon. Morocco cannot be ruled *against* the working-class (or against the Istiqlal, for that matter) any more.'

'Will the Sultan have to reckon with them?' I said, pointing at the Sultan's portrait in a golden frame, hanging above Mahjoub's desk.

'Yes,' said Mahjoub with an air of genuine conviction. 'The Sultan is an extraordinary man, a marvellous man, our rampart against dictatorship. He symbolizes our country just as the President of the United States symbolizes his ... And the Sultan, who received me in audience yesterday, knows the importance of the trade unions. We've got trade unions today even at Marrakesh —could anything be more feudal and obscurantist than Marrakesh a few years ago?'

I recalled the Glaoui's autocratic régime that I had seen functioning in Marrakesh in 1953, and asked Mahjoub what they were proposing to do about the *droit Berbère* and the Glaoui's old claim to own the mineral wealth of Southern Morocco.

'That, and much else,' he said, 'will have to be cleared up and cleaned up once and for all. What we really need in Morocco today is Austerity. Morocco is still run along colonialist lines. We have a colonial economy: export of raw materials, import of manufactured goods. We've got to control credit and foreign trade. We must have a planned economy; and the present coalition government, symbolizing only our *political* liberation, has outlived its usefulness. We must have a homogeneous government; we don't mean a one-party government, but a homogeneous government agreed on a definite programme. Sixty per cent of our present budget is spent on administration— i.e., on paying officials. It's far too much. We must have productive capital investments instead. Why, for instance, should we keep in clover 30,000 French officials? Why should we spend £2,500,000 a year on giving them free holidays in France? We shall gladly pay any French technicians we need; but we can't afford to encourage officials to have two town houses, and three country houses and three cars and thirty-six servants. In order to build up a social security system, we've got to cut down on all these luxuries.

'Next, we've got to have the Treaty of Algeciras scrapped; with its "Open door" it's paralysing our industrial development. We are willing to give full protection to medium industries, regardless of their owners' nationality, provided some of the profits are reinvested in Morocco. The bigger industries we must nationalize. We shall also carry out a land reform, complete with the nationalization of the property of the feudal lords—the caids and pashas—who grabbed thousands of acres not belonging to them. And, of course, the French gendarmes and the 90,000 French troops must go. We are a rich country; but an enormous number of our people are living in abominable conditions; and there are 150,000 unemployed whom, in the absence of any social security, we are in no position to help. But our country, unlike Tunisia, is a country of immense possibilities. And we have every chance of having a *travailliste* system—welfare state and all ...'

It was extraordinary to listen to this self-taught little Arab railway-man from Meknès talking in these terms. Clearly, Mahjoub represents something very 'Western' in Morocco. His passing reference to the USA, on which the Sultan was supposed to be modelling himself, was curious in itself. I was reminded of this when, at the French Embassy a few days later, I was told that the Americans were showing 'an unhealthy interest' in the Moroccan trade unions—'more even than in the Istiqlal'. And the French also complained of the rudeness with which the Moroccans were demanding the evacuation of the French troops from Morocco, and comparing it with the politeness with which (for financial, but no doubt also for political reasons) they were offering the Americans a 'ten years' transition period' before the four of five big air bases in Morocco became the property of the Moroccan State . . .

There was much talk at Rabat about Mauretania as part of Greater Morocco. This was what Larousse said about it:

> *Mauritanie* . . . French colony, created in 1921, and forming part of French West Africa, North of Senegal. 834,000 sq. km. 325,000 inh. Chief town: *St. Louis;* Princely residence, *Port Etienne.* Country mostly desert, chiefly inhabited by nomads. Gum, dates, cattle, fisheries.

Apart from this French Colony, the Moroccan nationalists insisted that Rio de Oro and other Spanish enclaves formed part of Great Morocco. *Al Allam*, the Istiqlal paper, wrote florid articles on Chenguit (the Moorish name for Mauretania), on the loyalty of its inhabitants to H.M. the Sultan, etc. It published on August 20, 1956, a long statement made to it by 'Ahmed Horma Ben Babana, well-beloved leader of the people of Chenguit'. It dealt with the Chenguit peoples' feeling of revolt against the French colonialists, who had made it a criminal offence for anyone in Mauretania to fly the Moroccan national flag . . . And the statement ended with an appeal to 'Dear Comrades of the Chenguit Tribes, who refuse to be humiliated'.

> I praise Allah for the satisfaction I feel at the manifestation of your great national consciousness. We are happy to learn of your oath of allegiance and devotion to His Majesty Mohammed V, Prince of the Faithful. For this King has sacrificed his person and his Throne for the good of his people and his country. Follow his example and be worthy of his confidence in you. May Allah guide you . . . Act in accordance with the words of Allah: 'O ye

Believers, obey Allah, obey the Prophet and your Rulers'. For
these are the words of the Koran . . .

It is easy to smile at all this archaic naiveté. All this seemed a
million miles away from the enlightened Westernism of a Bourguiba,
or from the Socialism or 'Labourism' of Mahjoub Ben Saddik, the
head of the Moroccan trade unions. But then a different vocabulary
was needed for different audiences; and there were many different
audiences in Greater Morocco. The important point of all this could
be found as one looked at the map of Africa: the Arab world had territorial ambitions; the Sultan of Morocco now wished to rule over territories stretching all the way to Senegal; there were to be no more
'colonial enclaves' between Arab Africa and Black Africa . . . And the
mineral wealth that was supposed to exist in the deserts of Mauretania
was an important element in the 'Great Morocco' plans . . .

During August, there were several Congresses: that of the National
Council of the Resistance Movement; that of the Istiqlal; that of the
Parti Démocratique d'Indépendence. The last-named was much milder
and 'gradualist' than the other two. The resolutions passed by the
Resistance people and the Istiqlal were almost identical, and did not
much differ from the main lines of Mahjoub Ben Saddik's arguments:
they stressed the need for Austerity; they insisted on the elimination
of all that was 'feudalist' in Morocco; they dwelt on economic
development and the nationalization of the major industries; they
demanded the rapid 'Arabization' and 'Moroccanization' of the
Administration.

The attitude to Nasser was much more openly sympathetic than
in Tunisia: with great approval he was quoted in *Al Allam* as saying:
'The Suez Canal belongs not only to Egypt, but to all the Arab countries.' And on behalf of the Executive Committee of the Istiqlal,
Mohamed Lyazidi sent on August 15 a message to Nasser saying that
the Istiqlal Party had called, throughout Morocco, a 'Solidarity-with-
Egypt' strike on the previous day—a strike which had been observed
everywhere—and assuring Nasser of the Moroccan people's total support for Egypt in her struggle for the Canal.

Al Allam's editorial the same day gloated over the way Nasser had
'twisted the British lion's tail'; and said that if France and Britain
attacked Nasser, it would mean their suicide.

At the National Resistance Congress the tone of the speeches was
violently anti-French. There were references to 'our brethren, the
Tunisian fighters for freedom', to 'the revolution of our Algerian
brethren', and to the savagery of the Colonialists who 'in their insane

rage' had mowed down hundreds of Moroccans in the streets of Casablanca, Oued Zem, Marrakesh, Fez, Kenitra and Khenifra, and who had torture chambers attached to the police stations, filled with children, innocent young people and suspects ... 'By this classical colonialist method they were trying to persuade the outer world that they still had the situation well in hand in Morocco.'

I had many talks with various members of the Istiqlal both at Rabat and Casablanca. I soon found that there were really two different types of Istiqlal people: some were 'spiritualists' (i.e., men believing in a specifically Mohammedan and Koranic culture and way of life, with a great sympathy for the Arab League and Nasser) and others who were 'materialists'. But the dividing line between the two was seldom very clear. One thing, however, seemed certain: the Sultan was scared of a preponderant influence of the Arab League and of Egypt, and was preferring to play ball with the West. Similarly (though for other reasons) the Trade Unions were looking to America, rather than to Egypt for moral (and perhaps financial) support. (The French, at any rate, were pretty categorical that the UMT was subsidized by the USA.)

The strongest pro-Egyptian tendency was represented by Allal el Fassi, who was living most of the time in Cairo, with frequent visits to Madrid. The rôle of Franco in the recent developments in Morocco was hard to assess; but he had created the legend of being more 'pro-Arab' than the French ...

Most of the Istiqlal people I saw were of the 'materialist', rather than of the 'spiritualist' school of thought. They were greatly taken with the 'Austerity' slogan, and spoke volubly of the 'feudal forces' which were now trying to 'regroup'. They hinted that there was 'definite collusion' between the PDI and certain feudal lords and the reactionary governors of certain provinces.

The French, they said, were, of course, still backing all that was 'most reactionary in the country'.

'Frankly,' one Istiqlal leader told me, 'we don't much believe in close collaboration with France; nor do we think that the French believe in it very much. "Interdependence" was merely a slogan invented by Edgar Faure to camouflage the awful fiasco of his Moroccan policy, when he *had* to bring the Sultan back. We are perfectly willing to be "interdependent" with all countries. And we certainly have some very nasty memories of the nefarious rôle played in Morocco in the last ten years or so by certain Frenchmen. And some of them—members of the *Présence*

Française—are still holding their posts in the Moroccan Administration; it's not good enough.

'Of course, we are perfectly willing to keep those French officials who will honestly and conscientiously contribute to the prosperity of Morocco. But we don't want this mob of 30,000 French officials we've still got here. It's a bit ironical that the Moroccan State should pay French officials the "insecurity bonuses" created in 1953—considering that the French themselves are to blame for the insecurity. And why should we have to pay their *tiers colonial* and their holidays in France, complete with children's governesses and what-not? As things are at present, no Austerity policy is possible . . . And why should Morocco continue to be the playground for all sorts of French profiteers and racketeers—for instance certain eminent Radical politicians (need I name them?) owning the gambling dens and the brothels of Fedala [the "Brighton" of Casablanca]. You've heard of the Sphinx, haven't you? And we are also pretty fed-up with having to pay pensions to retired French generals. They have to be paid 175,000 francs a month for doing nothing, while a baker's assistant has to live on 12,000 . . . The whole question of property must be reconsidered in Morocco.

'That old scoundrel, the Glaoui thought he could save his property for his family by crawling on his belly before the Sultan —when at last he realized which way the wind was blowing. Don't you make any mistake about it! All the things that the Glaoui stood for will be scrapped. It was a healthy sign when, last May, several supporters of the Glaoui were massacred in Marrakesh. His son Ibrahim escaped by the skin of his teeth.

'The administrative conventions with France, which will shortly be signed, give us a certain latitude, all the same, for reorganizing the administration. In our educational system there are still far too many Frenchmen: some have even recently been brought to Morocco. It's not true what some of the French say— that we are going to close down the French schools and prohibit the teaching of French in Morocco. But now that we are independent the French have got to submit. If they want to run specifically French schools for their children, we don't mind; but what business of theirs is it if our Minister of Education is what they call "*un arabisant*"?

'And then there's still the French Army here—90,000 men— and there's the French police. In theory, it's under the authority of the Moroccan Sureté—in reality, it's under the thumb of the French Embassy.'

Much of this talk was a little amateurish and unrealistic. The next few weeks were to show that the Sultan was in no hurry to give way to the Istiqlal all along the line. The Sultan was willing to become a 'constitutional monarch' in time; but he did not consider conditions ripe for an election on Western lines, and for a proper Parliament; he was, instead, in favour of setting up an Advisory Council of 76 members, representative of all currents of opinion, but appointed by himself. It was not likely that there would be a parliament before 1959 or 1960.

One day I had a long talk with Pierre Parent, a legendary character in Morocco. He had lost one arm in the 1914-18 war, had settled in Morocco soon afterwards, was a passionate pro-Moroccan, and, having no family of his own, had virtually adopted the 10 children of his Moroccan gardener and labourers. He was expelled from Morocco, as an Istiqlal sympathizer, in 1952 and was not allowed to return until 1955. Now he was working on the Moroccan State Radio.

How was it, I asked him, that the Sultan, who had been mercilessly kicked about by the French in 1953, still seemed to be on reasonably good terms with them?

'The Sultan really has a sort of mystical belief in himself,' said Parent. 'He has a deep sense of mission, and feels that his misfortunes were, somehow, an inseparable part of his historic destiny. Therefore he is not at all guided by personal grievances or a desire for revenge.'

Parent thought the Istiqlal—though he was fully in sympathy with them—were perhaps exaggerating the villainy of the Independents and the *Parti Démocratique*. The mass of the people were, of course, behind the Istiqlal; but much of the *petite* and *moyenne bourgeoisie* were more favourable to the Independents and the 'Democrats'. He did not think much of the French *fonctionnaires* in Morocco today. 'The *vieux Marocains* are disheartened by the results of the insane policy pursued by France in Morocco since the last war; and the younger people have just lost interest. They are hanging on for the time being, collecting their pay at the end of the month, but feeling it isn't really their show any longer . . .'

I could not help feeling a good deal of sympathy for some of the younger officials I met at the French Embassy—about the only building in the whole Residence quarter at Rabat still flying a French, and not a Moroccan flag. Some of them had come here with Grandval, and all of them spoke of the insane policy of 1952-55 which had landed France in its present predicament in Morocco. They still seemed to hope that the Sultan would not give way to the extreme demands of the Istiqlal. Some of the Istiqlal people were completely crazy. They, too, referred to the mad scheme put forward by the Arab League for creating a 'pool' of Arab technicians who would replace European technicians in all the Arab-speaking countries. Today 80 per cent of all technicians in Morocco were still French, and it would take years to replace them by Arabs. Even the Moroccan Army—now numbering 17,000—was largely French-trained; it was composed of Moroccan *cadres* who had served in the French Army, and of the *goums*, to whom had latterly been added certain elements of the Liberation Army.

I remarked that, as distinct from Tunisia, the Moroccans tended to 'talk big' about the immense wealth of Morocco.

'That,' said one of my French friends, 'is largely our own fault. It is we who built up this myth of the boundless wealth of Morocco. No doubt, Morocco has far greater possibilities than either Tunisia or Algeria, but it'll take an infernal lot of money to develop Morocco and especially what they call "Greater Morocco", and to raise the living standard of the Moroccan people.'

'What about French Big Business in Morocco; is it true that they want to stay and, if necessary, even to play ball with the Istiqlal, and with the "homogeneous" "Austerity" government of which there's so much talk today?'

'The industrial groups in Morocco are living in hopes. They are not liquidating their property in Casablanca and other places. They're hoping, but without much conviction, that everything will turn out all right. In some enterprises relations between French and Moroccans continue to be quite correct; but in others they are pretty strained. And if there *is* a "homogeneous" government with its vast social programme, its land reforms, its sequestration of "irregularly acquired property", it'll become hard for business firms to hang on . . .'

'How are your personal contacts with Moroccans?' I asked.

'Well, there are Moroccans and Moroccans. In the days of Arafa personal contacts between French and Moroccans stopped practically completely. Now there is a marked improvement. Contact has been re-established between French and Moroccan intellectuals. There's a French-trained—even if anti-French—élite among Moroccans who like to mix with the French. But, politically speaking, this doesn't go very far . . . And things have lately got worse again, because of Algeria. They've started screaming a good deal about Algeria; and now that they think that Nasser is getting away with it, many Moroccans are becoming pretty arrogant again—I mean those who adopted a very cautious and discreet line when it seemed Britain and France were going to crack Nasser over the head, good and hard . . . From the French point of view, it was very important that there should be a sharp reaction from the West. It'll be a great pity if, in the end, Nasser *does* get away with it.'

Flying over the uniformly brown Spanish landscape in the Casablanca-Bordeaux plane some days later, I tried to sum up my impressions of those two months in North Africa. And I could not think about it without a touch of melancholy. Looking down at Spain (we had just seen the dim silhouette of Toledo in the distance) I recalled my own experiences in Spain in 1937. How strongly one felt about things in those days! How beautifully clear-cut the issues were! We had to fight Fascism—and that's all there was to it. We were on the side of the angels. But North Africa? Who was right? Who was wrong? I put to myself the hypothetical question: if you had to choose between fighting for the Arabs against the French, or the French against the Arabs, which side would you choose? There could be no question of wanting to fight for the 'colonialists', for Borgeaud and Blanchette. But there could be no question either of fighting against French conscripts.

For better or for worse, the Arab world was in a state of upheaval and revolution. Perhaps progressive forces would gain the upper hand. Men like Bourguiba and Mahjoub Ben Saddik were immensely impressive. Colonialism was dying; but would *they* replace it? Would North Africa, in the end, co-exist constructively with Europe, with economic advantages being gained by both?

One thing was certain: it was essential to put an end to the war in Algeria. And then, only then could France hope to make the Arabs forget the errors and follies of the last century, and especially of the last decade. Perhaps then, too, the Arabs would feel that they had something to be thankful for to France.

*　　*　　*

Looking back on this North-African inquiry a year later, it is obvious that the human, political, racial, social, economic and trade union problems have remained the same—still unsolved, but rendered still more acute in all three countries by the perpetuation of the war in Algeria.

PART VIII

THE SUEZ DEBATE
ALGERIAN WAR FOR EVER?

THE SUEZ DEBATE
ALGERIAN WAR FOR EVER?

THE two most characteristic features of France during 1956 and 1957 were her obsession with Algeria and her anti-Islam *mystique*. Apart from the Communists (who were taking the usual doctrinaire anti-colonialist line) there was extremely little opposition to either the pursuit of the war in Algeria or its corollary, the Suez Adventure. The Mollet Government were even more keen on this than the British Government, and Mauriac was right when he wrote that 'if, in the past, the British usually had us in tow, this time it is the feeble and inept Mollet Government which converted that nice gentleman, Sir Anthony Eden, to its own way of thinking.'

'Crack Nasser over the head, and it'll be the end of the war in Algeria'—or what Lacoste called *le préalable égyptien*—had become an *idée fixe* with Mollet, Pineau and so many other French leaders, who fully shared the views so widely expressed to me when I was in Algiers in August 1956.

There was in France nothing to equal the Labour opposition to the Suez operation. Even Mendès-France seemed for a time to hesitate and to have become conscious of the anti-Nasser feeling in the country, which had been created by practically the entire press, including even such previously unorthodox papers as *Combat* and *Le Monde*. He pulled his punches. It was not until a few days before the Suez operation was to be launched (and this had by now become almost an open secret) that he called on Mollet and warned him against the terrible dangers of a fiasco. He proposed a top level Four Power conference, only to be told by Mollet that 'it would be insane to allow the Russians into the Middle East' in this manner. When, a few days later, Mollet announced before the National Assembly the Anglo-French ultimatum to Egypt 'and Israel', Mendès-France publicly refrained from speaking up; and, when the Suez operation failed, he did not contest that there was justification for the attack on Egypt, but confined himself to saying that it should have been launched immediately after Nasser's seizure of the Canal, and not three months later. . . .

391

Mendès was uncertain of himself. The Radical Congress at Lyons at the beginning of October had proved one thing: which was that the *mendésisme* of the Party had made no headway. Although the diehard *anti-mendésistes* had been eliminated a year before, a new strong anti-Mendès opposition had now crystallized, with M. André Morice as its leader. Worse still, practically all the Radical Ministers in the Mollet Government were hand-in-glove with Mollet, and were not taking the slightest notice of Mendès, whereas the Minister of Defence, M. Bourgès-Maunoury, ranked as one of the most determined Algerian and anti-Nasser diehards. This Congress marked, indeed, a further pulverization of that Radical Party which Mendès had tried to unify: a large fraction, led by Morice and Queuille simply formed a 'new' Radical Party, independent of Mendès.

Over the Socialist Party and its deputies Mollet continued to hold a firm grip, and the 'rebellion', led by André Philip, Daniel Mayer, Robert Verdier and a few others, was less effective than had been the opposition to the Mollet-Lacoste policy at the Socialist Congress at Lille in June. Even after the failure of the Suez operation, a large part of the French Socialist Party continued to share in Mollet's obstinate assertions that it had been right to embark on preventive action against Egypt. Nor did Mollet seem unduly perturbed by the violent criticism with which the French Socialist Party had met from the other Socialist Parties at the international meeting at Copenhagen in November. My-country-right-or-wrong moods, mixed up with all the *wrong* kind of anti-Americanism, were very strong in France after the Suez failure.

Nevertheless, when the great three-day debate on Suez opened at the National Assembly on December 18, the attitude to the Mollet Government was rather more critical than it had been before. The petrol shortage had demonstrated the Government's failure even to Mollet's best friends. It was also alleged that Mollet had deliberately misled Parliament.

In fact, on October 30, in announcing the Anglo-French ultimatum to Egypt and Israel, Mollet had said:

Our objectives are: to establish ourselves temporarily in the Canal's key positions: Port Said, Ismailia and Suez, in order to guarantee the free passage of ships of all nations;

On November 7, he had declared:

We consider that our targets have been satisfactorily reached. In a few hours our forces occupied Port Said and Port Fuad and are controlling a large stretch of the Canal. France and Britain have ordered their troops to cease fire.

And on December 4, Mollet had announced that the Suez affair had been handed over to U.N. and that the Anglo-French forces would be completely withdrawn. All these three decisions, on the face of it so strangely at variance with each other, had been taken without Parliament having been consulted in advance.

Moreover, more and more precise news had been leaking out about the collusion between France and Israel, prior to the Israeli attack on Egypt, complete with numerous details of the French airmen who had taken a more or less active part in this victorious operation against the Egyptian army in the Sinai desert.

As for North Africa, there were two outstanding facts: in October the French had seized the *Athos* off the coast of Orania; this ship was running arms to the Algerian rebels and was known to have come from Egypt.

Secondly, there was the famous case of the Sultan of Morocco's plane which, having been diverted from its course, was captured by the French military authorities of Algiers, with Ben Bella and four other leaders of the Algerian resistance on board. This was a serious matter. With the knowledge of Guy Mollet, the Sultan of Morocco had invited these rebel leaders to Rabat, where conversations had taken place in preparation for an unofficial conference at Tunis. Here the rebel leaders, the Sultan of Morocco and Bourguiba were to work out the basis of a general North African settlement, which would then be submitted to the French.

On October 22 the Sultan, Prince Moulay Hassan and the Algerian leaders were to fly from Rabat to Tunis. The Moroccans travelled in one plane, the Algerians in another. The latter plane belonged to Air-Atlas, a company owned by the Moroccan Government. The crew were, however, French, though, in a strictly legal sense, employees of the Moroccan State. After refuelling at Palma, Majorca, the two planes flew off to Tunis. It was then that a wireless message was received from Algiers by the pilot of the plane carrying the Algerian rebel leaders, instructing him to land at Algiers, instead of taking his passengers to Tunis. The French crew, feeling it was 'their duty to France' to obey the order, acted accordingly, the air hostess going so far as to announce, just as the plane was about to land at Algiers, that 'in a few minutes we shall land at

Tunis'. The man who had taken direct responsibility for this trick was M. Max Lejeune, Under-Secretary for War, and M. Lacoste hastened to 'cover' him. Mollet, impressed by all the hee-hawing this 'good practical joke' had produced, also hastened to approve, even though it meant another victory of the Algerian diehards over the supporters of a negotiated solution on the lines of the 'Bourguiba Plan' which the latter had already outlined to me in August.

The 'practical joke' ceased, however, to be funny before long. There were anti-French riots in Tunis and, worse still, large-scale massacres of French settlers in Morocco, particularly in the Meknès area. The Sultan, who looked upon the Algerian leaders as his guests, whose safety he had guaranteed, was mortally offended, and relations were practically broken off for a time between France on the one hand and Tunisia and Morocco on the other. M. Savary, the chief supporter in the French Government of a negotiated solution, resigned in disgust. Photographs appeared in all the papers of Ben Bella and the four other rebel leaders being taken handcuffed to prison in Algiers; and some days later they were flown to Paris and locked up at the *Santé*.

The whole gravity of the 'practical joke' was to become even more apparent later: the Ben Bella group *were* men who were willing to talk; they were to be replaced at the head of the rebellion by much more fanatical and irresponsible people.

Mollet had throughout been playing a 'double game' in the sense that he maintained indirect contact with the Algerian rebels. This was done partly to reassure any potential opposition inside the Socialist party; but, whatever his real intentions, he always submitted in the end to the diehard elements inside his own Party and his Government majority. Full details of Mollet's contacts with the Algerian rebels were published in December in the *Action* of Tunis, closely reflecting the views of Bourguiba.

In the course of 1956, said *Action*, the French Government had arranged four meetings between its representatives and the delegates of the F.L.N. (*Front Algérien de Libération Nationale*)

The first took place in Cairo on April 12, 1956; the second in Belgrade on June 11; the third in Rome on September 2; and the fourth in Belgrade on September 22. The last thus took place exactly a month before the Tunis Conference, the culmination of all these negotiations, and a month before Ben Bella and his four companions, officially recognized as the plenipotentiary representatives of Algeria, were intercepted and arrested.

M. Commin, Acting Secretary-General of the Socialist

Party since Mollet had become Prime Minister, stressed in the course of friendly correspondence with the delegation of F.L.N. —the letters still exist—that these contacts were official. The French were understood to have recognized Algeria's legitimate and natural claim to independence and to have declared that they were authorized to negotiate on that basis, the problem being to find the best methods for persuading French public opinion to accept this claim. At the fourth and last meeting, held in Belgrade on September 22, 1956, it is said to have ended with the French representative asking for time to consult his Government, and the negotiators parting after having stated their 'points of agreement' and having recognized the need for further meetings.

Exactly one month later, M. Lacoste 'calmly violated' (as *Action* put it) international law by intercepting in a foreign plane the men to whom he had issued safe-conduct passes. Under Right-wing pressure, M. Mollet gave his full approval to this new course.

The substance of these revelations was not very different from what had transpired from other sources, inside and outside France, about these contacts between the Mollet Government and the French Socialists on the one hand and the Algerian rebels on the other.

Anyway, the Sultan of Morocco considered the 'joke' such an act of treachery on the part of the French Government—not to mention the French employees of the Moroccan State—that, for several weeks, he refused to meet any Frenchmen, with the sole exception of François Mauriac. During the hour the latter spent with him, the Sultan would speak of nothing except the appalling violation of the most elementary laws of Moslem hospitality of which, owing to the French, he (the Sultan) had been guilty *vis-à-vis* his Algerian guests. It was like an obsession with him.

*　　　*　　　*

A year had passed since the day when Mollet, as leader of the Republican Front, had declared:

The first duty of the Government that will be formed after the Election will be to re-establish peace in North Africa. What we must do before anything else is to stop lying, and stop falling into the old errors of Indo-China, Tunisia and Morocco. Of course, we must protect the Algerian populations, but we must stop all this blind and insane repression. All that the Algerians wanted was to be French, to be our equals inside a Republic truly based on liberty, equality and fraternity. But we lied to them, and they no longer believe us. What they want now is to be treated as free human beings. Theirs is not an isolated case. It is part of a world-wide movement.

And now, on December 18, the National Assembly was going to take stock of the situation that had arisen in the world as a result of Suez and as a result of the Hungarian revolt . . . and with the Algerian war still in full swing.

Little need be said about Hungary, which took up the first few hours of the debate. Numerous speakers denounced Soviet treachery, while M. Bidault concentrated on showing up the lamentable helplessness displayed by U.N. in the Hungarian tragedy. Others stressed the completely cynical attitude adopted by the French Communist leadership and the profound bewilderment caused by the case of Hungary among the Communist rank-and-file, and particularly among the intellectuals.

M. Pineau, the Foreign Minister, concluded on a more conciliatory note. While regretting that U.N. could impose its will on the Democracies, whereas it was helpless in relation to the Soviet dictatorship, he still hoped that, through arduous negotiations, the Western Powers might yet persuade the Russians to agree to a neutral, 'Austrian' status for Hungary.

The rest of the three-day debate was, however, devoted almost entirely to Suez. As was remarked in the French press, the debate was really a trial of the Mollet Government; but in the end, as was to be foreseen, it was acquitted.

Not that Mollet and Pineau were not spared some sharp criticisms even from many of those who voted for the 'acquittal' in the end; but, by and large, a certain feeling of 'national solidarity' in conjunction with less disinterested sentiments prevailed. For one thing, as Paul Reynaud remarked, with remarkable candour, in an otherwise highly critical speech, there was no use denying *that practically everybody in France had been anxious, in August, to 'have a crack at Nasser'*.

Moreover, there was another important psychological element that played into the hands of Mollet and Pineau: and that was the feeling that they had, as best they could, stood up to both U.N. and the United States. They had voiced France's grievances and her sense of 'solitude', and had protested against the 'lack of solidarity' shown by the U.S.A. in the case of Suez. Though fairly subtly, both Pineau and Mollet played on the anti-American string, and this went down well at the National Assembly.

And finally, there was this: the world situation had deteriorated to such an extent that the time had come for a variety of reassessments: what was to be the future of the Atlantic Alliance? What were to be future relations with the U.S.A.? After Hungary, the Cold War had threatened to start up again in Europe, and what was to be France's policy *vis-à-vis* Germany and N.A.T.O.? Various more or less new ideas were put forward; other, older ideas, were being revived. Mendès-France placed the emphasis on a New Deal in Africa; Robert Schuman on a New Deal in 'Eurafrica'; Paul Reynaud spoke in terms of reviving 'Europe' on a grander model than before.

Mollet had also tried to benefit from the traditional cynicism that had always existed on the Right in relation to international organizations like the League of Nations or U.N., a cynicism which, in this case, was widely shared by others. Nor did he even draw the line at defending the principle of preventive war and at invoking, in this connection, the authority of . . . Léon Blum! As a piece of French national psychology, the line taken by Mollet and Pineau to justify their Suez adventure is very curious to examine. Needless to say, neither of them tried to deny that Algeria had not played an important part in the French decision, and that, if the Suez adventure had failed, it was, *in the first place*, the fault of the non-conformism of the British Labour Party.

The debate on Suez proper started with a highly critical speech by M. Isorni, the leading *pétainiste* at the Assembly. He recalled that, on October 30, the Assembly had condoned the ultimatum to Egypt, 'though in silence, and without practically knowing anything about the circumstances surrounding it'. He now, however, wished to know why six days had elapsed between the ultimatum to Nasser and the landing of the Anglo-French troops in Egypt. If there were military difficulties, why had these not been foreseen? Also, why had no simultaneous landing been prepared at the south end of the Canal?

In addition to Bulganin's threat, had there not also been a secret American message? And was it proper that this operation should be carried out without the U.S.A. having been informed? *If* it was true that Israel was about to be attacked by Egypt, in conjunction with Soviet 'volunteers', then the Anglo-French action was legitimate; but what was the evidence? The trouble, in any case, was that, with the U.S.A. trying to prevent the Arab countries from joining the Soviet bloc, it was willing to sacrifice Algeria.

M. de Menthon (M.R.P.) said that the Suez adventure had ended

2A

badly; and he blamed the Government for not having taken any precautions in respect of France's oil supplies. The fact remained, however, that if the Anglo-French had not acted, and had tolerated the American and U.N. delaying tactics to continue, they would have been faced with an Egyptian *coup de force*. 'The Anglo-French operation has failed. But we cannot but appreciate the courage of *a decision which had, we must admit, been approved by French public opinion*.'

¦¦ The Suez affair had, however, demonstrated the failure of the *Entente Cordiale*, which was about as out-of-date a conception as *la France seule*. He therefore argued in favour of undertaking a rapid integration of Europe, complete with economic unity, Common Market and Euratom. Simultaneous political unification, he said, must also be pursued; if Suez put life into Europe, it would prove a good thing on balance.

The unification of Europe was also the keynote of M. Robert Schuman's speech. He thought that, as a result of Suez, France had entered a blind alley; and there was no possible return to the *status quo*. No doubt, he said, much had lately been said about a reform of U.N. and of a reform of the Atlantic Pact. But such a reform was impossible without the consent of the U.S.A.

> For our own part, we cannot accept a withdrawal of the Russian troops in Hungary and Poland in return for our withdrawal from Germany. This would only strengthen Russia's strategic position. As for West-European Union, none of the agreements provided for in the Paris Treaty have yet materialized. . . . A European Community must be formed which would be open to all free countries and to all countries hoping to acquire their freedom. It should be possible, right now, to give European citizenship, for instance, to the Hungarian refugees. The Government's plans for a common market and for Euratom should be supplemented by Eurafrica, without which we shall be building on sand.

And M. Schuman advocated the formation of a permanent European Council of Ministers, 'which would meet periodically and which would be consulted in any matter vital to the European community. This would strengthen Europe's position at U.N.' There should also, he said, be a European Assembly elected by universal suffrage.

More notable still was the speech by M. Paul Reynaud, who sharply criticized the manner in which the Suez affair had been conducted. The National Assembly, he said, had not wanted to

disavow the Government the day it had launched its ultimatum
to Nasser.

> *Let's face it: In August we were all extremely anxious to see
> the Government act and overthrow Nasser. But the manner in
> which this was to be done, and the timing were both of the utmost
> importance, and the Government's choice of these was most
> unfortunate. The Government had overlooked the fact that we
> are no longer in the days of the Crimean War.*
>
> France and Britain cannot act alone these days. It is in our
> interests to resume confident relations with the U.S.A. I know
> that, to produce applause these days at a public meeting, one
> has to be rude about the U.S.A. and about U.N.

On balance, M. Reynaud said, it was in France's interests to
stay at U.N. After all, the creation of a U.N. police force for Egypt
showed that even delinquents like France and Britain could be of
value to the cause of U.N.! But it was, of course, essential that the
U.N. force should stay in Egypt as long as no lasting peace had been
established between Israel and the Arab countries. And M. Reynaud
concluded on the 'European' note:

> If there had been a united Europe, there would have been
> no Suez operation. Let us quickly ratify Euratom and the
> Common Market, and let us also work on the political unifica-
> tion of Europe. . . . In twenty years from now there will be
> 48 million people in North Africa. France cannot by herself
> afford to develop and finance it. You must create Eurafrica.
> And I say to the gentlemen on the Government bench: 'Hurry;
> because your time is limited—in every sense.'

M. Pineau, the Foreign Minister, ill at ease, defended the Suez
operation as best he could. He argued that, in the case of Israel,
the term 'preventive war' did not apply. Nasser was aggressive both
towards Israel and towards France: the *Athos* affair had clearly
shown what his intentions were. Nasser, he then said, had threatened
to block the Canal, and in view of the helplessness of U.N., it was
essential for France and Britain to act. If they had rapidly captured
the whole Canal Zone, all would have been well.

Unfortunately, the British decided on a premature cease-fire,
which it was impossible for France to disavow. He attributed this
unhappy British decision to four factors, in the following order of
importance:

1. The uproar in Britain, so contrary to the usual unity of
British parliamentary and public opinion;

2. American pressure which, in this case, had rendered a poor service to the cause of peace;
3. Pressure from U.N., whose recommendations it was, after all, difficult for France to ignore; and finally
4. The Soviet threat.

Pineau made no reference to Bulganin's 'hypothetical' threat to bomb Britain, but merely said that the Russian threat was not a very serious one. The most the Russians could have done was to bomb Cyprus and Tel Aviv, but even this was unlikely; and even if they had, the Anglo-French forces, he said, could still have occupied the whole of the Suez Zone in a few days.

In short, he said, if Britain and France had not attacked Egypt, Nasser would have chosen his own time—and Moscow's time—for striking. No doubt the petrol shortage was bound to have a serious effect on France's economy, but it was a short-term problem; and what certainty was there that it would not have arisen in any case?

After a piece of bravado about Nasser's 'loss of face', M. Pineau rather meekly concluded that France had accepted the resolution of the Security Council, which had been vetoed by the Soviet Union. The principles which the Russians had not vetoed were not, however, sufficient to establish an international control over Suez, and alternative solutions would have to be thought of now that the 1888 Convention had been so ruthlessly violated by Nasser: for instance an intensification of oil prospecting in the Sahara and the building of new pipelines across Turkey and Israel.

Pineau then spoke more in sorrow than in anger of America's attitude; but thought the 'misunderstandings' were beginning to be cleared up. On the question of whether America had been informed of the Suez operation, he was extremely evasive, leaving this awkward point for Mollet to deal with.

Mollet, speaking with a somewhat artificial air of supreme authority (so typical of the manner he had developed in the last few months), began by admitting that *Algeria had, of course, a great deal to do with the French decision to intervene in Egypt.*

If France were to abandon Algeria, it would merely mean that she was abandoning the whole of Africa, and surrendering it to the Soviet Union. Russia which is already threatening to turn Europe's defences by way of the Middle East, could then encircle Europe by way of Africa.

Mollet denied, however, that Algeria had been the only, or even the chief reason of France's attack on Egypt; for whatever had been the result of the Suez operation, Algeria would still have remained a problem to be settled in agreement with its own inhabitants.

We were, first and foremost, guided by a sort of anti-Munich reflex . . . We were determined not to submit to Nasser's threats and blackmail . . . Those who think any comparisons between Nasser and Hitler far-fetched must remember that if Hitler had to wait till 1939 before he had his Soviet-German Pact, the Nasser-Shepilov agreement came much sooner.

Although Mollet did not make it at all clear what exactly this Nasser-Shepilov agreement had provided for, there was 'stormy applause on the Left, Centre and Right'. Again Mollet sounded the Israel theme.

Today there are some who blame Britain, France and Israel for what has happened. Israel is being blamed for having fore-stalled the attack on it; the others for having limited the damage. If we had done nothing, and Israel had been crushed, how much more we would have been blamed! Should we have waited for the day when we would have wrung our hands helplessly over a destroyed Israel just as today we are weeping over a martyred Hungary? (*Loud cheers*).

And then came the defence of the 'preventive war' principle. This defence took a strange form: Mollet, still sticking through thick and thin to the Nasser-Hitler parallel, recalled that in 1946 Léon Blum had declared that, 'in all conscience' he believed World War II could have been avoided if in 1933 France, Britain and Poland had occupied Germany! And the movement in favour of this operation, Blum had said, should have been conducted by the British and French Socialist Parties!

After referring to the petrol shortage which was, however, less serious in present circumstances than it would have been 'if the Soviet Union had moved its Nasser pawn at the height of some international crisis, thus depriving us of our oil supplies', and deploring the 'double standard' that U.N. was applying to the democracies and the dictators, Mollet criticized the United States for allowing itself to be deceived by the 'uncommitted' States, all of which were, however, playing a double or even a triple game. What was the use of trying to win over Nasser, who was completely in Russia's pocket?

Later, in answering M. Edgar Faure, M. Mollet was even more explicit about his attitude to the United States, and could not refrain from embarking on a curious piece of anti-American demagogy:

On July 27 France and Britain informed the United States that they were preparing for every emergency. We were convinced ever since that day that the nationalization of the Canal was merely a first stage. What the next stage would be we didn't know: it might be an attack on Israel or the Sudan, or the prohibition for British and French ships to sail through the Canal. We made it perfectly clear to the Americans that we would not tolerate this 'second stage' of Nasser's operation, whatever it was. *But when our final decision to act was taken, we did not inform the Americans. We were deeply convinced that if we had, there would have been new delays, new conferences, and that, in the process, Israel was in danger of being wiped off the face of the earth. . . . And when the Americans asked us to explain our attitude, I told them quite frankly: You would have prevented us from acting; and we did not want to wait again, as we had already waited from* 1914 *to* 1917 *and from* 1939 *to* 1942. (Loud cheers on Right, Left and Centre).

He concluded by saying that he had the impression that 'our American friends, in the end, had understood and appreciated France's motives'.

Perhaps the strangest thing of all about that debate on Suez was the fact that the two men who really attempted to get down to fundamentals should have been the two 'enemy brothers'—Edgar Faure and Mendès-France. Both of them, more than any other speakers, tried to examine what had happened against the background of the broader world situation, as it appeared to them at the end of 1956, and to draw conclusions which the others had evaded. Both, in particular, brought the Algerian skeleton out of the cupboard. Mollet and Pineau had concentrated so much on the virtues of the Suez operation that it almost looked as though they were trying to forget the one problem which would continue to haunt France for years to come if nothing decisive were done about it.

Edgar Faure had not spoken at the Assembly ever since the General Election of the previous January.

He began by saying that, of all the Powers concerned, Israel alone had come out of the Suez ordeal with a creditable record. Israel had rebelled against the refusal of U.N. or anyone else to support her just claims and had done much to lower Nasser's prestige by defeating the Egyptians in the Sinai desert. The Anglo-French, on the other hand, had merely given Nasser an excuse to explain away the defeat of his army by saying that Egypt had been attacked by two of the Great Powers. Their rash action had, more-over, undermined their strong case in favour of the internationaliza-tion of the Suez Canal.

France, M. Faure said, had one very strong case against Egypt, but only one: and that was the *Athos* affair. Instead of exploiting this case, France had based her action on much more dubious arguments: the need to safeguard the freedom of navigation (with results that were disastrous) and the need to stop hostilities between Egypt and Israel.

After criticizing Mollet's 'absurd policy *vis-à-vis* the U.S.A.', Faure declared that the operation had 'not only been badly con-ceived, but equally badly executed'. There had been lack of co-ordina-tion between the British and French Governments, both of whom might have foreseen all the factors which forced the premature cease-fire on them.

In short, France had lost her case; and what was particularly serious in this was the fact that France would be in a much worse position now to 'face her second trial': the discussion of Algeria before U.N. In order not to weaken the Government on the eve of this ordeal, M. Faure said, he was still willing to vote for it; but this did not invalidate his fundamental criticism.

M. Mollet angrily protested against this, saying that the line adopted by M. Faure tended to discredit the Government in foreign eyes and cast doubts on *the general support it was enjoying in the country*. He said he would rather Faure voted against the Government.

Actually, M. Faure's speech was one of the few genuine pro-tests against the atmosphere of 'national-unity-in-a-bad-cause' with which the Mollet Government had tried to surround the Suez debate.

In the course of his speech, M. Faure had raised another impor-tant point: the vital necessity for Europe to embark on a vast pro-gramme of economic aid to underdeveloped countries like Egypt, a programme in return for which these countries should refrain from embarking on military adventures and from becoming involved in power politics.

For the first time since the fall of his Government nearly two years before, Mendès-France made a major parliamentary speech. This was a trenchant analysis of the world situation and of the causes and consequences of Suez, all of which was in the best tradition of his Opposition speeches of 1951, 1952 and 1953.

He said that the end of 1956 marked a turning point in the diplomatic history of the post-war world. In the last ten years, the world had been dominated by the formation and, later, by the opposition of the Big Two Blocs. It was true that, since 1954, there had been a *détente*: but, unfortunately, nothing was done during this relatively short period to solve any fundamental problems in the world: such as Germany, Eastern Europe, or disarmament.

France, absorbed with her domestic and Algerian problems, had done no more than any other country to propose any far-reaching solutions on a world scale. The *détente*, instead of being constructive, had been merely 'passive and conservative'. For everybody, it had, no doubt, been a pleasant change from the Cold War; but it had gone no further. Both the Soviet Union and the U.S.A. seemed content to let the world live in a kind of pleasant but atrophied state. For the Big Two, at any rate, this *status quo*, while it lasted, was quite satisfactory, complete with a tacit understanding about their two respective spheres of influence.

It was not the same for countries like Britain and France, with their colonial empires in a state of ferment, their excessive military expenditure and a variety of other difficulties.

Yet the Big Two preferred that nothing should be done to upset the 'equilibrium', no matter how precarious. That was why (for it was scarcely a coincidence) Russia and America almost simultaneously refused to build the Aswan Dam.

Each one perhaps had realized that the scheme was so gigantic that the attempt by either of them to monopolize it would have such far-reaching political repercussions in a strategically-vital part of the world that the other was sure, sooner or later, to take exception to it. The unilateral domination of East Africa by any one of the Big Two would upset the 'equilibrium'.

But here, said Mendès-France, was another example which affected France even more closely: and that was the tacit decision by the Big Two not to show any serious interest in French North Africa, and to let France settle the problem there. It was a thousand pities that France had not made use of that dual Russian-American attitude during the greater part of 1956.

Both to Russia and to America the Anglo-French landing in Port Said was a flagrant violation of the 'equilibrium'. Russia could already see Britain re-established along the Canal; while the U.S.A., which, to appease the Russians, had abandoned the Aswan Scheme, was not going to condone something that was bound to worry the Russians far more than Aswan. *Suez, in short, did not divide Russia and America; on the contrary, it tended to unite them, at least for a time. This unity had lasted long enough to make the Suez operation the failure it was.*

Our aims were to internationalize the Canal, or at least to guarantee its freedom of navigation; to discredit Nasser and eliminate him from public life; and to intimidate the Arab world, above all in French North Africa, so as to facilitate an Algerian settlement. The failure has been complete all along the line. . . .

The consequences of all this, Mendès said, were very serious for France in many fields: the fact that French airmen had (secretly) taken part in the Israeli attack on Egypt would not be forgotten by the Arabs; and the destruction or confiscation of all the French schools in Egypt and Syria meant a tragic set-back for France's cultural influence in the Middle East; 60,000 pupils would, probably for ever, be deprived of a French education.

It was unfortunate that the Government should have resorted to the unworthy subterfuge of saying that the Anglo-French forces had 'forestalled' a Russian attack in the Middle East. The truth was—and that was Washington's view—that Russian military influence in Syria and Egypt had not become strong until the last few weeks— *since Suez.*

Mendès then criticized Mollet's defence of the principle of the preventive war: for France to accept such a principle was to break away from a very long and honourable tradition of legality; it was scandalous that such ideas should now be defended by the country of the Briand-Kellogg Pact.

Almost as strange was the campaign started against the Atlantic Pact—and at a time when France needed more than ever the political and economic support of the United States. No doubt America's attitude to Nasser had both encouraged and provoked him; and it was a pity that the U.S.A. should not have reacted m ore vigorously on July 26. But that was no reason why France should have ignored the U.S.A. in taking so grave a step as the Suez operation. The fact that France was now getting a little petrol from the U.S.A. did not signify that the crisis of the Atlantic Alliance was finished. France's position would remain particularly difficult so long as she had to depend on American oil supplies, and on U.S.A. dollar supplies to pay for them!

At the same time, the unilateral action in Egypt had gravely undermined France's position at U.N. where she had always ranked as a defender of international law and order. Now a vast anti-French bloc was being formed at U.N., and even in Europe many of France's friends had been discouraged.

And now Mendès came to one of his main conclusions (which at least on a short-term basis, was to prove wrong). Never had the situation at U.N. been less favourable for a discussion of Algeria there.

> For months I have been warning the Government against a U.N. discussion of Algeria, and have been urging it to find the necessary solutions independently of U.N. To do nothing, is to ask for trouble both on the spot and internationally. The coming U.N. debate has been a further excuse for doing nothing. What we should do, on the contrary, is to act promptly in Algeria itself, to get in touch with the Moslem masses, and take advantage of the help offered us in this by Morocco and Tunisia. Even if they do not see eye-to-eye with us on all points, we have many interests in common. . . .
>
> Like France, these two countries have reason to fear certain pressures from the East. Like Bourguiba, I believe in a North African federation which would work in close harmony with France and would constitute a West-Arab unit, which would itself constitute a barrier against pressure from Egypt and other Eastern countries.

Mendès-France said that he had, at one time, even hoped that Tunisia and Morocco would not press for a discussion of the Algerian problem at U.N.; unfortunately their temper changed as a result of the Ben Bella Incident.

All this part of Mendès's speech was interspersed with much heckling from the Poujadists:

> 'All right, let's all get out of Algeria!'
> 'You'll safeguard our interests as well as you safeguarded them in Indo-China!'
> 'Oh, tell him to stop! He makes us sick!'
> 'Oh, shut up!'

and similar pieces of amiable *badinage*.

He went on, however. While saying that he wasn't quite sure what the still unexplored oil reserves of the Sahara[1] really were, he thought that the development of the Sahara could not be carried on without the closest co-operation between France and the Mediterranean countries—Tunisia, Algeria and Morocco—through which the pipelines would inevitably run.

[1] Mollet had inflated the Sahara problem to such an extent that the current wisecrack in Paris was: '*L'avenir de la France, c'est le Sahara!*'

The trouble, he said, was that Algeria was poisoning France's relations with both the Arab world and with Israel—since France was still trying to appease the Arabs, in spite of everything. As a result Israel was being merely treated as a pawn by France, as well as by other countries. Yes, said Mendès-France, it would have been much more effective as a retort to Nasser if, instead of landing troops in Egypt, France had built a pipeline across Israel from the Gulf of Aqaba to Haifa—even despite the opposition of certain oil interests.

M. Pineau interrupted, and said that such a pipeline was, in fact, on the point of being started.

Mendès-France replied that, for once, he was glad to have been wrong.

He concluded by reiterating his regrets that his advice should not have been followed to press for a Big Four conference in October. Now, as a result of Suez, France's weight as a Great Power had greatly diminished, and there was also a constant danger of Russia and America reaching agreements over the heads of the smaller Powers.

And such agreements, I fear, might some day extend to matters that concern us directly, such as Germany and North Africa. . . . The very fact that the U.S.A. is not keen on a Big Four conference ominously suggests that it prefers a *tête-à-tête* with Russia.

And he called for a bold and imaginative French foreign policy; but before she could carry much weight in the world, France must quickly settle the Algerian conflict.

Then, and only then, will France's voice regain, in every corner of the globe, its past credit and authority, both of which are so necessary to the consolidation of world peace.

How different was the frigid reception given by the Assembly to Mendès's speech from the enthusiasm with which a large part of the Assembly used to listen to his speeches before and during his 1954 premiership! No doubt they listened with great attention, but when it was over, there was only some thin applause from some of the Radical benches, and from a few 'undisciplined' Socialists. And that was all.

As a deliberate demonstration, Guy Mollet had walked out of the Assembly just as Mendès-France was about to start his speech. 'I'm off. I've got work to do,' he said.

Although in the opinion of most, Mendès had pulled his punches, the Assembly still felt that he was not sufficiently conforming to the country-right-or-wrong attitude assumed by most. (Similarly, Edgar Faure had been given a very cool reception.)

Mendès-France who had once been called 'our most serious and lonely statesman,' was lonely, desperately lonely again. Apart from the Communists and the Poujadists (who now voted against the Government systematically) practically no one, except Mendès and fourteen other Radicals voted against the motion approving Mollet's foreign policy, including Suez.

A few days later, L'Express bravely tried to console itself by saying that the situation in France at the end of 1956 was typified by the loneliness of a few outstanding men. In the midst of the appalling conformism of the Mollet Epoch a few—very few—great lonely figures stood out: de Gaulle, and Mendès-France, and Paul Reynaud, and a small number of Socialists whose non-conformism had, however, been mercilessly crushed by the Mollet Machine (the Express might have added Edgar Faure, but didn't). Yet, it was only men like Mendès and Reynaud and André Philip, as the Express continued to point out, who, in these weeks after Suez, had done some hard and agonizing thinking on the wider issues of the complex and ominous world situation. All the others were either conformist in their dismal and unimaginative acceptance of the Mollet regime, or (like the Communists) equally conformist in their prefabricated criticisms. Mollet was meantime sticking to his 'triptych': cease-fire, Election, Negotiations for a New Statute. This was unacceptable to the Rebels, since it promised them nothing in advance.

* * *

As the year 1957 progressed, the solitude of Mendès-France in the French political scene was becoming almost absolute. The Radical Party had broken up into several splinter groups, and at the National Assembly Mendès had barely twelve followers; whenever he rose to speak, Guy Mollet invariably made a point of being absent.

Since Suez, financial, economic and international difficulties of all kinds had been piling up in France. Mendès-France now once again assumed the role of Cassandra; but this time he was a Cassandra almost without an audience. As Robert Barillon commented in the Monde of March 21 after Mendès's important speech the day before on the ominous economic prospects of France:

As usual, Guy Mollet wasn't there to hear Mendès speak. But those who were heard a moderate and well-constructed speech reminiscent of his Opposition speeches of 1950-53. . . .

In the past, such a speech would have aroused a storm of applause from hundreds of deputies. Now only some sixty deputies had taken the trouble to come at all, and out of these about ten clapped: a few Radicals, one or two Socialists and three or four Gaullists. . . .

For one thing, he had continued to make himself unpopular with the Mollet Government. He had trodden on its toes on the Suez issue; and he had made the most vital criticism of that Common Market, with which Mollet had sought to demonstrate once more his 'Europeanism'. But what was more damaging to him was the Paris by-election in January which showed not merely that Mendès had lost his old grip over Parliament, but that, for the time being, he had lost his popularity with a large part of the electorate.

The year had, indeed, begun badly for Mendès-France. The by-election in the First Paris sector (comprising the whole of the Left Bank) following the death of the Radical deputy, Moro-Giafferi, was like the low-water mark in Mendès-France's career. He wanted the dynamic J. J. Servan-Schreiber, newly back from Algeria, to stand as Radical candidate; but the local Radicals, many of them out of sympathy with Mendès-France, and even more so with Servan-Schreiber and all that L'Express stood for, would not hear of it, and put forward a rather colourless candidate, Stefanaggi. Although he had not been sponsored, in the first place, by Mendès-France, he called himself a 'mendésiste', and Mendès was prepared to do his best for him.

But already on January 5, at the first big meeting attended by Mendès, 'Fascist commandos' caused a major disturbance and almost broke up the gathering. The mass meeting at the Vélodrome d'Hiver, presided over by Mendès-France on January 10, was to prove still worse. The moment he appeared on the platform the Fascists (belonging to a group led by Tixier-Vignancour and Biaggi, a French-Algerian diehard), threw incendiary and tear-gas bombs into the crowded hall; chairs were thrown about; several persons were injured, there was a panic rush to the exits, and with the police arriving in force, the meeting was broken up in disorder, without anybody having been able to say a word—except Mendès-France, and he had only succeeded in shouting, 'Vote for Stefanaggi!' into the microphone. Several million francs' worth of damage was caused by the incendiary bombs.

The result of the election was to show a deplorable decline in the 'Mendès mystique' of January 2, 1956. The total of the Mendès vote had dropped from 17.5 per cent. in January 1956 to a mere 6 per

cent. in 1957. The Communist poll had dropped from 26 per cent. to
20 per cent.—which was a smaller drop than many had expected
after the crushing of Hungary. One had only to go to any of
Tardieu's (the victorious right-wing candidate's) meetings to hear
the whole emphasis placed on France's determination to 'keep
Algeria' and on the denunciation of the alleged 'policy of surrender'
practised by men like Mendès-France. At such meetings the patriotism of Mollet was praised at least as highly as at the meetings of
Mme Osmin, the Socialist candidate.

Mendès-France commented:

> Throughout the history of Paris, there has existed in the
> city a strong national or even nationalist current. The Socialist
> Party has improved its position. This election is a success for
> the Government, which has seen its Algerian policy approved.
> The electorate is thus likely to stimulate the Government's
> Algerian policy—a policy of which, as you know, I do not
> approve. The Press has not done its duty in enlightening the
> public on the real state of affairs in Algeria. We must make a
> special effort to persuade the public what must be done there,
> before it's too late. . . .

The great majority of public and parliamentary opinion persisted
in its determination to cling to Algeria, and it was this Algerian issue
which was, somehow, prolonging the unexpectedly and unusually
long life of the Mollet Government, and—although there was no
public enthusiasm for 'Europe' and the Common Market (any more
than there had been, in the past, for the Schuman Plan), Mollet, by
being a 'European', managed to secure for himself continued support
at least from the M.R.P. On the other hand, financial and economic
difficulties were piling up, and it was not the platitudinous optimism
of M. Ramadier that could disprove unpleasant hard facts of France's
dwindling foreign exchange assets, of a stupendous budget deficit
piling up for 1957, and of increasing all-round inflationary pressures.

After the U.N. Assembly—which was like a delayed-action
warning to France that something must be done about Algeria in
the coming six months—a rather morose atmosphere set in in Paris;
M. Lacoste was no longer quite the legendary Clemenceau-like
figure he had been; he had, for one thing, assured France, once
too often, that this was 'the last quarter-of-an-hour', of the war in
Algeria. But, on the other hand, there were the *ultras*, the violent
diehards in Algeria who, unmindful of the international aspects of
the whole problem, were embarking on terrorism and repression in
a big way.

Paris was to see in March–April a wave of angry protests against the 'tortures in Algeria'; but these protests were, in the main, still limited only to intellectuals who had read with sympathy and horror P. H. Simon's little book on the tortures practised by the police and the paratroopers in Algeria or the series of articles in *L'Express* by J. J. Servan-Schreiber (who had served for six months as a lieutenant in Algeria) on the trigger-happy ways of so many of the French troops there. These protests produced a wave of counter-protests from what the *Monde* was to describe as that 'new extreme-Right' which organized some violent demonstrations in the Champs-Elysées, smashed the plate-glass windows of the *Express* offices, and shouted words of savage abuse at Mauriac and Mendès-France. For, to these people, Mendès-France continued to be the favourite symbol of anti-patriotism, defeatism, and 'un-French activities'.

In fact, all the stories of tortures and wanton killings that were to be published for some weeks still failed to create a nation-wide movement in favour of peace in Algeria, or even a nation-wide moral protest.

With a gesture of discouragement, a close friend of Mendès's remarked to me one day: 'Although history books suggest that the whole of France was in a state of uproar over the Dreyfus case, the truth is that the general public didn't give a hang one way or the other. It's the same with these tortures in Algeria—a very similar issue, when you come to think of it. Perhaps 200,000 in the whole of France feel really strongly about it, and that's putting the figure very high.

'People feel,' he added, 'that nobody, except possibly the Swiss and the Swedes, is qualified to preach any sort of morality to us. Neither the Russians, nor the Germans, neither the British with their Cyprus nor the Americans with their South Korea.'

Occasionally, during these months, Mendès-France would speak at the National Assembly—as soundly and often as vigorously as in 1950–53, but with no longer the same audience.

On January 19 he attacked, in his best style, the whole conception of the Common Market. He said he was in favour of building an 'organic Europe'; but this must not be done at France's expense.

The government's statement on the free circulation of persons (he said) had lacked in clarity. There was a danger of France being flooded by cheap Italian labour at all times, and by German labour if there were an economic depression in

Germany. As regards the circulation of goods, the danger was as great, if not greater: countries with lower costs and smaller social expenditure than France, were liable to flood the French market with their goods. The draft treaty did not provide for uniform family allowances, after the French model, in the five other countries. In view of the privileged position of German industry to produce cheaply, there would be an irresistible tendency on the part of French capital to emigrate. Moreover, the supra-national authority was liable, in certain conditions, to enforce a devaluation of the franc on France, against her will . . .

Mendès-France also protested against the haste with which the Mollet Government was trying to put the plan into operation, and against its reluctance to bring in Great Britain, on terms acceptable to her.

One has the impression that a race is being run between your Common Market and that Free Trade zone, comprising the six countries, Britain, Austria and Scandinavia, proposed by the British.

The British scheme, he suggested, was much less dangerous, because it wasn't based, as the Common Market was, on Nineteenth century cut-throat competition. A few days later, during a speech by M. Pierre Cot, Mendès clashed with the Foreign Minister, M. Pineau:

Christian Pineau: It wasn't until we had started preparing the Common Market that Great Britain proposed the Free Trade zone.
Mendès-France: The British Government asked, over and over again, that it be associated with the negotiations. It met with a refusal.
Christian Pineau: All the time we kept the British informed. Also, our delegation in Brussels was instructed not to subscribe to any clause that might prevent the British from adhering.
Mendès-France: At the beginning of December last Mr. Macmillan sent a Note to the six governments asking that there be a common discussion on tariffs and contingents 'before the negotiations for a Common Market had reached too advanced a stage'. On December 10, the Six decided that the formation of a Common Market must come first . . .

It soon became clear that Mendès was right; during Mr. Macmillan's visit to Paris in March, it became only too obvious that the prospect of Britain joining the Common Market were as remote as ever, especially in view of the insistence with which the Mollet Government had secured from its partners the inclusion in it of France's overseas territories. Once again in his political career Mendès seems to have proved right—once too often—while the Mollets and Lacostes, though inconsistent and beset with failures, survived errors and blunders without end. . . . And yet Mollet was still firmly in the saddle. Was Edgar Faure's review, *La Nef*, right when it wrote in February:

> One wonders how the devil Mollet has lasted so long. He didn't keep any of his promises. In what he undertook, he invariably failed. Peace in Algeria is more remote than a year ago. The effects of the Suez adventure are still with us. And yet the Mollet Government is still going strong. . . . Really, one would think that failure consolidated our governments. Eden has gone, but Mollet is still there. This isn't necessarily a recommendation for our parliamentary system . . .

And yet there seemed no doubt that whereas Mollet did not suffer from much opposition in Parliament, he was enjoying an even more positive kind of support in the country:

> The ordinary Frenchman sees in Mollet the reflection of his own self, just as he saw it in M. Pinay a few years ago. No doubt, he broke his promises about peace in Algeria, but then he's such an honest guy! His Egyptian expedition was a failure, but that wasn't his fault. It was the fault of the Russians and the Americans. Our troops had to reimbark, but, after all, they weren't defeated! He sends our boys to Algeria, but (fortunately) casualties among them aren't high. He deprives us of petrol, but we muddle through all the same. He calls himself a Socialist, but puts France's national requirements first. In short, an honest guy, who's doing what he can . . .

In fact, it was Guy Mollet, with a highly disciplined though largely discontented Socialist Party behind him, and not Mendès-France or Edgar Faure, brilliant individuals with the wreckage of the old Radical Party as their background, who remained at the head of France during the restless year of Algeria and Suez—and, indeed, long after. He was pursuing in the main a Right-wing policy, a curious case of government by proxy. His respect for the freedom of speech and of the Press was highly dubious, as could, for instance, be seen from his attempt to strangle the *Monde* financially by threatening to seize its financial assets for having dared to increase its price from 18 to 20 francs. His legalistic—but highly dubious—

excuse for this was that such an increase represented a violation of
the controlled-prices legislation and so a conspiracy against the
cost-of-living index! (An index which he, together with his Finance
Minister, had, for months, been subjecting to the most fantastic
hanky-panky.) Or when he ordered that *La Tribune des Journalistes*,
a regular feature on the French radio, be stopped because it created
opportunities for broadcasting dangerously non-conformist thoughts.

Yet nothing is eternal in this world—not even the Mollet
Government. In May it was overthrown on the financial issue.
Mollet himself scarcely made a secret of the fact that he was willing
to let somebody else try to raise fresh taxes and to clean up the
financial mess (at least temporarily), after which he would be ready
to come back at the first convenient opportunity. It was even
whispered that he was expecting the situation in Algeria to deteriorate
so badly during the summer that he could then re-emerge as the
'saviour'—with a new Algerian Plan, which might—for a while—
keep both the United States and the badly-rattled rank-and-file
of the French Socialist Party quiet.

During the last weeks of the Mollet Government, things had been
going from bad to worse in Algeria. FLN terrorism was assuming
alarming proportions. At Melouza, the entire adult male population
—over 300 men—was massacred in somewhat mysterious circumstances: the most probable explanation was that the FLN had
decided to make this massacre an object-lesson to any Moslem towns
or villages whose population had 'fraternised' with the French,
or had sought French protection. The twin reaction that this
horrible slaughter produced among the French diehards was that
(*a*) these people were savages, with whom any negotiations were out
of the question; and (*b*) the 600 or 700,000 troops already in
Algeria were insufficient to protect loyal populations against
massacres. The implication was that even more troops were needed.
(All of which was scarcely logical in view of the extreme reluctance of
the Assembly to provide new funds for the Algerian war.)

Just as bad, in a different way, as the Melouza massacre was the
increase in terrorism in Algiers itself, where bombs now started
blowing up at tram stops, in cafés and *dancings*, causing numerous
and indiscriminate casualties.

At the same time, acts of violence increased among the Algerians
in France itself; and one of the first steps taken by the new Government, under the premiership of M. Bourgès-Maunoury, was to
demand 'special powers' which would apply not only in Algeria,
but also in Metropolitan France. Although this was not stated
explicitly in the new law, this implied, nevertheless, that the

Government would have the right to create concentration camps in France—or internment camps, as they were more politely called—to which any person who had served a prison sentence, but who continued to be 'suspect' in the eyes of the authorities, could be sent for an indefinite period. Though the law was accompanied by a variety of 'safeguard clauses', the *Monde* thought the principle of the thing extremely ominous. Never, it said, had there existed internment camps under the French Republic in peacetime before. The *Canard Enchainé* came out with a cartoon showing 'Bourgès's 1957 Holiday Camp', among whose prisoners could be easily recognized Mauriac, Sartre, Mendès-France, and the anti-Mollet 'rebels' in the Socialist Party.

It was, indeed, significant that Mollet should have been succeeded in June 1957 not by anyone anxious to arrive at a liberal solution in Algeria, but by Bourgès-Maunoury, the forty-three-year-old *polytechnicien*, grandson of Marshal Maunoury of 1914 fame, member of countless governments, one of the moving spirits of the Suez adventure and an Algerian diehard if ever there was one.

And, equally significantly, the Assembly not only granted Bourgès the additional taxation it had refused Mollet, but allowed him additional powers of repression.

Mendès-France was, politically, now almost as isolated as before. Having repeatedly failed to secure any sort of discipline from the parliamentary Radical group, he threw up in June his post of First Vice-Premier. At the Radical Congress in May he had squarely condemned Mollet's Algerian policy; but had, after that, disappointed most of his followers by not insisting on Bourgès-Maunoury and the other Radical Ministers in the Mollet Government resigning their posts. He was, on that occasion, even accused of falling into the bad old Radical ways of thinking up *nègre-blanc* solutions in the best let's-have-it-both-ways tradition of the late Edouard Herriot.[1] However, it no longer mattered one way or the other. The Mollet Government was, clearly, on its last legs, and Bourgès-Maunoury and the other Radical Ministers would not have been, for more than a few days, diverted from their Algerian course by whatever Mendès said or whatever motion was carried by the Radical Congress.

[1] Herriot had been consistent to the bitter end. The G.O.M. of the Radical Party died at the end of March, aged 83. Both before dying, and in his will, he had declared that he wished neither a religious funeral, nor a 'national funeral'; however he had added in his will that he wished his widow to do whatever she thought best; so, in the end, he got both a religious and a national funeral, much to the disgust of some of the old anti-clericals who could still be found in the Radical Party!

Was there any sign, despite the apparent triumph of the diehard policy, as personified by the new premier, Bourgès-Maunoury, of a change of heart in France with regard to Algeria in the summer of 1957? Yes and no. On the one hand, the 'defeatism', associated with names like Mendès-France, Mauriac, and a few others was clearly spreading not only inside the Socialist Party, where (as the Toulouse Congress in June showed) the opposition to Mollet had grown appreciably, but also to certain elements on the Right and in the French business world. Significant was the almost simultaneous publication in June of two books sharply criticizing Mollet's (and, *ipso facto*, Bourgès's) Algerian policy—one by a Socialist, André Philip, *Le Socialisme trahi*, the other by the right-wing editorialist of the *Figaro*, M. Raymond Aron, whose *Problème algérien* was a plea in favour of granting independence to Algeria. It was also known that *in private* many leading businessmen as well as certain right-wing or MRP political leaders were now saying that the Algerian war 'ought to be wound up'. But still it was hard to see how, in parliamentary terms, this was possible. A coherent left-wing majority was as difficult to imagine as ever. The tragedy of the French Left was that no such majority was possible *without* the Communists; but it was almost equally impossible *with* them— especially after Budapest. Would Mollet in the end re-emerge as the 'saviour', as already said? Would he, supported by the MRP and— just in this particular case—by the Communists, think up an Algerian solution? There was, in the summer of 1957, some wishful thinking on these lines; but that was not the impression Mollet gave to those who saw him at the Toulouse Congress or who saw his right-hand man, Pierre Commin, at the meeting of the Socialist International in Vienna soon afterwards. Both continued to defend the Mollet-Lacoste policy of repression.

*   *   *

Not that an easy solution was in sight any longer, as there had been in January 1956. The mutual killings of the last eighteen months had deepened the gulf between the two communities. The 'practical joke' played on Ben Bella and his companions had had an unexpected result: if it was still possible to negotiate with the Ben Bella group (and their talks with the Moroccans in the autumn of 1956 showed that it *was* possible) others had since taken over the leadership of the FLN, and Bourguiba, anxious to find at least a basis of discussion, found them wholly uncompromising in their demands for immediate Algerian Independence. His attempt in April 1957, to talk to them proved a complete failure. Meantime the Ben Bella group, hidden away in the Santé prison, had lost their hold over the Algerian rebels.

For one thing, French propaganda had something to do with this attitude of the new Algerian rebel leaders: it had been drummed into everybody that the Sahara contained untold wealth: oil and thorium and uranium. Consequently, Algeria was no longer a poor country, which would have to depend on French charity; an Independent Algeria could sell its wealth to the highest bidder—France perhaps, or Russia, or Germany, or, most likely of all, the United States.

And in France, even among the *petit peuple*, even among the working class there continued a strong suspicion that 'the Russians and/or the Americans want to take Algeria away from us'. And, among certain French business groups, whose views were well reflected in the National Assembly, one often heard, in the early days of the Bourgès-Maunoury Government, this kind of dog-in-the-manger argument: 'At least so long as the Algerian war lasts, nobody else can get hold of the Sahara. It prevents us from developing the Sahara; but it prevents others even more from doing so!' This, in their view, had now become the main reason for trying to prevent the internationalization of the Algerian war!

Why then shouldn't the Algerian war go on for ever? Why not? Hadn't Bourgès-Maunoury remarked—in jest or in earnest, nobody quite knew—'After all, what's wrong with it? It doesn't cost us much more than the annual deficit of the French railways!'

But in fact, it can't go on for ever—except under a war-time or near-Fascist economy. And the French intellectuals, at any rate, have been increasingly aware of the seeds of a new French Fascism inherent in the Algerian crisis. Mendès-France was one of the first to draw attention to the danger. Will there be a sharp and organized reaction in France against this danger? By the end of 1957 or in the early months of 1958 we might know.

It is not certain that outside pressures would necessarily diminish this danger, or hasten the end of the Algerian war; they might, with France in her present mood, have the opposite effect.

On July 22 Mendès-France tabled at the National Assembly a *proposition de loi* (the equivalent of a Private Member's Bill) calling on the Government 'to open general negotiations with Morocco and Tunisia with a view to putting an end to all the disputes . . . between France and the countries of North Africa, and to laying the foundations of a Franco-North African Community which, on the basis of equal rights and duties . . . would provide for the social and economic progress of these countries through the joint development

of the natural wealth of North Africa, and of the Sahara in particular.'
In the preamble to the Bill, Mendès-France stated that there was no
time to lose, since foreign powers and international organizations
would soon try to act as arbiters between France and North Africa,
and to inflict upon them solutions beneficial to neither of them.
Mendès claimed that France was more inclined than any other
country to improve the lot of the under-developed countries associated with her, and the development of the Sahara would facilitate
this policy. It was absurd to try to maintain 'France's presence' in
North Africa by brute force, when free negotiations with the countries concerned were the obvious thing to attempt. Mendès then
argued that, even before any final decisions had been taken concerning
the future status of Algeria, there was no reason why an attempt
should not be made, in co-operation with Tunisia and Morocco,
to draw up the plan for 'a great human community of a new type'—in
which Algeria's place would be 'reserved'.

While hesitating to advocate direct talks with the F.L.N. at this
stage, Mendès was, in fact, trying to revive something fairly similar
to the 'Bourguiba Plan' (which had come to nothing owing to the
kidnapping of Ben Bella on his way to the Tunis Conference in
October). Mendès seemed to think that once a 'basis of discussion'
had been elaborated by France, Morocco and Tunisia, the Algerian
rebel leaders could be drawn into the talks.

M. Bourgès-Maunoury's only comment was that 'Mendès-France
himself knew perfectly well what difficulties his proposals would come
up against.' He added that there could be no question of Algerian
Independence being accepted by France in the sense given to the
word by international law.

And at Algiers, M. Lacoste said on August 21: 'One more effort,
and we'll have saved both Algeria and France!' He warned the
Europeans of Algiers that 'although this may take some time',
they must, above all, guard against two dangers: defeatism in France
and international plotting at U.N.

This was going even further than M. Bourgès-Maunoury who,
with his new *loi-cadre* for Algeria, was at least trying to keep up
U.N. appearances.

Meantime in France prices were rising, the black-market dollar
had shot up to 460 francs, and a new Algerian-bred devaluation
was round the corner. 'Cassandra' had foreseen it.

But then, as old Henri, the old Verdun *poilu*, and my favourite
waiter in the Boulevard St. Germain remarked: 'Devaluation and
colonial wars: both are an old French custom. As long as I can
remember, we've always had one or the other, or usually both.'

INDEX

INDEX

421